THE HEALTH

Society and Law b

The human world is changing. Old social structures are being overwhelmed by forces of social transformation which are sweeping across political and cultural frontiers. A social animal is becoming the social species. The animal that lives in packs and herds (family, corporation, nation, state ...) is becoming a member of a human society which is the society of all human beings, the society of all societies.

The age-old problems of social life – religious, philosophical, moral, political, legal, economic – must now be addressed at the level of the whole species, at the level where all cultures and traditions meet and will contribute to an exhilarating and hazardous new form of human self-evolving.

In this book Philip Allott explores the social and legal implications and potentialities of these developments in the light of the general theory of society and law which is proposed in his groundbreaking *Eunomia: New Order for a New World.*

PHILIP ALLOTT is Professor of International Public Law in the University of Cambridge and a Fellow of Trinity College, Cambridge. He was formerly a Legal Counsellor in the British Foreign and Commonwealth Office.

THE HEALTH OF NATIONS

Society and Law beyond the State

PHILIP ALLOTT

PUBLISHED BY THE PRESS SYNDICATE OF THE UNIVERSITY OF CAMBRIDGE
The Pitt Building, Trumpington Street, Cambridge, United Kingdom

CAMBRIDGE UNIVERSITY PRESS
The Edinburgh Building, Cambridge CB2 2RU, UK
40 West 20th Street, New York, NY 10011-4211, USA
477 Williamstown Road, Port Melbourne, VIC 3207, Australia
Ruiz de Alarcón 13, 28014 Madrid, Spain
Dock House, The Waterfront, Cape Town 8001, South Africa

http://www.cambridge.org

© Philip Allott 2002

This book is in copyright. Subject to statutory exception
and to the provisions of relevant collective licensing agreements,
no reproduction of any part may take place without
the written permission of Cambridge University Press.

First published 2002

Printed in the United Kingdom at the University Press, Cambridge

Typeface Adobe Minion 10.5/13.5 pt *System* LaTeX 2ε [TB]

A catalogue record for this book is available from the British Library

Library of Congress Cataloguing in Publication data
Allott, Philip.
The health of nations : society and law beyond the state / Philip Allott.
p. cm.
Includes bibliographical references and index.
ISBN 0 521 81655 6 (hardback) – ISBN 0 521 01680 0 (paperback)
1. Sociological jurisprudence. 2. Civil society. 3. International law. 4. Idealism.
I. Title.

K370 .A43 2002
340′.115 – dc21 2002023423

ISBN 0 521 81655 6 hardback
ISBN 0 521 01680 0 paperback

pathemata mathemata

for my dearest brother Roderick
(1936–1999)

speculum in speculo

Vain is the word of a philosopher which does not heal any suffering of man. For just as there is no profit in medicine if it does not expel the disease of the body, so there is no profit in philosophy either, if it does not expel the suffering of the mind.

Epicurus (341–270 BCE), Fragment 54, in C. Bailey, *Epicurus. The Extant Remains* (Oxford, The Clarendon Press; 1926), p. 133.

Natural health is the just proportion, truth, and regular course of things in a constitution. 'Tis the inward beauty of the body.

Anthony Ashley Cooper, Earl of Shaftesbury (1671–1713), *Characteristics of Men, Manners, Opinions, Times* (1711) (ed. J. M. Robertson; Indianapolis, Indiana University Press; 1964), II, pp. 267–8.

Truly, the earth shall yet become a house of healing.

Friedrich Nietzsche (1844–1900), *Thus Spake Zarathustra* (tr. R. Hollingdale; Harmondsworth, Penguin; 1961), pp. 102–3.

CONTENTS

PREFACE

The social species

The landscape of the human world is changing. A social *animal* is becoming a social *species*. Human social consciousness is becoming the social consciousness of the whole human species. Among all the species of social animals, one species is becoming the social species.

Biological history tells the story of the evolution of the human species by natural processes. *Human* history is the story of the self-evolving of the human species through the work of the human mind. The self-evolving of the human species is a by-product of the self-ordering of human beings, within the private mind of each human being and within the public minds of all human societies.

The three co-ordinates of our self-consciousness – as individual human beings, as intermediate societies, as the society of all-humanity – are the ordering structures of the ceaseless process of our self-constituting as persons and as societies. As the human species re-creates itself as the social species, the human mind faces new challenges, new in kind and new in scale, at every level of human self-constituting, at every level of human self-consciousness.

Social pathology

We are excited by the new possibilities of human self-constituting at the level of the species. Unused reserves of human potentiality can be released and realised, bringing into fruitful collaboration new levels of human energy, creativity, intelligence, to serve the highest aspirations and the highest ideals of all-humanity. We know that we will be writing a new page in the better story of human self-evolving.

We know also that there is another story within human history, the story of the social effects of evil. The private minds of human beings and the public minds of human societies interact in the process of their mutual self-constituting. It is a process which is wonderfully productive and creative but which includes also a vicious cycle of reciprocating pathology, as every form of human evil is reproduced and magnified at the social level.

As a social animal becomes the social species, we are anxious about the new possibilities of social pathology, as social systems take power over every aspect of all human life everywhere, as they take power over our minds, our wills, our hopes, our ideals, our species-nature, our species-consciousness, and as they take power, finally, over our idea of what it is to be human. The globalising of human society is also a globalising of social evil.

Social idealism

Societies constitute themselves in the form of ideas. *Nation, state, government, family, war, peace, justice, law, health, happiness.* These, and countless others like them, are structures of ideas. We live and die for ideas. Ideas are the biology of the human mind. As a social animal becomes the social species, the challenge to the self-creating and self-ordering human mind has never been greater.

Each human society is an infinitely complex and dynamic structure of ideas. The health of a society, its degree of well-being, is determined by the ideas which take actual effect in the process of its day-to-day self-constituting as a society. To reform or redeem a society is to change those determining ideas. Our quality of life is a function of the quality of our ideas.

The unifying theme of the studies contained in the present volume is a philosophy of *social idealism,* a belief in the capacity of the human mind to transcend itself in thought, to take power over the human future, to choose the human future, to make the human future conform to our ideals, to our best ideas of what we are and what we might be.

Practical theory

The ideas which take actual effect in the process of day-to-day social self-constituting are, in the first place, what we may call *practical theory.* Practical theory is a society's way of explaining itself to itself, explicitly or implicitly, in the course of its everyday activity. As a carpenter applies practical theory to the making of a table, so a society applies practical theory to the making of its own social reality.

Behind practical theory lies what we may call *pure theory*, a society's way of explaining its practical theory to itself. A theocracy may explain itself in terms of a particular religion. A democracy may explain itself in terms of a particular theory of social contract. A capitalist society may explain itself in terms of a particular theory of human behaviour. A geometer can explain the pure theory of the carpenter's practical theory. Behind pure theory lies what we may call *transcendental theory*, a theory of theory, our way of explaining to ourselves the nature of explanation, the nature of ideas, the nature of the mind.

In *Eunomia. New Order for a New World*,[1] I have sought to provide, at the levels of *transcendental* and *pure* theory, a philosophical basis for the new international society, the society of all human beings, the society of all societies. The essays in the present volume are intended to provide the groundwork of the possible *practical theory* of the new international society, that is, the practical theory of the social self-constituting of humanity at the level which lies beyond the self-constituting of states and nations.

Law

In the drama of a society's self-constituting, law plays the leading structural role. It is for this reason that the future of international law is crucial to the future of international society. The interaction of social reality and society's ideas produces *law*, so that law can act as the anatomy and the physiology of the body politic within which social reality can develop in co-operation with society's ideas.

Law creates an infinitely complex network of legal relations linking every single member of a society with all other members – relations of a relatively settled character, conditioning human behaviour, individual and social, within relatively settled limits. In this way, social reality develops, within relatively settled limits, in accordance with society's ideas as they are enacted in the law and as they are expressed through its day-to-day interpretation and application.

[1] Throughout the present volume, references to '*Eunomia*' are to P. Allott, *Eunomia. New Order for a New World* (Oxford, Oxford University Press; 1990/2001).

In the European Union, an attempt has been made to transcend the society of nation and state by constructing a complex legal system, enacting and expressing certain political and economic ideas. The grave problems besetting the process of European integration prefigure the problems which will beset the self-constituting of an international society which is self-consciously the society of all societies, transcending all subordinate forms of society.

The challenge of creating purposively a new European social reality formed by and forming a new kind of European public mind is mirrored and greatly magnified at the level of international society. The problem of creating the theoretical basis for a true international law of a true international society, formed by and forming a new public mind of all-humanity, is as daunting as it is exhilarating.

The other human future

Humanity cannot continue on its present self-destructive course, a course determined and distorted by large-scale socio-pathological phenomena – scandalous social injustice, chronic instability and violence within and between societies, widespread and deep-rooted public-realm corruption, the dehumanising of the human individual by morbid social forces.

Human self-perfecting through the unlimited potentiality of the better forms of human self-socialising remains as a permanent challenge, in an everlasting struggle between public good and public evil. Humanity's capacity for such self-transcending depends on the ideas which it forms of itself and of its possibilities, of its reality and its ideals. The present volume seeks to assist in the making of a better human future by contributing to that necessary process of human self-imagining and self-creating.

Method

This volume is radically syncretic in aspiration, drawing together ideas from many different fields. A major purpose is to encourage younger scholars and intellectuals, in particular, to have the courage to cross the arbitrary and artificial mental frontiers which have done so much harm to the creative potentiality of the human mind. Holistic diseases of the human world need homeopathic remedies produced from within the total potentiality of the human mind.

The author's hope is that younger scholars and intellectuals, in particular, will be inspired to reconnect with their intellectual inheritance, to explore new and better lines of thought, to search out new and better connections between ideas, ideas which may still be of redemptive value even if they are ancient ideas. Nothing could be more necessary or more urgent. Knowledge is not merely to be known, but also to be used.

Dare to think! Dare to know! Dare to speak! Dare to hope!

Trinity College, Cambridge

ACKNOWLEDGEMENTS

The following chapters of the present volume are revised versions (in some cases, substantially revised versions) of chapters or articles published elsewhere and published here with any necessary copyright permission.

Chapter 1. 'Kant or won't? Theory and moral responsibility': The British International Studies Association Lecture 1995, revised version in 23 *Review of International Studies* (1997). Chapter 2. 'Making sense of the law. Lawyers and legal philosophy': in 108 *Cambridge Review* (1987). 'Líbranos del mal social' (Deliver us from Social Evil): in 221 *Revista de Occidente* (1999) (special Pinochet number). 'The Emerging universal legal system': in 3 *International Law Association FORUM de l'Association du Droit International* (2001), 12. Chapter 3. 'Globalization from above. Actualizing the ideal through law': in 26 *Review of International Studies* (2000). Chapter 4. 'The nation as mind politic': in 24 *Journal of International Law and Politics* (1992). Chapter 5. 'Law and the re-making of humanity': in N. Dorsen and P. Gifford (eds.), *Democracy and the Rule of Law* (Washington, DC, CQ Press; 2001). Chapter 6. 'European governance and the re-branding of democracy': in 27 *European Law Review* (2002). Chapter 7. 'The crisis of European constitutionalism. Reflections on the revolution in Europe': in 34 *Common Market Law Review* (1997). Chapter 8. 'The concept of European Union. Imagining the unimagined': in 2 *Cambridge Yearbook of European Legal Studies* (2000). Chapter 9. 'The conversation that we are. The seven lamps of European Unity': in H. Cavanna (ed.), *Governance, Globalization and the European Union* (Dublin, Four Courts Press; 2002). Chapter 10. 'The concept of international law': in 10 *European Journal of International Law* (1999); and in M. Byers (ed.), *The Role of Law in International Politics. Essays in International Relations and International Law* (Oxford, Oxford University Press; 2000). Chapter 11. 'International law and the idea of history': in 1 *Journal of the History of International Law* (1999), 1. Chapter 12. 'Intergovernmental societies and the idea of constitutionalism': in V. Heiskanen and J.-M. Coicaud (eds.), The *Legitimacy of International Organizations* (Tokyo, United Nations University Press; 2001). Chapter 13. 'International law and the international *Hofmafia.* Towards a sociology of diplomacy': in W. Benedek, H. Isak and R. Kicker (eds.), *Development and Developing International and European Law* (Frankfurt-am-Main, Peter Lang; 1999). Chapter 14. 'International law and international revolution. Re-conceiving the world': Josephine Onoh Memorial Lecture 1989 (Hull, Hull University Press; 1989; and in D. Freestone, S. Subedi and S. Davidson (eds.), *Contemporary Issues in International Law* (The Hague, Kluwer Law International; 2002)).

PART I

Society and law

What is society? What is law?

1

The will to know and the will to power

Theory and moral responsibility

Theory and Istopia – Theory and society – Theory and the university – Theory and the philosophers – Theory and imagination – Theory and pathology – Theory and Eutopia

Given the role that ideas play within the self-constituting of human beings and human societies, what is the social responsibility and what is the moral responsibility of those whose function in the social division of labour is to think, the social engineers of human consciousness?

They cannot claim that the supposed ideal of intellectual objectivity absolves them from social and moral responsibility, if they claim that intellectual objectivity requires them to treat the actual – actual social and moral concepts, actual social and moral values, actual social and moral behaviour – as inevitable, rational and self-justifying.

Thinking in a social context is necessarily moral action, because it is liable to determine the lives of those whose consciousness is modified by that thinking, that is to say, by ideas acting as social forces. Our general social and responsibility now includes a duty to re-imagine the human world and human reality in the light of new ideas and new ideals.

Theory and Istopia

1.1 The human world is humanity's self-made habitat, a mind-world created by the human mind from its own substance. The reality of the human world is a species-specific reality made by human beings for human beings. The history of the human world is the history of the making of human reality, a self-consciousness of the self-creating activity of human consciousness, the mind's mirror of the mind. To say such a thing is not merely to take a certain view of the metaphysics of history or of the epistemology of historiography, aligning oneself, perhaps, with a sect of idealist historians.[1] To say such a thing is itself a significant event within the history of the making of human reality, an event whose ironical power is centred in the word *is*. To say what *is* is to change human reality.

1.2 The human world is constructed from the word *is*, an Istopia. The master-builders of Istopia are those whose task in the social division of labour is the fabrication of *is*-sentences. A special burden of social and moral responsibility rests on the shoulders of those of us who are paid to think in the public interest, the social engineers of the human mind-world.

1.3 To change human consciousness is to change human reality. To change human reality is to change the course of human history.[2] It

[1] Aligning oneself, perhaps, with R. G. Collingwood. 'All history is the history of thought.' 'Historical knowledge is the knowledge of what mind has done in the past, and at the same time it is the redoing of this, the perpetuation of past acts into the present.' *The Idea of History* (Oxford, Oxford University Press; 1946), pp. 215, 218. In *An Autobiography* (Oxford, Oxford University Press; 1939), Collingwood said: 'My life's work . . . has been in the main an attempt to bring about a rapprochement between philosophy and history' (p. 77). Collingwood was influenced by the Italian philosopher-historian Benedetto Croce (1866–1952), who had taken up from Vico and Hegel the idea of historiography as the history of the actualising of consciousness, inextricably linking ideas and events, the ideal and the real. For further discussion of the history of historiography, see ch. 11 below.

Ernst Cassirer, another philosopher-historian, aligned himself with Voltaire in proposing that 'the true object of history is the story of the mind'. E. Cassirer, *The Philosophy of the Enlightenment* (1932) (trs F. Koelln and J. Pettegrove; Princeton, Princeton University Press; 1951), p. 217. Cassirer contrasts Voltaire with Montesquieu, for whom political events still occupy the centre of the historical world, and the spirit of history coincides with the spirit of the laws: 'In Voltaire, on the other hand, the concept of mind has gained broader scope. It comprises the entire process of inner life, the sum total of the transformations through which humanity must pass before it can arrive at knowledge and consciousness of itself. The real purpose of the Essay on Manners is to reveal the gradual progress of mankind toward this goal and the obstacles which must be overcome before it can be reached.' Voltaire's *Essai sur les moeurs et l'esprit des nations* (Essay on the manners and the spirit [mind] of nations) (1756) was published eight years after Montesquieu's *De l'esprit des lois* (The Spirit of the Laws).

[2] 'Every day I become more convinced that theoretical work achieves more than practical work. When the realm of representation [*Vorstellung*] is revolutionised, reality cannot hold out.' G. W. F. Hegel, letter to Niethammer (23.X.1808), in J. Hoffmeister (ed.), *Briefe von und an Hegel* (Hamburg, Meiner; 1962–81), I, pp. 253–4 (present author's translation). 'Without revolutionary theory there can be no revolutionary movement.' V. I. Lenin, *What is to be Done?* (1902) (Moscow, Progress Publishers; 1947), p. 25. Lenin quotes F. Engels: 'Without German philosophy, which preceded it, particularly that of Hegel, German scientific socialism – the only scientific socialism that has ever existed – would never have come into being' (p. 27).

follows that, if it is our purpose to make a new human reality, we must find a way to stimulate the self-consciousness, the sense of social responsibility, the moral awareness, and the intellectual creativity of the ruling class of Istopia and, especially, of those who hold responsible positions in the mental service-industries – religion, politics, administration, commerce, the law, mathematics and the natural sciences, literature and the fine arts, the media of information and entertainment. It is they whose responsibility is not merely to imagine a new human reality but also to transform the human world as it is into the human world as it will be.

1.4 Thinking in the public interest is a social function which rests on two far-reaching philosophical assumptions. In the first place, we thinkers are saying that reality is not as it is but as we conceive it to be. Secondly, we are saying that reality as we conceive it to be is a possible human world, a world we human beings can choose to inhabit.

1.5 The assumptions underlying all public thinking are, for most people and for most of the time, subliminal, but they are not unconsidered and they are certainly not uncontroversial. The history of *philosophy* in the particular tradition established in Greece by the end of the fourth century BCE is the history of the self-contemplating of human consciousness, a history of human consciousness considering the possibility of human consciousness. It is, in particular, the history of the work of those whose function in the social division of labour is to think about thinking, that is to say, of *philosophers*, of those who think about what thinking *is*.[3]

1.6 We may call it *the Parmenides Moment*, that moment of self-enlightenment when the self-examining human mind recognises the problem of what it is to say that anything *is*, whether we say it of a god or gods, of justice, of the state, of our own being, of our own mind. And, for each human being, the Parmenides Moment is an ever-present

[3] Hegel referred to philosophy as 'the Thinking of Thinking', in the Introduction to *The Philosophy of History* (tr. J. Sibree; New York, Dover Publications; 1956), p. 69. He took the view that 'history', as opposed to historiography, is the march of the Universal Spirit towards Freedom.

Summarising his own philosophy of history, Ernst Cassirer said: 'Human culture taken as a whole may be described as the process of man's progressive self-liberation. Language, art, religion, science, are various phases in this process. In all of them man discovers and proves a new power – the power to build up a world of his own, an "ideal" world. Philosophy cannot give up its search for a fundamental unity in this ideal world.' *An Essay on Man. An Introduction to a Philosophy of Human Culture* (New Haven, Yale University Press; 1944), p. 228.

possibility of self-enlightenment. We ourselves may never experience it. Or, having experienced it, we may choose to ignore it. But humanity cannot escape from it. The human mind cannot unthink the self-imposed problem of its own functioning.[4]

1.7 *We perceive. We conceive. We become. We speak.* Such is one possible expression of the reality of our reality-forming capacity. It is an expression which can be constructed as a product of twenty-seven centuries of the great philosophical tradition, as a product especially of the intense self-examining of the human mind in the period since the enlightenment of the twelfth century, when the residues of the thought of Greece and Rome became available again to intellectuals throughout Europe. The human mind accumulates its self-consciousness. We are the ever-entitled beneficiaries of that inheritance, able to draw on the current state of that accumulation at any time. The possible progress of the human mind is the potentiality of its self-consciousness at any given time.

1.8 *We perceive.* If *being* is the way in which some part of reality presents itself to us, then it is possible to take the view (traditionally associated with the iconic name of George Berkeley)[5] that, at least so far as we humans are concerned, *being* is nothing more than being *perceived* by us. To be is to be perceived. Perceived reality is in the mind of the perceiver. *We perceive reality.*

1.9 *We conceive.* If *perceiving* is an activity of the mind, then it is possible to take the view (traditionally associated with the iconic name of Immanuel Kant)[6] that it is something in the self-ordering of the mind which allows it to conceive reality as an orderly world – a world of space

[4] The obscure and intriguing ideas of Parmenides (*c.* 515–*c.* 440 BCE) inspired several different branches of Greek philosophy by raising the problem of *being* through denying the possibility of talking about not-being. Does this mean that by saying that something 'is' we are necessarily saying that it exists other than as a thought in our minds? For a variety of interpretations of his ideas, see F. M. Cornford, 27 *The Classical Quarterly* (1933), pp. 97–110; M. Furth, 'Elements of eleatic ontology', in 6 *Journal of the History of Philosophy* (1968), pp. 111–32; S. Austin, *Parmenides – Being, Bounds, and Logic* (New Haven, Yale University Press; 1986); L. Brown, 'The verb "to be" in Greek philosophy: some remarks', in *Language* (*Companions to Ancient Thought* 3) (ed. S. Everson; Cambridge, Cambridge University Press; 1994), pp. 212–36. Plato discusses ideas attributed to Parmenides in two of his dialogues: *The Sophist* and *Parmenides.*

[5] George Berkeley (1685–1753) took the extreme 'idealist' position that, since the mind can only know its own contents, including the perceptions based on the data of the senses, the only reality we can know is the reality of our own thinking.

[6] Immanuel Kant (1724–1804), seeking to reconcile idealism and empiricism, supposed an interactive effort between the ordering capacity of the mind and the putative order of a putative non-mind reality.

and time, of energy, things, persons, life, death. To be is to be conceived. Conceived reality is reality remade in the mind of the conceiver. *We conceive reality.*

1.10 *We become.* If our perceiving of reality and our conceiving of reality are an interactive activity between the human mind and what we conceive of as reality, then it is possible to take the view (traditionally associated with the iconic name of G. W. F. Hegel)[7] that the making of human reality is itself a part of the continuous self-ordering of reality. To think is to become. Reality-for-us is a process of reality's self-constituting within human consciousness. *We become reality.*

1.11 *We speak.* If our making of human reality is an activity of mind, it is also an activity of minds. We think socially. The human mind has recognised the idea (now commonly associated, in particular, with the iconic name of Karl Marx)[8] that a society of human beings is a socialising of thinking and not merely a socialising of action. And we must take account of the view (now commonly associated, in particular, with the name of Ludwig Wittgenstein)[9] that the reality-for-us which is formed when human minds communicate with each other has characteristics which are determined not merely by the mind's capacity for perceiving and conceiving and becoming reality. It is determined also by the particular nature, and limitations, of our capacity to communicate. To speak is to act. To be is to be spoken about. In speaking about the world-that-is-for-me we make the world-that-is-for-us. *We speak reality.*

1.12 Such is the unprecedented self-consciousness of the human mind which is available to us as an inheritance at the beginning of the twenty-first century. We possess a form of philosophical self-consciousness which has not been available to any of our predecessors. Our intellectual inheritance is also an intellectual burden. We cannot unthink

[7] Georg Wilhelm Friedrich Hegel (1770–1831), in what was intended as a final reconciliation of idealism and empiricism, supposed that mind and what seems to be a non-mind reality are aspects of a third thing (*Geist*; Spirit or Mind) which manifests itself as *inter alia* an active force in both human thought and the products of human thought (human history).

[8] Karl Marx (1818–83), in what was intended as a final reconciliation of idealism and materialism, took the view that the activity of the human mind cannot be separated from the rest of human-made reality, in particular that part of human reality which involves the transformation by human beings of material reality. Theory is practice and practice is theory.

[9] Ludwig Wittgenstein (1889–1951) reflected a general crisis in the self-examining of the human mind, a crisis which concerned the status of all kinds of knowledge, including even the knowledge generated by the natural sciences. How can the human mind transcend itself to find the grounds of its ideas of truth and value when those ideas themselves are merely products of the mind?

what we have remembered of what we have thought. It has made our task of reality-engineering easier and more difficult. We have a more complex idea of ourselves, but it is an idea which makes us expect more of ourselves as we speak, publicly and in the public interest, about the nature and content and potentiality of human reality. We can think as nobody before us has thought. We can make a human reality which has never been made before. It is an intimidating power.

1.13 Friedrich Nietzsche (1844–1900), driven to distraction by the potentiality of human reality in the twentieth century, said that those whom he called genuine philosophers are commanders and legislators, saying 'thus it shall be'.[10] For once, he understated the case. Philosophers, including the kind of philosopher whom Nietzsche deplored, are commanders and legislators even when, especially when, they say, not 'thus it shall be', but 'thus it is'.

1.14 If they are theorists of the *human mind*, they are saying to human beings in general: 'these are the limits and the possibilities of your mental life, because this is what the mind is'. If they are theorists of *society*, they are saying to all those who participate in societies, that is, all human beings: 'these are the limits and the possibilities of your communal life, because this is what society is'. And if they are theorists of *international society*, they are saying to all those involved in international society, that is, the whole human race: 'these are the limits and the possibilities of human species-life, because this is what the life of humanity is'.

Theory and society

1.15 If thinking publicly is a social function, then public thinking is a system of social power with its own place in a society's constitutional structure and its own place in a society's history. A society's *public mind* is

[10] F. Nietzsche, *Beyond Good and Evil* (tr. W. Kaufmann; New York, 1966), § 211, p. 136. 'With a creative hand they reach for the future, and all that is and has been becomes a means for them, an instrument, a hammer. Their "knowing" is *creating*, their creating is a legislation, their will to truth is – *will to power*.' He was contrasting them with 'philosophical labourers', among whom he included Kant, who see it as their task merely to rationalise already received ideas. John Locke had said, with a modesty corrected by posterity, that, in the commonwealth of learning, not everyone can be among the 'master-builders, whose mighty designs, in advancing the sciences, will leave lasting monuments to the admiration of posterity...; 'tis ambition enough to be employed as an under-labourer in clearing ground a little, and removing some of the rubbish that lies in the way to knowledge.' *An Essay Concerning Human Understanding* (1689), Epistle to the Reader.

the place where a society constitutes itself ideally.[11] The history of public thinking is an integral part of the history of a society's self-constituting as a society. An analysis of the distribution of mental power in a society is as necessary, for an understanding of the functioning of that society, as an analysis of the distribution of political and legal power. In many societies, and many of the most successful societies, there has been a 'separation of mental power' analogous to the 'separation of powers' which has determined the distribution of political and legal power, with a mental ruling class which is functionally distinct from the classes which dominate political and legal power.

1.16 The class which dominates the means of mental production, distribution and exchange in a given society is an organ of its constitution. It is also a system within a society's economy. To produce commodities is to re-produce the idea of production and the idea of commodity, and to re-produce ideas in the form of commodities. To consume commodities is to consume the idea of consumption and the idea of commodity, and to consume ideas which have been re-produced in the form of commodities.[12] The monopolising of a society's mental power is as much of a threat to freedom as the monopolising of its political or economic power. A failure in the creative energy of a society's mental production, a decline in the value of its gross mental product, is likely to be a symptom, sometimes even a cause, of that society's general decay. The corruption of a society's mental production by an intellectually or morally corrupt ruling class is likely to be a symptom, sometimes even a cause, of a society's general corruption.

[11] For discussion of *ideal* self-constituting as one of the three interlocking dimensions of a society's self-constituting, see *Eunomia*, ch. 6. In its *ideal* constitution a society constitutes itself in the form of ideas. In its *real* constitution a society constitutes itself through the day-to-day social struggle of actual human beings. In its *legal* constitution a society reconciles its ideal and real self-constituting in the form of law.

[12] 'The production of ideas, of conceptions, of consciousness, is at first directly interwoven with the material activity and material intercourse of men, the language of real life. Conceiving, thinking, the mental intercourse of men, appear at this stage as the direct efflux of their material behaviour. The same applies to mental production as expressed in the language of politics, laws, morality, religion, metaphysics, etc., of a people. Men are the producers of their conceptions, ideas, etc. – real, active men . . . Morality, religion, metaphysics, all the rest of ideology and their corresponding forms of consciousness, thus no longer retain the semblance of independence. They have no history, no development; but men, developing their material production and their material intercourse, alter, along with this their real existence, their thinking and the products of their thinking. Life is not determined by consciousness, but consciousness by life.' K. Marx and F. Engels, *The German Ideology*, ch. 1, in K. Marx and F. Engels, *Selected Works* (Moscow, Progress Publishers; 1969), I, pp. 24–5.

1.17 Can a successful and dynamic society survive as a successful and dynamic society without an *intellectual aristocracy*? Western society, having dispensed with an intellectual aristocracy, is now the scene of a hazardous experiment which will provide an answer to that question.[13] Even as recently as the late nineteenth century, an intellectual aristocracy was able to speak to the political ruling class with authority because they were normally, in origin or by assimilation, members of the same social class. But there was also a new dominant socio-economic class, an intensely energetic and productive middle class, with new values and no instinctive respect for an old, seemingly unproductive intellectual class, an intellectual class speaking with the authority of an accumulated intellectual inheritance which seemed exclusionary to the new class. The French Revolution had shown that the exclusionary customs of an aristocracy (its 'privileges') can come to seem like an unnecessary and unjustifiable abuse to those who are seeking to destroy an old regime. The French Revolution had also shown the way in which ideas generated by a small intellectual elite can flow into a much more general process of social transformation.[14]

1.18 But there were two other classes competing for a new kind of dominance over the forming of the public mind – the ever-increasing mass of the urbanised working class and the new self-identifying and self-judging elite of the professional bureaucracy.

1.19 For Robert Owen (as for Plato, Bacon and Rousseau, among others), the radical re-forming of the contents of the 'public mind' had

[13] 'If the convulsive struggles of the last Half-Century have taught poor struggling Europe any truth, it may perhaps be this as the essence of innumerable others: That Europe requires a real Aristocracy, a real Priesthood, or it cannot continue to exist.' T. Carlyle, *Past and Present* (1843) (London, Oxford University Press (The World's Classics); 1909), p. 247.

[14] '[T]he French Revolution derives from the force, truth, and universality of the ideas which it took for its law, and from the passion with which it could inspire a multitude for these ideas, a unique and still living power; it is – it will probably long remain – the greatest, the most animating event in history'. M. Arnold, 'The function of criticism at the present time' (1875), in *Essays in Criticism* (ed. R. Supor; London, Macmillan; 1962), pp. 258–90, at p. 265.

The question of the role of ideas in the making of the French Revolution has been the subject of intense study and controversy. The Revolution is a continuing social and mental phenomenon, generating a permanent debate as to its significance. Among more recent contributions to the debate, see G. C. Comninel, *Rethinking the French Revolution. Marxism and the Revisionist Challenge* (London, New York, Verso; 1987) (especially ch. 1); W. Doyle, *Origins of the French Revolution* (Oxford, Oxford University Press; 3rd edn, 1999) (especially pt. 1 and ch. 7); F. Furet, *La Révolution en débat* (Paris, Gallimard; 1999) (especially ch. 2).

been an essential part of the making of a new kind of social order.[15] In his passionate excoriation of the new industrial bourgeois-led society, Thomas Carlyle spoke of the new self-consciousness of the exploited urban masses, 'these wild inarticulate souls, struggling there, with inarticulate uproar, like dumb creatures in pain, unable to speak what is in them!'[16] John Stuart Mill referred to 'the political consequences of the increasing power and importance of the operative classes' and said that 'the prospect of the future depends on the degree in which [the poor] can be made rational beings'.[17] In Britain, it was an intellectual aristocracy within the new bourgeoisie who would raise the cry 'educate your masters' and bring about the beginnings of universal compulsory education in the Education Acts of 1870 and 1876.

1.20 On the continent of Europe, the new imperative of rational and ends-directed education had long since established itself, but in a social order in which popular democracy would not be the impetus for change. The new class of the professional bureaucracy were the successors-in-function of the old-regime political class who were themselves in direct line of descent from the councils and courts of kings. It was to be an elite specially selected and trained to exercise rationalistic social power through public decision-making. Their task was conceived as being meta-political, not merely acting as the interpreter and agent of dominant social values, but representing and enacting some sort of universal meta-cultural value-system.[18] Their social status seemed to be in

15 R. Owen, *A New View of Society, or, Essays on the Principle of the Formation of the Human Character, and the Application of the Principle to Practice* (1813–16).

16 'And, first of all, what belief have they themselves formed about the justice of it all? . . . Revolt, sullen, revengeful humour of revolt against the upper classes, decreasing respect for what their temporal superiors command, decreasing faith for what their spiritual superiors teach, is more and more the universal spirit of the lower classes.' T. Carlyle, *Chartism* (London, J. Fraser; 1840), pp. 6, 40.

17 J. S. Mill, *Principles of Political Economy* (1848) (ed. J. Riley; Oxford, Oxford University Press (The World's Classics); 1994), pp. 136, 139. Mill referred to the view held by some people, a view which he labelled the theory of dependence and protection and which he rejected, to the effect that 'the lot of the poor, in all things which affect them collectively, should be regulated *for* them, not *by* them. They should not be required to think for themselves, or to give to their own reflection or forecast an influential voice in the determination of their destiny. It is supposed to be the duty of the higher classes to think for them' (p. 132).

18 The reform of the Prussian administration by Baron von Stein (1757–1831), the rational reformism of Napoleon and the central place assigned by Hegel to the 'universal class' in his newly conceived rational 'state' led Europe into a form of bureaucratism which, a century later, would be the focus of the prophetic anxiety of Max Weber. See further in ch. 6 below, at §§ 6.20ff.

the tradition of an intellectual aristocracy, but classless or beyond class, with the arrogance of the old monarchies transmuted into a new spirit of paternalism. They were the inheritors of some of the nostalgic prestige of the old intellectual aristocracy – medieval Schoolmen, Renaissance humanists, the French Academy, the 'natural philosophers' and mathematicians of the (British) Royal Society (with equivalent bodies in other European countries), the French *philosophes,* the master-minds of the Scottish Enlightenment.

1.21 The survivors of the shipwreck of the old intellectual ruling class diagnosed the early stages of a profound cultural crisis. At first the cultural crisis was analysed (in the 1830s, by Coleridge and others) as a problem of the relationship between religion and society.[19] But the true nature of the problem was detected, with characteristic prophetic clairvoyance, by Alexis de Tocqueville. As the democratic principle of social equality takes possession of society, the intellectual and moral centre of gravity of the public mind, and hence control over society's dominant ideas, comes to be located in aggregative social forces rather than in the minds either of the self-appointed *aristoi* or of the thrusting new middle class or of the most socially mobile members of the working class.[20] Democracy contained within itself a new risk, the 'tyranny of the majority'.[21]

[19] There was a theory that it was religion, especially Evangelical rather than Anglican Christianity, which had allowed Britain to escape violent social revolution after 1789. Coleridge proposed that a specially educated semi-secular clergy, a *clerisy,* should be posted around Britain to diffuse and protect good morals and the right values which were under threat from the more or less peaceful social transformation which was destroying the old order of society. In the troubled mental development (intellectual, religious, moral, sexual, political) of W. E. Gladstone (1809–98), four times British Prime Minister, we can see a vivid epitome of the revolutionary reconstituting of the British social mind. See, in particular, John Morley's biography of Gladstone (1903), a liberal rationalist writing sympathetically about a liberal believer. It is interesting that Coleridge's moral argument (rather than Hegel's idea of the universal class or even the impressive precedents of the new Prussian bureaucracy) seems to have been the spark which inspired Gladstone in his commissioning of the Northcote-Trevelyan report (1854), leading to the creation of a highly selective 'administrative' class in the British civil service.

[20] 'Thus intellectual authority will be different, but it will not be diminished; and far from thinking that it will disappear, I augur that it may readily acquire too much preponderance and confine the action of private judgment within narrower limits than are suited to either the greatness or the happiness of the human race ... [so] that, after having broken all the bondage once imposed on it by ranks or by men, the human mind would be closely fettered to the general will of the greatest number.' A. de Tocqueville, *Democracy in America* (1835–40) (London, David Campbell Publishers (Everyman's Library); 1994), pt 2, ch. 2, p. 11.

[21] '[I]n political speculations "the tyranny of the majority" is now generally included among the evils against which society requires to be on its guard ...; there needs protection also

1.22 Culture-critics frantically condemned the detranscendentalising, the philistinising and the materialising of the mental life of society, the crude mental hegemony of the actual, the popular, the practical, the material, the economic.[22] By the 1920s the struggle seemed to be lost. The French culture-critic Julien Benda, writing in 1928, called it the Betrayal or the Treason (*la trahison*) of the intellectual class (*les clercs*). Coleridge's natural *clerisy*, whose ideal function was to perfect their 'inward cultivation' on behalf of society as a whole, and so to take responsibility for society's higher thinking, had been swamped by mass phenomena and economic phenomena. The new masters of the social mind were preaching a new anti-transcendental metaphysic – the cult of the particular, scorn for the universal; adoration for the contingent, and scorn for the eternal.[23]

1.23 Theory had become dominated by *politics*. The central problem of purposive social organisation had become the problem of politics.[24] In the period between the World Wars, the problem of politics became the problem of *ideology*.[25] After 1945, after the experience of totalitarian ideologies (nationalism, militarism, nazism, fascism, Stalinism), the idea of 'the end of ideology' presented itself as a liberating ideology. Lippmann's 'good society' and Popper's 'open society' postulated an ideal in which the individual 'is confronted with personal decisions', a society in which individuals 'base decisions on the authority of their own intelligence',[26] a society in which the autonomous individual is free

against the tyranny of the prevailing opinion and feeling; against the tendency of society to impose, by other means than civil penalties, its own ideas and practices . . . ; to fetter the development, and, if possible, prevent the formation, of any individuality not in harmony with its ways . . . ' J. S. Mill, *On Liberty* (1859) (London, Dent (Everyman's Library); 1910), ch. 1, p. 68.

22 '[M]umbling to ourselves some vague janglement of Laissez-faire, Supply-and-demand, Cash-payment the one nexus of man to man: Free-trade, Competition, and Devil take the hindmost, our latest Gospel yet preached'. T. Carlyle, *Past and Present* (fn. 13 above), p. 175.

23 J. Benda, *La Trahison des clercs* (1927) (Paris, Bernard Grasset; 1977), pp. 244, 245; *The Treason of the Intellectuals* (tr. R. Aldington; New York, Norton; 1969), pp. 99, 100. Benda compares modern Europe to the brigand in a story by Tolstoy. After he had made his confession to a hermit, the hermit said: 'Others were at least ashamed of being brigands, but what is to be done with this man, who is proud of it?' (pp. 319, 183 respectively).

24 Thomas Mann and Max Weber addressed the problem of politics at a time when the fate of Germany as a democratic society was in the balance. See P. Gay, *Weimar Culture* (New York, Harper & Row; 1970), ch. 4.

25 The seminal work is K. Mannheim, *Ideology and Utopia. An Introduction to the Sociology of Knowledge* (London, Routledge & Kegan Paul; 1936).

26 K. Popper, *The Open Society and its Enemies* (London, Routledge & Kegan Paul; 1945; 5th edn, 1966), pp. 173, 202.

to design a personal way of living. It was an ideology which, during the Cold War, could conveniently define itself simply as a negation of the evidently 'closed' societies of Marxism-Leninism.

1.24 By the end of the twentieth century, we had learned another meaning of 'open society'. We found ourselves living in societies in which reality is, for the individual society-member, a heteronomy, societies so complex that we can no longer identify the processes by which social reality is formed, societies in which the public mind contains, in a turmoil of mutual conditioning, the despotism of rationalistic bureaucracy, the anarchic order of extra-parliamentary politics, the imperious order of the market-place, and the fantasy-forms of popular culture.

Theory and the university

1.25 The decline of high culture coincided with the rise of the professionalised university. It coincided also with the astonishing rise in the social significance of mathematics and the natural sciences, with the rise of totalitarian capitalism, with the decline of religion as a dominant social force. The professionalising of the universities coincided also with the emergence of the modern omnipotent state-system, that is to say, the rise of rationalistic bureaucratic absolutism in some European countries, the rise of rationalistic democratic absolutism elsewhere. So many coincidences suggest that they are the outward signs of some more general social transformation. But it is possible also that the new social role of the universities was itself a major causative factor in the general transformation of the public mind.

1.26 Germany was already the land of universities (more than 200 of them) when Savigny helped to reform the University of Heidelberg in the 1790s, when he and Humboldt founded the University of Berlin in 1810. In Britain, after the founding in the late 1820s of what would be a serious modern university in London,[27] an intense and remarkably clear-minded debate was joined about the reform of the older universities. What is a university for? What is education for? The debate was closely related to a much wider debate about the state of the public mind in the new social order, a debate which Matthew Arnold caused to be focused on

[27] University College and King's College were authorised to grant degrees in 1836 as 'the University of London'.

the idea of 'culture'.[28] The ideal of a 'liberal education'[29] was becoming as anachronistic as the nostalgia for 'medieval' arts and crafts. A more or less fantasised nostalgia for high culture and humanist higher education was meeting the pragmatic imperatives of the new social order and, in Britain, a perennial anti-intellectualism.[30]

1.27 When the question of the reform of the Universities of Oxford and Cambridge was referred to Royal Commissions in 1849,[31] a central theme of the ensuing great debate was whether or not to follow what was seen as the German model of a 'professors'' university. Should university professors, following the German model, 'devote themselves to the pursuit of special departments of knowledge, and acquire high

[28] Arnold defined culture as 'a study of perfection, and of harmonious perfection, general perfection, and perfection which consists in becoming something rather than in having something, in an inward condition of the mind and spirit, not in an outward set of circumstances'. M. Arnold, *Culture and Anarchy. An Essay in Political and Social Criticism* (London, Smith Elder; 1869), p. 14. Culture is 'particularly important in our modern world, of which the whole civilisation is, to a much greater degree than the civilisation of Greece or Rome, mechanical and external' (p. 15). And it was above all necessary in Britain: 'Indeed nearly all the characters of perfection meet in this country with some powerful tendency which thwarts them and sets them at defiance' (p. 15). (See M. Arnold, *Culture and Anarchy and Other Writings* (ed. S. Collini; Cambridge, Cambridge University Press; 1993), pp. 62–3.)

[29] 'A liberal education has for its object to impart the highest culture, to lead youths to the most full, vigorous, and harmonious exercise, according to the best ideal attainable, of their active, cognitive, and aesthetic faculties.' H. Sidgwick, in *Essays on a Liberal Education* (ed. F. Farrar; London, Macmillan; 1867), p. 222.

[30] Arnold divided British society into three classes – the barbarians (the aristocracy), the philistines (the middle class) and the populace (*Culture and Anarchy*, ch. 3). He quoted *The Times* newspaper: 'Art is long, and life is short; for the most part we settle things first and understand them afterwards. Let us have as few theories as possible; what is wanted is not the light of speculation . . . The relations of labour and capital, we are told, are not understood, yet trade and commerce, on the whole, work satisfactorily' (p. 233).

Cf. Walter Bagehot: 'I fear you will laugh when I tell you what I conceive to be about the most essential mental quality for a free people whose liberty is to be progressive, permanent, and on a large scale; it is much stupidity.' 'I need not say that, in real sound stupidity, the English are unrivalled . . . In fact, what we opprobriously call stupidity, though not an enlivening quality in common society, is nature's favourite resource for preserving steadiness of conduct and consistency of opinion.' W. Bagehot, *Letters on the French coup d'état of 1851* (letter 3: 'On the New Constitution of France, and the Aptitude of the French Character for National Freedom') (1852) in *The Collected Works of Walter Bagehot* (ed. N. St John-Stevas; London, The Economist; 1968), IV, pp. 50–1, 52. Bagehot was later to be an editor of the *Economist* newspaper and the author of *The English Constitution* (1865).

[31] The Royal Commissions on the Universities of Oxford and Cambridge of 1852–3 were followed by Royal Commissions on the Universities of Durham (1863), London (1911) and again on Oxford and Cambridge (1922).

eminence in learning'?[32] Or was the purpose of the university to perfect the whole person of the student?[33] In the end, a characteristic compromise was found,[34] a compromise which haunts universities to the present day. University professors would aim to optimise both learning and teaching.[35]

Theory and the philosophers

1.28 One of the fears expressed by those who had taken the trouble to inspect the German 'professorial' universities was that the obsessive and rigorous pursuit of 'learning' leads to a 'widespread doubt of the certainty of any knowledge, alike in theology and philosophy'.[36] Whether

[32] This was the view of Henry Vaughan of Oxford, a leading protagonist in the debate. Benjamin Jowett, Master of Balliol College (who was not unlearned and knew it), said that Vaughan was advocating an 'intellectual aristocracy', whereas the university's job was to teach the governing and professional elite. T. Heyck, *The Transformation of Intellectual Life in Victorian England* (London, Croom Helm; 1982), p. 165.

[33] Edward Pusey was Vaughan's antagonist. 'The object of Universities is, with and through the discipline of the intellect, as far as may be, to discipline and train the whole moral and intelligent being. The problem and special work of an University is, not how to advance science, not how to make discoveries, not to form new schools of mental philosophy, nor to invent new modes of analysis; not to produce works in Medicine, Jurisprudence, or even Theology; but to form minds religiously, morally, intellectually... Acute and subtle intellects, even though well disciplined, are not needed for most offices in the body politic. Acute and subtle intellects, if undisciplined, are destructive both to themselves and to it, in proportion to their very powers. The type of the best English intellectual character is sound, solid, steady, thoughtful, patient, well-disciplined judgment. It would be a perversion of our institutions to turn the University into a forcing-house for intellect.' E. Pusey, *Collegiate and Professorial Teaching and Discipline: in Answer to Professor Vaughan's Strictures* (Oxford, Parker; 1854), quoted in H. Liddon, *The Life of Edward Bouverie Pusey* (London, Longmans Green; 1894), III, p. 390.

[34] It seems that the compromise was designed, not least, to preserve the college system of Oxford and Cambridge, whose graduates were prominent in the government which introduced the relevant legislation in 1854.

[35] For further accounts of the debate, with its painful contemporary relevance, see S. Rothblatt, *The Revolution of the Dons. Cambridge and Society in Victorian England* (Cambridge, Cambridge University Press; 1968); S. Rothblatt, *Tradition and Change in English Liberal Education. An Essay in History and Culture* (London, Faber and Faber; 1976); M. Wiener, *English Culture and the Decline of the Industrial Spirit 1850–1980* (Cambridge, Cambridge University Press; 1981).

[36] E. Pusey, quoted in H. Liddon, *Life* (fn. 33 above), p. 382. Pusey, in the language of another era, said: 'Intellect, by itself, heightened, sharpened, refined, cool, piercing, subtle, would be after the likeness, not of God, but of His enemy, who is acuter and subtler far, than the acutest and the subtlest' (p. 390). Another of his prophetic observations was that German professors seemed only to concern themselves with books published in the past twenty-five years. That is, they were only reading each other's books, and not the great books of the past.

or not this opinion was correct at the time, it has proved to be remarkably prophetic of a major effect of the professionalising of the modern university. But the process by which such a profound intellectual and moral effect has been produced within general social consciousness has been extremely complex.

1.29 Large numbers of intelligent scholars, and some genuine intellectuals, are abstracted from the rest of society and are made to inhabit a world apart, to cultivate an academic *hortus conclusus*. And the hidden garden of this New Monasticism is a strange parallel unmoral universe whose high values are not moral values, but academic values – intercommunicative values of neutrality, objectivity, detachment, rigour, propriety, loyalty, professional ambition. Other social systems and forces determine what, if any, social effect can be given to the mental production of the universities. In the academic division of labour, the three classes of academics (artists, labourers and entrepreneurs) sell into such differing mental markets as are available to them. The potential social utility of mathematics and the natural sciences was very soon recognised, both in the wider mental markets of commerce (making possible products and processes) and government (serving the rationalistic arrogance of public decision-making). But the social utility of the academic activities bearing the obscure brand-name of 'the arts and humanities' has always been uncertain. What soon became clear is that their proper social function is not to prophesy, to enlighten, to lead or to elevate the human spirit. Least of all are they expected to sit in judgement, to aspire to be the guardians of society's guardians. The controllers of the political and economic public realms can be confident that our graduates, cultural orphans, will pose no threat to established social order by reason of anything that they have learned or experienced at a university. They leave us with added-value, but what values have we added?[37]

1.30 Professionalisation, as predicted by the Victorian elite, has meant ever-increasing specialisation, as the realm of the mind is partitioned into ever-smaller intellectual territories, each an island entire unto itself, protected by the territorial sea of its own exclusionary

[37] Virginia Woolf described university graduates as 'pale, preoccupied and silent'. She went on to say that it was as if, during their three years at Cambridge, 'some awful communication had been made to them, and they went burdened with a secret too dreadful to impart'. L. Gordon, *Virginia Woolf. A Writer's Life* (Oxford, Oxford University Press; 1984), p. 123. We may be inclined to reveal that the secret communicated to them is that the university has no secret to communicate – a sad secret, at least.

academic method and discourse. It soon became virtually impossible to cross the academic frontiers, let alone to look down, in the tradition of Renaissance humanism, on the whole edifice of the self-contemplating and self-creating human mind. The human mind came to contain the anguished presence of an absence, the absence of an image of its own achievement.

1.31 Learning for its own sake became cosmopolitan, not merely mathematics and the natural sciences, which are nothing if not universal, but also the arts and humanities. Samuel Johnson's world-wide 'community of mind', formed by the educated classes of all advanced societies,[38] became the global campus of an invisible college.[39] The globalising of learning, good and natural in itself, also carries a heavy price in the deracinating and alienating from their own society of scholars and, more importantly, of intellectuals, that is to say, of scholars who recognise the social and moral responsibility attaching to thinking in the public interest.

1.32 And, fatally, even philosophers professionalised themselves. Professional philosophers (surely, a contradiction in terms) have devoted themselves, obsessively and rigorously, to *studying* philosophy, rather than *doing* philosophy.[40] And, such was their intellectual rigour, they came to convince themselves, after much self-examination, that philosophy is, after all, impossible. We must salute this as a remarkable achievement of twenty-six centuries of European philosophy – the

[38] J. Boswell, *Life of Johnson* (ed. R. W. Chapman; London, Oxford University Press, 1904/53), p. 1,143 (entry for 8 May 1781).

[39] It seems that Robert Boyle invented the term Invisible College, rather than Francis Bacon, with whose name it is usually associated. Bacon's imagining of Salomon's House (of natural philosophers) in New Atlantis, his various recommendations for the internationalisation of learning through co-operation among European universities, and the general spirit of his new philosophy of science were factors in the creation of scientific societies which preceded the founding of the Royal Society, including a Philosophical College, which was also called the Invisible College. See M. Purver, *The Royal Society: Concept and Creation* (London, Routledge & Kegan Paul; 1967), chs 2 and 3. See also F. Bacon, *Advancement of Learning*, in *Bacon's Works* (eds J. Spedding, R. Ellis, and D. Heath; London, Longman; 1858), bk II, III, pp. 323–4, 327; and the preface to the second book of Bacon's *De augmentis scientiarum* (1623), in *Works*, IV, pp. 285–6.

[40] Wittgenstein insisted that the job of a philosopher is to 'philosophize' or to 'do philosophy', rather than to study or write about philosophy, and he himself made very little reference to the work of previous philosophers. '... from the bottom of my heart it is all the same to me what the professional philosophers of today think of me; for it is not for them that I am writing'. Letter of 8 August 1932 to M. Schlick; quoted in R. Monk, *Wittgenstein: The Duty of Genius* (Harmondsworth, Penguin; 1990), p. 324.

impossibility of philosophy philosophically demonstrated. The American Willard Quine put the matter cheerfully and chillingly in his John Dewey Lectures: 'I hold that knowledge, mind, and meaning are part of the same world that they have to do with, and that they are to be studied in the same empirical spirit that animates natural science. There is no place for a prior philosophy.'[41] An *is*-sentence with overtones of the Cretan Liar. Schelling, philosophical bridge between Kant and Hegel, would have said (and did say): 'without philosophy he cannot know that there is no philosophy'.[42]

1.33 The ethos of the professionalised university produced its own post-mystical religion, the religion of naturalism. The human being, a being-for-itself, product of human consciousness in human consciousness, became a being-in-itself, an object, not of self-contemplating, but of study. Subjectivity became an object. The universities created a material human world to be studied by the 'human sciences' or the 'mind-sciences' (*Geisteswissenschaften*), a world in which we are not morally engaged through value and purpose, in which everything human is present, other than the moral responsibility of the observer for the situation of the observed.

1.34 Derrida has called it heterological thought, humanity studying itself as an object.[43] Humanity became for itself a thing, a thing which speaks about itself (to borrow a phrase from Lacan).[44] And there was certainly a lot of speaking. The poverty of philosophy proved to be remarkably rich in the philosophy of human impoverishment. The unphilosophers went rushing in again, where angels had feared to tread – utilitarianism, positivism, pragmatism, behaviourism, phenomenology, logical positivism, analytical philosophy, structuralism, post-structuralism. Derrida calls all these -isms *empiricism* – a thousand times

[41] W. V. Quine, 'Ontological Relativity', in *Ontological Relativity and Other Essays* (New York, Columbia University Press; 1969), p. 2.

[42] F. W. J. Schelling, *Ideas for a Philosophy of Nature* (1797/1802) (tr. E. E. Harris and P. Heath; Cambridge, Cambridge University Press; 1988), p. 45.

[43] J. Derrida, *L'écriture et la différence* (Paris, Seuil; 1967), p. 224. Derrida has recently called for a 'profound transformation' of international law, to get beyond the concepts of state and nation: *Specters of Marx: the State of the Debt, the Work of Mourning, & the New International* (tr. P. Kamuf; New York, London, Routledge; 1994), pp. 58, 84ff. The possible transcendental significance of Derrida's thought, the possibility that he may himself be among the thousand prophets of human self-transcending, is a tantalising possibility for those whose wish it would fulfil. But see fn. 49 below.

[44] M. Borch-Jacobsen, *Lacan – le maître absolu* (Paris, Flammarion; 1990), p. 139.

denounced, he says, but still going strong.[45] We may call it *naturalism*, which is also the word used by Husserl to make much the same point.[46] Marcuse called it academic sado-masochism, self-humiliation, self-denunciation.[47] We might also call it the philosophy of misanthropy, misanthropology. The academy has surrendered itself to a masochistic and misanthropic ecstasy of human self-denying.

1.35 It was not, as is so often supposed, simply that human studies adopted the methods of the natural sciences, nor even that they adopted what Quine, in the sentence quoted earlier, called 'the empirical spirit' of natural science (as if the natural sciences were a single intellectual phenomenon), or even what Georges Canguilhem called the scientific ideology, which, as he said, is something supposed by philosophers of the non-sciences, rather than by natural scientists themselves.[48] The religion of human naturalism, the religion of the universities, is expressed rather in those most sinister words in the Quine sentence: 'knowledge, mind, and meaning are part of the same world that they have to do with'.

1.36 Terrifying words. They deny the possibility of human self-transcending. They condemn humanity to become the by-product, the surplus social effect, of its totalising systems. Human consciousness and human language become merely an object of study like any other. Epistemic relativism becomes what Quine called ontological relativity. All we can know about the nature of things is what we can say to each other 'usefully' about them, which is not very much.

1.37 Or we might recall one of Rorty's charming sayings: 'the very idea of a "ground" for "propositional attribution" is a mistake'. 'A concept is just the regular use of a mark or noise' which human beings use 'to get what they want'.[49] This reminds us also of the notorious description of

[45] J. Derrida, *L'écriture* (fn. 43 above), p. 224.

[46] P. Ricoeur, *Husserl: An Analysis of his Phenomenology* (tr. E. G. Ballard and L. E. Embree; Evanston, Northwestern University Press; 1967), p. 59. See also on the development of the human sciences since Kant: M. Foucault, *The Order of Things: An Archaeology of the Human Sciences* (London, Tavistock Publications; 1966/1970), pp. 309, 341, 387.

[47] H. Marcuse, *One-Dimensional Man. Studies in the Ideology of Advanced Industrial Society* (London, Routledge & Kegan Paul; 1964), p. 173.

[48] G. Gutting, *Michel Foucault's Archaeology of Scientific Reason* (Cambridge, Cambridge University Press; 1989), p. 44.

[49] R. Rorty, 'Is Derrida a transcendental philosopher?', in *Essays on Heidegger and Others* (Cambridge, Cambridge University Press; 1991), pp. 125–7. For Rorty, all talk about 'transcendental philosophy' – whether of Plato, Kant, Hegel, or anyone else – is nonsense, crazy, delusion, a gimmick. It seems that, for Rorty, Derrida's thought would continue to

abstract concepts which Ogden and Richards offered years ago: 'symbolic accessories enabling us to economize our speech material'.[50] Academic naturalism is dogmatic anti-transcendentalism, as dogmatic as any old religion. It is philosophy for the unphilosophical. In Lewis Carroll's *The Hunting of the Snark*, the ship's crew of snark-hunters were grateful to the Bellman for bringing a large map representing the sea, without the least vestige of land: 'And the crew were much pleased when they found it to be,/A map they could all understand.'[51]

Theory and imagination

1.38 The human species is the species that tells stories – stories about gods and heroes, about the forces of nature, about the history of a nation, about our selves. We re-present our experience to ourselves in the mirror of our own consciousness. And it is not only the experience we have experienced, but unlimited possibilities of experience. We can imagine that which has not existed and that which could not exist. Imagination allows us to invent reality at will, and the reality we invent may become part of the human reality of the human world in which we actually live our lives.

1.39 Plato was much troubled by the problem of the place of works of the imagination in the ideal society. Works of the imagination present

have value only if he could still be counted among the naysayers or, perhaps, among the not-say-either-wayers.

Cf. J. Bentham: 'While Xenophon was writing his History and Euclid teaching Geometry, Socrates and Plato were talking nonsense, on pretence of teaching morality and wisdom and morality.' *Deontology*, in *The Collected Works of Jeremy Bentham: Philosophy* (ed. A. Goldworth; Oxford, Clarendon Press; 1983), p. 135. (Euclid was not a contemporary of Socrates or Plato.) M. Arnold said that reading this passage 'delivered me from the bondage of Bentham! The fanaticism of his adherents can touch me no longer; I feel the inadequacy of his mind and ideas for being the rule of human society, for perfection.' *Culture and Anarchy* (fn. 28 above), p. 45.

[50] C. K. Ogden and I. A. Richards, *The Meaning of Meaning. A Study of the Influence of Language upon Thought and of the Science of Symbolism* (London, Routledge & Kegan Paul 1923 /1969), p. 96.

[51] L. Carroll, *The Hunting of the Snark* (1876), Fit the Second, lines 7–8. Francis Bacon defined 'metaphysics' as 'the investigation of forms, which are (in the eye of reason at least, and in their essential law) eternal and immutable'. *The New Organon and Related Writings* (1620) (ed. F. H. Anderson; Indianapolis, New York; 1960), p. 129. Of 'the received and inveterate opinion' that the human mind cannot find out the 'essential Forms', he said that such knowledge is 'of all other parts of knowledge the worthiest to be sought, if it be possible to be found. As for the possibility, they are ill discoverers that think there is no land, when they can see nothing but sea.' (*Advancement of Learning* (fn. 39 above), bk II).

an *is*-world whose essence is its non-existence but whose non-existence may be indistinguishable from existence. In the epistemology of Plato's theology there was no coherent place for the fictional. *God – the world of the Ideal – the world of the mind – the world of the actual – the world of appearances.* The mind mediates between what is above it and what is beneath it to produce true knowledge. Through education the mind can realise its potentiality for true knowledge. Fiction can confuse the mind, at best, but, more probably, it will corrupt the mind, making it incapable of true knowledge.[52]

1.40 For Plato, the corrupting power of the imaginary was not only epistemological. The imaginary could be a form of moral corruption. Virtue is an aspect of true knowledge. The crux of the problem was in the Homeric inheritance, a sublime soap-opera of the lives of gods and heroes. The Homeric *is*-world was all-too-human in its situations and its moral ethos, but was confusing in its representation of causation and motivation, with the incomprehensible interaction of the human and the super-human, of fate and guilt. Something of the same thing could be said of the Greek tragedians. Their effect was achieved through emotional identification on the part of the audience, the recognition of possible truths about the human world, rather than through the higher, dialectical power of the mind, finding more universal truth through the universalising of more particular truths. And, still more practically, how can a society be an ordered realm of human flourishing if the minds of the people are a junk-heap of sense and nonsense, fact and fiction?

1.41 All works of the imagination contain human consciousness, the consciousness which has given them their material form, in stone and paint and sounds and words and physical movement and projected image. The imagination-work modifies the consciousness of the spectator, the modification being the net product of the work of the two minds and of countless contextual circumstances. In a spectrum ranging from high art through functional art (including the making and selling of commodities) to entertainment-art, works of the imagination modify the state of private minds and of the public mind of society. We may reassure

[52] One of Plato's discussions of the matter focuses on a painting of a couch. What is its relation to reality? 'The painter, then, the cabinetmaker, and God, there are these three presiding over three kinds of couches.' Like 'the maker of tragedies', the painter is 'three removes from nature'. *Republic* (tr. P. Shorey), x. 597b, in *The Collected Dialogues of Plato* (eds E. Hamilton and H. Cairns; Princeton, Princeton University Press; 1961), p. 822.

Plato by saying that high art, including Homer and the Greek tragedians but also including works of Mozart and Turner and Dostoevsky, enables us to philosophise, inwardly and perhaps unconsciously, to contemplate ourselves, our human-made reality, and consciousness itself. But Plato was surely right in supposing that art-as-entertainment, including high art presented as entertainment, is much more than mere entertainment. It becomes pure experience, adding to the sum of personal experience of the spectator, modifying the spectator's consciousness, and thereby the collective consciousness of society, often in profoundly structural ways, conveying implicit epistemologies (what is true?), implicit ontologies (what is real?) and implicit moralities (what is good?), but conveying them in ways whose power over consciousness is proportional to the intellectual and moral passivity of the spectator.

1.42 Francis Bacon, seeking to establish a new foundation for the whole activity of the human mind, recognised that the major obstacle lay in the nature of the ideas which are already fixed in human consciousness, ideas which people worship and will be reluctant to give up: ideas flowing from the nature of the human mind itself (*idols of the tribe*, as he calls them),[53] ideas flowing from the mind of each individual human being (*idols of the cave* of personal consciousness, in which the light of nature is refracted and distorted),[54] ideas formed socially (*idols of the market-place*, where words 'force and overrule the understanding and throw all into confusion').[55] 'Lastly, there are Idols which have immigrated into men's minds from the various dogmas of philosophies . . . These I call *Idols of the Theatre*, because in my judgment all the received systems are but so many stage plays, representing worlds of their own creation after an unreal and scenic fashion.'[56]

1.43 Human reality contains mind-made fiction and mind-made non-fiction in seamless confusion. Like the dreaming and the waking state of the mind, the distinction seems to be important, if not in what seems to be the relative realness of each, then in our behavioural responses to them. We dream with our eyes open, but we also see with our eyes open. We can be deluded by illusions, but we can also decide that what we see is not an illusion. Our ideas of fiction, dream and illusion are the necessary negation of our ideas of non-fiction, of being awake, and

[53] 'And the human understanding is like a false mirror, which, receiving rays irregularly, distorts and discolours the nature of things by mingling its own nature with them.' F. Bacon, *The New Organon* (fn. 51 above), Aphorism XLI, p. 48.

[54] *Ibid.*, Aph. XLII, pp. 48–9. [55] *Ibid.*, Aph. XLIII, p. 49. [56] *Ibid.*, Aph. XLIV, p. 49.

of our capacity to see clearly and distinctly. The realness-for-us of human reality contains the richness of both sets of ideas, their opposition, and their enriching of each other.

1.44 A society in its ideal self-constituting[57] generates a story of its own self-constituting which we may call the *theory* of that society.[58] The question of the epistemological status of the theory is secondary. That question may be raised as a critique, as a pretext for social, even revolutionary, change. But the theory – divine right, social contract, the sovereignty of the people, sovereign equality of states, religious fundamentalism, countless others – proves itself for everyday practical purposes simply by establishing itself as a necessary condition of that society's continuation as a society.[59] The *industrial* revolution in Europe (from 1760) was not merely the emergence of new methods of production. It contained a new *idea* of the totality of society as an economic system. The *political* revolution (from 1815) was not merely a re-arrangement of institutional power. It contained a new *idea* of the nature of all public power.

1.45 A *cultural* revolution since 1918 has been not merely the triumph of mass socio-economic phenomena. It contains a new *idea* of the relationship between the individual and society, between the private mind and the public mind, between the private realm and the public realm and, not least, a new idea of the nature of human reality, the relationship between fact and fiction, truth and falsehood. We might identify this cultural transformation as *the Phenomenal Moment*. The Parmenides Moment (§ 1.6 above) is the awakening of our awareness of the problem of the nature of reality. The Phenomenal Moment is the beginning of the end of our ability to distinguish between fact and fiction. Actual social experience is made fictional as it happens. The 'news' becomes a

[57] See fn. 11 above.

[58] For further discussion of a society's *theory*, see *Eunomia*, §§ 2.44ff.

[59] Peter Winch rightly condemned Karl Popper's view that 'models' of social phenomena are merely intellectual fictions. 'Popper's statement that social institutions are just explanatory models introduced by the social scientist for his own purposes is palpably untrue. The ways of thinking embodied in institutions govern the way the members of the societies studied by the social scientist behave. The idea of war, for instance, which is one of Popper's examples, was not simply invented by people who wanted to *explain* what happens when societies come into armed conflict. It is an idea which provides the criteria of what is appropriate in the behaviour of members of the conflicting societies.' P. Winch, *The Idea of a Social Science* (London, Routledge & Kegan Paul; 1958/1990), p. 127.

'story'. Fictional experience presents itself as real, indistinguishable from fictionalised actual social experience.[60]

1.46 It is touching to watch Plato, in one of his last dialogues (this time, without Socrates as an interlocutor), wrestling with the problem of the distinction between reality and unreality, trying to remain true to Parmenides' interdict against the idea of the *is*ness of the *is-not*. He uses once again the idea of the 'sophist' as the embodiment of the un-philosopher, the merchant of 'opinion' masquerading as 'knowledge', not least the opinion that there is no ground for distinguishing between the 'true' and the 'not-true'.[61] In so doing, Plato helps us to understand the Phenomenal Moment, that is to say, the self-disabling of the public mind in the twentieth century.

1.47 Plato discusses a possible distinction between an image which is a representation of something (an *eikon*) and an image which represents something but which does not picture it (a *phantasma*).[62] In the twentieth century it was in the arts that the distinction between fact and fiction most evidently collapsed, as the *phantasma* came to be treated as an *eikon*. In painting, from post-impressionism through cubism, expressionism, abstract art, abstract expressionism, pop art, performance art and installation art, the picture itself became the subject-matter of the art-work. In the 'modernist' novel and poem, in the various post-classical forms of music (including twelve-tone music, *musique concrète*, synthesised music), the significance of the process of composition or performance became the primary significance of the music-work.

1.48 The twentieth-century obsession of professional philosophers with *language*, the phenomenal level of philosophy, was another symptom

[60] '[I]nformation exhausts itself in itself and absorbs its own purpose. Television says the same thing: I am an image, everything is image. The Internet and the computer say the same thing: I am information, everything is information... It is the sign that turns itself into a sign... It is now a long time since the media and information crossed the frontier of "neither true nor false"... If there is no longer the true or the false, lying becomes impossible...' J. Baudrillard, *Le Paroxyste indifférent* (Paris, Bernard Grasset; 1997), pp. 134–5 (present author's translation).

[61] 'The audacity of the statement lies in its implication that "what is not" has being, for in no other way could a falsehood come to have being. But, my young friend, when we were of your age the great Parmenides from beginning to end testified against this, constantly telling us what he also says in his poem, "Never shall this be proved – that things that are not are"'. *The Sophist*, 237a, in *The Collected Dialogues* (fn. 52 above), p. 980. We may see the modern professional philosopher (or misopher) as the successor-in-function, if not in-title, of Plato's sophist.

[62] *Ibid.*, 236a–b, p. 979.

of the self-disabling of the public mind.[63] Phenomenology limited the possibility of philosophy to the rationalising of phenomena as events in the human mind, as opposed to the rationalising of the reality of which the phenomena are a manifestation. Semiology and structuralism saw the problem of philosophy as the problem of rationalising the forms in which collective human consciousness presents ideas to itself, rather than the rationalising of those ideas. Analytical philosophy reduced philosophy to the investigation of speech-habits. Neo-pragmatism sought to redefine rationality as a possible by-product of human communication in society, rather than as a proper subject of study in itself. Postmodernism went to a third stage of phenomenology, seeking to do no more than to offer possible *re-presentations* of the *pictures* of *phenomena* which arise in the course of all kinds of human communication.

1.49 All this in a century which saw war, genocide, oppression, exploitation and the physical and mental degradation of human beings on an unprecedented scale, all in the name of ideas. All this in a century in which fantasy-forms, new mythologies, came to be the dominant form in which the ruling classes, political and economic, communicate with the people. A godless world is, once again, full of gods, to echo Thales, the pre-Socratic philosopher. Max Weber said that the old gods, with their magic taken away, rise up from their graves, in the form of impersonal forces.[64] The Hundred Names of God[65] are now the names of the re-mystified social powers which infest our public–private minds.

And then Inflation Rate, descending in cloud, speaks and says: I will spread Unemployment among the people like a plague. But Non-Trade-Balance, hearing this from afar, rose up and gathered to her side Short-term Interest Rates, and smiled upon the decision-makers and the opinion-formers. And they all Felt Good. And the people greeted with grateful eye the dawn-light of Renewed Business Confidence.

The mythology of capitalism. The social poetry of a new absolutism.[66]

[63] We may regard Wittgenstein as a true mirror of the cultural revolution if, in Platonic terms, we characterise his move from a 'picture' view of language (*Tractatus Logico-philosophicus*, 1921) to an 'activity' view of language (*Philosophical Investigations*, 1953) as a move from an iconic theory to a phantasmic theory.

[64] M. Weber, 'Science as a vocation', in *From Max Weber: Essays in Sociology* (trs and eds H. H. Gerth and C. Wright Mills; New York, Oxford University Press; 1958), p. 149.

[65] The title of a book by Fray Luís de León, a hero of Spain's Golden Century.

[66] 'The world enters language as a dialectical relation between activities, between human actions; it comes out of myth as a harmonious display of essences. A conjuring trick has taken

Theory and pathology

1.50 Psychopathology is a product of the imagination. Among the unlimited number of human realities which we can create for ourselves, as individuals and as societies, there are realities which are dangerous. We can be made to suffer as much by what we think with our minds as by what we experience with our bodies. To suffer in the mind is a suffering at least as painful as suffering in the body. When the pathological reality is that of an individual mind, its effects may be limited to the patient and to those who have direct contact with the patient. When the pathological reality is that of the mind of a holder of public power or is the reality contained in the public mind of a whole society, then its effects may extend to many people, to millions, to all humanity.

1.51 Michel Foucault, in his study of the way in which the dichotomy madness–sanity became established as social reality, shows how this development reduced to silence all other possible conceptualisations.[67] It is a silence which haunts all our treatment and mistreatment of people deemed by society to be mad. The conceptualisation itself can act as a source of evil. The *possible* contained in a particular human reality becomes the *necessary* of social human action. The converse of Foucault's analysis is that the 'sane' reality becomes unable to recognise its own 'insanity', its reality seems natural, rational and inevitable.[68] At the social

place; it has turned reality inside out, it has emptied it of history and has filled it with nature, it has removed from things human their human meaning so as to make them signify a human insignificance. The function of myth is to empty reality... It is now possible to complete the semiological definition of myth in a bourgeois society: *myth is depoliticized speech.* One must naturally understand *political* in its deeper meaning, as describing the whole of human relations in their real, social structure, in their power of making the world ... ' R. Barthes, *Mythologies* (tr. A. Lavers; Frogmore, Paladin; 1973), pp. 142–3.

67 M. Foucault, *Madness and Civilization: A History of Insanity in the Age of Reason* (tr. R. Howard; London, Routledge; 1971). 'I have not tried to write the history of that language, but rather the archaeology of that silence' (p. xiii). This construct may be seen as part of the great dialectical tradition in philosophy which goes back, beyond Plato, to Heraclitus and Pythagoras. It has become newly fashionable in the post-Hegelian world, in a fruitful constellation of ideas which includes *negation* in Hegel, *bracketing* in Husserl, *nothingness* in Sartre, *silence* in Foucault, *différence* in Derrida. Hegel acknowledged his debt to Spinoza, in particular to his saying: *omnis determinatio est negatio* (all affirmation is negation). S. Rosen, *G. W. F. Hegel: An Introduction to the Science of Wisdom* (New Haven, London, Yale University Press; 1974), pp. 73, 110.

68 'We are told that when the asylum at Charenton was shelled in the Franco-Prussian War of 1870, the lunatics saw reflected in the bursting bombs, each in a different way, his own madness.' I. Babbitt, *Rousseau and Romanticism* (1919) (New York, Meridian Books; 1955), p. 229. Those outside the asylum no doubt saw the bombing as sane.

level, we have witnessed countless examples of realities, both religious and political, whose inner perspective was absolute moral certainty and whose outer expression was morally outrageous behaviour.

1.52 Freudian psychology is not merely a phenomenology of mental events, although mental events are the material which it studies. It is rather a biology of the human mind and a philosophy of the human mind.[69] It seeks to explain the *functioning* of the human mind and it seeks to explain the *products* of the human mind. Its significance in the *cultural revolution* of the twentieth century (§ 1.45 above) is thus more complex than that of the work of the professional philosophers and its effect within the self-contemplating (the philosophising) of the human mind has surely been greater. It has had extraordinary effects in the public mind, far beyond the circle of those who have sought to study Freud's obscure and protean ideas at source. From day to day, physiology and biology modify the mind's conception of itself by providing new insights into the physical correlates of mental states and into the surviving inheritance of our biological evolution. They cannot explain the actual contents of consciousness, that is to say, the actual products of the infinite range of possibilities made available by the working of the brain and nervous system of an individual human being.[70]

1.53 Freud did not invent the idea of the *unconscious* but, by making it a central conception of his work, he changed the nature of the mind's self-contemplating. It requires us to believe that the mind contains an area which it cannot know, except by its effects, but whose effects are strongly determinative of all other mental events.[71] It is akin to the

[69] Of particular value, among countless other studies of the status of Freud's ideas, are: F. J. Sulloway, *Freud, Biologist of the Mind* (New York, Basic Books; 1979); P. Rieff, *Freud: The Mind of the Moralist* (Chicago, University of Chicago Press; 1959/1979); P. Gay, *Freud for Historians* (New York, Oxford University Press; 1985).

[70] In particular, the physical sciences, however far they had advanced, would not be able to *predict* the precise content of a particular work of art, such as Mozart's *Don Giovanni*, or the precise content of a particular book, such as D. Dennett's *Consciousness Explained* (1992). It is, perhaps, an instance or an analogy of Gödel undecidability. The human mind (brain) cannot, in principle, create a predictive theory of the whole of its own functioning. 'For physics may explain, in some measure, the mechanism of the senses and the formation of ideas; but in the power of willing or rather of choosing, and in the feeling of this power, nothing is to be found but acts which are purely spiritual and wholly inexplicable by the laws of mechanism.' J.-J. Rousseau, *A Discourse on Inequality* (1755), in *The Social Contract and Discourses* (tr. G. D. H. Cole; London, J. M. Dent & Sons; 1913/1973), p. 54.

[71] 'The oldest and best meaning of the word "unconscious" is the descriptive one; we call a psychical process unconscious whose existence we are obliged to assume – for some such

'state of nature' concept in social theory, pre-normative but haunting the making and breaking of all norms. It implies that conscious behaviour is intrinsically repressive of something, that mental life is necessarily a struggle and it seems to define sanity (or what was once called 'happiness') as some sort of successful integration of the conscious and unconscious aspects of the mind, and that social life is, in some way, an unnatural suppression of our natural selves.

1.54 In short, the idea of an unconscious level within the human mind, which is surely confirmed by our own introspection and experience, seems to imply that we have within us, as the ultimate source of our behaviour, a sort of hidden god or demon, wilful and inscrutable, acting as an ultimate explanation both of the need for social and moral order and of our relentless propensity to violate social and moral order. And, since the public mind of a society flows out from and back to the private minds of society-members, we may expect that human societies will reproduce on a large scale the structural characteristics and hence the pathological potentialities of the mind of the individual human being.[72]

1.55 The Freudian scheme presents consciousness as dynamic, flowing from the past through the present to the future in a process of ceaseless self-re-creating. But it is the past which dominates the whole process, a past which is remembered or repressed or imagined. On this view, psychopathological conditions may arise from a relationship with the past which gives rise to existential problems in the present. A society has a specific relationship to its past. At any particular time, its own self-understanding, its own theory of itself, includes an idea of its own history, partly remembered, partly repressed, partly imagined. Very easily, a society's self-idea can become distorted in a way which causes it to fail to adapt to the realities which transcend it, including its relationship with other societies and its relationship with the ideas and aspirations of its members (subordinate societies and

reason as that we infer it from its effects –, but of which we know nothing.' S. Freud, *New Introductory Lectures on Psycho-Analysis* (1932–3), in *Standard Edition of the Complete Psychological Works of Sigmund Freud* (tr. and ed. J. Strachey; London, Hogarth Press and Institute of Psycho-Analysis; 1964), XXII, p. 70.

[72] 'Is it not, then, said I, impossible for us to avoid admitting this much, that the same forms and qualities are to be found in each one of us that are in the state? They could not get there from any other source.' Plato, *Republic*, 435e, in *The Collected Dialogues* (fn. 52 above), p. 677.

individual human beings).[73] And the eternal presence of a distorted past may lead, in societies as in individuals, to 'repetition'[74] – for example, re-enacting behaviour appropriate to imperial power, an *ancien régime*, an era of religious orthodoxy, or an era of unchallenged cultural superiority.

1.56 When social psychopathology takes the form of collective fantasy-thinking, repressing the unthinkable, believing the unbelievable, then social psychotherapy may be impossible if society succeeds in suppressing all alternative thinking. The discrepancy between the fantasy and the reality may be very great but the society will tend to interpret the discrepancy as a demonstration of the reality of the fantasy, as the paranoid mind finds endless confirmations of its special reality. Democracy and capitalism are remarkable examples of a reality whose axes are 'liberty' and 'equality' but whose lived experience is of intense social control and glaring inequality, so that another possible self-idea would be that they are systems designed to enable the few to dominate the many. Similarly, religious theories of individual salvation, expressed perhaps as a reward in an after-life, may generate, in practice, extreme systems of social control, physical and mental.

1.57 To tell a psychotic person that their fantasy of omnipotence is not a fantasy but is part of reality, and that they are right to believe that they are exempt from morality, legality and rationality, might be a reasonable course of action in a very short-term situation. To persist in such a course of action could only mean that you yourself had checked into the asylum. And yet that is what responsible people have told the masters of the societies called 'states'. It is little wonder that the human world, in possession of such a reality, has been filled with the works of madness and evil which have characterised the history of so-called 'international relations' for the last seven centuries, including the madness

[73] Mannheim discusses such distortions under the heading of 'false consciousness' through which a society's particular 'reality', based on an 'ideology' inherited from the past, may not correspond with the new reality within which the society must exist. *Ideology and Utopia* (fn. 25 above), pp. 84ff. It is the overall contention of the present volume that this is exactly what has happened in the relationship between the theory and the reality of international society.

[74] In accordance with Freud's hypothesis that 'all the organic instincts are conservative, are acquired historically and tend towards the restoration of an earlier state of things'. S. Freud, *Beyond the Pleasure Principle* (1920), in *Standard Edition* (fn. 71 above), XVIII, pp. 37–8.

and the evil of war and the madness and evil of socially organised human oppression and exploitation.

1.58 If a particular kind of society, say the 'state', is taught to see itself as being the ultimate source of morality, then it seems also to follow that that society as a whole is beyond moral judgement and, as a second corollary, that the *inter se* co-existence of such societies is beyond moral judgement.[75] If a society is taught to see itself as the ultimate source of law, then it seems to follow that society as a whole is beyond the rule of law, except to the extent that it consents, by agreement with other such societies, to submit itself to law-like constraints.[76]

1.59 And, at last in the twentieth century of all centuries, the siren voice of professional philosophy whispers some interesting ideas into the ear of those who govern and those who are governed: (1) there is no rational ground for rationality; (2) the actual is necessarily rational; (3) the actual is always rationalisable; (4) truth emerges from actual practice; (5) truth proves itself in practice; (6) values are an epiphenomenal aspect of relations of power; (7) values are social conventions; (8) values are rhetorical conventions; (9) the mind is nothing more than a function of physiology and biology; (10) ends are justified means.

1.60 Morally sensitive human beings cannot find it in their hearts to judge, still less to condemn, those human beings who are afflicted with the terrible suffering of psychosis. Should we judge and condemn the sickness of whole societies, perhaps now even the impending sickness of the society of the whole human race? Should we, at least, judge and condemn those of us who fail to try to treat the sickness of human society, those of us who fail to try to make a better human reality?

[75] 'For the History of the World occupies a higher ground than that on which morality has properly its position; which is personal character – the conscience of individuals – their particular will and mode of action.' G. W. F. Hegel, *The Philosophy of History* (fn. 3 above), pp. 66–7.

[76] 'International law governs relations between independent States. The rules of law binding upon States therefore emanate from their own free will as expressed in conventions or by usages generally accepted as expressing principles of law and established in order to regulate the relations between these co-existing independent communities or with a view to the achievement of common aims. Restrictions upon the independence of States cannot therefore be presumed.' France *v*. Turkey (*The Lotus*), Permanent Court of International Justice, series A, no. 10 (1927), pp. 18–32, at p. 18. The view that international law is simply an aspect of power relations is, ironically, known as 'realism'. A *locus classicus* is H. J. Morgenthau, *Politics among Nations: the Struggle for Power and Peace* (New York, McGraw-Hill; 6th edn, 1985).

Theory and Eutopia

1.61 In the light of all that has been said above, we can at least identify rather precisely the painful moral situation of anyone who does seek to make a better human reality. The essence of that situation is that the obvious means of making a better human reality are not available.

(1) *Religion*, the sublime capacity of human self-transcendence, is not religion but religions. What seems like truth and moral certainty seen from within a given religion may seem like madness from outside that religion. For this reason, religions have proved to be a major part of the problem of humanity's inhumanity.

(2) *Science and mathematics*, which makes science possible, are the greatest achievements of the human mind. But they are a realm of means without ends. The purposes to which the ideas and the practices and the products of science may be put must be determined by other means, through the activity of other systems within the human mind. And the abuse of the fruits of science is another major part of the problem of humanity's inhumanity.

(3) *Philosophy*, the sublime potentiality of the human mind to improve its own functioning by means of its self-contemplating, has also proved capable of disabling that capacity and of assisting the mind in the exercise of its other power, the power to do great evil, and to convince itself that, in so doing, it is doing good.

(4) The former *intellectual class* in society, of those who recognise a social and moral responsibility to use the power of the mind for the improvement of human reality, has been marginalised and has marginalised itself, losing its self-confidence and even its self-consciousness in the face of the terrible events of the twentieth century and the rise of the overwhelming forces of mass-consciousness.

(5) The *universities*, the realm devoted to the study of both ends and means, whose ideal function is to use the capacities of the human mind to their limits in human self-knowing and self-creating, and to convey that potentiality from generation to generation, have lost sight of that function, becoming either efficient servants of imperious socio-economic systems or else obsequious rationalisers of the social actual.

(6) The *common sense* of the human species, the better voice of accumulated experience and self-evolutionary aspiration within each human mind, has been overwhelmed by another human voice, speaking through

the mass consciousness of the public mind as it universalises humanity's capacity for a form of thinking which is dehumanising, degrading and self-destructive.

1.62 And yet, how can any morally sensitive person, knowing what happened in the twentieth century and seeing the prospects of the twenty-first century, fail to recognise a heavy burden of moral responsibility to do whatever can be done to improve human reality? Must we deny our feelings of righteous *anger* at the social evil that plagues the human world, of *pity* for the immeasurable suffering caused by the acts and omissions of holders of public power, of invincible *hope* that a better human world is possible?

1.63 The will to know is a will to power. As we *conceive* what we *perceive*, so we *speak* and so we *become* (§§ 1.7ff. above). We think, therefore we are. To utter a new kind of *is*-sentence is an act of power and, as an act of power, it necessarily engages our moral responsibility, our responsibility for the way in which we use our moral freedom, our responsibility for the human world which we choose to make. We can, if we choose, undertake a new journey, the journey from Istopia to Eutopia, to a new human world filled with the idea of the ideal.[77]

1.64 We have Immanuel Kant to help us, the master of all those who know,[78] the Virgil who may lead us out of a world without ends, out of a tragic phase in the long-running human comedy. Kant suggested that it *is* possible for the rationalising human mind to know the possibility of rational knowledge.[79] He suggested that, with our innate and inescapable knowledge of our own moral freedom, we can know that the duty which conditions our freedom *is* the duty to make our will into an agent of an hypothetical universal will.[80] And he suggested that, as organic systems, our life *is* the unfolding of purpose and, as thinking beings, it *is* open to us to determine our purposes in the light of values and ideals.[81] To recognise such ideas as a theory of theory within the making of human reality is to recognise a new potentiality and a new responsibility for human beings.

1.65 To reconceive human reality is to make a new human world and unmake an old human world. To affirm is to deny. To conceive of

[77] On the Eutopian project, see further at §§ 5.63ff.

[78] Dante said this of Aristotle: *Divine Comedy – Inferno*, canto IV, line 131.

[79] *Critique of Pure Reason* (1781). [80] *Critique of Practical Reason* (1788).

[81] *Critique of Judgement* (1790).

theory as the capacity of the human mind to create and to re-create the human world is to deny the idea that theory *is* nothing more than an illusion generated by practice (the present chapter). To conceive of *law* as a complex form of rationality available to serve an unlimited variety of human ends is to deny the idea that law *is* merely an act of will of institutional power (chapter 2 below). To conceive of *globalisation* as the universalising of the potentiality of society-under-law is to deny the idea that international society *is* merely an aggregation of national societies (chapter 3). To conceive of *society* as the product of a process of human self-constituting-in-consciousness is to deny the idea that society *is* merely an institutional arrangement of social power (chapter 4). To conceive of a new human *enlightenment* is to deny that humanity *is* doomed merely to repeat its past (chapter 5).

1.66 To conceive of the European Union as a new kind of human *society*, intermediate between the state-societies and the society of all-humanity, is to deny the idea that the EU *is* doomed to be a tepid confusion of diplomacy and democracy (chapter 6). To conceive of the self-constituting of the EU as a dialectical struggle among *different conceptions of society* is to deny the idea that the EU *is* condemned to be a super-state or to fail (chapter 7). To conceive of the EU as the product of a particular process of self-constituting within the *historical experience* of Europe is to deny the idea that the EU *is* merely an instrumentally determined institutional artefact (chapter 8). To conceive of the EU as a reconstituting of an accumulating European *self-consciousness* is to deny the idea that the EU *is* doomed to be merely a system of European government, an alien presence in the minds of the people of Europe (chapter 9).

1.67 To conceive of *international law* as the true law of a true international society is to deny the ideas that international law *is* not law or *is* not the law of a society (chapter 10). To conceive of *history* as a possible story of all human collective self-constituting is to deny the idea that there *is not,* and cannot be, a history of international society (chapter 11). To conceive of the institutional arrangements of interstatal international society as possible institutions of an international *society-under-law* is to deny the idea that international government *is* merely the externalising of national government (chapter 12). To conceive of the history of interstatal society as the history of the *abuse of public power* is to deny the idea that diplomacy *is* the natural default-system for organising a world of 'states' (chapter 13). To conceive of *international society* as the society of all human beings, and the society of all societies, is to deny the idea that the human world *is* a state of nature in which all human beings must continue to pay the terrible price of unsocialised power (chapter 14).

2

The phenomenon of law

I. Making sense of the law. Lawyers and legal philosophy

It is surprising that social philosophers and sociologists feel able to offer explanations of society which do not assign a central place to law. It is surprising that legal philosophers and lawyers can speak about law as if legal phenomena were self-contained and capable of being isolated from social phenomena in general.

Law seems to have a special status among social phenomena by reason of its forms, its rituals, its specialised language, its special rationality even, and its specific social effects. But, on the other hand, law is clearly embedded in the totality of the social process which is its cause, and on which it has a substantial determinative effect, not least in providing the continuing structure of society, its hardware programme.

Legal philosophy is law's own self-philosophising, another closed world, familiar to some lawyers, more or less unknown to general philosophers and social scientists.

II. The emerging universal legal system. The law of all laws

Law is a universal social phenomenon – or, rather, legal systems seem to be, and to have been, a characteristic feature of social organisation. The ancient debate about whether law is a single generic phenomenon with countless local specific forms has never been resolved. That debate is now being overtaken by new real-world developments.

National legal systems are beginning to merge as a result of forces acting from two directions. On the one hand, there is a dramatic increase in international legislation and collective government, including socially sensitive law (international human rights law), socially transformatory law (international economic law and administration), and socially structural law (international public order law).

On the other hand, the greatly increased volume of transnational transactions, especially economic transactions, means that national legal systems are operating more and more in relation to extra-national situations, and that the structures and substantive contents of national systems are tending to converge.

III. Deliver us from social evil. International criminal law and moral order

Our experience of extreme social evil is the most painful psychological burden that we have inherited from the twentieth century. Social evil arises as a totalised product of the functioning of social systems. The problem is that a social system is not a moral agent and, although particular individuals who are principal actors in a social situation may seem to bear exceptional responsibility for social evil, it does not seem right to attribute that responsibility to them in isolation from the social situation. But human society, especially the international society of all-humanity, cannot begin to redeem itself unless it can find a way to reduce the incidence of social evil.

There is a trend in international society which seeks to attribute to individuals, not merely moral responsibility, but some form of criminal responsibility, national or international, for extreme acts of social evil. The policies which justify the crudities of the criminal law in national societies – deterrence, retribution, rehabilitation – depend on ideas which are inseparably linked with the total value-system of a given society. International society is not ready for such a thing.

Crude extrapolation to the global level of the criminalising of the antisocial conduct of individuals is a cynical distraction from the true problem, that is, the problem of the evil done by evil social systems. The solution to that problem lies beyond the proper limits of law and legal systems.

I. Making sense of the law. Lawyers and legal philosophy

Law's reality

2.1 What is law? A mystery to many people who are not lawyers, the law is a puzzle to itself. The citizen is deemed by the law to know the law.

Ignorantia juris haud excusat.[1] As a citizen, even the lawyer is deemed to know the law. As a lawyer, the lawyer knows that law is not a thing that can be known. All that the lawyer knows is forms of legal perception. To learn the law is not to learn law but to learn to be a lawyer. To be a lawyer is to live through a particular looking-glass, inside a law-world with its own law-mind and its own law-reality.

2.2 It is not easy to communicate any worthwhile concrete impression of the elusive inner world of the law, which is the familiar everyday world of the lawyer. Consider the following five legal puzzles.

2.3 (1) Does section 1 of the (British) Criminal Attempts Act 1981 mean that you are guilty of an offence if you attempt to commit an offence which is impossible but which, at the time, you did not know to be impossible? In 1985 the House of Lords thought not. Professor Glanville Williams, of Cambridge University, disagreed strongly in an article in the *Cambridge Law Journal.* In 1986 the House of Lords changed its mind.

2.4 In the 1985 case the accused had bought a video recorder believing it to have been stolen. In fact there was no evidence that it had been stolen. The House of Lords agreed with the magistrates, who had dismissed the case, that the mistaken belief of the accused could not turn her behaviour into the offence of dishonestly attempting to handle stolen goods. In 1986 the House of Lords upheld the conviction of a man for dealing with and harbouring a controlled drug. The man had believed that the substance in the suitcase which had been delivered to him was illegally imported heroin or cannabis. In fact the substance was snuff or some similar harmless vegetable matter. On this occasion it was evidently the accused's own admission of his own mistaken belief that caused him to be convicted of a criminal offence.

2.5 (2) Do you commit the offence of conspiracy under the (British) Criminal Law Act 1977 if you take part in arranging the escape of someone from prison with the intention to deceive your co-conspirators and to leave the country before the escape is effected, taking the money you have been paid in advance?

2.6 The statutory definition of conspiracy requires that the agreement among the conspirators must necessarily involve the commission of an offence 'if the agreement is carried out in accordance with their

[1] 'Ignorance of the law is no excuse.'

intentions'. In 1985 the House of Lords answered the question in the affirmative. 'Intentions' did not mean the several intentions of the different conspirators. But the House of Lords indicated that this would not necessarily mean that 'some innocent person' would be regarded as committing the offence if he collaborated in a conspiracy, which had come to the notice of 'the police or of some honest citizen', with the intention of exposing and frustrating the criminals involved. No doubt there are other interesting distinctions to be found in the single phrase about 'intentions' in the 1977 Act. For instance, it would be interesting to know whether you could commit an offence of conspiring with others to defraud yourself, you yourself sharing the intention of the other participants to defraud someone but not their intention to defraud you.

2.7 (3) If the local authority building inspector inspects the foundations of a house before they are covered to see that they satisfy building regulations, can you claim damages from the local authority if he makes a negligent inspection and the house, of which you are a subsequent owner, eventually proves to be unsound?

2.8 The relevant legislation did not expressly provide for such a claim. In 1972 the Court of Appeal answered in the affirmative. In another case in 1977 the House of Lords agreed with the Court of Appeal's conclusion but placed that conclusion on its 'correct legal basis'. In 1972 Lord Denning had stressed the novelty of the case. It was a statute of 1936 (the Public Health Act) which had created the relevant building inspection scheme, but apparently no one had previously made a claim against a local authority in respect of the negligence of its inspectors. Lord Denning placed the claim in the context of a series of cases in which the courts have imposed a common-law duty (that is to say, not deriving from any statutory provision) of reasonable care on people who cause loss or damage to those who rely on their expertise and to others who suffer loss or damage from a failure to use such care in the exercise of such expertise by the manufacturer of ginger beer in relation to the ultimate consumer (decision in 1932); a merchant bank in relation to a customer of a bank which had obtained from the merchant bank an opinion on a fourth party's creditworthiness (decision in 1963); the Home Office in relation to a yacht-club whose property was damaged by Borstal boys[2] who had not been properly controlled (decision in 1970).

[2] 'Borstal' was formerly the name of a young offenders' penal institution in the United Kingdom.

2.9 The House of Lords analysed the series of cases referred to by Lord Denning but preferred to see the duty in the case of building inspection not as the general common-law duty of care but as a special duty of reasonable care attaching to the statutory power to inspect, the duty being to exercise reasonable care to see that the building regulations were complied with. In the merchant bank case, Lord Devlin said that he would not himself offer a statement of the general rule on liability in such cases, but was prepared to accept any of the (four different) statements of the other Law Lords in the case and Lord Denning's (different) formulation of it in a case in 1951. In a case in 1984 the House of Lords warned against 'the tendency in some recent cases to treat... as being themselves of a definitive character' the syntheses of earlier cases made by the House of Lords in the Borstal boys case and the building inspector case.

2.10 (4) (Case A) In 1941 the Home Secretary, Sir John Anderson, determined that a certain person who called himself Liversidge was a person of hostile associations and ordered that he be detained under Regulation 18B of the (British) Defence (General) Regulations 1939. To have legal authority to do so, the Secretary of State was required to have 'reasonable cause to believe' that the person was of hostile associations. Could the courts, on application by the detained person, consider and determine whether the Home Secretary had in fact had reasonable cause?

2.11 The House of Lords said no. The matter concerned something essentially within the knowledge and exclusive discretion of the Home Secretary. It was enough if he were acting on what he thought was reasonable cause and in good faith. Dissenting, Lord Atkin thought that the phrase 'if A has reasonable cause to believe' is like the phrase 'if A has a broken ankle'. The latter phrase does not mean 'if A thinks he has a broken ankle'. He said that he knew of only one authority which might justify the method of construing the phrase adopted by the majority of the House of Lords, namely, Humpty Dumpty, *Through the Looking Glass*, ch. 6.

2.12 (4) (Case B) In 1964 the House of Lords had to face an analogous problem. Section 1 of the (British) Official Secrets Act 1911 makes it an offence to enter a prohibited place 'for a purpose prejudicial to the safety or interests of the State'. Would you commit an offence if, as a member of the Campaign for Nuclear Disarmament, you enter an RAF (Royal Air Force) station and sit, with others, on the runways with the purpose of preventing aircraft, probably carrying nuclear weapons, from taking off? The government considered such behaviour to be prejudicial to the safety or interests of the state. You considered that it would, on the contrary, serve the safety and interests of the state by helping to bring about nuclear disarmament. How could the courts judge between such views? The House of Lords held that the purpose which the 1911 Act had in mind was the immediate purpose (entering the RAF station and so on) not the ulterior purpose lying behind that purpose (to bring about nuclear disarmament). To judge whether the relevant purpose was prejudicial to the interests of the state was a matter for the courts. Ministers do not 'have any inherent general authority to prescribe to the courts what is or is not prejudicial to the interests of the State'. To hold otherwise would mean that 'the reasoning in Liversidge *v.* Anderson would, in effect, be part of the common law instead of the exegesis of an emergency regulation'. However, the methods of arming the defence forces and the disposition of those forces are at the decision of Her Majesty's Ministers for the time being. It is not within the competence of a court of law to try the issue of whether it would be better for the country that the armament or those dispositions should be different. In other words, the courts, rather than the government, should determine the legal question of what is prejudicial to the interests of the state but should not treat as a matter of judicial decision what is the best way of arming the armed forces. In all normal circumstances, therefore, the courts should, as courts of law, decide that that behaviour is prejudicial to the interests of the state, within the meaning of the 1911 Act, which interferes with what the government, as a matter of policy, determines to be the way of arming the forces.

2.13 (4) (Case C) In 1984 the House of Lords had to consider whether it should accept the government's judgement on the threat to national security which might have resulted from consulting certain interested persons before issuing instructions which would lead to preventing employees at a government communications establishment from belonging to a trade union.

2.14 The House of Lords decided that a court could require evidence from the government that its decision not to consult was based on reasons of national security, but would treat the question of whether or not the reasons of national security were adequate to justify the decision as being a non-justiciable question. Lord Diplock said that national security is the responsibility of the executive government. 'What action is needed to protect its interests is, as the cases cited by my noble and learned friend Lord Roskill establish and common sense itself dictates, a matter on which those on whom the responsibility rests, and not the courts of justice, must have the last word. It is par excellence a non-justiciable question. The judicial process is totally inept to deal with the sort of problems which it involves.'

2.15 (5) In 1868 the Fourteenth Amendment to the US constitution was adopted, providing that 'no State [of the United States] shall . . . deny to any person within its jurisdiction the equal protection of its laws'. In 1896 the US Supreme Court decided that racial segregation laws in the southern states, if they treated black citizens as separate but equal, did not violate the equal protection clause. In 1954 the Supreme Court decided that racial segregation failed to provide equal protection and that it should be terminated 'with all deliberate speed'. The Court said that, if its decision was inconsistent with the 1896 decision, then the later decision could be regarded as having overruled the earlier decision.

2.16 Five features of these examples may be readily apparent.

(1) They use ordinary language (*innocent*, *purpose*, *reasonable*, *intention*, *equal*) in a special way. It seems to be a private language which must have evolved alongside the mainstream of the English language. There would evidently be little point in a non-lawyer trying to enter the legal debate using the same terms in their ordinary-language meanings.

(2) They seem like the reports of a game. Evidently those taking part are extremely serious-minded. They remind us of the serious little Swiss children whom Jean Piaget lets us observe. Evidently there are rules of the game – a sort of rationality parallel to the rationality of the everyday world. But, once again, it might not be fruitful for an outsider to join in the debate using everyday rationality.

(3) They seem to be above but not beyond politics. They are clearly dealing with difficult social problems and making difficult social choices, and yet the discussion is not in ordinary political terms. Once again, we seem to be observing some parallel activity to everyday politics, a purified sort of politics, above the fray, Olympian in aspiration or, at least, in tone.

(4) They seem to reveal a notably dynamic activity. Nothing seems to be fixed or clear or final. Everything is open to further argument, reclassification, reconceptualisation, reinterpretation, re-evaluation. Everything is on the move from the past to the future (which will no doubt contain further, different decisions). What was seemingly the case

at one time (the effect of a statutory provision or a court decision or, at least, perceptions of that effect) is apparently not the case at another time.

(5) They seem to be progressive. There is some sort of negative entropy at work. Those involved seem to regard each decision as an increase in the quality of the system or, at least, as designed to achieve such an increase. Each state of the law seems to be intended as a surpassing of what has gone before which had itself surpassed something else – better understanding, better conceptualisation, better judgement. There seems to be a sense of direction in this ceaseless negation of negation, even if there is no obvious goal, a constant effort at greater orderliness in the face of the infinite variety and natural disorder of real-world facts, an instance, perhaps, of what Immanuel Kant had called the 'purposeful purposelessness' of organic systems.

2.17 Such immediate impressions would be correct impressions of the inner world of the law. To the lawyer law is a series of possible representations of something in the past and a series of representations of possibilities in the future. The superficial appearance of the law-world is, like the superficial appearance of the physical world, the appearance of a collection of discrete objects which are for some practical purposes regarded as static and self-standing. Legislative texts and decided cases are set out in a standard form in codes and statute-books and law reports and treatises and textbooks, like two-dimensional pictures of a putative real-world which has a form which corresponds to, if it is not fully represented by, such pictures. But there is no fixed object, no settled reality which corresponds to the legislative text or the decided case. Every statutory provision and every reported decision of a court may be supposed to have an efficient cause, located in the real-world of Parliament and the law-courts, and every other kind of cause in the total system (practice and ideology) of society, in the physiology and psychology of human beings, and ultimately in the whole structure of the material universe. But legislative texts and reported cases are not themselves the law. They do not even contain the law. The law is somewhere else and something else. The reality of the law is the reality of being perceived as law.

2.18 Every apparent object in the law-world – every apparent rule of law – is merely a transient wave in the field of legal forces which extends across the whole of the law and, beyond that, to the whole structure of causation which determines the successive conjunctures of the particular field of forces which is the law. The lawyer is the privileged observer within the field of legal forces. It is the interaction of his perception with those forces which constitutes the reality of the law. It is not the lawyer's perception which makes the law. But there is no law without his perception of law. It is not the law which the lawyer perceives. But there is no law unless the lawyer perceives something separate from his perception. And that something – the other which the lawyer perceives – includes not only the statutory provisions and decided cases; it also includes the perceptions of other lawyers.

2.19 This relativity of the law means, on the one hand, that the existing field of legal forces provides the possibilities of law. It means, on the other hand, that, in perceiving the law, the lawyer modifies the future possibilities of law. From the existing possibilities of law the lawyer determines the future possibilities of law. The categories in which the lawyer knows the law-world are the forms of his perception of it and those forms of perception are themselves liable to be modified by the perceptions of the law which other lawyers have had. Statutory provisions and decisions of courts are mediating structures between the whole system of social causation which causes them and the lawyer who perceives them, but the lawyer also perceives the perceptions of those structures by other lawyers and their perceptions of those perceptions. In this way the multi-dimensional network of the law grows organically and exponentially in internal and self-organising complexity.

2.20 The 'real' reality behind the perceived reality of the law-world is thus, like one view of the reality of the physical world, a hypothetical reality which can never be known otherwise than as hypothetical. The trouble is that the elusive hypothetical reality of the law produces dramatic real-world effects. If rules of law have causes in society which cause the field of legal forces to take on transient states of actuality in the minds of lawyers, then those transient states perceived by lawyers act, in their turn, as very efficient causes in the world beyond the law, transforming the very non-hypothetical lives of very real citizens. The door of the prison-cell is bolted. The fine and the damages are paid. The keys of the house are handed over. The deceased person's property is distributed. The employee is dismissed. The child is taken from his parents. The convict is executed.

2.21 The law mediates between two less hypothetical realities – the social forces which generate the law and the social events which the law generates. The law mediates reality through obscure mental events in the minds of lawyers. The citizen is deemed to know the law. He is not expected to know the mind of the lawyer. And yet his life may be transformed by the mind of the lawyer. To use Jeremy Bentham's image, men are killed by judges for not having guessed the judges' dreams.

2.22 Not all lawyers are aware of the strangeness of their enterprise. Most lawyers feel no need to make any further sense of it. But some lawyers have found it necessary to seek some higher-level rationalisation of their activities. The result has been the development of a series of specialist legal philosophies intended for consumption by lawyers – in-house, esoteric, hermetic, private legal philosophies. Over the last two centuries, there have a number of leading brands of special legal philosophies in the Anglo-American legal world. They have had, and will continue to have, an important effect on the self-consciousness of lawyers and thereby a significant effect on the development of society and on the life of every citizen.

Lawyers' philosophies

2.23 An attempt has been made above to give an impression of the strange inner world of the lawyer, with its special relativistic reality, separate from, but parallel to, the rest of social reality and in which a rule of law is best regarded as a sort of probability-wave, transient but undetachable from the total reality. Immersed in this special reality and living it as the everyday reality of their professional lives, lawyers in the Anglo-American law-world have found it necessary, over the last two centuries, to invent their own specialised form of legal philosophy.

2.24 These special legal philosophies have four common characteristics. (1) Each of them creates a model of the law in terms of which the peculiar phenomena of the law may be seen to be orderly and rational. (2) They do so by stressing one or other familiar feature of the law as its salient characteristic, making that feature axiomatic, so that other legal phenomena become explicable more or less derivatively. (3) In terms of intellectual method, they appeal to a sort of legal common sense. They depend on the introspection of the lawyer and his willingness to look sensibly and coolly at the legal phenomena with which he is perfectly familiar and to assent to reasonable explanations when he hears them. (4) Accordingly, their value is pragmatic (helping the law to improve its functioning) or heuristic (helping the law to improve its self-examination) rather than philosophical (purporting to offer some explanation which coheres with all higher-level explanations). They do not claim to be contributing to the mainstream of general Western philosophy. They ignore, or mention only incidentally, all the traditional and daunting problems of philosophy, especially the problems of epistemology, moral philosophy and social theory. They also ignore the study of law made by other disciplines, especially anthropology and sociology.[3]

2.25 William Blackstone (1723–80) served several useful intellectual functions, not the least of which was to ignite Jeremy Bentham. But his influence on lawyers is still far from finished. In a time of revolutionary intellectual and social change he managed to convey to Anglo-American lawyers an aristocratic belief in two things which were above time and circumstance – a common law and a parliament whose numinous power came from their deep roots in English history. Blackstone is the Livy, the Cicero and the Newton of Anglo-American law. English law is not necessarily irrational for being disorderly. The disorder of English law is not its true reality, when the underlying pattern of its development is brought to light. A constitution is not only the axiomatic source of law. The constitution is a temple. The law of the judges and the law of parliament are the admittedly human voices of priest and prophet. The history of English law is its future. Understand the true nature of the constitution, as a developed organism, and you will understand the law. Legislators and judges and practising lawyers and legal commentators might thereby all increase in legal virtue.

2.26 Blackstone was thus a representative figure of the eighteenth-century Enlightenment. He believed in a historism which was not nineteenth-century historicism. It was history as the study of causes not of iron laws. He believed in the enlightening power of knowledge. He believed in the possibility of order discovered in the depths of disorder.

[3] One school of legal thought in the US seeks to establish a close link between law and economics (and hence puts itself outside our present class of self-contained lawyers' philosophies), seeing law-behaviour as essentially analogous to economic behaviour in a sort of law-market. And there are many examples of lateral legal study with titles having the generic form 'law and such-and-such' which seek to build inter-disciplinary bridges rather than to create universalising theories of law.

Like his contemporary Edmund Burke, he believed in the wisdom of the natural. He gave a Roman self-confidence to English and American lawyers in the special rationality and dignity of their work, allied with a Roman piety together with an earnest purpose of improvement.

2.27 John Austin, writing in the early 1830s, was a pale shadow of the depressing Thomas Hobbes and the manic Jeremy Bentham – Hobbes and Bentham made safe for healthy practising lawyers. Bentham, whose ideas and influence went far beyond the special philosophical problems of lawyers, had turned Blackstone on his head. For Bentham and Austin, the law was, indeed, capable of being a rational science. But the law's future did not lie in its past. The past was full of lessons, almost all of them lessons by way of negative example. Legislation – intentional law-making – was to become the general paradigm of law. Legislation was reason made law. Law is made by an act of will, not found by an act of magic. Austin reduced these ideas to simple formulas, comprehensible to the most unintellectual of lawyers. Law, as Hobbes had long since said, was to be seen as a species of command whose validity derived from the fact of the sovereign's power and the fact of the subject's obedience. The common law was a law tolerated by the sovereign and, therefore, was rightly to be regarded as ersatz legislation, the continuation of legislation by other means. The idea-complex of sovereignty, command, sanction and obedience was all the lawyer needed to know about the theory of law.

2.28 What came to be called Austinian legal positivism was thus the means by which the general cultural phenomenon of positivism was allowed vestigially to affect the minds of lawyers. Law could be explained without reference to the extra-legal, the mysterious, the ideal or the moral. The Austinian orthodoxy was also prophetic, as the partly reformed parliament (after 1832) became, or came to seem to be, the engine for the revolutionary transformation of British society. The common law could take on a new dignity by association of ideas and by joining in as a vigorous partner of the new, purposive law-making. Giving practical effect to the will of parliament and, thereby, to the will of the people could also be a dignified task. In the last quarter of the nineteenth century, the court system was rationally reformed, the law-reports were properly established, and the study of everyday law became a regular university discipline, alongside the traditional studies of Roman law and Canon Law, instead of being a matter to be learned in the four Inns of Court. The common law could now also take on not only the purposive character of legislation but also special qualities of complexity, sophistication and rationality. The common law could now also weave its mystifying webs around the unquestionable but too-innocent words emitted as legislation by parliament. The result was that the common law began to take on a quality of massiveness and authority which would amaze even a resurrected Blackstone. With the reform of the law at the end of the nineteenth century, the doctrine of *stare decisis*, binding precedent, allowed the common law to take on a significance, so different in degree from the traditional respect of the law for 'decided cases', as virtually to amount to an innovation. The common law, through its self-chosen rule of precedent, could aspire to be a truly systematic structure. The judge could take on a new lease of Byzantine authority not only as the logothete executing the imperious will of the people but also as the oracle speaking and applying the accumulated wisdom of the judges.

2.29 Over the same period of time, law in the United States had undergone a parallel but separate development. The numinous character of the United States written constitution, drawing from the deep spiritual sources of the English unwritten constitution, had long since given to the idea of law a unique position in American political self-consciousness. Law is evidently and necessarily the rock on which the American nation is built. It followed that legal decision-making was necessarily of two kinds – the will of the people expressed in acts of the Congress and of the state legislatures; and the judicial process. More openly than in England, the judge had to be both arbitrator and decision-maker. Ultimate guardian of the constitutional order, the judge must settle disputes by choosing between competing claims to the protection of law, and he must interpret and apply the constitutional order by deductive decision-making, applying its generalities to the specific problems of everyday life. As a result, it was observed from the earliest days of the republic that the law and the lawyer occupied a special place in American society, as compared with England or the continent of Europe. The law and the lawyer have a high Blackstonian function to perform in the United States but they are to perform that function as an integral part of the system of social and political development. They are parallel to the directly political processes, as in Europe, but they are in no sense remote from them. The American people and all their institutions are engaged in the endless process of making the American nation and the judges are participating, directly and explicitly and actively, in that process.

2.30 Positivism did not cause in the United States the frisson which it caused in Europe. The idea that society might be understood mechanistically, or at least might be studied mechanistically, had in Europe an aura of iconoclasm about it, the thrill of insulting the gods of the tribe. The gods in question were as much intellectual gods as the gods of religion. In the United States society was much more evidently a man-made and man-determined creation. There was no intellectual or political or class necessity to cherish supersensible obscurities. So far as the religious gods of the American tribe are concerned, they have, from pre-independence days to the present day, been a tough sort of god. They have taken the measure of positivism. The spirit of legal positivism was not difficult to reconcile with the Blackstonian inheritance. The precise formulas of Austin were not appropriate, however, because one of the central features of the United States constitution is precisely the absence of a sovereign. The perverse American image of George III as tyrant had done its work. The separation of powers was so ingeniously built into the constitution of 1787 that it is impossible to say that any organ of the constitution is supreme (unlike the supposed and mistakenly supposed 'sovereignty' of the Queen in parliament in the United Kingdom). And the historical subtleties surrounding the origin of the constitution mean that, to this day, there can be no simple answer to the question of the repository of ultimate power. The confederation of states became a federal state, but which is master, the states or the United States?

2.31 In the first decades of the present century, some American lawyers suffered a realist paroxysm, a cyclical phenomenon in the history of Western philosophy from at least the days of the pre-Socratics. One particular form which it took was what has come to be known as American Legal Realism. In a spirit which is recognisably also that of American (philosophical) Pragmatism, American lawyers began to say, what not many Americans had really doubted, that law is not a mystery. Or, if it is, it is a dispensable mystery. Law is what lawyers do. Rules of law are perceived regularities in legal decision-making, especially adjudication, which, like observed regularities in the natural world, may sensibly be used as the basis for extrapolated predictions. Lawyers have a professional, moral and social duty to be explicit about the considerations which go to the making of legal decisions. Adjudication, like legislation, is a debate followed by a decision. Law is a purposive social phenomenon like any other. To improve law, and hence to improve society, it is only necessary to see what law is and laws are and, as with any other social problem, to do one's best in co-operation with everyone else.

2.32 Even lawyers were embarrassed by the conscious naivety of such a view, but there is no doubt that it articulated an element in their unarticulated self-perception. What every lawyer knows best is that law is a practical activity. What legislators, judges and lawyers do with the law is, in the eyes of any well-adjusted lawyer, very much more important than legal theory, whether of Blackstone or Austin, seemed to allow. It might be said that there was also a 'return to American values' aspect of the new approach. It echoes, implicitly if not explicitly, the populist and egalitarian and secular elements in the American political consciousness.

2.33 Realism was a luxury which Britain could not afford – in the first decades of the twentieth century any more than at any other time since the days of the British Solon, King Alfred, in the ninth century. British politics has never been able to bear too much reality. Britain lives in a perpetual state of suppressed revolution. Vague, collusive fantasies are the still-point of a turbulent political world. In such a context, political realism of the social-engineering variety is not possible. Political choices present themselves as choices of ideas, not choices of practicalities. Naive pragmatism, the optimistic belief in a society in which law is a series of open agreements openly arrived at, has simply not been available as a philosophical choice. What was observed in the first decades of the twentieth century was that parliament had, indeed, proved to be an excellent instrument of social change but that the executive branch of government had now taken power over parliament and thus that the supposed 'sovereignty' of parliament had become available to the political party, and especially its leader, having a bare majority in the House of Commons. The people's power over government now resided, if anywhere, in the infinitely complex new phenomenon of mass democracy, especially mass-media democracy.

2.34 Mass democracy elsewhere, in the paradoxical forms of fascism and Stalinist communism, certainly took a realistic view of the law. The law as an instrument of power, as the command of the sovereign, was an evident reality. It might have been expected that, after 1945, there would have been a surge of anti-positivism, a return to some sort of idealism. And, indeed, all over the world constitutionalism, on the model of the US constitution, was the instrument of the new democratisation of some societies and the coming-to-independence of many others. Human rights, in national constitutions and in international instruments, were to be a means of asserting ultimate values against the practical values of the positive law. The concept of human or natural or fundamental rights is not easy to square with legal positivism. In many advanced countries, the judges also began to assert the power of the law in relation to the vast new powers of executive government. It was recalled that democratic government is also government under the law, a principle which has come to be called the Rule of Law. In Britain and the United States, a whole new area of law – administrative law – rapidly developed to become a structure of great complexity and sophistication, controlling in the name of the law the powers which legislatures had given to the government in the name of social progress.

2.35 Legal theory in Britain took what was, in the circumstances, a surprising turn. In 1961 Herbert Hart published *The Concept of Law*. Hart is Hamlet without the King, Austin without the sovereign, Bentham without the zeal, positivism without the frisson. The paradigm of all law is not legislation but a rule of law. Understand why a rule of law is law and you will understand why all law is law. A rule of law is law because it satisfies criteria laid down by law. Those criteria are themselves rules of law, but rules whose function is distinguishable from the function of the primary rules of law. They regulate the making and changing and application of law. One of these secondary rules might be regarded as ultimate, saying what is the ultimate source of law although it need not name a 'sovereign'. But its content is itself determined contingently and extraneously, like the content of all other rules of law. It is the form and not the substance of a rule of law which must satisfy the criteria of legal validity. A legal system is a legal system because, as seen from within the legal system, it has a self-contained systematic coherence. The general relationship of the legal system to the other systems of society (political, economic, moral, religious) is also contingent and extraneous. It is not a necessary constituent of the legal character of the legal system. If you have a legal system functioning as a legal system, then it must contain a structure of rules of the two kinds, such that the structure coheres and persists and works.

2.36 Once again, this was very much a model which lawyers could recognise. The legal system of an advanced society does seem to be remarkably efficient, even though nobody has any clear idea of how the other social systems operate and, still less, of how the legal system is connected with those very problematic systems. If law is self-explaining, then that is not only intellectually reassuring; it is also just as well, since we are still waiting for an explanation of the other systems. Also, law does seem to persist by its own momentum regardless of the extraordinary conflicts and changes of the rest of society, as if it were a neutral arena for the social drama. Given the endlessly changing substance of law, experience does seem to suggest that law is a more or less empty framework capable of taking more or less any substantive content.

2.37 However, notwithstanding its popularity with law students, Hart's theory is of minimal theoretical or practical value. (1) It lacks the Hobbesian realism of the theory it explicitly rejects – that of John Austin. But to those involved in or with the law, law *does* seem like a system of commands to the breach of which a threat of unpleasant consequences is attached. And Hart's theory lacks the illuminating Kantian background of the theory which it tacitly resembles – that of Hans Kelsen, for whom law is a special system of self-consistent rationality. It leaves as tantalising loose ends the problem of those aspects of the law whose essence is that they are *not* seen as wholly validated within the given legal system (for example, what used to be called 'natural law' or what are now called 'human rights') and the problem of the relationship of law, if it is perversely seen as a set of 'rules', with other systems of rules, in particular morality. (2) So far as common-law legal systems are concerned, it misses the sublime essence of the common law – the idea that law *cannot* be stated as a set of existing rules but is a permanent process by which a potentiality of law is turned into an actuality as each case is decided, and as each case produces the potentiality of law for subsequent cases. This process, which retains the ancient virtues of customary law in societies in which legislated law has come to predominate, is becoming a universal feature of law as courts generally (including the European Court of Justice, the International Court of Justice, and even courts in the Civil Law tradition) make ever greater use of decisions in previous cases as a source of law. (3) As a matter of social practice, Hart's theory tends to enhance the social isolation and the self-satisfaction of the law and of lawyers.

2.38 Over the last thirty years Ronald Dworkin has been developing a fifth lawyers' philosophy. He has bridged the Atlantic with teaching posts in the United States and Britain. Dworkin is to Hart as Hart was to Austin. Dworkin is positivism with a human face. The paradigm of law is adjudication. What judges do is a great deal more than to apply rules of law. Indeed, the important question about the law is not why the judges see a rule of law as law but how they decide a case in terms of law. Is it possible to rationalise the very complex substance of the law without exiting from the law, as the legal realists would propose, and without bracketing out all the content of judgements which is not merely a recital of legal rules? The importance of the question is that, as Bentham so passionately believed and as Dworkin repeatedly invites us to remember, the law is dealing with matters of life and death in the lives of real people. All that the people have as their defence against the law is the rights which the law should see it as its duty to defend. Dworkin has concentrated on what might be called the substantive structures of the law, that is, the legal content which is not merely formal and not merely political. His is a theory of value in the law, a theory of value not of values. It treats a concept of value as being neutral enough to be included in the essential structure of law, even if values are otherwise contingent and extraneous and changeable. Dworkin believes that it is possible to rationalise the vast agglomeration of the law in terms of the nature and purpose of society. Law is designed to cause a society to flourish in accordance with its own highest aims, to cause it to be or to become a community.

2.39 Dworkin's approach can still be termed positivist in that the value in the legal system is, precisely, in the legal system. It is inherent and structural. His is, therefore, still a theory which treats law as self-contained and self-coherent, but neither an essentialist view of the 'real' nature of all law nor merely a semantic theory about the common usage of the word 'law'. To the criticism that his theory is provincial, a theory of an idealised version of Anglo-American or even merely of American law, his answer would be disarming. He would say that he has no wish and, perhaps, no competence to determine the real nature of all legal systems all over the world and through all time. He would also say that in the Anglo-American tradition, or at least in American society, law must be taken to have found its highest expression, in the most advanced or the most satisfactory form of political system. In other words, he would, on this issue, take up a position alongside John Rawls and Robert Nozick who, in the field of political theory as opposed to legal theory, are vulnerable to the same charge of provincialism. They may seem to be offering only theoretical models to encourage the self-awareness and self-confidence and self-esteem of those who have more liberal or more conservative attitudes to one and the same thing, namely liberal democracy of the capitalist variety. But they would regard that as no unworthy or unfruitful function, given the peculiar theoretical uncertainties of those who supposedly support that system and the unarguable superiority in principle of that system.

2.40 In the second half of the twentieth century there arose in the United States another lawyers' philosophy. The Critical Legal Studies movement was in the spiritual tradition of American philosophical Pragmatism, spliced (and spiced) with a long-distance affinity with Humean scepticism and European socialism. It is legal realism plus the spirit of critical philosophy. That is to say, it invited the lawyer to stop taking the mythology of the law on its own terms and to see the social and political realities which determine every aspect of the law. But it went further and joins the spiritual tradition of Marxism (itself drawing on Hegel and Kant and much that preceded them) in believing that to see a new reality is to change reality. In terms of intellectual style, the Critical Legal Studies movement has been hampered by using the American *macho* academic style (tough text; voluminous footnotes), which is an unworthy heir to the style of the High Renaissance of German university culture in the nineteenth century, itself a radical departure from the characteristically more lyrical style of French, Italian or British culture and of German culture before and since. In terms of intellectual apparatus, Critical Legal Studies makes fleeting promiscuous sorties into any other intellectual activity of the demystifying kind – praying in aid a varied collection of European thinkers of different schools and differing merit, especially those who in recent decades have sought to focus attention on the medium of the message and on the radical relativity of the significance of the message (loosely referred to as *postmodernism*). Since law is language in action, critical study of the law can naturally join with any study of language which treats language itself as problematic, opaque and uninnocent.

2.41 Disarmingly, CLS acknowledged the paradox of its position. Whilst seeing clearly the self-deluding tyranny of existing social values in the law, it nevertheless hoped that analysis can be made to transcend and dissolve the illusions of the law (and not merely to replace them by other illusions). Disarmingly also, it did not claim to be a general philosophy of law phenomena within the mainstream of general Western philosophy. Nor did it claim to be socially revolutionary in the extreme sense. It is interested in radically altering legal education and the self-perceptions of lawyers within the context of what may still broadly be recognised by an outsider as the world-view of liberal democracy (keenly sensitive as CLS itself is to the fantasy-form popularly known as liberalism). Once again, as with Legal Realism and Dworkin, there seems, to an outsider, to be an important ingredient of 'return to American values', a self-administered therapy, to restore a saner and clearer understanding of those values. It is hard to avoid drawing a parallel between CLS and a strain in Christian theology over the last century-and-a-half: Biblical Criticism (especially the Higher Criticism), Modernism at the turn of this century, Liberation Theology today. In a devastating aphorism, Loisy, a leading Modernist, said: 'Christ proclaimed the kingdom; there came the Church.' CLS seems to say: 'America proclaimed justice; there came the law.'

2.42 Critical Legal Studies led to acrimonious dissensions in those American university law schools where some faculty members had been affected by it. It has given rise to far-reaching debate about the purpose of legal education. Is its purpose to train good Wall Street lawyers or to educate? There are some British universities where Jurisprudence (legal theory) is not a compulsory subject for law students. This means that lawyers can leave the university and take up practice as lawyers without ever having considered at the second level, as a subject of study in their own right, the source of the validity of law, the special nature of legal rationality and the conceptual structures used by the law (especially the nature of rights and obligations), let alone the relationship of legal ideas to other structures of ideas or the relationship of law to other social systems and phenomena. Such lawyers must treat the actual in the law as inevitable and natural and as presumptively rational. Critical Legal Studies is right in saying that such an attitude is itself an aggressive policy and not merely an innocent side-effect of education. Those lawyers who have studied legal theory are not condemned to be revolutionary lawyers or even radical lawyers. They are merely more conscious lawyers – more conscious, in particular, of the special duty they owe to society by reason of the extraordinary trust which society places in them and their arcane mysteries.

2.43 Lawyers' philosophy is thus only one small part of legal philosophy, itself only one small part of philosophy in general. But there is a deep-structural, albeit unconscious, connection between the special lawyers' philosophies and general legal philosophy. Legal philosophy, an inheritance of more than twenty-seven traditions in the Western tradition, a still more ancient inheritance in other traditions, seems to be an overwhelming profusion and confusion of conflicting and competing ideas about a bewildering diversity of legal systems.[4] But it may also be seen as a more or less orderly exploration of the legal dimension of humanity's social self-constituting. As if programmed by the needs of human self-evolving, the conflicting sets of ideas can be seen as coherent if they are seen as seeking to explain legal systems in relation to a series of receding mental horizons.

(1) A legal system seen from within as a self-contained system of representation and rationality. Law as law. (For example, positivism.)
(2) The legal system as one of the systems of a society's self-constituting, alongside moral, political, economic and other such systems. Law as social superstructure. (For example, Marxism.)
(3) The legal system seen as the self-ordering structure of society as a whole. Law as society's legal self-constituting. (For example, Aristotle, social contract theory.)
(4) The legal system of a society as a manifestation of supra-societal phenomena, ideological or biological. Law beyond society. (For example, natural law theory.)
(5) The legal system as a means of participating in a realm of order which transcends society and integrates it with universal order. Law and the ideal. (For example, Plato, theologies of law.)

To look at law in relation to all of these horizons is to begin to know something about the phenomenon of law.[5]

II. The emerging universal legal system. The law of all laws

2.44 It is remarkable that the human species has managed to survive for almost 250 years in the grip of the bizarre Vattelian legal worldview.[6] In the twentieth century, the crazy idea that the human race

[4] For an exceptionally broad overview of the ideas and realities of legal systems, see A. N. Allott, *The Limits of Law* (London, Butterworths; 1980).

[5] The present author's *Eunomia* seeks to give effect to such an approach, which is reflected also in the present volume.

[6] E. de Vattel's *Le droit des gens, ou, Principes de la loi naturelle: appliqués à la conduite et aux affaires des nations et des souverains* was published in 1758.

might not survive was treated as a suitable topic for rational discussion and rational decision-making. People who are otherwise sane and sensible could talk about Mutual Assured Destruction and the End of Civilisation. People who are otherwise sane and sensible could make and manage total war, wars with no necessary geographical limit, no effective limit to the methods of death and destruction, no limit to the suffering to be endured by powerless and blameless human beings. In the twentieth century, people who are otherwise decent and caring could regard it as regrettable, but natural, that countless millions of human beings should live in conditions of life which are a permanent insult to their humanity, or in chaotic societies dignified by the name of 'state', or in subjection to criminal conspiracies dignified by the name of 'government'.

2.45 The fact that, for so long, such madness has been mistaken for sanity is a tribute to the power of simple ideas, and to the power of those who have power over public consciousness. The simple ideas in question – the Vattelian international system – seem infantile by comparison with the complexity and subtlety of the ideas that we have developed to explain and to guide our national systems. But, for those who have power over the national systems, the very simplicity of the international system has been its special charm. It has allowed them to escape from the tiresome burdens of their national political systems into the rarefied upper-atmosphere of 'foreign policy' and 'diplomacy', into a prelapsarian world in which there has been no French Revolution, not even an American Revolution, a world in which 'states' represented by 'governments' co-exist in a state of nature which is Lockeian when things are going well, and Hobbesian from time to time, when things get out of control or when there is no other way to sort things out. In John Locke's benign pre-society, human beings are in 'a state of perfect freedom to order their actions, and dispose of their possessions and persons as they think fit, within the bounds of the Law of Nature, without asking leave, or depending upon the will of any other man'.[7] In the non-benign unsociety of Thomas Hobbes, 'during the time men live without a common power to keep them all in awe, they are in that condition which is called war; and such a war, as is of every man, against every man'.[8]

[7] J. Locke, *Two Treatises of Government* (1690) (ed. P. Laslett; Cambridge, Cambridge University Press; 1960), II, § 4, p. 309 (spelling and punctuation modernised).

[8] T. Hobbes, *Leviathan* (1651) (London, J. M. Dent & Sons (Everyman's Library); 1914), ch. 13, p. 64 (spelling and punctuation modernised).

2.46 For Hobbes, the myth of the state of nature was, in one sphere at least, not a myth but a fact. 'But though there had never been any time, wherein particular men were in a condition of war one against another; yet, in all times, kings and persons of sovereign authority, because of their independency, are in continual jealousies, and in the state and posture of gladiators.'[9] And Locke had a simple answer to what he calls the 'mighty' objection that there never have been men in a state of nature: '[S]ince all princes and rulers of independent governments all through the world are in a state of nature, it is plain the world never was, nor ever will be, without numbers of men in that state.'[10]

2.47 It was Vattel who made the myth of the state of nature into the metaphysics of the law of nations. 'Since Nations are composed of men who are by nature free and independent, and who before the establishment of civil society lived together in the state of nature, such Nations or sovereign States must be regarded as so many free persons living together in the state of nature.'[11] And the reified abstractions inhabiting the international state of nature are not fictions. They are persons. 'Such a society has its own affairs and interests; it deliberates and takes resolutions in common, and is thus become a moral person having understanding, and a will peculiar to itself, and susceptible at once of obligations and of rights.'[12]

2.48 These pseudo-persons have what Vattelians call 'international relations', pseudo-psychic conditions of amity and enmity, as petulant and whimsical as the personal relations of medieval monarchs or oriental potentates. They play 'the great game' of diplomacy, as they call it, a game whose arcane contests must sometimes be decided by what they call 'the ultimate reason of kings', that is to say, armed force. The only 'law' they recognise is a form of self-regulation, providing minimum conditions of co-existence among neighbouring landowners, the rules of the game.

2.49 The peculiar consequence of these strange ideas is that the human species lives in two separate mind-worlds, two forms of human

[9] Hobbes, *Leviathan*, p. 65. [10] Locke, *Two Treatises*, II, § 14, p. 317.

[11] E. de Vattel, *The Law of Nations, or the Principles of Natural Law applied to the Conduct and to the Affairs of Nations and Sovereigns* (tr. C. G. Fenwick; Washington, DC, Carnegie Institution; 1916), p. 3. The semantic confusion in Vattel between 'state' and 'nation' proved to be of great significance when, in the nineteenth century, it became possible to cause ordinary citizens to confuse their allegiance to their nation with their obligations to the systematic state, a state-system which might cause them to die by the million.

[12] *Ibid.*, p. 1.

reality, one societal and one pre-societal, one highly socialised and one barely socialised, one primitive and one sophisticated. We live with two conceptions of justice, two conceptions of social justice, two conceptions of morality, two conceptions of law, two conceptions of public order and of public administration, and two conceptions of social organisation, one internal and the other external.

2.50 It has been the task of diplomats and international lawyers to do what they can to construct bridges between these two mind-worlds, reconciling the internal and the external. They have sought inspiration in a ragbag of high-voltage ideas designed to redress the ideological poverty of the Vattelian worldview: cultural hegemonism (why cannot foreigners be more like us?); Gladstonian liberal internationalism (foreigners are human beings, after all); naïve constitutional extrapolationism (institutions which are effective nationally can surely be effective internationally); utilitarian risk-assessment (those with the most to lose from international lawlessness have the most to gain from international order); enlightened economic self-interest (we will probably profit, perhaps disproportionately, from maximising the general wealth of nations); and semiotic pragmatism (talk about international law or international morality is a good thing if it causes other people to modify their behaviour in useful ways).

2.51 Over the course of two exceptionally eventful centuries, the international state of nature became a wilderness of ever-increasing unreality and endless danger. At the beginning of the twenty-first century, at long last, two centuries late, there is reason to think that we are witnessing the first stages of a great metamorphosis of the international system, a change in the metaphysical groundwork of international law, a beginning of the end of the Vattelian worldview. We are witnessing the emergence of a universal legal system.

2.52 The transformation involves a tectonic shift in the relationship of the 'law' phenomenon at three levels: the national legal systems; the (transnational) co-existence of the national legal systems; and the international (universal) legal system. It forms part of a much wider, more general reforming of the relationship between the national and the international, the internal and the external. The notional national–international frontier is evaporating. Social reality is now flooding in both directions across that frontier, including economic transactions and consciousness transactions (religious, cultural, political). Internal social reality in most countries is now being substantially determined by external social reality. The word 'globalisation' does not adequately reflect the two-way character of the process. The word 'interdependence' does not adequately reflect its intensely dynamic character.

2.53 A major component of the two-way free-flow of social reality consists of legal phenomena. A striking effect of the triumphalist expansion of democracy-capitalism in the 1990s, after the end of the Cold War, has been that national legal systems have become a matter of international concern. International human rights law had already sought to universalise concern about the performance of national legal systems, but the expansion of democracy-capitalism has transformed that concern into a strictly practical matter. We had hardly noticed, or we had forgotten, that advanced capitalism, whatever its rhetoric of 'freedom' and its naturalistic self-understanding, is a wholly artificial form of social system, requiring vast volumes of law and public administration. Advanced capitalism involves a structural transformation of society, including a transformation of the national legal system and the adoption of new legal institutions, systems, principles, rules and procedures of every kind.

2.54 Legal systems and legal services have become commodities in international trade, as legal experience is transferred from one country to another. It is now possible to get an economic advantage in international trade by ensuring that your trading-partner's legal system is more like your legal system than like those of your competitors. An investor's risk assessment necessarily includes an assessment of the adequacy of the legal system where the investment is to be made.

2.55 Liberal democracy is also an artificial form of social system or, rather, set of forms, since there are so many different kinds of democracy. Its social transformation includes the adoption of complex public law and intricate political and administrative systems, together with all the other subtle supporting systems of an 'open society'. In the 1990s we witnessed energetic international efforts to cause democratic social transformation in one national society after another, a genuinely well-intentioned international liberation movement, but one which might also help to make the world safe for capitalism, since a properly functioning democratic system is a wonderfully efficient way to provide the law and administration required by capitalism.

2.56 Transnational transactions of every kind, including economic and cultural transactions, involve the interaction of national legal systems, including the rules of those systems determining the law applicable to transnational transactions. International society now contains an infinitely complex network of overlapping national-law legal relations, in which the internal and the external are inextricably confused. The internationalising of social transactions is an internationalising of the national legal systems which make them legally possible.

2.57 We are also seeing an internationalising of national constitutional systems in the formation of a vast international public realm, as the national executive branches of government come together to regulate collectively every area in which the function of government extends beyond national frontiers and where the activities of governments overlap. The acceleration and intensification of international intergovernment, as we may call it, means that there are now, in effect, two forms of international law. Old international law is the modest self-limiting of the potentially conflictual behaviour of governments in relation to each other, as they recognise the emergence of new 'states', settle the limits of each other's land and sea territory and the limits of their respective national legal systems, resolve disputes and disagreements which may arise in their everyday 'relations'. New international law is universal legislation.

2.58 New international law is made in countless international forums, implemented through countless international agencies, interpreted and applied by countless new international courts and tribunals. And new international law is re-enacted by national legislatures, implemented by national executive branches of government, enforced in national courts. We are now beginning to see that old international law was essentially a rudimentary international constitutional law, providing the fundamental structures of a primitive form of international society.

2.59 The dramatic development of the international public realm and the denationalising of the national legal systems together raise, in an exceptionally acute form, the age-old problem of constitutionalism. How can we, the people, take power over the power of the social systems which govern us? How can we make government politically and legally accountable for what it does on our behalf? How can we achieve this at the level of international society, the society of all societies? The problem of international constitutionalism is the central challenge faced by international philosophers in the twenty-first century.[13] It involves

[13] For further discussion of constitutionalism in the international context, see ch. 12 below.

a fundamental reconceiving of international society. The first and most important step in meeting the challenge of international constitutionalism is to remake our international legal worldview, to begin to articulate the eventual structure of a universal legal system, the legal system of all legal systems.

- *International constitutional law*: the principles of the international constitution, fundamental rights, international legal persons, international law-making processes, the relationship between international law and national law, the relationship between national legal systems.
- *International public law*: the powers of international legal persons, the powers of international institutions, international public order law (international security).
- *International administrative law*: controlling the exercise of powers delegated by international law.
- *International economic law*: (*inter alia*) international commercial law, international environmental law, international intellectual property law, international competition law, international securities law.
- *International transnational law*: the international dimension of national legal systems.
- *International criminal law*: national jurisdiction over foreign offences, extradition, international criminal prevention and detection systems, jurisdiction over offences under international law.

2.60 International social reality has overtaken international social philosophy. The Vattelian mind-world is withering away under the impact of the new international social reality. The reconstruction of the metaphysical basis of international law is now well advanced. The deconstruction of the false consciousness of politicians, public officials and international lawyers is only just beginning.

III. Deliver us from social evil. International criminal law and moral order

2.61 To believe that we do anything from a free decree of the mind is to dream with our eyes open. Such was Spinoza's way of denying what he believed to be a false idea of moral freedom, and his way of affirming another idea of freedom, namely, the overcoming, through the power of the mind, of the decrees of the body. Since mind and body are, for Spinoza, merely two ways of conceiving of humanity's participation in the natural order of the universe, acting immorally and acting morally are merely two aspects of being human. We do good and we do evil because that is our nature.

2.62 The intellectual response to the problem of evil was taken further by the idealist-empiricist Kant and by the philosopher-biologist Freud. For the one, the solution to the problem is to be found in the transcending of the autonomous self by the idea of the universal self. For the other, the solution lies in the capacity of the self (the *ego*) to take power over its internal other (the *id*) by means of a transcendental form of the self (the *super-ego*).

2.63 Other self-examining human minds have suggested that moral freedom is an illusion, or that the search for a rational foundation for morality is illusory, or else they have disposed of the philosophical problem by reformulating it as an empirical problem, a social problem, or a linguistic problem. The mind that is haunted by its knowledge of good and evil reflects on its own knowledge and is able to convince itself that there is no problem or no answer or no possibility of an answer. The fact of human evil is apparently beyond human self-redeeming. We accept the non-human redemption offered by religion, or else we must simply accept the fact of evil, as we accept the facts of sickness and natural disaster. We know the good and we do evil. Why? We do not know.

2.64 The mind of society is more robust than the mind of the philosopher. Society's philosophy is social action. Social practice overcomes the hesitations of the self-contemplating mind. *Evil. Sin. Crime.* Society produces its own idea of *evil* as it condemns *sin* and punishes *crime.* And society's ideas are idea-forces, to borrow Fouillée's concept, ideas with the power to control human lives. The redeeming of evil becomes an aspect of the functioning of social systems. But, if society is to be the judge of evil, who is to be the judge of society? In the light of our experience of the long and tempestuous twentieth century, it is this question which has become the crux of a new form of the problem of evil.

2.65 We do evil socially. We judge evil socially. But what, in Spinoza's terms, is the place of society's decrees in the order of nature? How, in Kant's terms, can society find heteronomy within its autonomous self?

Where, in Freud's terms, can society find a self-controlling other within its idea of its self? In terms of the philosophies of all times and all places which have recognised the problem of evil, how can we explain the fact that societies, and not merely individual human beings, know the good and do evil? How can human beings who have disempowered themselves intellectually in the face of the problem of evil take power over the power of society to do evil and to judge evil? To believe that society does anything from a free decree of the mind is to dream with our eyes open. To believe that society's mind has an authority which we do not accord to the mind of the philosopher is to prepare the way for a form of human self-dehumanising, as the future of the human species becomes nothing other than a by-product of the social systems that it has created, social systems to which we accord a moral omnipotence if we believe that we cannot transcend them by the power of mind.

2.66 When the evil in question is said to be a *crime against humanity*, and the judging of that evil is by, or on behalf of, *international society*, the society of all societies, then the problem of social evil has reached its limiting case, the ultimate challenge of human self-knowing, self-judging, self-transcending and self-redeeming. And, at that level, the attempt to criminalise social evil raises three particularly painful problems.

2.67 (1) As Beccaria and Bentham suggested, a criminal sanction is itself a counter-crime, the doing of intentional violence to a human being. To justify the imposition of a criminal sanction requires a theory which reconciles very many things, practical and moral and psychological. Criminal law is no better than the theory which justifies it. And a justificatory theory of the criminal law is no better than the theory which justifies that theory. In other words, the social repression of the form of evil which is socially identified as crime is inseparable from the justification of the society which organises that repression. Except in a theocracy or a tyranny, the justificatory theory of criminal law in a given society is the object of social struggle. As international society develops its own system of criminal justice, how will it find its justificatory theory, the theory which justifies its judgement of evil and the theory which justifies its power to judge, unless through the arbitrary imposition of a theory by those with exceptional international social power, or else by the fortuitous application of the theory of a national criminal justice system which chooses to act as the agent of international society?

2.68 Criminal justice is a form of injustice. For Aristotle, legal equality is the great gift of law to the polity. In the criminal law, however, it takes on a sinister artificiality. Its artificiality is in its decontextualising. The offender and the offensive event are abstracted from the rest of the personal situation of the offender, and from the rest of the social situation of the event. The law even abstracts the person and the event from their participation in the natural world, imposing its own ideas of motivation and causation. When criminal law is applied internationally, or nationally in the name of international society, then the injustice of decontextualising is at its extreme. Each subordinate society – state or nation or people – is a unique product of a unique history. International society is full of disparities in every aspect of social development – spiritual, intellectual, moral, legal, political, economic. Artificial equality before the criminal law of an international society which still is a Many, and not yet a Many-in-One, is a limiting case of injustice.

2.69 Criminal justice is the admission of a failure in the socialising of society-members. It was in the philosophy of ancient China that it was first noticed that the cause of crime is the criminal law. If there were no criminal law, there would be no crime. In the absence of the idea of crime, anti-social behaviour might be regarded as an instance of social or personal failure, a human disaster, or else it might be reproved as sin, subject to any number of diffuse social and psychic sanctions. To criminalise a human being is a denial of love, of the possibility of the redeeming power of love. In love, I am the other, and the other is part of me. The murderer and the torturer, and those who procure murder and torture in the public interest, are me and part of me. *That art thou*, to borrow the formula of the Upanishads. The true *telos* of the criminal law is not deterrence or retribution, as generally supposed, but exclusion. It is a system of exclusion from the affective bonds of the social family and the human family. The *telos* of society, on the other hand, is the offer of affective inclusion. A society which seeks to increase inclusion to the maximum has the possibility of reducing crime to a minimum.

2.70 The introduction of international criminal jurisdiction into the present state of international society is a crude extrapolation of the most primitive, the least efficient, and the most morally dubious of systems for socialising human beings, namely, the criminal law. International criminal law might follow, but cannot precede, the establishing of the idea of the international rule of law, including international administrative law, to control directly the abuse of power and the anti-social behaviour of governments and public officials. And the establishing of the international rule of law will follow, but cannot precede, the coming-to-consciousness of the idea of human sociality, the species-consciousness of the human species.

2.71 (2) Corrective justice, in Aristotle's conception of it, is remedial justice, a remaking of the past. The legal remedy cures in the present a defect in the past. The effort to introduce the notion of international criminal justice into international society is one aspect of a remarkable *fin-de-siècle* (if not *fin-de-millénaire*) phenomenon, a cultural movement which we may call *corrective history*. Corrective history does not seek merely to tell the story of the past in a new way, which is the perennial task of historiography. It seeks to redeem the past by remedying past injustice. Rather as the psychoanalyst assists the patient to recover a personal past, so the historian now is called upon to recover a social past, to assist in a process of collective confession and, if need be, penitence. As St Augustine, in his *Confessions*, sought 'to wind round and round in my present memory the spirals of my errors', so whole societies are being constrained to frame an 'accusation of oneself' and to weep 'the tears of confession'.

2.72 Augustine, in his remarkable proto-Freudian self-analysis, said that 'man is a great depth' and that 'there is in man an area which not even the spirit of man knows of'. And yet historians, when they act as the confessors of societies, are required to throw light into the depths of the public mind of society, with a methodological and forensic assurance which no one now would bring to the exploring of the private mind. Francis Bacon said that 'the government of the soul in moving the body is inward and profound'. No less obscure is the government of society by many souls. Those who share responsibility for social evil and those who bear the greatest responsibility for the greatest social evils committed in the public interest – colonial oppression, slavery, genocide, methodical terror, war – are two-souls-in-one: a private mind moved, perhaps, by tender family-feelings or a scrupulous religious sensibility, and a public mind systematically integrated with the public mind of society, with the distinct drives and desires of society's mind, and its distinct ideas of rationality and morality. The mind of government has reasons which the reasoning mind does not know.

2.73 A possible social function of history-writing is to teach us about ourselves. 'In history a great volume is unrolled for our instruction, drawing the materials of future wisdom from the past errors and infirmities of mankind.'[14] Quite another thing is to suppose that we can *take responsibility* for the past. We cannot take responsibility for what we did not do, nor for what was done in the past by, or on behalf of, the society to which we now belong. We can feel shame, as human beings and as beneficiaries. We can feel pity, anger and disgust. We can take responsibility for correcting the continuing consequences of the past. We can resolve to do better in the future. More cannot be expected of us. The past is beyond redemption.

2.74 The past is beyond resurrection. The arrow of human time cannot be reversed. The past cannot be re-enacted or relived. The dead, murdered in the public interest, cannot be reborn. The tortured cannot be un-tortured. The disappeared cannot be made to reappear. We cannot avoid forming a judgement of the public interest of other societies and other times by reference to our own ideas of the public interest. We cannot suspend our moral sense. But to enact the process of judgement using conventional legal process, using corrective history to achieve retrospective corrective justice, is social evil added to social evil. It is injustice masquerading as justice.

2.75 There is pathetic irony in the fact that the retrospective application of corrective justice involves a betrayal of those who are the victims of past social evil. Corrective justice, as its name implies, in some sense corrects an evil. To some degree, the perpetrator is absolved. A price is paid. Suffering is compensated. Feeble old men and their seedy subordinates shuffle into the court-room, shrunken figures bearing no physical relationship to the physical scale of the suffering for which they are responsible. The half-theatrical, half-religious rituals of the law are performed. Due process. Verdict and sentence. History has been corrected. The causes and the effects of extreme social evil remain, its human price, but our moral outrage is clouded by the charade of judicial retribution.[15]

[14] E. Burke, *Reflections on the Revolution in France* (1790) (London, Dent (Everyman's Library); 1910), p. 137.

[15] 'The ordinary actors and instruments in great public evils are kings, priests, national assemblies, judges, and captains. You would not cure the evil by resolving that there should be no more monarchs, nor ministers of state, nor of the gospel; no interpreters of law; no

2.76 (3) The most painful irony is that the introduction of criminal justice into international society will have the incidental effect of seeming to legitimate the social evil that it does not condemn. It will catch in the net of its legalism only a minute proportion of the social evil which fills the human world. The false innocence of legal impunity will encourage the evil-doers in their arrogance. And, when public interest permits of no other course of action, governments and public officials will continue to do social evil. They cannot do otherwise. To do evil is to do good, if that is their professional duty, as they understand their duty. Their self-justifying will increase in sophistication, as the challenges to their self-justifying become more sophisticated. Legalism breeds legalism. Legalism does not, and cannot, redeem.

2.77 The disorder of an evil social order can only be overcome by a higher moral order. Evil is to the human world what entropy is to the physical world. Human order, moral and social, is a perpetual negating of disorder. The actual is made better only by the power of negation which is present in our knowledge of the good. Our tragic sense of human life reveals our sense of its other potentiality. Our moral awareness – the *synderesis* of medieval philosophy, Schopenhauer's *bessere Erkenntnis* – allows us to will a better world in forming the idea of a better world. Our *voluntas* includes a *noluntas*, to borrow a word from José Ortega y Gasset, our power to exempt ourselves from the General Will, to overcome the omnipotence of society's public mind, to transcend the apparent necessity of the actual.

2.78 The governments of states, acting in relation to each other, are at an infantile stage of moral development. The most optimistic view of the rush to introduce international criminal justice, ostensibly with the support of governments, is that it is a sign of a new maturing of the moral sense of the public mind. The fact that it has led governments, like the seven-year-old children studied by Piaget, to adopt, for the time being, an inappropriate form of social ordering may be less significant, in the long run, than the fact that they have exposed themselves to the possibility of a maturer moral consciousness, to an understanding, centuries overdue, that moral heteronomy is indivisible.

general officers; no public councils . . . Wise men will apply their remedies to vices, not to names; to the causes of evil which are permanent, not to the occasional organs by which they act, and the transitory modes in which they appear.' *Ibid.*, p. 138.

2.79 There is only one moral order, for human individuals and human societies.[16] The power of the self-controlling mind may overcome also the apparent necessity of the decrees of society. Social evil is also evil.[17]

[16] 'Thus we recognise that, in our most secret motives, we are dependent upon the *rule of the will of all*, and there arises in the community of all thinking beings a *moral unity*, and a systematic constitution according to purely spiritual laws.' I. Kant, *Dreams of a Spirit-Seer Illustrated by Dreams of Metaphysics* (1766) (tr. E. Goerwitz; London, Swan Sonnenschein; 1900), p. 64 (emphasis in original).

[17] We already have an eloquent example of an effort to assert a higher moral order, above and beyond the criminal law, in relation to gross social evil. South Africa's Promotion of National Unity and Reconciliation Act 1995, establishing a Truth and Reconciliation Commission, might be seen as a model *mutatis mutandis* for the moralising of international society, and for the forging of a new international moral consciousness in the face of seemingly invincible large-scale social evil. Section 3 of the Act provides as follows.

'3. (1) The objectives of the Commission shall be to promote national unity and reconciliation in a spirit of understanding which transcends the conflicts and divisions of the past by – (a) establishing as complete a picture as possible of the causes, nature and extent of the gross violations of human rights which were committed during the period from 1 March 1960 to the cut-off date, including the antecedents, circumstances, factors and context of such violations, as well as the perspectives of the victims and the motives and perspectives of the persons responsible for the commission of the violations, by conducting investigations and holding hearings; (b) facilitating the granting of amnesty to persons who make full disclosure of all the relevant facts relating to acts associated with a political objective and comply with the requirements of this Act; (c) establishing and making known the fate or whereabouts of victims and by restoring the human and civil dignity of such victims by granting them an opportunity to relate their own accounts of the violations of which they are the victims, and by recommending reparation measures in respect of them; (d) compiling a report providing as comprehensive an account as possible of the activities and findings of the Commission contemplated in paragraphs (a), (b) and (c), and which contains recommendations of measures to prevent the future violations of human rights.'

3

Globalisation from above

Actualising the ideal through law

Becoming – Minds – Realities – Constitutions – The ideal – The legal – The real – Globalisation from below – Globalisation from above

Society is made in the mind, reproducing the characteristics of our mental processes in the form of social consciousness, the public mind of society, and in the form of social systems capable of thinking and of acting in accordance with their thinking.

One particular form of idea – the ideal – enables the human mind and human societies to imagine a better future and to choose to enact a better future. Law is a special way in which society thinks with a view to modifying the willing and acting of subordinate societies and of individual human beings who are the society-members.

The history of international society is the history of the arbitrary suppression of creative social thinking beyond the level of the nation and state, the repression of the idea of the ideal, the avoidance of the society-making power of a true legal system.

Can the potential international society of the whole human race, with its primitive systems and exiguous social consciousness, redeem its mind in the name of newly conceived ideals of its human self-constituting beyond the level of the nation and state?

> How beauteous mankind is! O brave new world,
> That has such people in 't!
>
> William Shakespeare, *The Tempest*, Act v, sc. 1

Becoming

3.1 We, human beings and human societies, are processes of becoming. We are what we have been and what we will be. What we have been, what we call our *past*, exists nowhere else than as an idea in our minds. What we will be, what we call our *future*, exists nowhere else than as an idea in our minds. What we call the *present* is the vanishing-point between the past and the future, a mere idea within our minds of the relationship between what we have been and what we will be. In the continuous present of our idea of our becoming, we present the past and the future to ourselves as a contrast between an actuality and a potentiality.

3.2 In the continuous present of our idea of our becoming, we can constantly re-imagine the actuality of our past, through the mental processes which we call personal *memory* and social *history*, but that is the limit of the potentiality-for-us of the past. Otherwise the past is beyond our power. And we can imagine, and constantly re-imagine, the potentiality-for-us of the future, imagining what we could become, what we will be. But, in the case of the future, the human mind understands its relationship to the future in the form of a strange paradox, a strange feature of the way in which the human mind seems to have evolved within the evolution of all living things, within the development of the universe of all-that-is. We can make the future but we cannot determine it. What will be will be what we do, but not only what we do. The future will also be made by the willing and acting of other human beings and other human societies, and by all other organic and inorganic processes of becoming, as they actualise themselves within the becoming of the universe of all-that-is.

3.3 So it is that the strange paradox of our relationship to the future is also a strange fate. We can imagine the future; we can choose to actualise this potentiality rather than that; and we can will and act to actualise our chosen potentiality. But we cannot be certain that our chosen future will become an actuality, a presence within our past. We may be able only to console ourselves by imagining what might have been, or by re-imagining and re-evaluating, through personal memory and social history, what has been, making it conform, so far as we are able, to the potentiality which we chose or might have chosen – the road we might have taken, the words we might have spoken, the unintended effects of wanted and unwanted events, the war we won by losing it or which we lost by winning it, the revolution which created new possibilities by destroying old potentialities, the suffering which made us better. The future of the human species is within the power, and beyond the power, of the human species.

3.4 The strangest feature of our paradoxical relationship to the future, the central fact of our evolved destiny, lies in the fact that the vanishing-point which we call the *present* is filled with the idea of *responsibility*, the permanent and inescapable burden of choosing the future, of choosing what to do next. Our life, as it presents itself to our minds, as human individuals and as human societies, is a process of becoming, but, above all, it is a process of choosing to become. The human species is a species of *moral* beings, because we cannot avoid the burden of choosing, of willing with a view to acting. Moral freedom is moral duty.[1]

3.5 The way in which we understand the past affects the future because it affects the way in which we understand the potentialities of the future, and hence the way in which we understand our moral responsibility in relation to the future. In this sense, the past is always an active presence in the present, in the place where we are doomed to play our part in making the future. The moral burden of choosing the future includes the moral burden of choosing our idea of the past, of forming our idea of what we were, as individuals and as societies. We are what we have been, whether we remember it or not. But what we remember, and the way in which we choose to remember it, are added to what we have been in making what we will be. Memory and history shape the process of our becoming, up to and including the becoming of all-humanity.[2]

Minds

3.6 International society is a society like any other human society, except that it is the society of the whole human race, the society of all societies.[3] A society is a socialising of the human mind. From the society

[1] 'We human beings do not possess freedom; . . . freedom possesses [*besitzt*] us.' M. Heidegger, *Wegmarken* (Frankfurt-am-Main, Vittorio Klostermann; 1967), p. 85 (present author's translation). Heidegger's discussion of 'the nature of freedom' formed part of a lecture (on the nature of truth) first given in 1930 and included in this volume in a revised version first published in 1943.

[2] On the nature and possible social function of *history* in international society, see ch. 11 below.

[3] For an exposition of this conception of international society, see *Eunomia*.. Since the Reformation of the sixteenth century no single reified unifying conception of the social aspect

of the family, through the society of a nation or state, to the international society of the whole human race, a society is a form of functioning of the human mind. The mind of a society – social consciousness or the *public mind*, as we may call it – functions in ways which are characteristic of the functioning of the *private mind* of the human individual and in ways which are particular to the public mind of society. The role played by the mind in the *becoming* of a society is accordingly concordant with, and distinct from, the role of mind in the becoming of the human individual.

3.7 As human individuals, we have four minds. We have the *personal consciousness* by which we constitute our self within our ultimate solitude. We have the *interpersonal consciousness* by which we constitute our self in contact with the minds of others. We mutually construct each other. We have the *social consciousness* by which our mind participates in the public minds of societies, and by which the public minds of societies enter into our personal and interpersonal consciousness. We have the *spiritual consciousness* which integrates and transcends all the other forms of consciousness and which manifests itself in, but not only in, religious belief and practice.

3.8 The public mind of a society is also a multiple mind. Human societies have a *personal consciousness* by which a society constitutes its self in communion with itself, through its own social processes, including the private minds of society-members and the public minds of the subordinate societies which it contains. A society also has an *interpersonal consciousness* through which it constitutes itself in contact with the public minds of other societies – for example, a nation or state in its relations with other nations and states. Societies mutually construct each other. A society also has a *social consciousness* formed as the society participates in the public minds of the super-ordinate societies to which it belongs – including, for example, intergovernmental organisations – up

of human existence has established itself, leaving the speculative field open to competing ideas: a universal society of human beings or of states or nations, an international society of states, the international community, an anarchical society of states, the international system, world order. Greek and Roman thought, and pre-Reformation Christian thought, had produced many such ideas: *homonoia, kosmopolis, humanitas, humana civilitas, humana universitas, universitas humani generis, civitas maxima, concordia, the earthly kingdom, the City of Man, Christendom.* There was one last hopeless revival of the idea in the work of Christian von Wolff (1679–1754), who, in his 'natural law' exposition of the law of nations based on a *civitas maxima* (universal society), carried the best ideas of the intellectual worlds of the Middle Ages and the Renaissance into the new intellectual world of the eighteenth-century Enlightenment. See further in ch. 14 below.

to and including the international society of all-humanity, the society of all societies. Finally, a society shares in the integrating power of *spiritual consciousness*, not least, but not only, because of the extreme socialising of religion in human practice.

3.9 All human consciousness, individual and social, is thus both an aspect of the *phylogeny* of the human species, our shared evolutionary inheritance, and an aspect of the *ontogeny* of each individual organic system, human being or human society, the product of its own life-history.

Realities

3.10 The reality of reality has forever been the central question of philosophy, that is to say, the central question raised by the self-contemplating of the human mind. All cultures – and, especially, all religions – have sought to find a satisfactory way of resolving the question. In the Western philosophical tradition, originating in the philosophy of ancient Greece, it was very soon accepted that there could be no one answer, let alone one final answer. On the contrary, the clash of opposing solutions to the problem itself became the means of powerfully enriching the substance of human self-contemplating, especially the philosophy of being (metaphysics – what is it to use the word *is*?) and the philosophy of knowing (epistemology – what is it to say that I *know* that something is or is-so?).[4] The dialectic of idealism and realism, and of the countless intermediate positions, continues to the present day.[5]

4 'One party is trying to drag everything down to earth out of heaven and the unseen . . . and strenuously affirm that real existence belongs only to that which can be handled and offers resistance to the touch. They define reality as the same thing as body, and as soon as one of the opposite party asserts that anything without a body is real, they are utterly contemptuous and will not listen to another word . . . and accordingly their adversaries are very wary in defending their position somewhere in the heights of the unseen, maintaining with all their force that true reality consists in certain intelligible and bodiless forms . . . and what those others allege to be true reality they call, not real being but a sort of moving process of becoming. On this issue an interminable battle is always going on between the two camps.' Plato, *Sophist* (tr. F. M. Cornford), 246b–c, in *The Collected Dialogues of Plato* (eds. E. Hamilton and H. Cairns; Princeton, Princeton University Press; 1961), p. 990.

5 The negating of idealism has been called, at different times: sophism, pyrrhonism, scepticism, empiricism, nominalism, materialism, relativism, nihilism, positivism, naturalism, realism, pragmatism, logical positivism, phenomenology, neo-pragmatism, postmodernism. For contemporary examples of characteristically American fundamentalist anti-idealism, see: J. B. Watson, *Behaviorism* (London, Kegan, Paul; 2nd edn, 1931); H. S. Sullivan,

3.11 The problem of the reality of reality presents itself in a quite special way in relation to the reality which the human mind has itself made. Human beings inhabit a *human world*, entirely made by the human mind, a world parallel to the natural world, a self-made second human habitat, a human mind-world with its own *human reality*. Human reality is one reality and countless realities. On the one hand, human reality is constructed collectively through the interaction of consciousness in the activity of what have been referred to above as our interpersonal, social, human and spiritual minds. The becoming of international society – the society of all-humanity and of all human societies – contains the actuality and the potentiality of a universal human reality. But, on the other hand, the human world also contains countless particular human realities. Every person's idea of human reality is 'my reality' or a 'reality-for-me'. Like a Leibnizian monad, every human being and every human society has its own unique point of view from which the human world is seen, a perspective which contains the whole human world seen from that point of view.[6]

3.12 Over the course of the last three centuries, significant intellectual attention has been devoted (if not always *eo nomine*) to the problem of *human reality*, and we may regard ourselves as now being exceptionally well placed to offer a fruitful response to that problem. That we are able to do so may be seen as a side-effect or after-effect of what might crudely be called a Kantian revolution, a revolution which, as is the way with revolutions in general, was a restoration and a recapitulation rather

The Interpersonal Theory of Psychiatry (New York, Norton; 1953); H. J. Morgenthau, *Politics among Nations: the Struggle for Power and Peace* (New York, McGraw-Hill; 6th edn, 1985); R. Rorty, *Philosophy and the Mirror of Nature* (Princeton, Princeton University Press; 1969); E. O. Wilson, *Sociobiology* (Cambridge, MA, Harvard University Press; 1975); R. A. Posner, *Economic Analysis of Law* (Boston, Little, Brown; *c.*1986); D. Dennett, *Consciousness Explained* (London, Allen Lane; 1992).

[6] 'And so, since what acts upon me is for me and for no one else, I, and no one else, am actually perceiving it... Then my perception is true for me, for its object at any moment is my reality, and I am, as Protagoras says, a judge of what is for me, and of what is not, that it is not.' Plato, *Theaetetus* (tr. F. M. Cornford), 160c, *Collected Dialogues* (fn. 4 above), p. 866. Plato's Socrates is here speaking about a subjectivist conception of the reality of reality (i.e., of universal reality, not merely of what we are here calling human reality). G. W. Leibniz (1646–1716) conceived of the universe as being formed from ultimate indivisible 'monads' each of which contains the whole order of the universe organised around its unique 'point of view' (*point de vue*), so that each 'simple substance' is 'a perpetual living mirror of the universe'. *The Monadology*, §§ 56, 57, in his *Philosophical Papers and Letters* (ed. and tr. L. E. Loemker; Dordrecht, D. Reidel; 2nd edn, 1969), p. 648.

than a new beginning, a provocation rather than a programme.[7] We have come to understand much more clearly the way in which human reality – including, of course, the reality of international society – is constructed. In particular, we are able to identify more clearly the existence and the interaction of four *vectors* of human reality-making – the rational, the social, the unconscious, and the linguistic.

3.13 (1) It is possible to accept the idea that there is a *rational* component within human reality without taking any fundamental metaphysical or epistemological position relating to reality in general. The idea merely acknowledges that the human mind constructs relatively stable representations of reality, natural and human, which are communicable from mind to mind and which are thus able to have effect in all aspects of human consciousness from the personal to the spiritual, including social consciousness.[8] In social consciousness, such *models* of reality acquire world-changing power, equivalent not only to the most effective hypotheses of the natural sciences but even to the natural forces which those hypotheses rationalise. It is to such creative rationalising that we owe all the flora and fauna of the human mind-world – *state, nation, people, law, treaty, rule, war, peace, sovereignty, money, power, interest,* and so on and on.

3.14 (2) The *social* component in the making of human reality means that a given society – from the family to the international society of all-humanity – constructs a mental universe, a social worldview, which has the extraordinary characteristic that, although it is necessarily the product of particular human minds at particular moments in time, it somehow takes on a transcendental life of its own, in isolation from any

[7] Kant compared his own work to the Copernican revolution, resituating the human observer in relation to universal reality by making the human mind an integral part of the constructing of the reality of the universe. I. Kant, *Critique of Pure Reason* (1781/87), 2nd edn, preface (tr. N. Kemp-Smith; London, Macmillan; 1929), pp. 22, 25. 'What a Copernicus or a Darwin really achieved was not the discovery of a true theory but of a fertile new point of view [*eines fruchtbaren neuen Aspekts*].' L. Wittgenstein, *Culture and Value* (tr. P. Winch, ed. G. H. von Wright; Oxford, Blackwell; 1980), p. 18e.

[8] In the philosophy of the natural sciences, the Kantian point of view was reflected in the influential ideas of Ernst Mach (1838–1916) for whom science is a product of biological evolution which enables us to create 'economical' (simple, coherent, efficient) representations (primarily mathematical) of the universe, the 'necessity' of the universe being logical rather than physical. See R. Haller, 'Poetic imagination and economy: Ernst Mach as theorist of science', in J. Blackmore (ed.), *Ernst Mach. A Deeper Look. Documents and New Perspectives* (Dordrecht, Kluwer Academic Publishers; 1992), pp. 215–28. For an exposition of the analogous role of *models* in the social sciences, see P. Winch, *The Idea of a Social Science and its Relation to Philosophy* (London, Routledge & Kegan Paul; 1958/90).

particular minds and persisting through time, as society-members are born and die, join and leave the society. It is the mental atmosphere of the society within which the society forms itself and which forms the minds of society-members, that is, the public minds of subordinate societies and the private minds of individual human beings. It is retained in countless substantial forms – buildings, institutions, customs and rituals and conventions, the law, literature, the fine arts, historiography, cultural artefacts of every kind. It contains a network of aspirations and constraints – moral, legal, political, and cultural – which are internalised by society-members and take effect in their everyday willing and acting.[9]

3.15 (3) Whatever theory of the structure and functioning of the human mind we may accept, if any, it is difficult now not to acknowledge a powerful *unconscious* component in the formation of human reality. The mind finds within itself a *self-consciousness*, in which it seems to be aware of itself, the master of its own reality, the writer, the director, and the actor in its own drama. And, in each of our minds, there is an area which surpasses and eludes us, off-stage, out-of-sight – the *unconscious mind*, as it has come to be called – the area behind and beneath and beyond self-consciousness.[10] And we have reason to believe that there is the same duality in the minds of those we meet in interpersonal consciousness, in the public mind of society, and in the spiritual mind, the mind of all minds. It means that psychic reality is analogous to the putative real reality of the physical universe (the *noumena*, to recall the Kantian term),[11] in that the ultimate contents of our minds are unknowable. Our

[9] 'The phantoms formed in the human brain are also, necessarily sublimates of [active man's] life-process, which is empirically verifiable and bound to material premises. Morality, religion, metaphysics, all the rest of ideology and their corresponding forms of consciousness, thus no longer retain their independence.' 'Consciousness is, therefore, from the very beginning a social product, and remains so as long as men exist at all.' K. Marx and F. Engels, *The German Ideology. Part One* (1845–6) (tr. W. Lough, ed. C. J. Arthur; London, Lawrence & Wishart; 1977), pp. 47, 51.

[10] 'I received the profoundest impression of the possibility that there could be powerful mental processes which nevertheless remained hidden from the consciousness of men.' 'But the study of pathogenic repression and other phenomena which have still to be mentioned compelled psycho-analysis to take the concept of the "unconscious" seriously. Psycho-analysis regarded everything mental as being in the first instance unconscious; the further quality of "consciousness" might also be present, or again it might be absent.' S. Freud, *An Autobiographical Study* (1925), in *Standard Edition of the Complete Psychological Works* (ed. J. Strachey; London, Hogarth Press; no date; revised version of translation published separately in 1935), xx, pp. 17, 31. In the first sentence quoted, Freud is recalling the effect of his observation in 1889 of the effects of hypnosis.

[11] For Kant, the *noumena* (plural of *noumenon*) are conceived by the mind (*nous*) as that of which the *phenomena* are the appearances available to us.

self-consciousness is placed between two unknowable realities.[12] We live our lives with an unknowable world within us, a social order which we make but which is both within us and beyond us, and a natural universe of which we form part but which we cannot know except as we represent it to ourselves in our minds. The power of the unconscious mind is nowhere more apparent than in social reality, including the reality of international society, as feeling and imagination lend to rationally formed ideas the social power of life and death, and socialised forms of the psychopathology of the individual mind inflict suffering of every kind and degree on individual human beings.

3.16 (4) Although the role of *language* in the formation of human reality was an obsessive subject of study in the twentieth century, the general problem of the nature and origin of language is as old as philosophy, and as crucial as ever in humanity's never-ending search for self-awareness. We may usefully distinguish between language as a biological phenomenon present in many species of animal, language as a specific system within human consciousness, and language as a necessary component of social reality.[13] Biological evolution has conferred certain species-characteristics on human language, and the socialising of human language has transformed it into the means of expressing a specific form of human reality. Connecting the personal mind, where we speak to ourselves in isolation, to the interpersonal and social minds, and by integrating the personal and social minds with the spiritual mind, language has made the human species what it is for-itself and what the universe of all-that-is is for us human beings.

3.17 For those who have lived in the long twentieth century (from 1870), amazing and terrible as it was, the world-making and world-changing power of words is a lived and vivid experience. The human world is a world of words. Nouns and names rule our minds. We live and die for words. They give form to our feelings, determine our willing

[12] 'The unconscious is the true psychical reality; *in its innermost nature it is as much unknown to us as the reality of the external world, and it is as incompletely presented to us by the data of consciousness as is the external world by the communications of our sense organs.*' S. Freud, *The Interpretation of Dreams* (1900), in *Standard Edition* (fn. 10 above) (1953), v, p. 613 (emphasis in original).

[13] Saussure proposed analogous distinctions (*langage, langue, parole*) which have been influential in the modern study of language. F. de Saussure, *Course in General Linguistics* (1915, posthumous) (tr. W. Baskin, eds C. Bally and A. Sechehaye; New York, Philosophical Library; 1959).

and acting, define our possibilities, as individuals and societies. The long history of the philosophy of language – mind contemplating the possibility of the public mind – now offers to the public mind of the twenty-first century a powerful collection of ideas on the nature and origin of language, an unprecedented opportunity for a new human self-enlightening, a New Enlightenment.[14]

3.18 The metaphor of enlightenment has been a dominant archetype of many religions and philosophies across the world. It affirms the possibility that the human mind can raise itself by its own effort, can speak to itself, and about itself, in qualitatively new ways, and hence that humanity can repeatedly re-humanise itself.[15]

Constitutions

3.19 A society does not have a constitution. A society is a constituting, an unceasing process of self-creating. A society constitutes itself simultaneously in three dimensions – as ideas, as practice, and as law.

[14] The history of ideas about language is a striking instance of what Augustine and other optimists have called 'the education of the human race'. (1) In an exceptionally inconclusive dialogue worthy of the later Wittgenstein, Plato's Socrates says: 'How real existence is to be studied or discovered is, I suspect, beyond you and me. But we admit so much, that the knowledge of things is not to be derived from names. No, they must be studied and investigated in themselves.' Plato, *Cratylus* (tr. B. Jowett), 439b, *Collected Dialogues* (fn. 4 above), p. 473. (2) Aristotle proposed a conventionalist view of language. 'A noun is a sound having meaning established by convention alone . . . No sound is by nature a noun; it becomes one, becoming a symbol.' *On Interpretation* (tr. H. P. Cooke; London, Heinemann (Loeb Classical Library); 1938), II, p. 117. (3) A naturalist view of language was proposed by Lucretius. 'But the various sounds of the tongue nature drove them to utter, and convenience (*utilitas*) moulded the names for things.' *De Rerum Natura* (trs. W. H. D. Rouse and M. F. Smith; Cambridge, Harvard University Press (Loeb Classical Library); 1975), V.1028–9, p. 459. For the view that the way in which language expresses meaning has an evolutionary origin, see R. M. Allott, *The Motor Theory of Language Origin* (Lewes, Book Guild; 1989). (4) For the view that it is possible to establish the logically necessary *substantive universals* of language, see N. Chomsky, *Language and Mind* (New York, Harcourt Brace Jovanovich; 1968/*c.*1972). (5) For the view that language, as social reality, is a set of languages, connected by 'family resemblances', see L. Wittgenstein, *Philosophical Investigations* (tr. G. E. M. Anscombe; Oxford, Basil Blackwell; 1974).

[15] In the cultural history of Western Europe, five enlightenments, at intervals of three centuries, have been identified since the end of the Roman Empire in the West: western monasticism (sixth century; the Rule of St Benedict); the Carolingian renaissance (ninth century; centred on the court of Charlemagne); the twelfth-century renaissance (centred on the University of Paris); the fifteenth-century renaissance (centred on Italy); the eighteenth-century Enlightenment. For the idea of a twenty-first-century enlightenment, see ch. 5 below.

Each society, including the international society of all-humanity, the society of all societies, is a unique but ever-changing product of its threefold self-constituting. In its *ideal* constitution, a society presents its becoming to itself as actuality and potentiality, forming a *reality-for-itself* which includes its *history,* its self-explanatory *theories* and its *ideals.* In its *real* constitution, the willing and acting of individual human beings is socialised as they exercise *social power* in the course of their own personal self-constituting. In its *legal* constitution, social power is given the form of *legal power*, so that the willing and acting of individual human beings may serve the *common interest* of society in its self-constituting.[16]

3.20 Since a society is a socialising of the human mind, there is a direct and necessary concordance between the self-constituting of a society and the self-constituting of an individual human being. The constitution of a society is its personality. The personality of human beings is their constitution. My personality, which includes my reality-for-myself, is also a unique and ever-changing product of my ideas, my practice, and my law-for-myself, that is, my moral order. Like my reality-for-myself, society's reality-for-itself contains social poetry as well as social prose, the contribution of the imagination and the unconscious to the work of rationality.[17] Social practice is a product of ideas and law. Law is a product of ideas and practice. The ideas which take the form of *theories* within a society's ideal self-constituting and which help to form its reality-for-itself are that society's explanation of itself to itself, a society's philosophy-for-itself, one part of the totality of the self-contemplating of the human mind. As *practical* theory, they express themselves in the

[16] For further discussion of the three dimensions of a society's self-constituting, see *Eunomia*, ch. 9.

[17] The term 'social poetry' is particularly associated with the names of Giambattista Vico (1668–1744), for whom historiography is the social reconstructing of the story of the social self-constructing of human consciousness, and Georges Sorel (1847–1922), for whom social consciousness is both a weapon and the target of revolutionary social change. '[As] force is always on the side of the governed, the governors have nothing to support them but opinion. It is therefore, on opinion only that government is founded.' D. Hume, 'Of the first principles of government', in *Essays Moral, Political, and Literary* (eds. T. H. Green and T. H. Grose; London, Longmans, Green; 1875 /1907), I. IV, p. 110. 'For a society is not made up merely of the mass of individuals who compose it, the ground which they occupy, the things which they use and the movements which they perform, but above all is the idea which it forms of itself.' E. Durkheim, *The Elementary Forms of Religious Life* (1912) (tr. J. W. Swain; London, George Allen & Unwin; 1915/76), p. 422. Wondering at the social poetry of the nation and the state we may be reminded of Shakespeare's image of the poet who 'gives to airy nothings / A local habitation and a name'. *A Midsummer Night's Dream,* Act V, sc. 1.

course of social practice, the programme of actual willing and acting. As *pure theory*, they act as the theory of practical theory, the programme of society's programmes.[18] As *transcendental theory*, they act as the theory of theory, a society's epistemology.

3.21 The present essay is proposed as a contribution to the self-explaining of international society at the level of transcendental theory and pure theory, with a view to modifying the practical theory of international society, and thereby the willing and acting of all who participate in its real and legal self-constituting. The history of human societies contains many examples of revolutionary change not only in the real constitutions of societies but also in their ideal self-constituting, revolutions in the mind. Such events are moments of human self-enlightenment which transform the potentiality and the actuality of those societies. There is no reason why international society should be incapable of such self-enlightening, and every reason, derived from the lamentable history of its own self-constituting, why it should find a new potentiality for human self-creating at the level of all-humanity, the self-evolving of the human species, a revolution in the human species-mind.

The ideal

3.22 The potentiality of human self-creating takes the particular form of the *ideal* when the mind *conceives* of the present in the light of a *better* future, when the mind *judges* the actual by reference to a *better* potentiality, when the mind dedicates its moral freedom to the *purpose* of actualising that *better* potentiality. The ideal is the better potentiality of the actual, acting as a moral imperative in the present, with a view to making a better future. The idea of the ideal was made possible by three developments in the self-knowing of the human mind.

3.23 (1) It was first necessary for philosophy to produce the idea of *rationalised abstraction*. Reflecting upon the thesis of Heraclitus that all reality is *change*, Greek metaphysics and epistemology identified a capacity of the human mind to postulate the unchanging in the midst of change, that to which the process of becoming applies. It did so by postulating the universal aspect of every particular process of

[18] This distinction between pure theory and practical theory is analogous to Aristotle's distinction between speculative reason and practical reason (*Politics*, VII.14) or, as he expresses it in the *Nicomachean Ethics* (I.vii), the difference between the thinking of the geometer and the thinking of the carpenter. For further discussion, see *Eunomia*, §§ 2.52ff.

becoming – from the becoming of material objects (whose formal substance remains) to the becoming of living things (whose integrating form remains) to language itself (whose structure of rationality remains beneath the infinite diversity of actual communication). In this way, every single particular element in the universe could be seen as an instance of something more general, up to and including the universality of the universe itself (*kosmos* or *god*).

3.24 It became possible to see a particular collection of human beings living together as a particular instance of a universal idea of *society* (*koinōnia*) and, perhaps, of a *constituted society* under *law* (*polis*). It thereupon became possible to compare particular instances by reference to a universal model – Athens and Sparta, Greek and Egyptian, the governors and the governed, monarchy and oligarchy, oligarchy and democracy. It became possible to objectify and even to personalise particular cases of the generic universal (this state, that nation, all-humanity). It became possible to universalise and substantiate standards of comparison (values) – freedom, tyranny, justice, the rule of law, well-being. It even became possible to universalise the standards behind the standards of comparison, the value of values – the good, the true, the beautiful, virtue, happiness.

3.25 (2) Reflecting on another insight of Heraclitus, that change is the product of negation, the human mind became conscious of another remarkable feature of its functioning, namely, its propensity to present ideas to itself in the form of *duality*. It seems likely that we are biologically programmed – perhaps literally so, in some binary process within the systematic functioning of the brain – to construct reality by integrating opposing ideas ($1 + 1 = 1$). Philosophy very soon identified and appropriated this mental process as the amazing universal power of *dialectical thought*.[19] What may be an aspect of the physiology of the human brain, which has determined the functioning of the human mind, and which has been reproduced in the structure of human language through the long process of socialising, has given to human reality a peculiarly *dualistic* structure – life and death, being and nothing,

[19] The idea of the dialectic, made explicit in Plato's dialogues, retained its extraordinary power within pure theories of society up to and including the work of Hegel and Marx in the nineteenth century, and has continually haunted practical theories of society, up to and including the power-legitimating political parties and elections of democracy and the value-determining competitive struggle of capitalism.

appearance and reality, essence and existence, mind and matter, good and evil, pleasure and pain, true and false, the past and the future, the actual and the potential.

3.26 The dyad of *appearance and reality* has allowed us to make a human reality which is a mental reconstruction of a reality which we suppose to be not mind-made, enabling us to take power not only over the physical world (through the mental reconstruction effected by the natural sciences) but also over the human world (through the power of thought communicated through language). The dyad of *the actual and the ideal* has allowed us to make human reality into a moral order in which the actual can pass judgement upon itself by reference to its better potentiality, which is the ideal.

3.27 (3) Reflecting on human practice, especially social practice, philosophy was able, finally, to see that the power of the ideal stems from the fact that the idea of the better contains both the idea of the possible and the idea of the desirable. It generates a powerful attractive force inclining us to seek to actualise it. It engages, in our spiritual mind, something which is akin to physical love in our interpersonal mind. As evolutionary biology has used the power of physical love to negate physical separation with a view to the creation of new life, so it has made possible the power of spiritual love to negate the opposition between the present and the future with a view to the creation of better life, including better life in society. From the spiritual mind, energised by the idea of the ideal, come our most passionate moral feelings – of anger (for example, in the face of injustice and oppression), of hope (for example, for freedom and self-fulfilment), of joy (for example, in the face of the good and the beautiful) – feelings capable of inspiring limitless self-surpassing and self-sacrifice. Moral freedom is moral desire.[20]

3.28 These developments have given a particular form to *human reality*, the world made by the human mind. It is a form which we so much take for granted that it is difficult to see that it might have been

[20] '[Love] is the ancient source of our highest good ... For neither family, nor privilege, nor wealth, nor anything but Love can light that beacon which a man must steer by when he sets out to live the better life. How shall I describe it – as that contempt for the vile, and emulation of the good, without which neither cities nor citizens are capable of any great or noble work.' Plato, *Symposium* (tr. M. Joyce), 178 c–d , in *Collected Dialogues* (fn. 4 above), p. 533. 'We live by Admiration, Hope and Love; / And, even as these are well and wisely fixed, / In dignity of being we ascend.' W. Wordsworth, 'The Excursion' (1814), IV, lines 763–6.

otherwise – and that, at different times and in different places, it has been otherwise. Humanity discovered within itself a self-transcending power of self-conceiving, self-evaluating, and self-making, an inexhaustible source of human progress, of the self-evolving of the species. The idea of the ideal is the permanent possibility of the moral transformation of human beings and human societies, the permanent possibility of revolutionary human self-perfecting. We would not be as we are without the idea of the ideal. We will not be what we could be without the idea of the ideal.

The legal

3.29 The idea of the ideal has entered into the *ideal* self-constituting, and the revolutionary transformation, of countless societies. It has had a particularly powerful effect in the *legal* self-constituting of societies. It is present, if at all, only embryonically and immanently, in the *legal* self-constituting of international society, the society of all societies.

3.30 The law is another of the wonderful creations of the human mind. It enables a society to carry its structures and systems from the past through the present into the future. It enables a society to choose particular social futures from among the infinite range of possible futures. Above all, it enables society to insert the *common interest* of society into the willing and acting of every society-member, human individuals and subordinate societies, so that the energy and the ambition, the self-interest of each of them may serve the common interest of all them. Law is the most efficient instrument for the actualising of the ideal, universalising the particular in law-making, particularising the universal in law-application, a primary source of a society's survival and prospering within the self-perfecting of all-humanity.[21]

[21] 'How can it be that all should obey, yet nobody take upon him to command, and that all should serve, and yet have no masters, but be more free, as, in apparent subjection, each loses no part of his liberty but what might be hurtful to that of another? These wonders are the work of law. It is to law alone that men owe justice and liberty. It is this salutary organ of the will of all which establishes, in civil right, the natural equality between men. It is this celestial voice which dictates to each citizen the precepts of public reason, and teaches him to act according to the rules of his own judgment, and not to behave inconsistently with himself. It is with this voice alone that political rulers should speak when they command; for no sooner does one man, setting aside the law, claim to subject another to his private will, than he departs from the state of civil society, and confronts him face to face in the

3.31 It is possible to identify rather precisely the way in which law achieves its wonder-working. Within general human reality, and within the social reality of a particular society, there is a *legal reality* in which everything without exception – every person, every thing, every event – has legal significance. Legal reality is created by means very similar to the way, discussed above, in which the human mind constructs human reality generally – that is to say, by re-presenting to itself in the form of ideas what it conceives as being the 'real' world. Legal reality is a language-reality, made from words. Law is a language-world, in which special words, and words from other language-worlds, have their own self-contained life-process. Law shares in general ideas of human psychology, but has its own methods of explaining behaviour and attributing responsibility. Law shares in general rationality, but has its own methods of analysis, argument, and proof. In particular, legal relations are a special application of the capacity of the human mind for abstract generalising, followed by the substantialising and even personalising of abstract ideas.

3.32 Legal significance is given to that idealised reality in the form of what are called *legal relations* – that is, rights, duties, freedoms, powers, liabilities, immunities, disabilities – conferred on legal persons (human beings or legally recognised social forms). Legal reality is a network of infinite density and complexity in which everything, without exception, is the subject of countless legal relations.

3.33 My *freedom* to conclude a contract engages with your *freedom* to conclude a contract, and the resulting contract creates *rights* and *duties* upon each of us; gives me the *power* to invoke the protection of a court of law, if you fail to carry out a *duty* under the contract (unless you have an *immunity* from legal proceedings); gives to the court the *power* to make orders which alter the *rights* and *duties* of the parties to the contract, including, perhaps, the imposing on you of a *duty* to pay damages; thus giving a *power*, and imposing a *duty*, on a court official to enforce the court orders; all because a legislator exercised a *power* to enact a law about contracts and a law about courts; and because someone exercised a *power* to appoint judges and court officials under legislation on those matters – and so on, *ad infinitum*.

pure state of nature, in which obedience is prescribed solely by necessity.' J.-J. Rousseau, *A Discourse on Political Economy* (1755), in *The Social Contract and Discourses* (tr. G. D. H. Cole; London, J. M. Dent & Sons (Everyman's Library); 1913), p. 124.

3.34 A legal relation is an abstracted pattern of potentiality into which actual persons and things and situations may be fitted. It is a *matrix* which identifies persons and things and situations in an abstract form distinct from their status in general reality (person, corporation, state, contract, treaty, judge, plaintiff, government, parliament, property, territory, money). It is an *heuristic* which connects aspects of those persons and things and situations to each other in a particular way (contracting parties, shareholders in a corporation, parties to legal proceedings, sovereign of territory, government of a state, voter in an election). It is an *algorithm*, a mini-programme of action, which triggers a succession of consequences (especially the application of other legal relations) when actual persons, things, and situations fit into the pattern of potentiality (you step onto a pedestrian crossing, you ratify a treaty, you speak falsely about another person, you put money into a slot-machine). When the legal relation is applied, social reality is modified accordingly, by the conforming behaviour of actual human beings, actualising a possible future which had been selected by society in the common interest. From the selection-by-election of the members of a parliament, through the way in which the accounts of a commercial corporation are presented, to where you park your car, every aspect of human behaviour may be modified by law in the common interest.

3.35 It is the function of the *legislative process* to insert the common interest into legal relations, by resolving conflicting conceptions of the common interest into a single conception reflected in the substance of the law. It is the function of the *judicial process* to interpret the common interest when the abstracted patterns of the law are applied to particular situations. It is the function of *politics*, in the most general sense, to provide the forum in which conflicting conceptions of the common interest are brought into the dialectical competition of the *real constitution.* It is the *ideal constitution* of the society, its total self-constituting in the form of ideas, which generates the values and purposes which are the raw material of politics and which may ultimately be reflected in the law.

3.36 There are three primary functions of the law which are especially significant for the actualising of the legal potentiality of international society.

(1) Law makes the economy. Whatever the naturalist fantasies of the pure theories of an economy, not least theories of free-market capitalism,

the economy is a legal structure, that is to say, an artificial structure, made possible by the creation by the law of all the paraphernalia of the economy, from property and money to the corporation. The common interest which is supposed to guide the invisible hand of the market must first make itself visible in the superstructure of the law. Crucial question for the future of international society – what is the legal basis of the global economy?

(2) Law makes the public realm. The public realm consists of legal powers which are to be exercised *in the public interest.* A legal power generally gives to the power-holder a choice of possible decisions within the limits of the power, which may include decisions which are chosen to serve whatever interest the power-holder chooses to serve (to vote or not to vote; to vote for this candidate or that). A *public-realm legal power* limits the choice of possible decisions to those which serve the public interest, as determined explicitly or implicitly by the terms of the power itself or by the status of the power-holder.[22] If we take seriously capitalism's own story about itself, namely, that private wealth-seeking is justified because it is public wealth-creating, then we should regard economic power as a form of public-realm power, to be exercised in the common interest. Crucial question for the future of international society – in whose interest are the international powers attributed to states and other international actors to be exercised?

(3) Law makes constitutionalism. In countless societies, throughout the course of human history, social theory has been able to generate ideas whose common feature is that they place the ultimate source of the authority of law in something other than the will of the person or persons currently making or enforcing the law.[23] All law, and especially public-realm power, is essentially a delegation of power. Crucial question for the future of international society – what is the ultimate source of the authority of law at the global level?

[22] Locke similarly defined *political power* as the right to make and execute the laws and defend the commonwealth from foreign injury, 'and all this only for the Publick Good'. J. Locke, *Two Treatises of Government* (1690) (ed. P. Laslett; Cambridge, Cambridge University Press; 1960), II, § 3, p. 286.

[23] The 'higher' source of everyday law has been identified, at different times and in different places, as divine order, the sovereignty of law, natural cosmic order, and natural social order – with the last idea being used in the pure theory of liberal democracy (social contract) and in the practical theory of many national constitutions. For further discussion of the idea of 'higher law', see ch. 12 below.

The real

3.37 Who or what has caused the scandal of international unsociety, the unsociety of all-humanity, an inhuman human reality of everyday social evil and social injustice, of cynical parodies of law and social order, an unnatural state of nature in which social predators oppress, abuse and kill human beings in their millions, a world seething with fraudulent democracies and criminal presidential monarchies, a social reality in which some human beings worry about the colour of the bed-linen for their holiday-home in Provence, while other human beings worry about their next meal or the leaking tin-roof of the shack which is their only home?

3.38 In a society's *real constitution*, a society creates itself through the actual day-to-day practice of actual human beings, including, above all, the decisions of the holders of public-realm powers, their behaviour being conditioned by every aspect of social reality, as society also creates itself, as ideas and as law, in its ideal and legal constitutions.[24] The real self-constituting of international society has produced a diseased social reality, a psychopathic condition which threatens the survival of the human species.

3.39 Given the relative simplicity and transparency of international society, it is relatively easy to explain the present tragic state of international society. The root cause has been the emergence, in the period since the end of the fifteenth century, of a discontinuity in human reality, a duality in the social self-constituting of the human species – a duality

[24] 'The laws reach but a very little way. Constitute Government how you please, infinitely the greater part of it must depend upon the exercise of powers which are left at large to the prudence and uprightness of Ministers of State . . . Without them, your Commonwealth is no better than a scheme on paper, and not a living, active, effective constitution.' E. Burke, *Thoughts on the Cause of our Present Discontents* (1770), in P. Langford (ed.), *The Writings and Speeches of Edmund Burke* (Oxford, Clarendon Press; 1981), II, pp. 251–322, at p. 277. '[T]he real constitution (*wirkliche Verfassung*) of a country exists only in the true actual power-relations which are present in the country; written constitutions thus only have worth and durability if they are an exact expression of the real power-relations of society.' F. Lassalle, 'Über Verfassungswesen' (On the nature of the constitution) (1863), in *Gesammelte Reden und Schriften* (ed. E. Bernstein; Berlin, P. Cassirer; 1919), II, p. 60 (present author's translation). Lassalle, a follower of Hegel and, less faithfully, of Marx, and the founder of the General Union of German Workers (the first political party of the working class), contrasted the real constitution with the written (or legal) constitution, the former but not the latter (in the Germany of the 1860s) being the expression of the real power of the nobles, great land-owners, industrialists, bankers and major capitalists.

reflected in *practice*, especially in the practice of war and diplomacy, as international society was isolated and insulated from the amazing development of national social systems; in *ideas*, especially through the conceiving of separate national and international human realities; and, not least, in *law*, as the development of international law was isolated and insulated from the amazing development of national legal systems.

3.40 (1) The universal and perennial dialectic of the duality of the One and the Many has shaped the constituting of human societies throughout human history. The development of the modern (European) idea of the 'state' is a world-transforming product of that dialectic. The post-medieval (Renaissance and Reformation) individualising of the human being was accompanied by an equal and opposite individualising of society, so that the historical development of particular societies would be an endless succession of particular resolutions of the forces of individualism and collectivism, and the historical development of international society came to be a mere side-effect of that process.[25]

3.41 (2) The One of the Leviathan state was then personalised through the operation of the universal and perennial dialectic of the self and the other which has shaped the self-constituting of societies throughout human history.[26] The holders of public-realm power, kings and public officials, could identify their self-interest with the public interest of the One they so nobly served, and could, by force or by mind-manipulation, induce the people to suppose that it was their patriotic and moral duty to kill and be killed by their neighbours on behalf of their own so-called commonwealths.[27] Again and again, the agonistic

[25] The leading role in Act One of the drama was taken by Thomas Hobbes (1588–1679), who managed to proceed from an heuristic model of the personality of the individual human being to the total socialising of the individual person in the individualising and substantialising and personalising of the 'commonwealth', that is to say, 'the Multitude so united in one Person'. The 'sovereign', to whom they have transferred their powers, 'may use the strength and means of them all, as he [or it, in the case of a collective sovereign] shall think expedient, for their Peace and Common Defence.' (*Leviathan*, ch. 17).

[26] The word 'state' acquired two senses, referring to an aspect of a society's internal constitution and, externally, referring to a society's participation in international relations. But the semantics of the word soon took on a great weight of additional semiotic significance. After 1789, the word 'nation (*Volk*)' also took on great semiotic power, referring to a society in its genetic individuality and subjectivity. For further discussion of the subjectivity of the *nation*, see ch. 4 below.

[27] 'The wonder of this infernal enterprise is that each leader of the murderers has his standards blessed and solemnly invokes God before setting out to exterminate his neighbour.' Voltaire, *Dictionnaire philosophique* (1764–5), article on 'War' (Paris, GF-Flammarion; 1964), p. 218

relationship has produced a third thing ($1 + 1 = 3$), a fantasy construct within the interpersonal consciousness of each society, a *folie à deux* which reached a sublime level of insanity in the so-called Cold War of the later twentieth century.

3.42 (3) The third Act was an act of omission. Social philosophers, despite their achievements in the revolutionary reconceiving of national society, mysteriously failed to extend their vision to encompass the condition of humanity as a whole. Philosophy is surely universal or it is not philosophy. Moral philosophy is surely universal or it is not moral philosophy. The moral order does not contain political frontiers.[28]

3.43 (4) Pure and practical theories of international law filled the vacuum left by social philosophy, dissolving the perennial and universal dilemma of justice and social justice into a vapid simulacrum of law. Spawning an exiguous vocabulary of concepts, adding fashionably 'democratic' overtones to their medieval feudal landholding, a new international language-world re-empowered the powerful in their relations with each other, using the language of the law to dignify, as right and duty, the self-seeking of those who could continue to behave externally as if they were *ancien régime* monarchs, more or less free from the tiresome requirements of political or moral accountability, free from the burden of any form of self-justification beyond the anti-morality of *reason of state*.[29]

3.44 (5) The becoming of international society came to be practised as a permanent game of social Darwinism, in which the national game of politics extruded a misbegotten form known as 'foreign policy' pursued through the rituals of diplomacy and war. In the nineteenth century, the game took on a substantial economic aspect, as industrial capitalism became a central feature of the national struggle to survive, a determining factor in the causes and the conduct of war.[30] The condition

(present author's translation). The heroes of Act Two of the drama were the masterful makers of the modern states: kings and courtiers and politicians and their obsequious acolytes. For further discussion of the making of the international real constitution, see ch. 13 below.

[28] The most striking failures of vision were those of Locke, Rousseau and Hegel.

[29] The benign *maître à penser* of the new world order was Emmerich de Vattel (1714–67) whose simplistic ideas were both comprehensible and delightful for the holders of public power. War remained, in the formula cherished by Louis XIV of France, the 'ultimate reason of kings' (*ultima ratio regum*).

[30] Herbert Spencer (1820–1903), anguished apostle of nineteenth-century optimism, believed that human progress is a form of biological evolution, including a Lamarckian inheritance

of all-humanity came to be a random by-product of the national struggle to survive. Social Darwinism is not merely an anti-idealism. It is an anti-philosophy, a pragmatic default-theory. Democracy-capitalism is the institutionalising of social Darwinism, with democratic *public opinion* and the capitalist *market* acting as dynamic myth-forms within a mental absolutism whose high-values (*consent* and *efficiency*) are functional rather than transcendental.

3.45 (6) In the twentieth century, the volume of the internationally abnormal came vastly to exceed the volume of what was supposed to be the normal. The externalising and the interpenetration of economic systems, and of the national legal systems which subtend the economic systems, were anomalous in relation to the continuing isolation of the national political systems. The assertion of high-level principles for controlling the exercise of public-realm power (human rights), and the naïve or cynical extrapolation of internal constitutional forms (courts, assemblies), were anomalous in relation to the continuing isolation of national constitutional systems. The development of conceptions of international public order was anomalous in relation to the continuing 'territorial integrity' of states. The development of complex systems of international government was anomalous in relation to the 'political independence' of states, and the emerging hegemonic international public realm was anomalous in relation to 'sovereign' national public realms. The bureaucratised international redistribution of wealth was anomalous in relation to the institutionalised *laissez faire, laissez aller* of the global economy. The formulation of masses of international legislation, in the form of treaties and decisions of international institutions, was anomalous in relation to a conception of international law as setting the minimum conditions of the co-existence of neighbouring feudal landowners. Above all, a gathering global revolution of rising expectations as to human flourishing, a moral revolution in people's ideas about the good life in society, was anomalous in relation to the structural inequality and injustice and atavism of the international system.

3.46 (7) In the twentieth century also, we experienced extremes of the pathology of human socialising, as evil minds corrupted the minds of millions, as episodes of insanity possessed the public minds of whole

of acquired mental characteristics. Competitive industrial capitalism could be seen as the continuation of war by other (better) means.

societies, and whole nations paid the price in suffering. The growing complexity of law and government, at every social level, revealed itself, as it has throughout human history, as the growing sophistication of structures of social inequality. So-called 'human rights' in legalistic formulations, and technocratic programmes of 'good governance', revealed themselves as new forms of the age-old mask which conceals the exploitation and the oppression of the many by the few.[31] Democracy-capitalism is a social system in which the many lead unsatisfactory lives in order that the few may have the possibility of leading satisfactory lives. The few then find a hundred ways to turn that possibility into a source of misery for themselves and for others. The twentieth century taught us once more a lesson which is as old as human society. The only constant in human social history is the ruthless self-protecting of social privilege. The only human right which is universally enforced is the right of the rich to get richer.[32]

Globalisation from below

3.47 The problem of social evil is as old as human socialising. Social evil is humanity's self-wounding and self-destroying through the operation of social processes, from war and genocide to social oppression and social injustice of every kind. Humanity in the twenty-first century has

[31] See further in ch. 6.

[32] 'Consequently, when I consider and turn over in my mind the state of all commonwealths flourishing anywhere today, so help me God, I can see nothing else than a kind of conspiracy of the rich, who are aiming at their own interests under the name and title of the commonwealth. They invent and devise all ways and means by which, first, they may keep without fear of loss all that they have amassed by evil practices and, secondly, they may then purchase as cheaply as possible and abuse the toil and labour of all the poor. These devices become law as soon as the rich have once decreed their observance in the name of the public – that is, of the poor also!... What is worse, the rich every day extort [*abradunt*] a part of their daily allowance from the poor not only by private fraud but by public law... and finally, by making laws, have palmed it off as justice.' T. More, *Utopia* (1516), in *The Complete Works of St Thomas More* (eds. E. Surtz and J. H. Hexter; New Haven, London, Yale University Press; 1965), IV, p. 421. 'Laws and government may be considered... as a combination of the rich to oppress the poor, and preserve to themselves the inequality of goods which would otherwise be destroyed by the attacks of the poor... The government and laws... tell them they must either continue poor or acquire wealth in the same manner as they have done.' A. Smith, *Lectures on Jurisprudence* (lecture of 22 February 1763) (eds. R. L. Meek, D. D. Raphael and P. G. Stein; Oxford, Clarendon Press; 1978), pp. 208–9. '[T]he art of becoming "rich", in the common sense, is not absolutely nor finally the act of accumulating much money for ourselves, but also of contriving that our neighbours shall have less.' J. Ruskin, *Unto This Last. Four Essays on the First Principles of Political Economy* (1860) (London, George Allen & Sons; 1862/1910), pp. 45–6.

inherited from the self-inflicted suffering of the turbid twentieth century an unprecedented and unbearable legacy of world-wide social evil.

3.48 Social evil is a systematic product of social systems, caused by human beings acting in their official capacity in the public interest, alienated from their moral responsibility as individual human beings, or caused by social systems so complex that their products can be attributed to no human beings in particular. Social systems and their products escape moral judgement. They are beyond good and evil. But the wages of social evil are paid in *suffering*, the suffering of actual human beings, of whole peoples, of all humanity. The price is paid in *corruption*, the corrupting of all human values, down to and including the values of the most intimate interpersonal consciousness of individual human beings. And the price is paid in *destruction*, the relentless degradation of the natural habitat of the human species.

3.49 It so happens that we have also inherited from the twentieth century an unprecedented degree of human socialisation, unprecedented possibilities of the good that social systems can do, unprecedented possibilities of social evil. What is called 'globalisation' is seen, like the political and economic imperialism of the nineteenth century, as an extrapolating of the national realm into the international realm. The risk now facing humanity is the globalising of all-powerful, all-consuming social systems, without the moral, legal, political and cultural aspirations and constraints, such as they are, which moderate social action at the national level.[33]

3.50 In particular, and above all, international society now contains the potentiality of a human future in which the globalising of economic and governmental social systems will be merged with a rudimentary international social system inherited from the past, a system which has been the cause of so much social evil, local and global. It is a social system in which the highest value continues to be the maximising of the advantage of the particular social formations known as 'states', and in which the maximising of the survival and prospering of each human

[33] In the parable of the Grand Inquisitor (*The Brothers Karamazov*, bk v), Dostoevsky expressed, with passionate intensity, what he saw as the paradox of Roman Christianity, that a liberating human enlightenment had become an absolutist social system. We need a Dostoevsky to express the paradox of democracy-capitalism, that a system dedicated to 'freedom' has produced social systems of totalitarian social power, systems that are now being globalised. 'High hopes were once formed of democracy, but democracy means simply the bludgeoning of the people by the people for the people.' O. Wilde, *The Soul of Man under Socialism* (1891) (ed. L. Dowling; London, Penguin; 2001), pp. 127–60, at p. 138.

individual and of all-humanity is conceptually secondary, in practice and in theory. It is an international system which, with the overwhelming political and economic energies generated by globalisation, is perfectly designed to maximise the risk of every form of international social evil.

Globalisation from above

3.51 So it is that international society now contains the potentiality of a human future determined by the unrelenting force of the social actual, unmoved by the self-surpassing power of the social ideal. It is a burden made almost unbearable by crude historicism, by self-disempowering in the face of the human future, by the belief that humanity is beyond self-redeeming, and that social evil is an unalterable fact of social life. The idea of the end of history is a vision of the end of humanity. The idea of the clash of civilisations is a vision of the end of civilisation. Social evil, and our despair in the face of social evil, are the symptoms of a diseased human reality. The great task of the twenty-first century is to install the idea of the ideal in dialectical opposition to the fact of the actual as a creative force in the making of the human future. International social idealism is the dialectical negation of international social Darwinism.

3.52 To redeem international society requires a fundamental reconceiving of our inherited international worldview, a psychological and philosophical reconstituting, a revolution-from-above in the public mind of all-humanity. It is possible already to diagnose the symptoms of diseased international social reality and so to prescribe a cure, identifying the guiding principles of a new international reality, a new ideal self-constituting of a true international society, a charter of international social idealism, a New Enlightenment.

- A social reality (international society or the international system) which is commonly supposed to be merely the interaction of instances of a certain kind of reified concept (states)[34] is a dehumanised social reality.

[34] A 'state', on this traditional view, is a generic society whose public realm is under the authority of a 'government' and which is recognised as a state by other governments. A 'state' is then treated as being an entity and a legal person, with some of the characteristics of a natural person (will, purposes, interests, etc.). The primary social process of the international society or system so formed is supposed to consist of intergovernmental behaviour, especially through the practices known as 'foreign policy' and 'diplomacy'.

- A social reality in which social consciousness is formed, not by the interacting of the private minds of all human beings and the public minds of subordinate societies, but primarily through the systematic interacting of agents of subordinate societies (governments), can never be a fully human social reality.
- A social reality conceived as the actualising through foreign policy, diplomacy and war of a pragmatic highest value (the prospering of each particular state) is a demoralised social reality.
- A social reality in which war and the use of force are seen as the ultimate instruments of social cohesion is an anti-social social reality.
- A social reality in which law is seen, not as the source, the limit, and the judge of social power but as merely an incidental by-product of social power, is an illegitimate social reality.

3.53 Globalisation from above means the application of every self-creating potentiality of human consciousness to the self-constituting of international society. It is to set the human-world-transforming attraction of the ideal in dialectical opposition to the human-world-affirming force of the actual, the universal in dialectical opposition to the particular.

- There is only one human world, one human reality, one moral order, and one social order extending from the family and the village up to the international society of the whole human race.
- Our culturally diverse ideals of human existence, our ideas of the good life as individuals and as societies, are, for each human being, one and indivisible. And those ideals include not only our ideas of justice and injustice, good and evil, but also our transcendental ideas of the particularity of human existence within the order of the universe of all-that-is.
- The rule of law is one and indivisible. All public power is derived from law, and is subject to the law, at the global level as at the level of individual societies. International law will be the true law of an international society truly conceived.[35]
- All legal power exists to serve the common interest. International law exists to serve the common interest of all humanity and of all subordinate societies.

[35] For the blueprint of a true international law of a true international society, see ch. 10 below.

- The common interest of international society is the survival and prospering of all human beings within a natural habitat shared by all.

3.54 Our capacity to form the idea of the ideal allows us to undertake our moral self-transforming, to actualise our revolutionary self-re-creating. Our spiritual consciousness allows us to desire human self-perfecting. Our moral freedom allows us to recognise a moral duty to make a better human future. We are what we think. We will be what we think. We must make a revolution-from-above in the name of the ideal, a revolution in the private mind of every human being, in the public minds of all societies, and, eventually and at last, in the public mind of the society of all-humanity.

4

The nation as mind politic

The making of the public mind

Humanism and naturalism – Nation and identity – Nation and state – Nation and pathology

The idea of human society as shared subjectivity is probably older than the idea of human society as political organisation. The nation presumably pre-existed the state. Society as mind politic probably pre-existed society as body politic.

The subjectivity of the nation means that there is a permanent flow of consciousness between individual consciousness and social consciousness, as the private mind of the individual finds an essential part of its identity in participation in the identity of society, and the public mind of society borrows the powerful idea of selfhood to establish its unique collective identity. The individual self of the citizen is mirrored in the selfhood of society, and the self of society is mirrored in the identity of the citizen.

The mutual self-constituting of the individual and society means that individual psychology and social psychology flow into each other. And where there is psychology there is the possibility of pathology, the social manifestation of individual psychopathology and the internalising in the individual of social psychopathology. Symptoms may go as far as the self-destruction of society, as it pursues the defence of its self against other selves, and the self-destruction of the individual, carried to self-sacrifice by loyalty to the greater self.

Humanism and naturalism

4.1 Hegel called it 'a glorious mental dawn'. 'Never since the sun stood in the firmament and the planets revolved around him had it been perceived that man's existence centres in his head, i.e. in Thought, inspired by which he builds up his world of reality.'[1] He was referring to a development of ideas which, he believed, stemmed from the French Enlightenment and the German *Aufklärung*. 'All thinking beings shared in the jubilation of the epoch.'[2] Two centuries after the dawn, we are inclined to be less euphoric. We have learned that man's head, as a source of reality, is a strange and dangerous place, as strange and dangerous as ever were the Universe or Nature or things-in-themselves or gods or God. And we have discovered some formidable obstacles in the way of thought-thinking-about-thought, obstacles which, by the end of the twentieth century, have made the human mind into a sort of ultimate unknowable, a *noumenon* within us, to use the Kantian term with sad irony.

4.2 Allowing the names of prophetic figures to stand as emblems for complex movements of thought which surpass their individual work, we may identify three challenging idea-complexes, and a fourth which is not yet realised to the same degree. With Wittgenstein, we have been forced to face the possibility that human communication is not the transfer of something called Truth through a neutral medium called Language. Communication would then have to be regarded as simply another form of human activity, sharing in the intrinsic and irreducible ambiguity of all human activity. With Freud, we have been forced to face the possibility that human beings cannot know, and so cannot control, the content of their own minds. On such a view, we would be condemned to be strangers to our selves, our individuality being merely a particular product of universal mental processes. With Marx, we have been forced to face the possibility that what we see as our personal life is rather a life lived in a reflexive continuum with our social circumstances, society forming us as we take part in the forming of society in consciousness. On such a view, our minds, our selves, would have to be regarded as communal property, aspects of a permanent communal building-project.

4.3 A fourth complex of ideas can be associated with the name of Charles Darwin but has not yet reached a decisive level of unifying coherence. It will force us to face the possibility that, as in the case of

[1] G. W. F. Hegel, *The Philosophy of History* (tr. J. Sibree; New York, Dover Publications; 1956), p. 447. The word 'him' in the quoted passage should be 'it' if the original German text is taken to be the following: '*Solange die Sonne am Firmamente steht und die Planeten um sie herumkreisen.*' G. W. F. Hegel, *Vorlesungen über die Philosophie der Geschichte* (Stuttgart, Reclam; 1961), p. 593.

[2] *The Philosophy of History*, p. 447.

any other animal, our minds, and hence our selves, are of the same nature as chemical reactions.

4.4 There are those who would regard such movements of thought not as obstacles to self-transcendence, but rather as precious moments of illumination, freeing us from infantile ideas about the mind and the self and society, creating the possibility of deeper self-conceiving, of richer self-socialising, of human self-empowerment. Or else they might even be seen as decisive steps towards a new transcendental philosophy of philosophy, the human mind transcending all previous transcending of itself in consciousness. One day, perhaps, a new Hegel will be able to greet another glorious mental dawn. In the meantime, we must face the fatigue and confusion of an oppressive noon.

4.5 At the very least, one might have expected that such formidable challenges to the capacity of the human mind to transcend thought through thought would have led to a certain reticence in the expression of ideas, to a certain caution in the application of ideas through social action. If we can no longer speak sensibly of Truth or Reason, no longer use the word 'I' or 'You' with confidence, no longer detach ourselves on any sound intellectual basis from society or from the physical world as objects of study, how can we say anything worthwhile about matters of society and psychology which cry out for creative understanding but which reach into the depths of our minds and our selves? May not silence be the only appropriate response to questions, however urgent, which surpass our capacity to speak?[3]

4.6 But the strange fact is that human beings still struggle to be persons, full of projects, of love, of suffering, of anger, of despair, of hope. Human beings still transform the natural world through the application of ideas. Human societies still struggle to survive and prosper in the name of ideas. Since 1789 ideas have poured forth as never before, flooding

[3] 'What we cannot speak about we must consign to silence.' L. Wittgenstein, *Tractatus Logico-Philosophicus* (1921) (tr. D. Pears and B. McGuinness; London, New York, Routledge; 1961), § 7, p. 74. 'We feel that even when all *possible* scientific questions have been answered, the problems of life remain completely untouched. Of course there are then no questions left, and this itself is the answer'; 'The solution of the problem of life is seen in the vanishing of the problem' (§§ 6.52 and 6.521, p. 73). Wittgenstein may have offered a possibility of transcendental thinking about such non-scientific philosophising in his own later philosophy. 'We remain unconscious of the prodigious diversity of all the everyday language-games because the clothing of our language makes everything alike.' *Philosophical Investigations* (tr. G. Anscombe; Oxford, Basil Blackwell; 1953), p. 224.

first the minds of the learned, then the minds of the privileged, and now the minds of the masses.

4.7 With 1789 it was possible to greet another new dawn, not in transcendental philosophy but in the application of ideas to the human condition, in human self-socialising and human self-creating. A whole generation experienced that 'Romantic enthusiasm' and thought that they were present at a new emancipation of the human spirit, a liberation which would release every human possibility, personal and social. Humanity would overflow with its own subjectivity and that subjectivity would recognise itself in the overflowing power of Nature. And it is true that, since that dawn, not only the individual subjectivity of the artist, the intellectual, and the man of action but also self-conceiving collective subjectivities of every kind (nations, states, cities, corporations, races, peoples, faiths, cultures) have conceived and reconceived their selves with manic mental energy and, with manic social energy, they have grown and fought and flourished, ceaselessly making and remaking and destroying, transforming the world.

4.8 Between the cold indeterminacy of transcendental philosophy and the extraordinary vitality of ideologised social practice the restless human spirit sought and soon found within itself a new form of self-knowing. The 'humane sciences' (*Geisteswissenschaften*) seemed to offer a way of rescuing humanity from its own excesses. Their *Ur*-prophets were Goethe, the intelligent heart, and Hegel, the passionate mind. The new University of Berlin[4] was a symbolic first altar of the new unreligion. First in political economy, then in historiography, then in sociology, then in anthropology, and finally in pre-Freudian psychology, they sought to apply to subjective phenomena (personal and social) that intellectual ethic of objectivity which they took to be the essential ethos of natural science. Academic professionalism and the scientific spirit might together provide a means of harnessing the boundless energy of humanity, as natural science had come to be a way of harnessing the inexhaustible energy of nature. At last the subjective would be made objective.

4.9 By using methods which had become characteristic of botany and biology, especially taxonomy and morphology, the humane sciences might thus find themselves able to say something about human

[4] For von Humboldt's conception of the new university, see P. R. Sweet, *Wilhelm von Humboldt. A Biography* (Columbus, Ohio State University Press; 1978), p. 66.

phylogeny (why nations exist, for example) and even about human ontogeny (for example, why this particular nation is as it is). By collecting facts about human behaviour and human societies, over time and space, by disciplined analysis and comparison and synthesis, it might be possible to find some tentatively universal laws or principles for the understanding of all the teeming particularity of human experience. Human subjectivity-for-itself might, to that extent, become human subjectivity-in-itself, a sort of objectivity. The humane sciences are the self-ordering of the human mind as Other.

4.10 The professionalised humane sciences have generated an effect which has made itself felt in the deepest recesses of human self-conceiving. The humane sciences have *naturalised* human phenomena. By evacuating subjectivity from the study of human phenomena, they have created a new reality which is neither the reality of the hypothetical world of matter studied by natural science nor the reality of human subjectivity, known immediately through experience and sympathy. This new reality of the natural world of the human is a middle kingdom in which everything human, both social and individual, exists of and for itself, neither merely as a side-effect of matter nor merely as an emanation of the human mind.

4.11 The human mind had tried other methods of transcending human phenomena through reality-forming. Religion was reality conceived as obligation, all reality conspiring to propose the right ordering of a human life. Mythology was reality conceived as will, all reality responding to the willing of agents and agencies whose resemblance to human beings went at least as far as their capacity to will action. Natural science was reality conceived as hypothetical necessity: the phenomena, which might have been otherwise, are real if, and to the extent that, they are found to be the source of regular effects. The new humane sciences proposed something more dramatic: a human reality conceived as actual necessity. The reality of the human world is, in this way, more real even than the reality of the material world, precisely because it presents itself as the reality that we live. Human naturalism, as this form of self-transcendence may be called,[5] is not merely a new professional activity nor merely a new intellectual method. It is a new metaphysic.

[5] The use of this term is intended to establish a difference from the word 'positivism' in the complex Comteian meaning of that word: see especially A. Comte, *Discours sur l'esprit positif* (1844) (Paris, Librairie Philosophique; 1974), pp. 41–2. The word has since been used in

4.12 The assertion of Hegel set out at the beginning of this essay is unHegelian; it is the voice of Hegel the hectoring historian. Hegel the ingenious metaphysician had a more complex and more significant view of the relationship of subjectivity and objectivity and, incidentally, thereby provided a possible metaphysical foundation for the human naturalism of the new humane sciences. Correcting Descartes and Kant and Fichte and Schelling among others, Hegel had (at least to his own satisfaction) abolished and transcended the opposition of subject and object which had plagued philosophy at least since Athens of the fifth century BCE.[6] In absolute spirit, the object is subject and the subject is object. The manifestation of the subjective (the rational) is not other than the manifestation of the objective (the actual). Fact, consciousness and spirit are not in a hierarchy of transcendence. They are one. There is no question of systems of human self-transcendence. Humanity is

many other intellectual contexts, not least in legal theory (see ch. 2 above). For a discussion of a distinction in Husserl between the 'personalistic attitude' and the 'naturalistic attitude' as 'two eidetically different modes of apprehension', see P. Ricoeur, *Husserl – An Analysis of His Phenomenology* (tr. E. Ballard and L. Embree; Evanston, Northwestern University Press; 1967), p. 59. On Husserl's discussion of the *Geisteswissenschaft-Auffassung* (human sciences apprehension) and the *naturalisation* of man, see Ricoeur, *Husserl*, pp. 68ff. Foucault also treats the period since Kant as radically new in relation to what he calls the Classical (post-medieval) period, and he also relates it to the development of the 'human sciences' in which nature and human nature are confused: M. Foucault, *The Order of Things. An Archaeology of the Human Sciences* (London, Tavistock Publications; 1970; London, Routledge; 1989), pp. 309ff. In what he calls the Sleep of Anthropology, philosophy has fallen asleep over the question 'What is Man?', a question which hopelessly confuses the empirical and the transcendental (p. 341). His conclusion is that 'man is a recent invention. And one perhaps nearing its end' (p. 387).

6 G. W. F. Hegel, *The Phenomenology of Spirit* (tr. A. V. Miller; Oxford, Clarendon Press; 1977), p. 55. This passage is discussed in A. Kojève, *Introduction à la lecture de Hegel* (Paris, Gallimard; 1947), pp. 453ff. Kojève's lectures on Hegel at the Ecole pratique des Hautes Etudes in Paris in the 1930s are often critical of Hegel and might be said, in Hegelian parlance, to amount to an impressive *Aufhebung* of Hegel. (Hegel himself regarded the *Phenomenology* itself as a preparatory work.) The lectures had an important influence on the notable French intellectual generation active after 1945, including Sartre, Lévi-Strauss and Lacan. In the same discussion, Kojève links Hegel's ideas with quantum physics (p. 454, fn. 1), and with the idea of science as a form of myth (p. 456).

For a particularly interesting interpretation of Hegel's treatment of rationality and actuality, see H. Marcuse, *Reason and Revolution. Hegel and the Rise of Social Theory* (1941) (2nd edn; London, Routledge & Kegan Paul; 1955), pp. 153ff. See also W. Marx, *Hegel's Phenomenology of Spirit. Its Point and Purpose. A Commentary Based on the Preface and Introduction* (tr. P. Heath; New York, Harper & Row; 1975), pp. 54ff.; and R. G. Collingwood, *The Idea of Nature* (Oxford, Clarendon Press; 1945), pp. 121ff.

naturally self-transcendent. Human history is natural history. History is self-justifying and self-judging.[7]

4.13 Such a view seems to integrate human subjectivity into a universal world-order which is neither mythological nor religious nor material. And it seems to ennoble and empower the human will. As actualised in post-1789 human naturalism, it has proved to be the unexpected source of a new and particularly disabling form of human alienation.

4.14 There is an important difference between the rationalism of post-medieval humanism, culminating in the eighteenth-century Enlightenment, and the human naturalism of the period after 1789.[8] Rationalism projects the human mind onto phenomena and makes the phenomena into a system of order reflecting the order of the mind. Rationalism is the self-ordering of subjectivity. And there is an important sense in which this is true even of mathematics and natural science.[9] The beautiful order of the universe which they reconstruct for the human

[7] '[T]he history of the world which is the world's court of judgment'. G. W. F. Hegel, *Philosophy of Right* (tr. T. Knox; Oxford, Oxford University Press; 1952), § 340, p. 216.

[8] Edmund Husserl considered that what he called 'objectivism' was responsible for the crisis of modern man and saw modern philosophy as a struggle between transcendentalism and objectivism. (See Ricoeur, *Husserl* (fn. 5 above), pp. 161ff.) He characterised positive science as a science of being which is lost in the world.

There have been a number of retranscendentalising attempts in the twentieth century (the century of scientism, relativism, materialism, populism and of both nihilism and fanaticism). To universalise the characteristic activities of man (language, myth, religion, art, science, history) rather than the 'essence' of man, see E. Cassirer, *The Philosophy of Symbolic Forms* (tr. R. Manheim; New Haven, London, Yale University Press; 1955). To redeem individual significance after Hegel, Heidegger and Husserl, see J.-P. Sartre, *Being and Nothingness. An Essay on Phenomenological Ontology* (tr. H. Barnes; London, Methuen & Co.; 1957). In his later work Sartre moved from the dominating influence of Hegel to that of Marx. To retranscendentalise philosophy after Hegel, Marx and Freud, see H. Marcuse, *One-Dimensional Man. Studies in the Ideology of Advanced Industrial Society* (London, Routledge & Kegan Paul; 1964). To regenerate humanism from a specifically Christian point of view in a world dominated by science, see J. Maritain, *Humanisme intégral* (1936) (tr. M. Adamson; London, G. Bles; 1938); P. Teilhard de Chardin, *The Phenomenon of Man* (1955) (tr. B. Wall; London, Collins; 1959). For an attempt to retranscendentalise the philosophy of society and law (after Hegel, Marx, Husserl, Habermas and Foucault), see the present author's *Eunomia*.

[9] Seventeenth-century rationalism (especially Descartes and Malebranche), in integrating the order of the mind in the order of the universe, followed in a Western tradition going back to Plato and beyond. For three forms of twentieth-century detranscendentalising of science and scientific method, see K. Popper, *The Logic of Scientific Discovery* (London, Unwin Hyman; 1959): T. Kuhn, *The Structure of Scientific Revolutions* (Chicago, University of Chicago Press; 2nd edn, 1970); and P. Feyerabend, *Against Method* (London, New York, Verso; 1975) (the most extreme and the most spirited of the three).

mind seems to be a mirror-reflection of a beautiful potentiality of order in the human mind. It may be only that. It may be more than that. We may never know.

4.15 Human naturalism, on the other hand, treats human phenomena, personal and social, as containing an order which is, in principle, independent of the observing mind. The evacuation of subjectivity from human phenomena seems to require that the specificity of human phenomena must be found not in their subjectivity but in their actuality. The rational is in the actual. The actual is not in the rational. The actual of the human world – say, the institutional arrangements of a particular society or the self-consciousness of a particular nation – exists nowhere else than in human minds, but, for the humane sciences, it is nevertheless a reality 'out-there'. It is a world made by human beings conceived only as makers of the actual. Human beings, on this view, become a sort of back-formation from the actual. The actual is prior to the human. To be human is to be the postulated cause of human effects.

4.16 The first consequence of this new human metaphysic is that the human mind attributes an equal measure of reality to all human creations. The necessity flowing from actuality has the effect of dignifying all human creations. A salute, a religion, a royal palace, an epic poem, a national anthem, a law, a life of self-sacrifice, a surgical operation, a death in battle, the burning of a witch, a nuclear weapon, the genocide of a people, world war, global warming. They are all actualisations of the human mind. They are all equally actual. They all equally call for explanation and understanding. In the eyes of human naturalism, they are all equally real. That they may be not real but merely collective fantasies, simply outward signs of a collective mental pathology, is a possibility that may be formally acknowledged but may then properly be bracketed out by the right-thinking humane scientist.

4.17 The second consequence is that humanity has become passive in relation to its own creations. The creations of the human mind are not merely reified, seeming, so far as the human mind is concerned, to have a thing-like reality in the world of human communication, capable of being the subject or object of a verb: 'England expects . . . The stock-market is nervous . . . They have chosen democracy . . . ' More than that, they are treated as autonomous sources of energy and significance, as if they were human actors full of human desire and human meaning, as if they were indistinguishable in principle from the sources of material effects which are thought to fill the physical world studied by natural science, and which science arranges into fields and systems and structures, in short, into 'things'.

4.18 Human passivity is painfully apparent in relation to the products and by-products of *natural science*. It is the personal ambition, the imagination and the ingenuity of scientists and engineers, fuelled by economic incentives, which now determine a substantial part of social development. Scientists and engineers oppress us with the relentless normativity of the actual. Humanity did not choose to work in systems of mass production, to travel over land and through the air at ever greater speeds, to fill the mind with images electronically generated on screens of various kinds, to prolong life and alter states of mind by the use of chemical compounds, to murder human beings by the million and destroy whole cities by the use of ever more ingenious weapons. The supply of such things created a demand, and the demand co-operated by rationalising and optimising their use. There is no way of knowing what another human world might have been, a world made by human desire and the human spirit and not by human skill and the spirit of scientism.

4.19 In the *economic* field, the field of the social transformation of the material world with a view to human survival and prospering, those who control great systems of social power are obliged to watch and wait as a totalised economic system, of a nation or of the world, a system which contains nothing but the willing and acting of human beings, alters direction or dynamic, perhaps cyclically, as if it were a slow-witted monster with instincts of its own, making and destroying human lives as random side-effects. In the case of capitalism, its first philosophy postulated a totalising phenomenon which, free of subjectivity, aggregates the willing and acting of countless individual human beings to serve immanent purposes of the system, of the so-called nation.[10] Since 1945

[10] Gellner has suggested that the appropriation of Adam Smith by economists has obscured the fact that Smith saw that the Hidden Hand had an effect on the whole structure of a society and not merely on its economy. In this sense, he argues, Smith was not merely an apostle of *laissez faire* but also a sort of economic determinist. E. Gellner, 'Nationalism and the two forms of cohesion in complex societies', in E. Gellner, *Culture, Identity, and Politics* (Cambridge, Cambridge University Press; 1987), p. 6. But perhaps, in this, as in other things, Smith was following the French Physiocrats, who believed that society could be reformed generally through economic freedom. On Smith's political views, see P. Gay, *The Enlightenment. An Interpretation: 2. The Science of Freedom* (London, Weidenfeld & Nicolson; 1970), pp. 362ff.

there has been a movement of thought which seeks to understand an economic system by reference to hypothetical human beings with hypothetical ideas and aims, rather than by reference to the subjectivity, the ideas and aims, of actual human beings.[11] And, at the end of the twentieth century, there is a tendency to elevate capitalism from being a practical economic theory which may be applied in a given society into a pure theory of economic activity in general, or even a transcendental theory about our knowledge of ourselves as desiring-machines, postulating a natural and, ultimately, unavoidable congruence between individual and collective desire, actualised through the mechanisms of the capitalist system.[12]

4.20 In relation to *political* structures, naturalism is a great deal older than the nineteenth century. Aristotle treated political systems as if they were botanical specimens or animal species.[13] The intellectual tradition flowing from Aristotle and from the Greek and Roman historians turned all humanity into spectators of a bizarre human comedy which happens also to be the story of our own lives. The antics of rulers and ruling classes, the long history of their crimes and follies, have been made to seem as rational, as real, and as natural as the long history of human achievement in the various forms of human self-transcendence.

4.21 What the new human naturalism has added to this old tradition is a new dignity, a new seriousness. The human comedy is the same; the audience has been reconditioned. We have learned to repress our spontaneous responses of irony and doubt and pity and bitter anger, to watch instead with the steady gaze of the entomologist as human beings are oppressed and exploited and killed to serve some national interest, as the wealth of nations becomes the poverty of the human spirit. It is the poor spirit of human naturalism which, at the end of the

[11] For a survey of Social Choice theory and literature, see R. Pildes and E. Anderson, 'Slinging arrows at democracy. Social choice theory, value pluralism, and democratic politics', in 90 *Columbia Law Review* (1990), p. 2,121.

[12] For the corrective view, that there is more than one kind of 'capitalism', see M. Albert, *Capitalisme contre capitalisme* (Paris, Editions du Seuil; 1991).

[13] It is tempting to see a parallel between Aristotle's confusion of morphology (forms of governments and political organs) and teleology (the ethical purpose of the state) and the confusion of form and function in comparative anatomy and botanical classification up to the time of Linnaeus (late eighteenth century). See W. Dampier, *A History of Science and Its Relations with Philosophy and Religion* (1929) (Cambridge, Cambridge University Press; 4th edn, 1966), pp. 167–8, 184–7.

twentieth century of all centuries,[14] can engender the idea that humanity has now found a political system, known as democracy, which ensures a natural congruence between individual and collective willing through the mechanisms of the democratic process. We are being led to believe that we have found at last the natural political habitat for the human species, a place called democracy.[15]

4.22 The third consequence of human naturalism, perhaps a by-product of the other two, is thus that human beings have found a means of detaching the human effect from its human cause. In this way, human beings could come to feel no further need for transcending ideas, of religion or mythology or morality, to explain and justify human effects. And so also they would be able finally to detach themselves from human responsibility for human effects. Human effects have come to be seen as the product of objective human activity, the work of the human species, rather than the products of human subjectivity. The mindless invisible hand of social evil is supposed to generate macro-evil from countless indifferent acts of public duty and private interest – the cunning of evil, to paraphrase Hegel. Humanity is losing the power to distinguish the reality which made humanity from the reality which humanity has made. Nations, races, democracy, religions, the family, the market-place, war, crime, so-called 'human nature' have become the given, the facts of human life, the flora and fauna of our habitat, which have evolved spontaneously and necessarily as macro-effects of all the micro-causes of actual human behaviour in the human world as it interacts with the physical habitat of the natural world. When humanity ceases to believe that it is responsible for humanity, we may say that humanity begins to cease to be humanity.

4.23 The history of the twentieth century has shown, with painful and repeated clarity, that that part of social development which is not

14 Isaiah Berlin, who observed the public affairs of his time with an exceptionally keen eye, expressed the view that the twentieth century had been 'the worst century that Europe has ever had' (in an interview entitled 'Two concepts of nationalism', in *New York Review of Books*, 21 November 1991, p. 22). (For corrections to the text, see *NYR*, 5 December 1991, p. 58.)

15 F. Fukuyama, *The End of History and the Last Man* (New York, The Free Press; 1992). The co-existence and the prestige within the culture of the US of theories such as those of J. Rawls, *A Theory of Justice* (1971) and R. Nozick, *Anarchy, State, and Utopia* (1974) suggest that democracy is not one single intellectual phenomenon even in the US, let alone throughout the world. On differing ideas of democracy in the US and Europe, see P. Allott, 'The European Community is not the true European Community', in 100 *Yale Law Journal*, p. 2,485 (1991).

determined by the application of science is now largely determined by the activity of collective subjectivities, especially nations and state-systems. In the world wars, in the countless local and internecine wars, in the surging idea-complexes of self-determination and nationalism, in the ending of the colonial empires and the formation of new nations, in the economic struggle of the state-systems, the fate of all human beings everywhere now rests on a set of human phenomena which take a leading place in the human reality conceived by human naturalism.

4.24 The nation is a prime example of all the metaphysical consequences of human naturalism. Any nation because it conceives of itself and is conceived of by others as a nation is dignified with a measure of human reality equal to that of any other part of that reality, including that of any other nation. The nation as self, with its self-conceived subjects, and the nation as other, in relation to those individuals and collectivities which are not conceived as part of its self, are treated as an actual modification of human reality, a natural source of actual effects, in relation to which all, self and other, must accommodate their self-conceived reality and their willed action.

4.25 And, most dire of all the consequences, the nation has detached itself from human subjectivity, human responsibility, human transcendence. Nations are a reality-for-themselves, a subjectivity-for-themselves. They are mind made matter. And human beings must simply accept that they live in a place which is inhabited also by these alien subjectivities, creatures which are half-human and half-thing. To invite human beings to begin to take control over the idea of the nation is thus to ask human beings to do something which may now no longer be possible, namely, to redeem human subjectivity by means of human subjectivity.

4.26 Such an undertaking would require that, going beyond the taxonomy and morphology of the humane sciences, we would reassert the psychic substance of social phenomena. We would have to learn once again to conceive of them with Romantic sympathy (*Einfühlung/ Mitfühlung*) as mind-for-mind, subjectivity seeing itself reflected in subjectivity. And we would have to face the challenges of Wittgenstein, Freud, Marx and Darwin, as they seem to decree that mind is the one thing that mind will never master.

Nation and identity

4.27 In what we know of the ancient world we can hear the human mind speaking to us, mind speaking to mind. And, in the ancient world, the self-identifying of nations seems to have been notably conscious and energetic and articulate, an impression which may in part be due to the fact that the *Prachtbauten* of public-realm self-identifying, architectural and artistic and literary remains, presumably make up a disproportionate amount of the relics available to us. Our knowledge of ancient Egypt, ancient Greece and ancient China happens to include a great deal of information about their idea of themselves. In the case of ancient Israel, we have extensive literary remains which reveal a people obsessed with the idea of themselves.[16]

4.28 In each of these cases, the nation finds a source of identity not merely in a present state of consciousness. We are as we are because we have been as we were. Furthermore, we may say that this retrospective self-nationising tends to take either a genetic or a generic form. In the genetic form, the nation sees the source of its identity in a story which may extend back into a mythico-religious realm (as in the case of Egypt and Israel). In the generic form (most perfectly exemplified by the Confucianised Chou kingdom of China, by the Pericleanised city-state of Athens and, in the modern world, by the United States of America), the nation sees the source of its identity in its idea of the special character of its land, its people, its institutions, its values, its traditions. Those features have formed a national identity which is also a national character and which is handed on from mind to mind, from generation to generation.

4.29 Identity is also alterity. The struggle for self-identity was also a struggle of other-identification. The genetic source of identity conferred a particular identity also because it was something that no other nation could claim. Mythic events which gave birth to the forefathers of this people, which conveyed the special favour of a god or gods (perhaps theophanised as pharaoh or emperor) by assigning this land and these boons to this people rather than to that were the source and the guarantee not only of identity but also of uniqueness. The ancient traditions

[16] Omitted from this group of nations are other ancient nations, especially India, Persia and the city-states of Mesopotamia, whose identity is too complex and obscure to include in the proposed paradigm.

and customs of a particular nation were so dense and complex and inexplicable, if not irrational, that no other nation could possibly match them. The generic source of identity conferred a particular identity also because it stood in stark contrast, highlighted and caricatured in story and art-objects, with the always strange and often despicable nature and behaviour of other nations: the Libyans, Asians and Africans for the ancient Egyptians,[17] the barbarians for the Chinese, Egypt and Persia and Sparta and Corinth for the Athenians, the gentiles for the Jews, the Europeans for the new Americans. We are who we are because, fortunately, we are not as other peoples are.

4.30 The self-identifying and the other-identifying were also a sort of self-ordering, calling forth particular social structures and functions and values. To defend the identity suggested itself as a primary interest of the nation (national security) and hence a primary responsibility of the ruler and ruling class. To enrich and to celebrate and to communicate the identity (education) was a primary responsibility of particular parts of the ruling class – a priesthood, a lay clerisy, craftsmen. To use the identity as an axiomatic basis for the derivation of legislation and executive action (government) was the primary responsibility of other parts of a ruling class – an assembly, a royal council, a mandarinate, a bureaucracy, a judiciary. To live and to die for the identity could then be put to the people as the primary responsibilities of those privileged to be members of the nation (citizenship).

4.31 If all the public life of the nation seemed to be bound up with the self-identifying of the nation, then it can be supposed that the whole of social consciousness would be a constant process of self-reinforcement reaching deep into the consciousness of the individual nationals. The result is that not merely the daily lives of the nationals, but their actual personal identity as individual human beings would become caught up in the overwhelming process of national self-identification. I am as I am because we are who we are.

4.32 It is, perhaps, in Rome that this totalitarian tendency is the most evident, as the Romans invented themselves with exceptional panache, trying (with the help of Virgil and Livy, the sacralisation of the emperor, and other rather unconvincing forms of religious behaviour) to fabricate

[17] H. Frankfort and others, *Before Philosophy* (Harmondsworth, Penguin; 1949), pp. 49, 122. Originally published as *The Intellectual Adventure of Ancient Man* (Chicago, University of Chicago Press; 1946).

a genetic Rome, but having to satisfy themselves with an overblown generic, fantasised Rome of dignity and order and law and freedom.

4.33 With the development of Christianity a new form of self-identifying took place. By an ingenious piece of symbolic reconceptualisation, a particular sect, who came to be called Christians, managed to detach an identity from the Jewish nation and reattach it to humanity as a whole, to universalise it. A prophetic figure, although conceived physically as the son of a Jewish woman, was reconceived mentally as the Son of Man, an idealised representative of humanity in general, and was then reconceived again, not merely as a God who spoke to and favoured his people and not merely as a mysterious theophany, but as a God who had, in some sense, become present in humanity, thereby repairing the separation between the divinity of the One-Good and a mankind which had been alienated from that divinity.[18] Christianity then developed an anti-national self-identification, as a City of God or 'a kingdom not of this world', a universal non-nation, even as the ecclesiastical organisation of the Church of Rome took on more and more of the attributes of a medieval nation or super-nation.[19]

4.34 Then, paradoxically, this universal religion became available also as a powerful instrument of national self-identification, in five notorious phases of world social development: first, with its acceptance by the Roman Emperor Constantine in the fourth century; then through its acceptance by the barbarian kingdoms of Europe formed after the collapse of the Roman Empire;[20] then under the dialectical pressure of Islam (from the seventh century), another universal religion rooted in ancient Israel which became available also as a powerful instrument of national self-identification and a powerful basis of mutual alterity; then

[18] Joseph Campbell has suggested that, in the ancient world, mythology divided into two streams, a division which still affects human consciousness, between an 'oriental' mode, based on an intrinsic union of the divine/natural/universal and the human/individual, and a 'near-eastern/occidental' mode, based on an intrinsic separation between the two. J. Campbell, *The Masks of God: Oriental Mythology* (New York, Viking Press; 1962), ch. 1. Hegel makes a similar point in relation to ancient Jewish thought: *Philosophy of History* (fn. 1 above), p. 195. See also E. Cassirer, *The Myth of the State* (New Haven, London, Yale University Press; 1949), pp. 37ff., and M. Weber, *Ancient Judaism* (Glencoe, Free Press; 1952), pp. 3–5.

[19] The *locus classicus*, apart from the New Testament itself, is Augustine (354–430), *The City of God*.

[20] For a corrective to the commonly held view that the early medieval nations lacked national consciousness, see S. Reynolds, *Kingdoms and Communities in Western Europe 900–1300* (Oxford, Clarendon Press; 1984), pp. 250ff.

as an element in the powerful development of distinct national identities in Europe after the Reformation of the sixteenth century; and, finally, as an element in the imposed reidentifying of colonised peoples in all parts of the world.

4.35 In the meantime, the self-identifying traditions of the tribes of Israel had become detached from their particular locus in Palestine, had been reconceptualised as Judaism, a sophisticated metaphysical and ethical structure which became the central feature of the self-identifying of a virtual nation, whose virtual nationals were dispersed throughout the world, until Zionism in the nineteenth century sought to reassert the geographical aspect of the national self-identifying.

4.36 We must learn to see these familiar phenomena not as events in history but as interesting expressions of human psychology, and sometimes as symptoms of psycho-pathology. It is an aspect of our own psychology, magnified but not beyond recognition, which is displayed through the art of self-justifying self-promotion practised by those who build nations in the mind and not merely on the battlefield. It is an art in which some nations have excelled above all others, especially, it seems, those nations which have found it useful to believe that their subjugation of other lands and peoples was a destiny consistent with the special nature of the nation.

'We are alone among mankind in doing men benefits, not on calculations of self-interest, but in the fearless confidence of freedom. In a word I claim that our city as a whole is an education to Greece, and that her members yield to none, man by man, for independence of spirit, many-sidedness of attainment, and complete self-reliance in limbs and brain.'[21]

'For thou art an holy people unto the Lord thy God: the Lord thy God hath chosen thee to be a special people unto himself above all people that are upon the face of the earth.'[22]

'Remember thou, O Roman, to rule the nations with thy sway; these shall be thine arts to crown Peace with Law, to spare the humbled, and to tame in war the proud.'[23]

[21] The text of the Funeral Oration of Pericles as reported, or reconstructed, by Thucydides may be found (in a translation of Wilamowitz's text) in A. Zimmern, *The Greek Commonwealth – Politics and Economics in Fifth Century Athens* (1911) (Oxford, Clarendon Press; 4th edn, 1924), pp. 200ff.

[22] Deuteronomy, 7.6.

[23] Virgil, *Aeneid* (tr. H. R. Fairclough; Cambridge, MA, London, Harvard University Press (Loeb Classical Library); 1986), bk vi, lines 851–3, p. 567.

'Britannia triumphant, her ships sweep the sea; Her standard is Justice her watchword, "Be free".'[24]

'Let our object be, our country, our whole country, and nothing but our country. And, by the blessing of God, may that country itself become a vast and splendid monument, not of oppression and terror, but of wisdom, of peace, and of liberty, upon which the world may gaze with admiration for ever.'[25]

4.37 Seen in a psychological perspective, what seems to be happening in such exemplary cases of national self-identification is a threefold process, three processes in one.

(1) projection of the individual's self-process onto the collectivity;
(2) *introjection* of the collectivity's self-process into the individual;
(3) the forming of a *subjective totality* identified as the collectivity (the nation).

4.38 The individual concerned may be a self-conceived participant in the collectivity (a national), or else a self-conceived non-participant (an alien), in which case the process is one of self-identification through alterity (such self-identification being then part of the self-identifying of all three parties – the national, the alien, the collectivity).[26]

4.39 By *projection* we would mean something loosely analogous to its meaning in Freudian psychology. The individual's personal struggle for self-identification seems to the individual to be mirrored in the self-identifying of the collectivity. And the individual not only focuses considerable psychic attention on the collectivity but also imputes to the collectivity the full range of individual psychic processes (identifying, constraining, directing, motivating processes), at all levels of consciousness and unconsciousness, so that the collectivity comes to have a psychic process which is congruent with, and a continuation of, the individual psychic process. By this means the individual's self-identifying comes to be part of the self-identifying of the collectivity. The nation becomes an inseparable part of our desiring.

4.40 By *introjection* we would again mean something loosely analogous to its meaning in Freudian psychology. The individual makes

[24] D. Garrick, *Heart of Oak* (1759).

[25] D. Webster, Speech at the Placing of the Cornerstone of Bunker Hill Monument, 17 June 1825.

[26] For the role of the 'perennial dilemma' of the self and the other in the self-constituting of a society, see *Eunomia*, ch. 4.

part of the self-forming process into something which, while being conceivable as 'other', is nevertheless also able to function as part of the individual's self-forming. Effects are produced in the individual psychic process which originate from that 'other' and acquire a sort of necessity, and certainly a special power, stemming precisely from the fact that they surpass the individual's psychic process, that they are part of a significantly autonomous psychic story which is not only the individual's own. By this means the self-identifying of the collectivity becomes part of the individual's personal self-identifying.

4.41 The *subjective totality* is generated by the interacting and integrating of the projection and introjection processes of many individuals (nationals and aliens). It is important to say that, on this view, the subjective totality (the nation) is neither a thing which is created and which then takes on a life of its own nor is it merely an illusion shared by an indefinite number of individuals. The subjective totality is and remains an integral part of the psychic process of the individuals but it always surpasses the process of any given individual. The individuals enter and leave the subjective totality, as they are born and die, as they are naturalised or expatriated. The nation is thus just one of those countless remarkable phenomena of the human reality, the reality made by the human mind, which depend on us to think them into existence and to maintain them in existence by our thinking but which at the same time think us into existence, and sustain us in existence.

4.42 A nation can become extinct as a self-identifying nation; if remembered at all, it then continues to exist only as an alterity, seen from the point of view of those who remember it. In this way, even a nation which is extinct as a self-identifying nation can have identifying effects, for example, Athens in relation to republican Rome, ancient Greece and Rome in relation to Renaissance Europe, ancient Rome in relation to Napoleonic France, Teutonic Germany in relation to the Germany of the nineteenth century, ancient national identities of some of the 'new' states which have emerged from imperialism after 1945.

4.43 To speak of a state-system as a body politic is as much to speak in metaphor as if one were to describe a state-system as a Leviathan or a Mortal God or the March of God on Earth.[27] To speak of a nation as mind politic is to use language in a different way. It is to propose a name for a

[27] For a discussion of the organic analogy between the state and the human body, see O. Gierke, *Political Theories of the Middle Age* (1881) (tr. F. Maitland; Cambridge, Cambridge University

theoretical model of a particular set of phenomena within human reality which we are attributing to a set of particular psychological processes. It is to propose that we find within ourselves, within our own struggle for personal identity, something which we recognise as being merely the continuation of that process, its extension or expansion beyond what we conceive to be our personal location in space and time. A nation is not something which is *like* mind organised politically. A nation *is* mind organised politically.

4.44 What we recognise in the nation is what we call in ourselves personality. What we must expect to find in the nation is all the possibilities of the whole human personality, of that subjective totality which is the integrated product of mind and which integrates us with the whole of the universe beyond our own locus in space and time. This means that we will find the unconscious mind at work in the nation, so that the reality conceived by the nation will be full of all the bizarre effects which the unconscious part of the mind can cause. It means that we will find neurotic and psychotic behaviour in the behaviour of the nation. It means, above all, that we will find that the nation is capable of good and

Press; 1900), pp. 22ff. (including the idea of humanity itself as an organism); E. Barker, *The Political Thought of Plato and Aristotle* (1918) (New York, Dover; 1959), pp. 276ff. (on Aristotle's use of the analogy, in particular). Hobbes uses the analogy in various ways for different purposes. In the Introduction to *Leviathan*, he carries the analogy to a rather absurd length, saying that the Leviathan or Commonwealth or State is 'but an Artificial Man', in which the sovereignty is 'an Artificial Soul, as giving life and motion to the whole body'. (London, J. M. Dent & Sons (Everyman's Library); 1914, p. 3). Locke uses Body Politic to refer to the political society as a whole (ch. 8 of the Second Treatise). He overuses it, in the same chapter, to assist his unconvincing argument in favour of majoritarianism. J. Locke, *Two Treatises of Government* (ed. P. Laslett; Cambridge, Cambridge University Press; 1960), II, § 96, p. 375.

The formula attributed to Hegel that the state is 'the march of God in the World' (*der Gang Gottes in der Welt*), is in an Addition (*Zusatz*) to § 258 of the *Philosophy of Right* (fn. 7 above), p. 279. Hegel uses the organicist view of the state at §§ 267ff. (including an Addition to 269) and analyses the subjective aspect of the state, including the nature of patriotism. In the 'Mind Objective', the second section of the *Philosophy of Mind* (tr. W. Wallace; Oxford, Oxford University Press; 1971), pp. 254–5, 265, he considers mind in relation to 'the spirit of a nation' (§ 514) and as Political Constitution, that is, 'the mind developed to an organic actuality' (§ 517). In § 539 he refers to the state as 'living mind'. However, it should be stressed that all these passages depend on a special concept of 'mind' or 'spirit' which, one might say, it is the aim of the whole of his philosophy to construct and which is only distantly related to the purely subjective concept of mind with which we are concerned in the present study. For Hegel's use of the concept of spirit or mind, see J. N. Findlay, *Hegel: a Re-examination* (London, George Allen & Unwin; 1958), ch. 2.

In the work of Herbert Spencer and Henri Bergson, social organicism finally surpassed metaphor and became metaphysics.

evil, because the nation is that same mind which, in each of us, is capable of good and evil. The human mind, acting as nation, can do good, ensuring the survival and prospering of its nationals without harming others. And the human mind, acting as nation, can do evil, great evil, all the evil of which the human mind is capable. So it is that our response to the nation cannot be merely that of the human naturalist observing human phenomena. The human mind as nation engages our moral responsibility as human beings.

Nation and state

4.45 In the spirit of post-medieval humanist rationalism, Hobbes and Locke (and other social philosophers of the same era) took up again an ancient tradition, of Plato and Aristotle and the Stoics and the theorists of natural law, to propose a denationalised, universalised theory of politically organised society. Such a society is as it is not because it is a subjective nation but because it is the actualisation of a particular structure of ideas, which can be represented in the form of a conceptual model conforming to the principles of logic, rather than as a story or a description reflecting the practical effects of human subjectivity. For such a theory, the ontology of a politically organised society is metaphysical not physical, philosophical not historical. A politically organised society is a manifestation of mind not of minds.

4.46 It is as well that the seventeenth century was able to develop theories of such a kind, since it made possible the existence of the modern state, a form of social organisation which is systematic in character, and which may or may not be the political organisation of a pre-existing nation. If a non-national state-society generates a national collective subjectivity, then it does so as a by-product of its successful self-organising as a state.

4.47 The reconceiving of the idea of the non-national state made possible, in particular, the conceiving of the United States of America, which was not created as a united nation or a union of nations but as an institutional structure-system, the essence of which was set out in the US constitution, an essence which was a refreshing blend of mildly puritan New England zeal and the best ideas available to a well-educated late-eighteenth-century gentleman from the long history of universalist thought about the good life in society. The United States, almost immediately, became an inspiration for all those who wished to create a state *de novo*, often as a purposive repudiation of something which had gone before, a degenerate genetic nation, a colonial regime, some other form of social system which had come to seem alien. Once established as a state, the US lost no time in trying to make of itself a nation.[28] It became a prime example of the single-minded and energetic creation of a generic nation through the manipulation of the minds of the people, as Plato and Hobbes had prescribed, in order to consolidate and sustain the existence of the state.[29] It also thereby initiated a development which was full of sinister potentiality, and which would affect state-systems and genetic nations and generic nations alike: namely, the systematic appropriation by the institutional authority of the state-system of the subjective energies of the nation.

4.48 Following in another tradition (set by the Greek and Roman and medieval historians and reinvigorated by Machiavelli), Montesquieu and Voltaire offered a dialectical correction to the transcendentalist view of the state. It is the utter particularity of every politically organised society which is, on the contrary, the basis of the ontology of politically organised societies in general. Such societies are unique manifestations of universal social forms,[30] but the specificity of a given society – as

28 See M. Jensen, *The New Nation. A History of the United States during the Confederation 1781–89* (New York, Knopf; 1950), pp. 85ff. Strangely, it seems that the Declaration of Independence did not acquire its status as an affirmation of the nation's specificity until, perhaps, 1812: G. Wills, *Inventing America. Jefferson's Declaration of Independence* (New York, Vintage Books; 1978), pp. 323ff. See also C. Becker, *The Declaration of Independence. A Study in the History of Political Ideas* (New York, Vintage Books; 1945), pp. 224ff.; S. M. Lipset, *The First New Nation* (New York, Basic Books; 1963).

29 Since, for Plato, the orders of the soul, of society, and of the universe are a coherent order, it follows that a society has to be interested not only in public matters but also in all that affects the life of the soul (poetry, music, myth, education in general). See, for example, *Republic*, III. 398ff; *Statesman*, 309.d; *Philebus*, 16.d.; *Laws* II.659d. For Hobbes, 'it is the unity of the representer, not the unity of the represented that makes the person one' (*Leviathan* (fn. 27 above), p. 85). A cause of the weakness and dissolution of states lies in various forms of fragmentation, including moral and intellectual fragmentation (pp. 173ff). It follows, incidentally, that universities must be kept pure in their teaching, free from 'the Venom of Heathen Politicians and the incantation of Deceiving Spirits' (p. 391).

30 It is important to recognise the universalising aspect of Montesquieu's approach, even when he is at his most particularising – 'In a nation [*sc.* England] so distempered by the climate as to have a disrelish of everything, nay, even of life, it is plain that the government most suitable to the inhabitants is that in which they cannot lay their uneasiness to any single person's charge . . . ' He is seeking to explain the remarkable political freedom of the English. Baron de Montesquieu, *The Spirit of the Laws* (tr. T. Nugent; New York and London, Macmillan; 1949), p. 231.

a function of geography, climate, culture, national character and as a function of the society-forming action of dominant individuals – explains the existence of that society, and is not merely part of a more or less picturesque, *ab extra* account of its nature and customs.

4.49 As practical theories influencing the actual life of given societies, both sets of ideas were full of tantalising ambiguity, as seen from the position of a ruler or a ruling class. Were they revolutionary or reactionary? The transcendentalist theory might dignify the status quo of a given society with the charisma of metaphysics, but it might also provide a supra-societal theoretical basis (such as natural law or natural rights) for seeking to transform a society, suggesting a *status quem*, as it were. The theory of contingency might dignify the status quo with the charisma of practical inevitability and might even allow a ruler to claim to be the embodiment of the true nation, but it also necessarily implied that contingencies, and hence social structures, might change in uncontrollable ways.

4.50 The development of a new theory of the nation, in the later eighteenth century, may be seen as a dialectical surpassing of transcendentalism and contingency in the conceiving of politically organised society. Herder's paradoxical idea of the nation is of something which is transcendentally specific.[31] All nations have in common their uniqueness. It is of the nature of a nation to be uniquely itself, its self having being formed by long and profound and mysterious processes, material and subjective, which have, as it were, secreted a nation from within themselves. The analogical discourse is organic rather than mechanical, where the organic phenomena in question are not merely bodies but the deeper life-processes of living nature. On this view, the nation is thus non-transcendental, in the sense that its whole explanation is to be found deep within itself. But the nation is also transcendental, in the sense that it is not a mere accumulation of contingencies; it has a unique pattern or genetic programme which unfolds in, and can only be known through, its actualised history. A nation is not a completed aggregate but a growing totality. A nation is self-transcending.

4.51 It is tempting to believe that there is some deep-structure connection between this individualisation of the nation and the

[31] Berlin takes a lenient view of Herder's responsibility for the excesses which would flow from the powerful idea of the *Volksgeist* (the spirit of a nation). I. Berlin, *Vico and Herder: Two Studies in the History of Ideas* (London, Hogarth; 1976), pp. 156ff.

contemporaneous development of the idea of the personality of the individualised human being.[32] The Romantic enthusiasm for the self-creating and self-fulfilling and self-transcending human being, spiritually rooted at the deepest level in all the processes of Nature, seems also to be present in the invigorating idea of the self-filled organic nation. Whatever the connection may be as a matter of intellectual history, there can be no doubt that the heightened subjectivity of the Romantic period flowed powerfully into the new idea of the nation.

4.52 The humane sciences of the nineteenth century played an ambiguous role in the aetiology of the dramatic social effects which flowed from the newly energised idea of the nation. While political science and sociology and pre-Freudian psychology were pursuing the grail or the snark of the universality of the human phenomenon, anthropology and historiography were doing that, but were also incidentally providing rich and abundant material to feed the spiritual hunger of the new national subjectivity. Savigny and the Historical Right School of historians in Germany were seeking not merely, as good human naturalists, some sort of historical 'truth'. Like good proto-Marxists they were also seeking a form of 'higher necessity', to be found in the history of a nation, a necessity which is incidentally the source of the authority of the legal system and of all other systems of social authority, including state-system authority.[33] In this way, the nation and the state are bound together in a holy union of transcendental reality.

4.53 As human naturalism lent to the idea of the nation the self-confidence of its new faith in the subjective-made-objective, there remained the problem of reintegrating the subjectivity of the individual into the subjectivity of the non-national state-system, into politically organised society considered in its universal, transcendental aspect. In the fertile obscurity of Rousseau and Hegel the conjunction of individual and social subjectivity was made possible, the integration of all human reality.

4.54 The 'problem' of Rousseau and the 'problem' of Hegel are remarkably similar. Were they passionate believers in human subjectivity

[32] For a discussion of this topic, with references, see P.-A. Taguieff, 'Le "nationalisme des nationalistes". Un problème pour l'histoire des idées politiques en France', in *Théories du nationalisme* (eds G. Delannoi and P.-A. Taguieff; Paris, Editions Kimé; 1947), pp. 64ff.

[33] H. Marcuse, *Reason and Revolution* (fn. 6 above), pp. 367ff. E. Cassirer, *The Myth of the State* (fn. 18 above), p. 182.

or passionate believers in social solidarity? The biographical question is of lesser importance, although, in the light of the evidence, it seems perverse to insist that, whatever the uses to which their ideas have been put in real-world social practice, their personal aim was to provide a basis for submerging the individual in an all-powerful state-society.[34] From very different philosophical points of departure, they are both saying that there is no reason to suppose a natural antagonism or even a natural duality between the individual and society. Not just any society, admittedly, but a good society or a more rationally achieved society could be a place where self-fulfilment was the same thing as social fulfilment, either because society as an agent of willed action is capable of conceiving of itself as the social manifestation of the citizen as agent of willed action, or because society as the actualisation of social potentiality is capable of conceiving of itself as the actualisation of the same spirit which actualises the potentiality of the individual through the processes of individual consciousness. Our ideal self as a person and as a citizen is, on either view, one ideal. The moral order and the social order are one. Human reality is a single reality.

4.55 By these various means, nation and state and individual were brought together in a potent compound which could enter, with mind-flooding energy, into the mind politic of any nation, and which could be used and abused by those controlling the institutional authority of any state-society. It is a development of the human mind which has,

[34] 'The *Philosophy of Mind*, and in fact the whole of the Hegelian system, is a portrayal of the process whereby "the individual becomes universal" and whereby "the construction of universality" takes place.' H. Marcuse, *Reason and Revolution*, p. 90. 'Hegel's whole philosophy turns its polemical edge against pure individuality, which the Romantic movement had raised on its banner at that time, with its "law of the heart", which this individuality was supposed to realize, but which for Hegel meant the descent into the "insanity of subjectivism".' Frankfurt Institute for Social Research, *Aspects of Sociology* (1956) (tr. J. Viertel; London, Heinemann; 1973), p. 42. The reference is to the chapter entitled 'The law of the heart and the frenzy of self-conceit', in Hegel's *Phenomenology of Spirit* (fn. 6 above), pp. 221–7. Ch. 3 of *Aspects* contains an account of the background to the nineteenth-century ambivalence towards individualism. The apparent ambiguity of Hegel in these matters is impressively treated in S. Avineri, *Hegel's Theory of the Modern State* (Cambridge, Cambridge University Press; 1972), esp. ch. 9. Rousseau's 'discrepancies', as they are called by L. Althusser in *Politics and History* (tr. B. Brewster; London, New Left Books; 1972), part 2, are convincingly treated in E. Cassirer, *The Question of Jean-Jacques Rousseau* (tr. P. Gay; Bloomington and London, Indiana University Press; 1954). Popper's one-sided view of Rousseau and Hegel (as of Plato and Marx) seems, by comparison, to be a caricature: K. Popper, *The Open Society and its Enemies* (London, Routledge & Kegan Paul; 1945). The early (1844) writings of Karl Marx might be seen as an effort to find a single solution to the ambivalences of both Rousseau and Hegel.

as things turned out, determined the subsequent course of European history, and then of world history.

Nation and pathology

4.56 It follows from all that has been said above that the moral problem of the behaviour of nations in the twentieth century – in particular, the evil which has been done by nations acting through state-systems and by nations at odds with state-systems – is a complex one. We have identified a set of powerful resistances which must somehow be overcome if we are to understand and to deal with the problem:

(1) the indeterminacy of transcendental philosophy undermines our capacity to understand the phenomena of the nation rationally and to judge them morally;
(2) the naturalism of the humane sciences detaches the phenomena of the nation from our subjectivity, including our moral consciousness, individual and collective;
(3) the naturalism of the humane sciences renders us passive in relation to the behaviour (political, economic, technological) of the nation, as passive as a remote tribe cowering before the omnipotence of Nature;
(4) and yet our minds are full of the overflowing subjectivity of the modern nation, of our own nation or nations, and of other nations;
(5) and the institutional authority of the state-systems relentlessly appropriates the phenomena of national subjectivity and transforms them into facts of power, instruments of power, commodities.

4.57 In short, we feel that we cannot judge the nation and its works, we cannot control the nation and its works, and yet we cannot escape the nation and its works.

4.58 To oppose such formidable forces, we have been able to summon up only a modest array of intellectual weapons:

(1) the idea that the mind which is involved in the mind politic of the nation is precisely the same mind as the mind which is involved in individualised human behaviour;
(2) the idea that self-nationising is the same process as self-personising, forming a subjective totality which feeds on the mind that it feeds;

(3) the idea that, having regard to (1) and (2), there is an indissoluble moral unity between the nation as mind politic and the person as mind individualised.

4.59 So it is that we find ourselves in the same condition – but what a different condition after three such centuries! – as the self-contemplating Descartes. The best efforts of philosophy, of academicism, of scientism, of economism and of state-power cannot separate us from that first hearth and last refuge which is our own consciousness. In our immediate and inescapable experience of our internal forum we must find the means to re-experience the public forum. In the communicating of our own self with itself, our most intimate experience, we must find the means to communicate with, and to cure, the self-communicating nation.

4.60 How to begin? We could try to re-experience, as if we were reliving some personal experience of our own, the development of the self-consciousness of actual nations. Using, as compass and map, our own conceptions of what it is to be a person, what it is to be a healthy or a virtuous person, what it is to be a diseased or an evil person, we might begin to imagine a way to find a sympathetic understanding of self-nationing, the kind of understanding which alone would entitle us to pass judgement on the behaviour of nations, and to condemn, if need be, the evil that nations do, and to propose therapies for the sicknesses that afflict nations and those whom they infect with their sicknesses. To make a start somewhere, we might consider, as a tentative and rudimentary thought-experiment, what is perhaps the most striking instance of modern times – the reconceiving of German national consciousness in the nineteenth century.

4.61 Beginning in the period of German Romanticism, Germans set themselves the task of rediscovering not only what it is to be human (a task that they shared with European Romantics everywhere) but also what it is to be German. They went in search of what Hegel would call 'the indwelling spirit and the history of the nation ... by which constitutions have been made and are made'.[35] It was a task made easier by the relative

[35] G. W. F. Hegel, *Philosophy of Mind* (fn. 27 above), § 540, pp. 268–9. Hegel was disparaging about the medieval mystifying of Germany's origins: Avineri, *Modern State* (fn. 34 above), p. 229, also at pp. 21–2. Gellner is dismissive, scornful even, of attempts to universalise the idea of the nation, to make of it a natural and inevitable category of human socialisation. The idea of the nation is a contingent thing, arising in particular ways in particular social conjunctures. See 'Nationalism and the two forms of cohesion', fn. 10 above, *passim*. 'The

sparseness of the information and by the passage of time, and it was a task which, for the same reasons, could be, at one and the same time, an enthralling exercise in dry-as-dust objectivity and a thrilling exercise in rampant subjectivity. With remarkable facility and with surprising certainty there could be conjured out of the cold northern mists of a remote Teutonic past a German self which was heroic and pure and creative and dynamic and masterful. In such an interesting mirror, it was possible to see and to judge a German self that had somehow, in the meantime, become petty and and provincial and bloodless and aimless. It was not difficult to see that Germany was a genetic nation which had collapsed into a patchwork of insignificant nations, together forming some sort of shadowy and unsatisfactory generic nation, a nation which had not remained true to its self but which could, perhaps, be made to become its true self once again.

4.62 In the office of official psychoanalysts to the German nation, the brothers Grimm, whom we may take as symbolic heroes of a movement which involved countless scholars, including adepts of the new human naturalism, were able by their vast labours to bring up from the depths of German unconsciousness a German soul which manifested itself uniquely in German language, German folk-tales, German literature, German art, German religion, and even a German mythology.[36] In a more Jungian framework, Richard Wagner (once again, a hero-figure standing for countless German artists and writers) transmuted the new consciousness through the magical processes of art into something which could return, as all art does, to take on a new universalised life in the depths of German unconsciousness.[37] By these means, German consciousness, at its most articulated and at its most secret, was changed.

4.63 The German case is merely an extraordinarily open and explicit and purposeful example of what all nations do all the time, in a much more disordered way. It raises, as all such cases do, the questions of why such a reforming of national self-consciousness occurs and what are its consequences.

great, but valid, paradox is this: nations can be defined only in terms of nationalism, rather than, as you might expect, the other way round.' E. Gellner, *Nations and Nationalism* (Oxford, Basil Blackwell; 1983), p. 55.

36 J. Grimm, *Deutsche Mythologie* (1835).

37 R. Wagner, *My Life* (tr. A. Gray; New York, Da Capo; 1983), pp. 280, 343.

4.64 In the case of Germany in the nineteenth century, it seems particularly perverse that a people should redefine themselves in so romantic a spirit when (a) German scholars were using the spirit of objectivity to carry the humane sciences and the natural sciences to the highest levels attained anywhere in Europe; (b) the Prussian state was leading Europe in the rational reorganisation of the social, if not of the political, aspects of society; and (c) German business and industry were applying the lessons of the British industrial revolution to generate an economy which was rapidly overtaking, in scale and sophistication, any other European economy.

4.65 Renan drew attention to the essential part that forgetting and error play in the formation of national consciousness.[38] The self-image may be based on false information about the past and present situation of the nation, and it may, probably must, involve the repression of much in that situation which is inconsistent with the ideal-self-image. We may go further and say that national self-consciousness is a form of private fantasy, a reality-for-themselves of the nationals whose relationship to the reality-for-non-nationals is secondary. However, in the case of nations, the private fantasy is necessarily a public fantasy. The development of German consciousness was as much a matter of interest for other Europeans, especially the French and the British, as was German material progress. Germans were fellow members of a European society, a European family, a European nation even, and their state of mind could not be a matter of indifference to the other members. To a greater extent with the French and to a lesser extent with the unreflective British, the development of a new German consciousness generated modifications in all non-German national consciousness.[39]

4.66 In these facts lie the roots of the pathology of national consciousness.

[38] 'Qu'est-ce qu'une nation?', in E. Renan, *Oeuvres complètes* (Paris, Calmann-Levy; 1947), I, p. 891.

[39] On Franco-German mutual self-nationalising, see Taguieff (fn. 32 above), *passim*; and P. Birnbaum, 'Nationalisme à la française', same volume, pp. 125–38. See also L. Dumont, *L'idéologie allemande. France-Allemagne et retour* (Paris, Gallimard; 1991). Compare Adam Ferguson: 'Athens was necessary to Sparta, in the exercise of her virtue, as steel is to flint in the production of fire.' *An Essay on the History of Civil Society* (1767) (ed. D. Forbes; Edinburgh, Edinburgh University Press; 1966), p. 59. Discussed in P. Gay, *The Enlightenment* (fn. 10 above), pp. 340ff. For a comparison of British, French and German national constitutional psychologies, see ch. 7 below.

4.67 In the age-old language of historians – a form of language which, strange to say, is still used by specialists in International Relations – *Germany was envious of the prestige of France and resented the world-power of Britain.* France had a priceless possession, its private fantasy, the French nation – *la France* – which had been brought forth from 1,000 years of history, a history which had to be transmuted from being a record of remarkably sustained cultural excellence of all kinds ('culture' in the high-culture sense, rather than in the anthropological sense) into a supposedly coherent history of a self-knowing and self-forming political nation. Britain, sub-Germanic in national origin, but a mongrel people, irrational and indolent in matters of social organisation, had, as a reward for no particular merit or effort, outplayed many other worthier players in the international power-game and had collected all sorts of undeserved advantages, including a blithe national self-confidence. *In order to be able to play in the world-power-game, Germany wanted to make itself into a world-power nation like France and Britain.* Such is the world-view of the human naturalists.

4.68 From such a viewpoint, these hypostatic bodies-politic, state-systems with personal names, are supposed to behave like real human beings in all but one respect. Their psychology is the psychology of the nursery, of books for children, of fairy-tales.

4.69 It was not a Gulliver called Germany which had taken a drink from the bottle of nationalism marked *Drink-Me*, in order to become a giant in a world of giants. It was the Germans who were re-forming their minds as collective subjectivity as they re-formed their minds as individualised personality, allowing the new subjective totality to overwhelm their long-cherished regionalism and diversity. The consequences of such a re-forming of consciousness are felt in the personal lives of individuals and also in the social life of the nation, its social life within itself and its social life in the company of other nations and their nationals. In order to be able to make the judgement that those consequences, in a given case, are diseased or evil, we must treat them not as the product of infantile personifications but as the everyday work of all-too-human human beings. To deal with the strange behaviour of nations we need, not iron laws of history or game-theories of power-politics or rational-choice theories of economics, but a nosology of the mental diseases of national identity.

4.70 A list of such diseases would include the following – *neurotic nationalism; psychotic nationalism; biological racism; hysterical xenophobia; religious fanaticism; terrorism; anti-Semitism.*

4.71 There must be an overwhelming presumption that not merely wickedness but mental disease is involved in human behaviour which leads to such terrible evil as the events of the two World Wars of the twentieth century. We may hazard the diagnosis that the First World War was a war of neurotic nationalism and that the Second World War (in Europe and in Asia) was a disease of psychotic nationalism.

4.72 The nationalist neurosis of the First World War was a sort of neurosis *à six*, an interactive neurosis involving most of the German, French, British, Russian, Austro-Hungarian and Ottoman Turkish ruling classes, together with some part of their respective masses, to the extent that they were manipulated by those ruling classes. If patriotism conceives the nation in fantasy, nationalism conceives the nation in obsession. The neurosis in question involves some unresolved conflict of self-identification and hence of self-esteem and hence of self-preservation. Such a neurosis is not a problem of acute social significance unless and until it involves other people, including the people of another nation, or involves an interaction at the subjective and/or practical levels between the different national obsessions, feeding on each other, reinforcing each other.

4.73 The Cold War was another example of such a neurotic interaction. Here the *folie à deux* was between the United States which, despite its relative antiquity, continued to conceive of itself as a generic nation, and the Soviet Union, which had been formed when a small part of the Russian ruling class chose to reform the old genetic nation into a generic nation, defined by its particular social structures and a particular set of universalist ideas (Marxism-Leninism) put to exceptionalist use. It is in the nature of generic nations that they must continually compete (in war or sport or trade or whatever), in order continually to reaffirm their exceptional nature. In the Jungian typology, they are closer to the extraverted end of the personality spectrum; in Riesmann's terms, they tend to be other-directed.[40] In the Cold War, the two nations drove each other (and the other nations who were infected by their neurosis) into

[40] D. Riesmann, *The Lonely Crowd. A Study of the Changing American Character* (New Haven, London, Yale University Press; 1950), pp. 17–25.

more and more irrational behaviour, above all into a wildly hypertrophic accumulation of military weapons – those fetishistic props of troubled identity, like a fast car or a young mistress. With the end of the Cold War, Russia reverted to an untidy genetic status, in which the sub-nation of Russia may once again come to imperialise some or all of the other sub-nations. The United States is left to struggle with its identity in new and especially difficult circumstances.

4.74 If the First World War was a neurotic episode, involving the newly genetic German nation, the Second World War was, from a clinical point of view, a very different thing.

4.75 Psychotic nationalism may be called madness, if we declare our grounds for continuing to use that terrible word.

4.76 Stunned into transcendental silence by the philosophical phenomena labelled above as Wittgenstein, Freud, Marx and Darwin, we must begin to find some way to incorporate them into a new way of speaking, at least of speaking at levels other than the transcendental level. We may try to find in them – separately and taken together – a new subjectivity-beyond-subjectivity, a new conception, if not of rationality or morality, then of sanity.

4.77 The Nietzschean resonance is no coincidence. Nietzsche, lonely prophet, saw the twentieth century and it drove him mad. Wittgenstein, Freud, Marx and Darwin are all, spiritually, post-Nietzschean. He saw that the products of the human mind, however sophisticated and self-assured, cannot be contained within the categories of rationality and morality, that all the efforts of the mind are nothing but a sort of permanent self-exploration in the dimension of sanity, that is to say, an exploration by the mind of the mind's reality-for-itself. Modernism in the fine arts and music and literature would be the twentieth century's exploration of the mind's reality through the power of creative imagination. Totalitarianism, of left and right, would be the twentieth century's exploration of the reality of the self-socialising mind through the power of the mind-filling institutional authority of the state-system.

4.78 The reality of the totalitarian nation is a possible reality for the self-nationing of the human mind. The twentieth century has demonstrated that. Nazi Germany might not have been Nazi Germany without a great European war. But Nazi Germany without a great European war might have become a German nation of perfected self-judging rationality and morality. Without a great European war and without the

Cold War, Stalinist Russia might have become as perfect a version of a greater-Russian nation as that difficult sub-continent may permit.

4.79 The psychotic personality of the human individual is similarly capable of apparently self-surpassing behaviour. The behaviour is self-surpassing from the perspective of public reality, the reality shared by most people and incorporated in the self-forming of society. But the behaviour is not at all self-surpassing, is rational and moral and sane, in the perspective of the private reality of the psychotic person. And in the processes of society, including self-nationing, psychotic reality can also be a public reality.

4.80 It is a phenomenon which has evidently existed throughout the whole history of human socialising, but it is a phenomenon which became of great practical significance in the twentieth century, given the intensity of the socialising of modern nations and the intensity of their social interaction. The private reality of a Hitler, a Stalin, a Mussolini – not to mention the dozens of other less successful but no less sinister holders of personalised institutional authority all over the world in the twentieth century – is also the public reality of a nation.

4.81 In the case of Hitler, the phenomenon is at its most acute and most sensitive. An aspect of the reality-for-itself of Nazi Germany was the discovery within the self-conceiving of the genetic German nation of an element which can only be called biological purity – and that element was also powerfully present in the reality-for-himself of the socially marginal Hitler. The German nation might then be said to be genetic, not merely in the metaphorical sense that we have been giving to the term, but in a descriptive sense. It has been rather rare for a nation to include a notion of biological purity as a primary element in its self-conceiving. (Oddly enough, Japan may be another example.) But there is frequently such an element latent somewhere in the self-conceiving of genetic nations and, perhaps, even in that of generic nations. (The treatment in the United States of native Americans and black Americans may be evidence of such a thing.) And such an element is probably a pathogenic factor in several of the mental diseases of national identity listed above.

4.82 Freud took a step which now seems to be irreversible when he removed the frontier dividing the mentally normal from the abnormal, the mentally healthy from the diseased. He also took the first step towards removing the frontier between personal psychology and social psychology, in two rather rudimentary attempts – on the one hand, using the work of previous psychologists who had studied 'crowd' phenomena;[41] on the other hand, constructing one of his myth-models, as one may call them, which would find at the root of society something analogous to the Oedipal myth-model at the root of individual personality.[42] What we are considering in the present essay is the possibility that there is no frontier at all between personal psychology and the social psychology of the nation as collective subjectivity.

4.83 After Freud, in the work of the supposedly Freudian Lacan,[43] but also in the work of those who have opposed the ideas and practices of Freud-based psychiatry,[44] the very idea of madness is being dissolved.

[41] S. Freud, *Group Psychology and the Analysis of the Ego* (1921), in *The Standard Edition of the Complete Psychological Works of Sigmund Freud* (ed. J. Strachey; London, Hogarth Press; 1953–74), xviii. The focus is on the effect on the psychology of the individual of participation in groups rather than on the nature of the group.

[42] See S. Freud, *Totem and Taboo. Some Points of Agreement between the Mental Lives of Savages and Neurotics* (1912–13), in *Standard Edition* (fn. 41 above), xiii. Having put forward his explanation of the origin of society, Freud says that it is surprising to him that the problems of social psychology should prove soluble on the basis of one single point – man's relation to his father (p. 157). He expresses concern that 'I have taken as the basis of my whole position the existence of a collective mind, in which mental processes occur just as they do in the mind of an individual.' He is recognising in advance the criticism that there is no generally accepted biological explanation for the species-inheritance of mental events as part of human phylogeny. He had been anticipated by Hume and Nietzsche in the idea of society as the product of the repression of natural instincts.

For three later works of Freud which explore the psychic aspects of society, see S. Freud, *The Future of an Illusion* (1927); *Civilization and its Discontents* (1930); and *Moses and Monotheism* (1939). They are written in Freud's broader, more Jungian mode and do not amount to a rigorous philosophy of the psychology of society. For an impressive response, especially to *Civilization*, see H. Marcuse, *Eros and Civilization. A Philosophical Inquiry into Freud* (1955) (Boston, Beacon Press; 1966).

[43] Lacan did not publish any exposition of a 'general theory' and rejected the idea of general psychological theory. This has not prevented publication of numerous Lacan texts nor the development of an academic extractive industry mining those texts (now at the tertiary level of writing about the secondary literature). We are still waiting for a general theory of the psychology of society. It may be hoped that, when it comes, it will be more exhilarating and empowering than the work of either Freud or Lacan. Especially on the philosophical resonances of Lacan, see M. Borch-Jacobsen, *Lacan – Le maître absolu* (Paris, Flammarion; 1990). See also M. Marini, *Lacan* (Paris, Pierre Belford; 1986); S. Felman, *Jacques Lacan and the Adventure of Insight* (Cambridge, MA, London, Harvard University Press; 1987); D. Macey, *Lacan in Contexts* (London, New York, Verso Books; 1988); M. Bowie, *Lacan* (London, Fontana Press; 1991) (with bibliography).

[44] There is a very substantial literature critical of Freud at all three levels of theory: transcendental (about his empirical-metaphysical-mythological method); pure (about the coherence and appropriateness of his concepts and structures); practical (about the social and psychic and clinical implications of his work). On the idea of levels of theory, see *Eunomia*, ch. 2.

It is a step which seems to be inherent in the work of Freud but which, for some reason, he appears to have been inhibited from taking. The uniquely privileged status of the public reality of normal society is being challenged; the irredeemably alien character of private realities, even psychotic realities, is being mitigated.

4.84 New conventions of self-determination will have to be established, new rules as to the forming of the reality of the individual human being within the self-forming of the societies to which the individual belongs. The concept of mental illness is a set of conventional limits on the right of self-determination of the human individual. On the hypothesis proposed in the present essay, the self-determining of nations is simply a special case of all human self-determining, and the self-determination of a nation must be seen as subject to conventional limits within the reality-for-itself of the society of all nations. With nations as with individuals, madness may be conventionally defined, in a form which is deliberately fashioned on the model of Kant's structuring of the rationality of morality, in the following terms. *The madness of nations is the self-forming of a nation within a reality-for-the-nation which could not become a reality for the society of all nations, the society of the whole human race.* In this sense, Nazi Germany was a mad nation.

4.85 Madness is contagious, and the Second World War was a contagion of madness. But sanity may also be contagious. A more optimistic hypothesis has been proposed in relation to individual mental illness – that a family-member may take on as a scapegoat, so to speak, the mental illness of a family, and so make sane the other family-members.[45] We might say that the European Community is the product of a European family made sane by the madness of Nazi Germany. But the European

On schizophrenia seen from a 'communications' aspect, see G. Bateson, 'Towards a theory of schizophrenia', in *Steps to an Ecology of Mind* (St Albans, Paladin; 1973), pp. 173ff. On psycho-pathology and language as a social phenomenon, see M. Foucault, *Madness and Civilization. A History of Insanity in the Age of Reason* (tr. R. Howard; London, Routledge; 1971). For an impassioned evocation (in almost impenetrable prose) of the socio-political implications of Freud, see G. Deleuze and F. Guattari, *Anti-Oedipus. Capitalism and Schizophrenia* (tr. R. Hurley, M. Seem, H. Lane; Minneapolis, University of Minnesota Press; 1983).

[45] 'From the observer's standpoint the ostracized or scapegoated person thus takes an important covert family role in maintaining the pseudo-mutuality or surface complementarity of the rest of the family.' L. C. Wynne *et al.*, 'Pseudo-mutuality in the family relations of schizophrenia', in 21 *Psychiatry* (1958), p. 214. 'One of the covert roles the patient takes in becoming overtly schizophrenic thus may be to allow other family members to achieve vicariously some measure of individuation' (p. 219).

Community is, at most, only a half-formed generic nation, defined by its peculiar social structures and formed by the fusing and transcending of the national state-systems in the state-system of the Community. It has not yet discovered itself as the genetic European nation. Until it does so, it will not be able to modify significantly the national self-conceiving of the participating nations. The danger of pathological national developments remains.

4.86 We might also say that the future of the whole world, as a society of nations and as a society of human beings, depends on finding a way of judging and modifying the behaviour of nations, of making the nations sane. Such a way will not be found by moral exhortation, social pressure, or the making of law. It will only be achieved by a reconceiving of the human society as a self-transcending nation of all nations, a reconceiving of the reality-for-itself of a humanity at last made sane by the age-old madness of nations. Democracy will be defined, not in terms of institutional arrangements and constitutional guarantees (which can so easily be a mask for illusion, corruption, exploitation, and decadence), but in terms of the health and happiness of the people. For the whole of self-socialising humanity, the redeeming ideal will be not world peace but world happiness, not the wealth of nations but the health of nations.

5

New Enlightenment

The public mind of all-humanity

THE CHALLENGE. The mind's freedom – Law's power – Millennial potentiality – Surpassing the past – The health of nations: human inhumanity – The health of nations: de-humanising humanity – The health of nations: re-humanising humanity
A RESPONSE. Self-resisting mind – Self-knowing mind – The misconceiving of democracy – Law and freedom – The *Eunomian* project – The *Eutopian* project

The peculiar human self-consciousness associated with the idea of a new century and the idea of a new millennium encourages us to make judgements about the past and to think about new possibilities.

At the beginning of the twenty-first century, we are exceptionally conscious of the remarkable development of human society through the last ten centuries of frenzied social experience. We are conscious of the power of social systems which have emerged from that experience, especially the systems known as democracy and capitalism. We are conscious also of the paradoxes of our social experience, all the good and all the evil done by and through the social systems which we have made.

We are conscious of our inherent freedom to reconceive and reform the social systems which we have made, and yet we seem also to be the slaves of the systems we have made. Two aspects of our experience offer us the hope of regaining and reusing our freedom – the role of law as the means of ideal-governed social self-constituting and the power of the mind to transcend itself in what we have experienced from time to time as 'enlightenment'.

Humanity has the need and the possibility of a New Enlightenment. The author's Eunomian project (reconceiving society and law) and his Eutopian project (reconceiving the human mind) are New Enlightenment projects.

I. The challenge

The mind's freedom

5.1 A new century. A new millennium. A time to look back – and a time to look forward. The future already exists, as a potentiality within the present, just as the present is an actualised potentiality of the past. In the words of Schiller's Wallenstein: 'in today tomorrow is already on the move'.[1] This is true of the future of the natural world and the future of the human world. But, in the case of the human world, there is an amazing difference. We make the human world. We choose the human future. We can choose to actualise *this* potentiality rather than *that* potentiality. The past offers us a range of possibilities, and we, individually and collectively, must make our choice among those possibilities.

5.2 We have a freedom of the mind which is like the freedom of the will. Using our freedom of the mind (reason and imagination and feeling), we make a human reality which is a presence of *mind* within a world which we suppose to be a world of *non-mind* and which we call the physical world. We make our mental habitat as we remake our physical habitat – unceasingly, inevitably.

5.3 We are morally responsible for what we think as much as for what we do. We cannot avoid the responsibility of choosing what we shall become, the burden of our self-creating freedom. Martin Heidegger said that we human beings do not possess freedom; freedom possesses (*besitzt*) us.[2] Nor can we escape our self-made past, the potentialities that we have made possible and the potentialities that we have destroyed. Samuel Beckett said: 'There is no escape from yesterday because yesterday has deformed us, or been deformed by us . . . [W]e are rather in the position of Tantalus, with this difference, that we allow ourselves to be tantalised.'[3]

1 F. Schiller, *Wallenstein. Ein dramatisches Gedicht. II: Wallensteins Tod* (1799) (Act v, sc. 3). (Stuttgart, Philipp Reclam jun.; 1969), p. 113. '[I]n dem Heute wandelt schon das Morgen'. St Augustine (354–430 CE) said: 'it might be properly said [of the activity of the reality-making human mind], "there be three times; a present of things past, a present of things present, and a present of things future".' *Confessions*, bk x (tr. E. B. Pusey; London, Dent (Everyman's Library); 1907), p. 266.

2 M. Heidegger, *Wegmarken* (Frankfurt-am-Main, Vittorio Klostermann; 1967), p. 85.

3 S. Beckett, *Proust* (1931) (London, John Calder; 1965), p. 13. In ancient Greek mythology, Tantalus was condemned by the gods to be perpetually hungry and thirsty while surrounded by food and drink which he could not reach.

5.4 The present essay is intended to set out a particular view of the present state of human reality and a particular view of human potentiality, at this time when we are unusually self-conscious, unusually conscious of our past and our future, of the burden of responsibility which rests on us, both the burden of our responsibility for the human past which we have made, and the burden of our responsibility for the human future which we will choose.

5.5 We must uncover a future which could be our future, a future which is ours to choose, if we have the collective intelligence and the collective courage to choose it.

Law's power

5.6 In the making of the human world, nothing has been more important than what we call *law*. Law is the intermediary between human power and human ideas. Law transforms our natural power into social power, transforms our self-interest into social interest, and transforms social interest into self-interest. Law universalises the particular, in law-making, and particularises the universal, in law-applying. These transformations are effected in the name of ideas, ideas generated within the human mind, in the private minds of human individuals and in the public minds of human societies.

5.7 Law defeats the passage of time by retaining choices made in a society's past, in a form – the law – which can take effect in a society's future. The law which is retained from society's past takes effect in society's present, as the law is interpreted and applied in the light of actual circumstances, and so helps to make society's future. The law carries the past through the present into the future. The law offers to society stability in the midst of ceaseless change, and change-from-stability as new human circumstances demand new human choices. You may not be able to step into the same Heraclitan river twice, but you can and cannot live in the same society twice. Society changes unceasingly, but something remains. Society's steady-state is also a state of change. It is, above all, the law which resolves that infinitely fruitful dialectic between stability and change which is the nature of human society. Law is a wonderful, and insufficiently appreciated, human invention.

5.8 The wonderful creative capacity of law is now available to humanity as a whole, as a potentiality, in the making of international society, the society of the whole human race, the society of all societies. And so we have now to consider an ultimate form of human potentiality and human choice – the role we might assign to law in making the human future, in remaking the human world, in remaking humanity.

Millennial potentiality

5.9 What have we learned, if anything, during the last millennium of human existence, and especially during these last two centuries, two centuries like no others in the story of human self-creating, two centuries during which the Library of Congress, in its own history, has been a true mirror of turbulent times, at the climax of a millennium full of the glory and the terror of the human world, the sadness and the grandeur of human reality?

5.10 A thousand years ago, everything in the human world was much the same as it is today, and everything was very different. A thousand years ago, ancient civilisations were in decay and decline, in different ways and to different degrees. Successor civilisations – Islam and Christendom, in particular – were full of a latent energy which would express itself in creative competition and sometimes in destructive rivalry. A thousand years ago, we in Europe had wasted our inheritance from Greece and Rome, if not our inheritance from ancient Israel. The human world was full of other peoples who had not known that inheritance, peoples with their own histories, their own realities, their own potentialities, their own intellectual and artistic cultures.

5.11 Who, in the eleventh century, could have imagined the potentiality of human reality, a potentiality which would be actualised over the succeeding centuries – a potentiality, we must say, for both great good and great evil? That potentiality must have been present, in the capacities of the human body and the human mind, and in the seemingly random residues of the past that had survived centuries of disorder and neglect.

5.12 It is hard to believe that, in the year 1000, we in Europe did not know of the idea of zero in mathematics; that we did not even have an agreed way of representing the numerals from 1 to 10; that, in the year 1600, all but a few Europeans believed that the sun orbited the earth; that, in the year 1700, Isaac Newton still believed that God had created the world in 4004 BCE. And yet we now know that, ten centuries ago, within an apparently unsatisfactory human reality, a latent and obscure potentiality must have contained the mathematics, the natural sciences, the arts and crafts, the philosophy, the social and economic systems which have made a new human world in the course of these last ten centuries, a ten-century frenzy of human self-evolving, a transformation which is now transforming all human reality everywhere.

5.13 There is no reason why the next century and the next millennium should be any less glorious, and every reason why they should be much less terrible, than the most recent chapters in the strange story of the self-evolving of the human species.

Surpassing the past

5.14 We may say that the one unmistakable lesson of the last millennium is that humanity can transform itself by its own efforts using the creative powers of the mind, and hence that the next century and the next millennium can, if we so choose, contain new transformations, a new kind of human existence.

5.15 The human past which humanity must surpass in the twenty-first century is its recent past, a past which has been made from ideas produced in the human mind and which remains as a powerful haunting presence within the human mind. The 'end of ideology' was a thing people hoped for in the twentieth century. By 'ideology' they meant the social enforcement of big ideas.[4] But one thing we have learned is that you cannot escape ideology. All societies enforce big ideas. In the year 2000 we were marching into a Brave Old World under four ideological banners which were perfectly familiar in the year 1900. *Great-power hegemony. Inter-state rivalry. Global capitalism. Science-led social progress.*

5.16 *Great-power hegemony* meant, and means, that a handful of countries – the US and the EU and one or two others – will dominate the future development of the world. *Inter-state rivalry* meant, and still means, that international co-existence is seen as the game of diplomacy punctuated by occasional sessions of what Clausewitz and others, before

[4] Karl Popper went further and argued that the roots of twentieth-century ideological evil were in the work of some of the philosophers who were supposed to have contributed most to the making of the Western mind. K. R. Popper, *The Open Society and its Enemies* (London, Routledge & Kegan Paul; 1945).

and since, have seen as the fascinating and invigorating game of war.[5] *Global capitalism* meant in the nineteenth century, and still means today, that the totalitarian social integrating of human effort, known as capitalism, cannot be confined within any limit short of the whole physical world and the whole human world. *Science-led social progress* seemed to the Victorians to be a wonderful thing. It meant then, and it still means today, that science and engineering have an inner and imperious momentum which must transform all human life systematically, a transformation to which human beings and human societies must simply adapt themselves, as if to a changing physical habitat.

5.17 These four ideological premises, taken together, mean that the social Darwinism of the late nineteenth century has ceased to be merely a tendentious optimistic dogma and has come to be seen as some sort of natural law of human existence.[6] We are apparently condemned to be social Darwinists, not by choice, but because there is nothing else left to believe. Our general failure of will and imagination may simply reflect an exhaustion of the human spirit. We have lived too much and thought too much in the long twentieth century. But, beyond moral fatigue, there is another symptom – an aching sense of spiritual confusion. At the end of the millennium, at the beginning of a new century, we are in two minds about human potentiality. Humanity is more than ever amazed at its own creative capacity. And humanity is more than ever uncertain of its ability to use that capacity well. It is this spiritual tension, in the depths of human consciousness, that we must try to diagnose.

5.18 Each of us lives at the imperceptible intersection between our private mind and the public minds of the societies to which we belong. It follows that the way we understand human society and the way we understand the human mind are two aspects of a single process of human self-knowing. It follows also that the task of remaking our idea of humanity contains two projects – reconceiving human society and reconceiving the human mind. We have done it before. We can do it again. The human mind has made the old human world in which we

[5] C. von Clausewitz, *On War* (1832) (tr. J. J. Graham (1908), ed. A. Rapoport; London, Penguin; 1968), p. 116.

[6] In his *Autobiography* (1904), it is possible to track the waning optimism of Herbert Spencer (1820–1903) as real-world social developments challenged his belief in the evolutionary nature of human progress, including his belief that competitive industrial capitalism could be the continuation of war by other (better) means.

are obliged to live. The human mind must make a new human world in which we would want to live.

The health of nations – human inhumanity

5.19 First, we must attempt the self-diagnosis of our chronic *fin de siècle* and *fin de millénaire* spiritual confusion. Looking back over the last two centuries, it is possible to observe three leading symptoms of our present morbidity. We may call them inhuman humanity, de-humanising humanity and re-humanising humanity.

5.20 *Humanity's inhumanity* remains a scandal and a mystery, a timeless scandal and a timeless mystery. Why do human beings continue to behave in ways which would shame animals? For long centuries, theologians and philosophers sanitised the phenomenon, calling it 'the problem of evil'. We who have experienced the twentieth century should be exceptionally expert now in the theology, the philosophy and the psychology of evil. And we have had particularly intense experience of what is, perhaps, the most troubling of all forms of evil, namely, *social evil.*

5.21 Social evil comes in two forms. There is the evil done by human beings in their official capacity and in what they believe to be the public interest – killing people, exploiting and oppressing people, individually and by the million, in the name of what they believe to be good ideas – with their good idea of the public interest sometimes conveniently coinciding with their idea of their private interest. And there is a form of social evil which we may call social-systematic evil, evil generated systematically by social systems and for which no individual human beings take moral responsibility.

5.22 These two forms of evil – evil in the public interest and social-systematic evil – pose an agonising problem, a problem whose scale and complexity cast much doubt on the well-meaning movement to internationalise or deterritorialise the criminal prosecution of national public officials for acts done within the context of social evil.[7]

5.23 In the twenty-first century, as part of our ambiguous millennial inheritance, we are dealing now with a planet-wide phenomenon, a pandemic of social evil which is more than merely an aggregation of

[7] One might see such proposals as a manifestation of the tendency to banalise evil. See H. Arendt, *Eichmann in Jerusalem: a Report on the Banality of Evil* (New York, Viking Press; 1965). On social evil, see also ch. 2 above, §§ 2.62ff.

the dysfunctioning of subordinate societies. The globalising of social systems is also a globalising of social morbidity. Human inhumanity will be, more and more, the collective self-wounding of the half-formed society of all-humanity. Social evil is the greatest social challenge which the twentieth century has bequeathed to the twenty-first century.

The health of nations – de-humanising humanity

5.24 In our new-century self-consciousness, we are acutely conscious also of something more pervasive, more intangible than human inhumanity, than evil in the traditional sense, namely, the relentless *de-humanising of humanity.* Human self-de-humanising has taken two main forms – social and intellectual.

5.25 Michel Foucault said that 'man is an invention of recent date. And one perhaps nearing its end.'[8] The ancient Greeks and Marcus Aurelius and Saint Augustine, among many others, were well aware of the significance of the human individual, long before the supposedly individualising effects of post-Reformation religion and early capitalism, but it is true to say that the intensity of human socialising over the last two centuries has created the possibility that human beings are becoming nothing but social epiphenomena. That is to say, the primary human reality is now so powerfully social that individual human beings have less and less significance, except as elementary particles within social force-fields. This is now, above all, an effect of *capitalism,* as Herbert Marcuse and many others have shown.[9] Capitalism has become a form of totalitarianism, in which every human individual is an economic actor with a role to play in the division of labour. And we now see that the so-called division of labour is, in fact, an aggregating of labour, a totalitarian integrating of human effort, including the totalitarian integrating of human consciousness.[10] One people, one market, one mind. *Ein Volk, ein Markt, ein Geist.*

[8] M. Foucault, *The Order of Things. An Archaeology of the Human Sciences* (London, Tavistock Publications; 1970), p. 387.

[9] See especially H. Marcuse, *One Dimensional Man. Studies in the Ideology of Advanced Industrial Society* (London, Routledge & Kegan Paul; 1964). On the psychology of the 'fascism' of social structures, see G. Deleuze and F. Guattari, *Anti-Oedipus. Capitalism and Schizophrenia* (1972) (tr. R. Hurley *et al.*; Minneapolis, University of Minnesota Press; 1983).

[10] 'Totalitarian movements are mass organizations of atomized, isolated individuals. Compared with all other parties and movements their most conspicuous external characteristic is their demand for total, uncritical, unconditional, and unalterable loyalty of the

5.26 The social integration of consciousness is not merely a side-effect of capitalism. On the contrary, it is of the essence of capitalism that human beings should internalise an appropriate economic world-view and, still more important, should internalise the social and personal values necessary for the efficient functioning of capitalism, aligning their life-determining desire with the desire of all other economic actors. But this process is intrinsic also to the successful functioning of *liberal democracy*, capitalism's necessary and super-efficient co-worker. Democracy unites the general will of society and the personal will of society-members, using an armoury of powerful structural ideas – self-government, consent, representation, participation – so that the vast volume of law and public administration required by capitalism can seem to be the product of one mind and one will. One people, one will, one mind. *Ein Volk, ein Wille, ein Geist.*

5.27 The necessary tendency of democracy-capitalism is to socialise the citizen by integrating systematically individual consciousness and social consciousness, the private mind of the human being and the public mind of society. Democracy-capitalism is the most advanced form of social oppression ever invented. The globalising of democracy-capitalism is the universalising of a form of absolute socialism.

5.28 No less troubling is the *intellectual* de-humanising of humanity. For two and a half centuries, we have been searching for some truths about ourselves, in the so-called human sciences. We have been trying to find what humanity is like by trying to study humanity objectively, as if we were natural phenomena of the natural world. A library is a repository of dead books, from which undying ideas rise up to take possession of living minds, forming that metaphysical Library of Babel, so memorably described by Jorge Luis Borges,[11] in which we are tempted to search for the catalogue of catalogues, the truth of all human truths – in history, anthropology, sociology, jurisprudence, biology, neurology, and all the other -ologies.

5.29 However, what we can discover in the Library of Babel is something else. After two centuries of what is sometimes called the

individual member.' H. Arendt, *The Origins of Totalitarianism* (London, George Allen & Unwin; 1951/1958), p. 323. The Internet is yet another social system of psychic dependency which nevertheless atomises and isolates the individual internaut.

11 'La biblioteca de Babel' (1941), in J. L. Borges, *Ficciones* (Madrid, Alianza Editorial; 1971), pp. 89–100. 'The Library of Babel' (tr. J. E. Irby; 1964), in J. L. Borges, *Labyrinths* (Harmondsworth, Penguin; 1970), pp. 78–86.

Enlightenment project, we have found no certain truths about ourselves, not even any universally accepted hypotheses, like the provisional certainties of the natural sciences. On the contrary, a reasonable dialectical response to the human sciences might now take the form of three great negations. There is no such thing as *human nature*. There is no such thing as a *natural human condition*. There is no such thing as *natural human progress*. All three are dangerous illusions. The dissolving of the comfortable illusion of *human naturalism* is the greatest intellectual challenge which the twenty-first century has inherited from the Enlightenment project.

5.30 The illusionary ideas of human nature, the human condition, and human progress are dangerous for two reasons. They seem to offer an excuse (*eine Entschuldigung* – a de-responsibilising) for human failure and human evil, individual and social. And, secondly, they disempower and depress the human spirit. They suggest that we are victims of our biological nature, that we cannot overcome our psychological nature (so-called human nature), or our social nature (the so-called human condition). They lead to fatalism, defeatism, nihilism, negativism, passivism, pragmatism and general despair. They suggest that war and injustice and exploitation, and all other forms of social evil, are natural, like epidemics or earthquakes. They powerfully re-enforce the idea that social evil is natural and inevitable.

5.31 The idea of natural human progress is now an article of faith in the theology of capitalism. And it is embodied now in the theology of the natural sciences as a social phenomenon. Natural human progress, it is said, is and will be an inevitable product of capitalism and science. But whatever capitalism and science may achieve in the long term, they are compatible with terrible horrors and miseries in the meantime. Capitalism and science are means, not ends. Human progress depends on human choice, on our intelligent and courageous use of our capacity for self-transcending and self-surpassing.

5.32 It is we as we are who do the things that we do. It is we human beings, our human minds, that make war, injustice, exploitation, corruption – not God or evolution or our genes or the market. The human sciences have tended to alienate humanity from itself, because they tend to deny the essential and overwhelming subjectivity of human beings. We are *not* merely natural phenomena; we create ourselves every moment of our lives through the amazing power of subjective consciousness, individual consciousness and social consciousness. The mind is a mirror in which we see ourselves as we seem to be.[12] Everything human is a mind-thing.[13] Every body politic is a mind politic.[14]

5.33 The relative failure of the Enlightenment project of human empiricism has had other important psychic side-effects. It has suggested that, if we cannot transcend the *human* world in thought, as we are able to transcend the *physical* world in thought, there is nothing left for us but to return to a state of primitive irrationality, on the one hand, or to submit finally to the natural sciences, on the other hand, espousing a *human biologism* which will find a physical basis for everything human, even for human consciousness. And that seems to be what is happening now. At the beginning of the twenty-first century, human self-consciousness seems to be subject to collective fantasy, on the one hand, and triumphalist natural science, on the other. They are both forms of collective alienation, not unlike the worst forms of mythology and superstitious religion and general ignorance, one thousand and more years ago. Mass culture in its most debased forms, together with the fantasy-reality generated by capitalism, and degenerate forms of religion: these post-Enlightenment atavisms are now alienating human beings yet again, in a new century and a new millennium.

5.34 The world-transforming achievements of *science and engineering* are also themselves having an alienating effect. The magic and the mysteries and the miracles of Faustian science, assisted by engineering,

[12] 'What seems to Be, Is, To those to whom / It seems to Be, & is productive of the most dreadful / Consequences to those to whom it seems to Be...' W. Blake, *Jerusalem* II.36 (*c.*1804), in G. Keynes (ed.), *The Complete Writings of William Blake* (Oxford, Oxford University Press; 1966), p. 478. Blake was a passionate Romantic critic of the de-humanising effect of scientistic rationalism (as opposed to imagination, feeling, and faith).

[13] '[E]in geistiges Objekt.' W. Dilthey (1833–1911), 'Der Aufbau der geschichtlichen Welt in den Geisteswissenschaften', in *Gesammelte Schriften* (Leipzig, B. G. Teubner; 1927) VII, pp. 79–188, at p. 86. Reprinted in W. Dilthey, *Die Philosophie des Lebens* (Stuttgart, B. G. Teubner; 1961), pp. 230–339, at p. 237. He explores the history and philosophy of the mind-sciences (*Geisteswissenschaften*), setting out his own position: the hermeneutic study of 'humanity' as 'human-social-historical reality' (pp. 81, 232).

[14] 'Among the delusions which at different periods have possessed the minds of large masses of the human race, perhaps the most curious – certainly the least creditable – is the modern *soi-disant* science of political economy, based on the idea that an advantageous code of social action may be determined irrespectively of the influence of social affection.' J. Ruskin, *Unto This Last. Four Essays on the First Principles of Political Economy* (1860) (London, George Allen & Sons; 1862/1910), p. 1. 'Political economy' was an earlier name for what came to be known as 'economics', especially after the publication of A. Marshall's *Principles of Economics* in 1890.

its ingenious familiar, are taking power over what we think and what we desire, over what we are and what we will be. Science is trying to tell us what it is to be human, what it is to be conscious. Only the irrational can escape the hegemonic explanatory power of natural science. But natural science can provide ever more efficient means for the world-wide propagating of the irrational and for the world-wide corrupting of the human spirit.

The health of nations – re-humanising humanity

5.35 Within human de-humanising it is possible to discover a paradoxical potentiality of *human re-humanising*. At last, at the end of this amazing millennium, we can *see* what is happening to us, we can begin to *understand* what is happening to us, and this new kind of self-knowledge is a possibility of a new enlightenment, a new kind of enlightenment.

5.36 One striking effect of capitalism has been a very great increase in what Adam Smith called the wealth of nations – that is to say, the *material* wealth of our nations. The idea of the totalised wealth of a nation is a metaphysical statistical concept, since national wealth is distributed, and distributed very unequally, among the members of the nation. But there is no doubt that the material life-conditions of the mass of the people, particularly in countries with capitalist systems, have vastly improved, including the range of their personal choices in their day-to-day lives. We must say that this has been a sort of humanising, or a re-humanising, of people de-humanised by centuries of slavery and serfdom and exploitation and poverty and ignorance.

5.37 Vast numbers of what for all recorded time has been a proletarian class in society, exploited and excluded from the full benefit of society-membership, have found a way of living which, in the past, was only enjoyed by a small privileged social class. But vast numbers of human beings remain exploited and excluded, a global proletariat, excluded from the full benefit of membership of the society of all-humanity, deprived of elementary possibilities of personal self-creating. A re-humanising of humanity could at last be a self-perfecting of all humanity, not merely of an exceptionally privileged class or exceptionally privileged nations.

5.38 The millennial challenge, and the re-humanising opportunity, is to maximise the wealth of nations in the widest possible definition of the word *wealth*. At long last, we must make the benefits of human socialising for all human beings exceed its costs, actualising the human potentialities which we have discovered within ourselves. To meet this challenge we must undertake to improve the quality of human consciousness, not only our consciousness as members of self-perfecting societies but also our personal consciousness as self-perfecting human beings. It is a challenge for every form of human society and, above all, for the international society of the whole human race, the society of all societies.

II. A response

Self-resisting mind

5.39 A challenge which is both a threat (to humanity's humanity) and an opportunity (to re-humanise humanity) calls for a response of self-surpassing intelligence and courage.[15] The self-surpassing task of social reordering at the global level requires the self-transforming power of *law*. And a response which consists of re-imagining our ideas and our ideals of human self-socialising (*society*) and human self-contemplating (*mind*) requires the self-transforming power of *philosophy*.

5.40 *Philosophy* is the socially organised self-contemplating of the human mind. At the beginning of the twenty-first century, we find ourselves in a strangely impoverished situation as self-contemplating human beings. The self-inflicted poverty of philosophy, at the beginning of the new millennium, is an effect of complex but ascertainable causes, a paradoxical disenlightening at the heart of the Enlightenment project. Alongside, and not unconnected with, the de-humanising effect of the human sciences and the spiritual hegemony of the natural sciences, philosophy has disabled itself by using its own activity to question its own possibility. Philosophy in the Western tradition has always contained

[15] The concept of *challenge and response* was a central feature of Arnold Toynbee's (controversial) hypothesis of the genesis of the historical *civilisations* which he identified. They used 'the virtues of adversity' to raise themselves to new levels of organisation and sophistication. A. J. Toynbee, *A Study of History* (London, Oxford University Press; 12 vols., 1934–61), esp. I and II. D. C. Somervell, *Abridgement of Vols. I–VI* (London, Oxford University Press; 1947), esp. chs 5 and 6.

within itself a dialectical negation of its own possibility.[16] From the middle of the nineteenth century, philosophy, one of humanity's greatest glories, came to be treated as a sort of human science, a professionalised activity within universities. Philosophy in the great tradition came to an end. And, incredibly, in the twentieth century of all centuries, self-denying philosophy came to be the academic flavour-of-the-century.

5.41 Through the power of thought we have been able to suggest to ourselves that thought is incapable of transcending the conditions of its production – the social condition, the psychological condition, the linguistic condition. *Felix culpa.* There has been a paradoxical benefit flowing from so much intellectual self-disabling. We may use the names of three particular people to stand for intellectual movements which go far beyond their own work. What they have in common is that, at one and the same time, they have been major figures in the fact of our intellectual de-humanising and yet they can also be major figures in the ideal of our intellectual re-humanising.

5.42 After Karl Marx, we cannot any longer ignore the *social* vector in the construction of human consciousness. After Sigmund Freud, we cannot any longer ignore the *unconscious* vector in the making of human consciousness. After Ludwig Wittgenstein, we cannot any longer ignore the *symbolic* vector in the making of human consciousness. Ancient philosophers knew all these things, but that knowledge is now available to us all, far beyond the field of professional philosophy, including to those engaged in the work of human self-redeeming.

5.43 How can we say that the work of these three people has been part of our *de-humanising*? Like Rousseau and Nietzsche and Weber, among many others, they all knew that their work was incomplete. This knowledge created great personal anguish in the minds of all three of them, a sense of failure. And, much worse from humanity's perspective, each of their half-complete systems, their intellectual half-revolutions, has had big real-world effects.

5.44 The idea of the *social* construction of consciousness could be abused to explain and justify the enslavement of society-members by those who control society and the mind of society, that is, the political and economic ruling classes. The idea of the *unconscious* construction of consciousness could be used to explain and justify every kind of evil

[16] See further in ch. 1 above, §§ 1.28ff.

and destructive behaviour, and to make us feel powerless in the face of the products of our own consciousness. The idea of the *symbolic* construction of consciousness could lead us to believe that there could be no transcendental basis for truth or for value, that all human ideas are equally worthy or worthless, because ideas are condemned to be expressed in nothing but arbitrary symbols, including the arbitrary symbols of language.

5.45 These deformed versions of half-formed ideas have had huge real-world effects in our societies, profoundly demoralising and dehumanising us as individuals and as societies, a major contributor to our profound spiritual confusion. But, at so great a cost, they may also be seen as offering us a very great potential benefit. They mean that we are now able to *see* more clearly than ever before how it is that we make the human world, how it is that we make human reality, and hence how it is that we may remake them. They allow us to know ourselves in a way we have never known ourselves before, demystifying our limitless creativity and our self-inflicted suffering. In beginning to uncover the roots of human evil-doing, they may have begun to reveal a new potentiality of human good-doing. When we can begin to *understand* our spiritual confusion, not only its symptoms but also its causes, then can we begin to find its cure.

5.46 There is no need for humanity simply to abandon itself to primitive fantasy and superstition, or to surrender to defeatism in the face of our inability to find natural laws of human behaviour. We do not need to give up hope in the face of the apparently hopeless phenomenon of social evil. And we do not have simply to submit to the iron will of capitalism, or to the imperious dictates of science and engineering. We can resist. Humanity can resist its own de-humanising. We can transcend and surpass ourselves once again. We have the capacity to redeem the human mind, to rescue it, to remake it, so that the new human mind is the mind we *want* to have, so that the human reality made by our minds is the human reality we *want* to have, so that we can inhabit a human world, a human habitat, that we *want* to inhabit.

Self-knowing mind

5.47 Our (post-Marxian) understanding of the *social* vector of human consciousness helps us to understand better the flow of energy between the private mind of the individual human being and the public mind of society. Society, like everything else in the human world, is manufactured in the minds of individual human beings but becomes a presence in the collective consciousness of society. As such, it returns as a decisive presence in the self-identifying and self-constituting of society-members. It follows that there is no reason in principle, whatever may be the tendency of historical practice, why the consciousness of individual human beings should not transcend and take power over the self-constituting of society. There is no reason why the self-knowing and self-surpassing power of human consciousness should not reassert its authority over the power of society, even at the level of the society of all-humanity.

5.48 Our (post-Freudian) understanding of the *unconscious* vector of human consciousness helps us to understand better both the internal limits on the freedom of the human mind and its apparently boundless creative energy. We surprise ourselves in what we think and in what we feel, and hence in what we do and what others do to us. In Pascal's hallowed formula, the heart has its reasons of which reason knows nothing.[17] In addition to the imperious phylogenic instincts which we attribute to our physiology, our minds contain ontogenic causes which are aspects not of the brain but of the mind. But unconscious consciousness is only one layer of the deep-structure of our minds. The species-characteristic of the self-ordering rationality of the mind is as great and as strange and as powerful a wonder as its self-surprising anomie. And it is a wonder shared by the rational mind of all human beings and the public mind of the society of all-humanity.

5.49 Our (post-Wittgensteinian) understanding of the *symbolic* vector of human consciousness helps us to understand better both the inherent limits and hazards of our capacity to communicate within ourselves and with others and also our apparently boundless capacity to construct a form of reality which is neither merely a photograph nor merely a dream, the second reality in which we live and die as thinking animals. In becoming conscious of language as a non-transparent, non-neutral, reflexive medium, we are able also to see better the role which *truth* and *value* play as ultimate structural axes in the making of human reality. The views of Richard Rorty and of many others notwithstanding, *truth* and *value* are neither delusions nor merely metaphors but existential

[17] B. Pascal (1623–62), *Pensées* (1670) (tr. A. J. Krailsheimer; London, Penguin; 1966), p. 154.

ideas and ideals. Within the human mind-world, including the mind-world of the society of all-humanity, they are what *space* and *time* are for the mind's idea of the physical world, that is, the necessary conceptual conditions of knowing and acting.[18]

5.50 It is for this reason that the two New Enlightenment projects are inseparable. The public mind of society and the private mind of the human individual are extensions of each other. Social evil arises at the intersection of the two, where the freedom of the mind and the freedom of the will of human individuals meets the freedom of the public mind and the freedom of the general will of society, and where the three vectors of human consciousness are integrated. It is at the same intersection that our new purposive pursuit of social good and of a better form of human society must originate. Transnational justice is not possible except as an ideal of a self-conscious society of all-humanity.

The misconceiving of democracy

5.51 A school of thought which has come to be associated with the name of Immanuel Kant (1724–1804) sees the only reasonable prospect of a peaceful and progressive international society in a natural confederalising tendency among 'republican states' – that is, among societies whose public realms are under the management of a 'government' and which are recognised as states by other governments, and which have transformed themselves internally into constitutional republics. International constitutionalism would be a side-effect of the constitutionalising of particular state-societies.[19]

5.52 It might be thought that our experience over the last two centuries had cast terminal doubt on such an idea, but Kant's consoling myth, as we may call it, has been revived in recent years in three forms of assertion: (1) that constitutionally reformed states have a natural tendency to recognise each other as members of an *international society* of states; (2) that there is a low-to-zero probability that 'democratic' states

[18] Immanuel Kant (controversially but cogently) identified space and time as necessary conceptual conditions of possible experience. They make possible the mind's structuring (our knowledge) of physical reality, and so make possible our purposive activity in the physical world. I. Kant, *Critique of Pure Reason* (1781) (tr. N. Kemp Smith; London, 1929), pp. 71ff.

[19] See I. Kant, 'Idea for a universal history with a cosmopolitan purpose', and 'Perpetual peace: a philosophical sketch', in *Kant's Political Writings* (tr. H. B. Nisbet, ed. H. Reiss; Cambridge, Cambridge University Press; 1970).

will go to war with each other; (3) that democratic societies are in some sense fulfilled in their social development, thus removing a perennial cause of international conflict (an 'end of history' view). At a more general level and in a less precise form, the Kantian view underlies the post-1989 triumphalism of the advocates of democracy-capitalism and the apologists of 'globalisation'.

5.53 Such naïve or self-interested evangelism overlooks or underestimates four things.

(1) The imperfection of democracy, especially as allied with capitalism, is not confined to the psychic totalitarianism which has been considered above. There are *diseases of advanced democracy-capitalism* of which we have much painful experience and which were foreseen by its early observers (including Jefferson, J. S. Mill, and de Tocqueville): the tyranny of the majority, the tyranny of minorities (factions and special interests), the corruption of politics (by money and crude populism), the devaluation of its own high values (liberty as a residue left by social regulation, equality as institutionalised inequality, fraternity as institutionalised selfishness), the devaluation of cultural values (anti-elitism, anti-intellectualism, anti-exceptionalism), the devaluation of spiritual values (the triumph of materialism, the commodification of ideas, of cultural products, and of education), the depersonalising of the human person. If the present condition of democratic-capitalist societies is the end of the history of human self-evolving, it is a tragic, if not farcical, end to the long experiment of human biological evolution.

(2) Democracy-capitalism is not a single or simple phenomenon. Democratic institutions are organic in character. They take on the characteristics of the ground in which they are planted. They take effect in a given society in a way which is specific to that society, a unique product of the physical characteristics, the history, the psychic ethos of that society, and its relationship to other societies. Like sects within religions, different democratic-capitalist orthodoxies may well see their supposed fellow-travellers as their most formidable adversaries.

(3) Like religious evangelism, the negligent imposition of institutional elements of democracy-capitalism on societies whose specific situation is thereby violated can lead to a gross form of social evil which will dominate the twenty-first century as it dominated the last decades of the twentieth century, namely *fraudulent democracy.* In such societies, recent experience suggests that democracy-capitalism readily transforms

itself into *plutocracy*, a form of internal colonialism in which the common interest of society is equated with the self-interest of an arrogant, greedy and criminal ruling clan, associated by birth or marriage or dependency, in which the common wealth of society is simply stolen by the plutocratic oligarchy, a society in which a class of selfish *nouveaux riches* sustains the system with obsequious cynicism, and over which some of the superficialities of democracy spread a veneer of worthless legitimacy.

(4) There are, and will continue to be, many such societies around the world. There are also countless subordinate human societies other than those managed by 'governments', in particular industrial and commercial corporations with world-wide interests. The problem of socialising the competitive but mutually dependent co-existence of human societies of all kinds far exceeds the capacity of the piecemeal aggregating of the self-interest of all such societies or the potentiality of a dream-world of self-ordering 'democracies'.

Law and freedom

5.54 The misconceiving of democracy makes necessary its reconceiving. Especially over the last two centuries, we have learned that the transformatory effect of *democracy* is not merely a matter of institutions or of a particular distribution of social power. The central ideal of democracy is better expressed as *nomocracy*, the rule of *nomos* (the law), rather than merely the rule of those who claim to represent the people (*dēmos).*[20]

5.55 The two daring core-paradoxes of the democratic ideal – freedom under law, self-government – rest upon the strange fact that law, which is the archetypal means of social constraint, is also our most reliable means of social liberation. Law, in the very act of distributing social power in the form of legal power, also sets the *legal limits* of social power. Law, with its own inherent substantive and procedural values, is also the enacting of society's *high values*, including its very-high-values of justice and social justice, whose function is to control the substantive and procedural content of law.

5.56 The hallowed ideal-characteristics of democracy are all better seen as ingenious methods for using law to restrain law. *Constitutionalism* is law about law, law above law, law before law. *Separation of powers* is a

[20] Nomocratic democracy can be seen as forming part of perennial world-wide traditions of law-based society. For further discussion of such traditions, see ch. 12 below.

division of legal labour, the interdependence of legal power. *Fundamental rights* are legal limits on the power of law in the name of society's highest values. *Representation* is the legal repersonifying of the holders of public-realm powers, that is, legal powers to be exercised in the public interest. *Accountability* is the extra-judicial control of the public-interest aspect of public-realm legal powers, with elections as a form of legally imposed social judgement. The *rule of law* is the judicial control of the legal terms and conditions of all public-realm powers. The *open society* is the legally imposed social inclusion of all citizens by means of legally organised education and legally protected social communication and other forms of social participation. (If we regard democracy and capitalism as inseparable social phenomena, with *economic freedom* as an eighth ideal-characteristic of democracy-capitalism, then it is a wholly artificial freedom which is the integrated product of every kind of law – international, constitutional, public, civil, criminal.)

5.57 Since 1945, a vast international public realm has been formed, as if by stealth, through the piecemeal co-operation of governments, determining the lives of all human beings everywhere. This largely unaccountable concentration of social power co-exists with the largely unaccountable social power of industrial and commercial corporations with world-wide interests, both of them subject only to the intermittent influence of so-called non-governmental organisations, whose representative authority may be as dubious as that of many governments. The need is apparent and urgent for a presence of the nomocratic ideal at the level of international society, acting as an enacting and enforcing instrument of universal ideals of justice and social justice. But the full paradoxical power of law can only operate at the level of all-humanity within an international society whose high values it enacts, including the values of justice and social justice.

5.58 Among global agents of the ideal must be all those who, by religion or tradition or in their own self-conceiving, recognise the idea of the ideal within their own social self-constituting. And, among these, a role of special potentiality and special responsibility is that of the people of the United States of America, a generic nation in which the idea of the ideal and the ideal of law continue to be living forces within its social self-constituting.[21] It is a responsibility based on the sheer facts of

[21] For the distinction between genetic and generic nations, see ch. 4, above, at § 4.28.

American military and economic and cultural power, and the extent of American economic and political and military investment in the rest of the world – that is to say, of American dependence and vulnerability in relation to the rest of the world.

5.59 It is a responsibility which rests on a second, more complex basis. The United States is an exceptional phenomenon in world history. It is itself a law-state. It is itself a world-state. The transformation of the American colonies into a new kind of society at the end of the eighteenth century was achieved through law. The United States was made as a law-state, a *Rechtstaat*. But, at some time in the nineteenth century, it began to become a world-state, a *Weltstaat*.[22] Instead of imperialising externally, in the manner of Rome or Britain, the United States imperialised internally. With amazing aggressive energy it took over the rest of southern North America, and set about peopling its vast new space with people brought in from outside, an internal American empire, composed of people from every part of the world, living together in the American law-state. The United States is a microcosm of the human world, of the actual human world, and of a potential Human World under Law.[23]

The Eunomian project

5.60 There cannot be law without society or society without law. There cannot be good law except in a good society. As a third thing, produced by and producing society's ideas, produced by and producing the everyday exercise of social power, law cannot be separated from the self-constituting of a given society.

5.61 The polemical and practical purpose of the New Enlightenment project of *reconceiving human society* is to show that international society – the society of all-humanity and all societies – need not be the crazy and archaic intergovernmental unsociety which characterised international relations throughout the last millennium, the archaism which led, in the last century, to more than 100 million unnecessary deaths and to unspeakable human suffering caused by holders of public power, and unspeakable human suffering caused by the disgraceful inequality

[22] *Rechtstaat* and *Weltstaat* are intended as neologisms, differentiated from *Rechtsstaat* and *Weltstadt*.

[23] For further discussion of this aspect, see P. Allott, 'The true function of law in the international community', in 4 *Indiana Journal of Global Legal Studies* (1998), pp. 391–413.

of social and economic development throughout the world, a structural injustice which is being perpetuated by the archaic and inhuman international system. In such an unsociety, international law was liable to be seen as little more than 'a science which teaches princes to what extent they may violate justice without injuring (*sans choquer*) their own interests'.[24]

5.62 As the emerging international society of the new century comes to be understood as a society, by human beings in general and by holders of public-realm social power in particular, international law will at last be enabled to act, at the global level, as an effective agent of human self-empowering and self-perfecting, through the distribution of social power in the common interest of society and in accordance with society's high values.[25] International society will be seen as a society of all human beings and all subordinate societies, not merely a coagulation of government-managed societies known as 'states'. And the common interest of society, which it is law's task to enact and then to disaggregate into the legal relations which determine the willing and acting of actual human beings and actual human societies, will be the common interest of all-humanity, the common interest of the human species as one species among many in a habitat shared by all.[26]

The Eutopian project

5.63 Prior to law is *politics*, the struggle to determine society's values and purposes, and the struggle to take control over the making and the implementation of the law which actualises its values and purposes. It follows that humanity will not socialise itself effectively under law until international society has its own form of politics and its own means of determining its own values and purposes.

[24] [C.-L.de Secondat, Baron de] Montesquieu, *Lettres persanes* (1721) (Paris, Librairie Gallimard (Pléiade); 1949), letter 94, p. 270. Montesquieu's Persian visitor to Paris is explaining the European concept of 'public law'.

[25] See generally the present author's *Eunomia*. The Greek word *eunomia* (good social order) came to be associated with the name of Solon (*c.*640 – *c.*588 BCE), a charismatic 'law-giver' of ancient Athens who laid down what was virtually a new social contract to resolve deep-structural social conflict. It was a new order which did not last (*absit omen*!). He was the author of an elegy entitled *Eunomia*, extolling the virtues of law-based social order.

[26] On the reconceiving of international law as the true law of a true international society, see ch. 10 below.

5.64 The New Enlightenment project of *reconceiving the human mind* thus includes the task of reconceiving the way in which we form our ideas, our values, and our purposes. We must overcome our self-imposed poverty of philosophy, and resume the great tradition of self-transcending philosophy which ended with strange abruptness, sometime in the late nineteenth century, like a majestic highway suddenly coming to an end, for no evident reason, in the middle of nowhere. We live in the human reality made by the perennial philosophical tradition, which gave us the social and mental structures that we take for granted, but we have perversely deprived ourselves of the possibility of renewing and surpassing that tradition.

5.65 We need a new intellectual discipline – *international philosophy* – in which minds from all traditions and cultures across the world can contribute to a reunderstanding of what it is to be a thinking being. What am I? asked René Descartes – a thinking thing. A thing, yes. But a thing that thinks. And a thing that thinks about its thinking.[27] The capacity of human consciousness that makes possible our collective self-reconceiving is philosophy – the mind thinking about itself, the mind creating itself as it thinks about itself, reflexive thought, the self-consciousness of human reality. Philosophy is to humanism what mathematics is to scientism, if by *humanism* we mean the study of humanity as a set of *mental* phenomena, and by *scientism* we mean the study of the universe, including humanity, as a set of *physical* (putatively non-mind) phenomena. Philosophy and mathematics, respectively, are the conditions of the possibility of humanism and scientism.

5.66 Those of us who work in universities should have it as our aim to make young people understand that all existing social systems have a history. None of them is natural or inevitable. We have made them all, including the disgracefully primitive international system. We have to remove from the minds of the young what Diderot called 'the sophism of the ephemeral' (*le sophisme de l'éphémère*) – the disempowering idea that what happens to exist now is inevitable and permanent. Maynard Keynes said: 'in the field of economic and political philosophy there are not many who are influenced by new theories after they are twenty-five or thirty years of age, so that the ideas which civil servants and

[27] R. Descartes, *Meditations on the First Philosophy* (1641) (tr. J. Veitch; London, Dent (Everyman's Library); 1912), p. 88.

politicians and even agitators apply to current events are not likely to be the newest'.[28]

5.67 The natural sciences cannot be instruments of human self-redeeming. They may tell us what we are; they cannot tell us what we might choose to be. No doubt physiology, genetics and micro-biology will explain the working of the human brain and the nervous system. The views of Daniel Dennett and of many others notwithstanding, the natural sciences will never explain the working of human consciousness. No scientist could ever predict, merely from the physiology of the brain, the emergence of the idea of Buddhist *satori* or of the Invisible Hand or the content of the present sentence, or any other idea whatsoever. The capacity of the mind infinitely exceeds the capacity of the brain.[29]

5.68 We know that our bodies are conditioned and determined by the physical processes of the material world. And yet we cannot escape the anguish and the excitement of deciding, from moment to moment, what to *do* next. We know that our minds are conditioned and determined by the physical processes of the brain and the nervous system. And yet we cannot escape the anguish and the excitement of deciding, from moment to moment, what to *think* next.

5.69 As a first great task for international philosophy, we must find ways to explain to ourselves, and to begin to overcome, our spiritual confusion and our self-inflicted unhappiness. Why are we not more happy, when we have the wonderful power to make our own world and to make our own reality? Why do we persist in choosing to do evil, individually and as societies, when we have the wonderful power to choose to do good? To understand this, we have to find a way of understanding the close correlation between the self-constituting of the private mind – our personality – and the self-constituting of the public mind – the constitution of a society. The self-constituting of the personality of a human being and the self-constituting of a human society are similar and connected processes. And that is, of course, because the private mind of

[28] J. M. Keynes, *The General Theory of Employment Interest and Money* (London, Macmillan; 1936), pp. 383–4. The saying of Diderot is taken from his *Le Rêve de d'Alembert* (1769; first published 1830) (ed. P. Vernière; Paris, Librairie Marcel Didier; 1951), p. 60.

[29] 'Learn that man infinitely transcends man.' B. Pascal, *Pensées* (fn. 17 above), pp. 64–5. '[N]or do I myself comprehend all that I am. Therefore is the mind too strait to contain itself.' St Augustine,*Confessions*, bk x (fn. 1 above), p. 212. Book x contains a remarkable proto-Freudian analysis of the human mind.

the human being and the public mind of society are extensions of each other.

5.70 The *second* great task and challenge for international philosophy in the next century is to think the ideal of the human future. The idea of the ideal has been the wonderful instrument of human self-evolving and self-perfecting. We can imagine and constantly re-imagine the ideal, as a dialectical *negation* of the actual which nevertheless affirms a *potentiality* of the actual. The ideal is the perfectibility of the actual. And we can constantly concretise the ideal in ideas which have the form of truth and value. And, in that form, the ideal can become the controlling principle of our action, our personal and social action, giving us the self-transcending power to overcome both social totalitarianism and social evil at every level of social organisation from the village to the international society of all-humanity. The ideal can determine the way in which we understand our potentiality for self-perfecting. It can then condition our choice among our potentialities, the potentialities which we choose to actualise, as individuals and as societies. The ideal is the efficient secret of human self-perfecting.[30]

5.71 In dialectical opposition to a human reality dominated by war, social injustice, the corruption of public power, alienation and money, we must establish a human reality dominated by the ideal, that is, by our intimate participation in the natural world, by our instinctive love of justice, truth, beauty and goodness, a human reality dominated by the wonder and enthusiasm and joy which are so natural to us, and by a species-quality which we might call *grace* – the psychic anti-entropic binding-force which holds together the personality of a happy human being and the constitution of a good society. Grace is the gravity of the better worlds that the human mind creates.

5.72 In Samuel Beckett's *Waiting for Godot,* a mysterious Boy comes with an equivocal message. 'Mr Godot told me to tell you he won't come

[30] The word *eutopia* (good place) is used here, in preference to the word *utopia* (no place), another invented word using Greek roots, to emphasise that the nature of the New Enlightenment challenge is to find and to enact the new ideals of a new human mind-world, rather than, as in Thomas More's *Utopia* (1516), to criticise the actual by reference to an imaginary alternative which, in More's own pessimistic words (at the end of book II), he wished rather than expected to see realised – echoing, perhaps, Cicero's comment in *De re publica* (II.30.52) on Plato's ideal republic: '[*civitatem*] *optandam magis quam sperandam*'. After the Eunomian project (reconceiving society) and the Eutopian project (reconceiving the mind), there remains the *Eusophian* project (reconceiving the universal, that is to say, religion).

this evening but surely tomorrow.' The play ends with Vladimir saying: 'Shall we go?' Estragon replies: 'Yes, let's go.' And then there is the final stage direction: '*They do not move*'.[31]

5.73 To remake humanity, we must move. We cannot wait for Mr Godot, whether Godot is the capitalist market, the globalising of democracy, the wonder-working of natural science, human science, or natural human progress. Somehow, in the new century and the new millennium, humanity has to find the courage to believe in its own self-transforming potentiality, its unlimited capacity for self-evolving and self-perfecting. Humanity is its own re-creator. We are what we think. This is the truth that our predecessors rediscovered during the course of this last millennium, which they rediscovered so intelligently and so courageously. Both New Enlightenment projects – new society and new mind – are a call to humanity to be intelligent and courageous, once again, yet again, before it is too late. It is a call to a human revolution, a revolution not in the streets but in the human mind.

[31] S. Beckett, *Waiting for Godot* (London, Faber and Faber; 1956), pp. 50, 94.

PART II

European society and its law

Can nations and states transcend themselves through law?

6

European governance and the re-branding of democracy

The governance of virtue – Who governs the governors? – The lure of anti-politics – The government of Europe – New Europe

The new usage of the words 'governance' and 'civil society' reflects a new trend in the theory and practice of liberal democracy. It is a trend which is reflected also in the use of the expression 'corporate governance' in the theory and practice of capitalism. It is a development which is presented as if it were benign and progressive. It may also be seen as sinister and reactionary.

In a White Paper on European Governance the European Commission has fallen in with such an approach. It is not likely to be useful in resolving the problem of the legitimacy of the institutions of the European Union. The Union's constitutional problem requires a fundamental reconceiving of the nature of the Union as a society and of the Union's relationship to the societies and constitutional systems of the member states.

European Union is a new kind of society with a new kind of constitution which is contained within but transcends the societies and the constitutions of its member states.

6.1 As the idea of *democracy* decays, the ideas of *governance* and *civil society* flourish. They are the superficially benign symptoms of a wasting disease which is affecting thinking about democracy at every level. It is a disease which is affecting the self-conceiving of traditional democratic societies and the reconceiving of societies recovering from Soviet-style communism and other morbid forms of absolutism. It is rampant in the international unsociety where a formless social consciousness feeds on the left-overs of national social philosophy, including ideas which are certainly not benign.

6.2 The European Commission's White Paper on European Governance[1] reminds us that the disease has taken hold in the intermediate international society of the European Union, seeping into the void of social philosophy which is European integration.

6.3 The semantic shift from *government* to *governance* and from *society* to *civil society* may seem to be slight, but its theoretical and practical implications are profound. *Governance* is government seen as the social function of a governing class whereas, in the liberal democratic tradition, *government* is seen as society's self-government. *Civil society* implies that there is a realm of collective non-governmental social action which is parallel to, but not an integral part of, the function of 'governance' whereas, in the liberal democratic tradition, it is *society* in its entirety which integrates all social systems in the process of public-realm decision-making. To disintegrate the integrity of *society* and to separate the people from their *government* is a theoretical counter-revolution against liberal democracy, a nostalgia for the bad old days of more and less enlightened absolutism.

The governance of virtue

6.4 It is no coincidence that there is a concordance of spirit and language between the Commission's White Paper on European Governance and the OECD Principles of Corporate Governance.[2] We are witnessing a peculiar convergence: the governmentalising of the corporation and the corporatising of government. The common feature is that each aims to be a normative rationalisation of a social system which has traditionally had quite another form of self-ordering. It is a new form of social domination which presents itself under the benevolent mask of a new 'ethics' applicable to the exercise of ultimate political and/or economic social power and in which 'good governance' and 'good corporate governance' are made into the immanent universal values of self-regulating systems.

6.5 The OECD Principles are part of an immense international effort, involving very many intergovernmental and non-governmental institutions, designed to spread the good news of *private enterprise* to

[1] COM(2001)428 final; 25 July 2001. The text is available on the European Union website.

[2] Drafted by an Ad-Hoc Task Force and endorsed by the OECD Council meeting at ministerial level on 25–7 May 1999. The text is available on the OECD website.

societies undergoing fundamental socio-economic transformation. Because it has proved tactically necessary to universalise the principles of private enterprise and not merely to preach them to the neophytes, the corporate governance movement has had a dramatic backwash effect within the mind-world of traditional capitalist countries, not least in those areas of the law which are most relevant to economic organisation (including corporation law and employment law), refocusing their conceptual structures in the light of the new normativity.

6.6 The OECD Principles reveal explicitly their dual motivational sources. 'A good corporate governance regime is central to the efficient use of corporate capital. Good corporate governance also helps to ensure that corporations take into account the interests of a wide range of constituencies, as well as the communities within which they operate, and that their boards are accountable to the company and the shareholders' (OECD's Long Abstract of the Principles). 'In addition, factors such as business ethics and corporate awareness of the environmental and societal interests of the communities in which it operates can also have an impact on the reputation and the long-term success of a company' (Preamble). 'If countries are to reap the full benefits of the global capital market, and if they are to attract long-term "patient" capital, corporate governance arrangements must be credible and well understood across borders' (Preamble).[3]

6.7 More problematic is the relationship between the European Commission's White Paper on European Governance and the immense international effort now being devoted to spreading the good news of *liberal democracy* to societies undergoing fundamental socio-political transformation.[4] The Commission's paper forms part of that effort, in so far as it is clearly intended to be read in the potential member states of

[3] We may recall de Tocqueville's comment on the phenomenon of religion in the United States. It is often difficult, he says, to ascertain 'whether the principal object of religion is to procure eternal felicity in the other world or prosperity in this'. A. de Tocqueville, *Democracy in America* (1835/1840) (D. Campbell Publishers (Everyman's Library); 1994), II, ch. 11, p. 127. The St Paul of the corporate governance movement is, perhaps, Robert Monks. See R. Monks and N. Minow, *Corporate Governance* (Oxford, Blackwell Business; 1995/2001).

[4] Leading intergovernmental actors in this effort (other than the European Commission itself) are the World Bank and the Organisation for Security and Co-operation in Europe (OSCE). 'Corruption, ineffective public institutions and a lack of coherent legal framework are some of the issues that affect economic stability and pose security risks in the OSCE area.' OSCE release concerning the Ninth OSCE Economic Forum on the theme 'Transparency and good governance in economic matters' (Prague, 15–18 May 2001; available on the OSCE website).

Central and Eastern Europe. But it is also aimed at a strategic challenge which the President of the Commission has identified as the making of 'a new, more democratic partnership between the different levels of governance in Europe'.[5] And the Commission has said that the White Paper aims 'to enhance democracy in Europe and to increase the legitimacy of the institutions'. So, here also, a universalising of principles demanded by an international crusade, this time in the name of democracy, is also speaking to the very special constitutional self-consciousness of the far-from-embryonic democracies of Western Europe.

6.8 The Commission lists five Principles of Good Governance: Openness, Participation, Accountability, Effectiveness and Coherence.[6] It says that the principles are 'important for establishing more democratic governance. They underpin democracy and the rule of law in the member states, but they apply to all levels of government – global, European, national, regional and local.'[7] The Commission says that the Union must also do more to involve 'civil society' in its decision-making, since civil society 'plays an important role in giving voice to the concerns of citizens and delivering services that meet people's needs'. A footnote tells us that civil society includes 'trade unions and employers' organisations ("social partners"); non-governmental organisations; professional associations; charities; grass-roots organisations; organisations that involve citizens in local and municipal life with a particular contribution from churches and religious communities'.[8]

6.9 Seen from the hallowed halls of the many-palaced *Hofburg* of the European Kakania,[9] the turbulent constitutional histories of the 'member states' and their complex constitutional psychologies may seem to be tiresome relics which must be overcome (*aufgehoben*, in Hegel-speak) in a new order of enlightened governance which surpasses the

[5] Romano Prodi, speech to the European Parliament, 15 February 2000. Text available on European Union website.

[6] We may be reminded of the four Cardinal Virtues of a previous European social order – Justice, Prudence, Temperance and Fortitude. We might rather have hoped to hear an acceptance by the European Commission of the aspirational Machiavellian principles of republican *virtù*.

[7] Section 2, p. 10. [8] *Ibid.*, p. 14.

[9] Kakania, with its unpleasant undertones in the Greek and German languages, was the name which the Austrian writer Robert Musil invented to evoke the multi-nation, multi-polity unity of the Austro-Hungarian Empire which had been formally structured around the 'k' words *kaiserlich* and *königlich*. R. Musil, *Der Mann ohne Eigenschaften* (1930); *The Man Without Qualities* (trs. E. Wilkins and E. Kaiser; London, Secker & Warburg; 1953), p. 32.

hard-won reality of liberal democracy.[10] Seen from another point of view, the greatest strategic challenge facing European integration seems rather to be the need, at long last, to integrate European integration itself into a European constitutionalism which far surpasses in complexity and importance the institutional structures of the European Union. It remains to be seen whether the attempt to re-brand free-market capitalism as a system of enlightened social welfare will succeed. The attempt to re-brand liberal democracy as a system of enlightened paternalism must be made to fail.

Who governs the governors?

6.10 The term 'civil society' has had three lives. The father of the first was Adam Ferguson who, with his friends David Hume and Adam Smith, was one of the leading-lights of the Scottish Enlightenment.[11] His *Essay on the History of Civil Society* (1767) should be required reading for the entrepreneurs of European integration. It is a study of the wise self-governance of a true society. For Ferguson, society is natural to human beings but *civil* society is a great human achievement, the realm of human self-development, an arena of struggle, uncertainty, energy, creativity, but also a realm of civic virtue, as human beings accept the mutual burdens and blessings of sociable behaviour.[12]

[10] In the spirit of Musil, we might give the name of Eunarchia to this brave new European order, with its obsessive use of the 'Eu' word: a complex, alien, and ultimately unknowable order which is commonly referred to simply as 'Europe'. Musil remarked that the Austro-Hungarian Empire, for all its multiplicity and complexity, was referred to in everyday speech simply as 'Austria' (*ibid.*, p. 33).

[11] Hobbes and Locke had used the term 'civil society' occasionally, but they were in (rare) agreement in the view that 'commonwealth' was the best English equivalent for the Latin *civitas* (*Leviathan*, ch. 27; *Two Treatises*, II, § 133). However, Locke's essential structural concepts were 'society' and 'government'.

[12] 'Our notion of order in civil society is frequently false: it is taken from the analogy of subjects inanimate and dead; we consider commotion and action as contrary to its nature; we think it consistent only with obedience, secrecy, and the silent passing of affairs through the hands of a few . . . When we seek in society for the order of mere inaction and tranquillity, we forget the nature of our subject, and find the order of slaves, not that of free men.' A. Ferguson, *An Essay on the History of Civil Society* (1767) (ed. F. Oz-Salzberger; Cambridge, Cambridge University Press; 1995), p. 254 fn.

Machiavelli had taken a similar view, arguing that Rome had been invigorated by its internal dissensions, including its endemic class-struggle. *Discourses on Livy* (1531) (trs. J. and P. Bondanella; Oxford, Oxford University Press (The World's Classics); 1997), bk I, chs 4 and 6, pp. 29, 36.

In such a society, law is 'the treaty to which members of the same community have agreed'.[13] Legislation does not succeed because of its rationalistic merits, but because it is concordant with the whole spirit of society.[14] And the slide into despotism is not always a product of the use of force. 'Societies easily pass from a condition in which each individual has an equal title to reign, into one in which they are equally destined to serve.'[15] In a 'search of perfection', government may pass from the hands of the statesman and the warrior into the hands of 'the mere clerk and accountant'. And 'this seeming perfection of government might weaken the bands of society, and . . . separate and estrange the different ranks it was meant to reconcile'.[16]

6.11 Most poignant of all is the fact that Ferguson himself rejects the very idea which is reflected in the particular use of the term *civil society* espoused by the Commission in its White Paper. '[T]he separation of professions, while it seems to promise improvement of skill, and is actually the cause why the productions of every art become more perfect as commerce advances; yet in its termination, and ultimate effects, serves, in some measure, to break the bands of society, to substitute "form" in place of ingenuity, and to withdraw individuals from the common scene of occupation, on which the sentiments of the heart, and the mind, are most happily employed. Under the *distinction* of callings . . . society is made to consist of parts, of which none is animated with the spirit of society itself.'[17]

6.12 Ferguson's book was translated into German and was read by G. W. F. Hegel who was the father of the second life of the term 'civil society'. Hegel turned Ferguson's idea of *civil society* on its head and gave birth to the idea of the Hegelian *state*. Ferguson's delight in the self-ordering disorder of society was replaced by Hegel's contempt for the irrationality of such a society, exemplified, not least, in the deplorable wilderness of British society and British law. Hegel admitted that a benign potentiality of the self-consciousness of civil society, where people's behaviour is socialised by the random aggregation of particular events

[13] *Ibid.*, p. 150.

[14] Of British *habeas corpus* legislation he says: 'No wiser form was ever opposed to the abuses of power. But it requires a fabric no less than the whole political constitution of Great Britain, a spirit no less than the refractory and turbulent zeal of this fortunate people, to secure its effects' (*ibid.*, p. 160).

[15] *Ibid.*, p. 72.

[16] *Ibid.*, p. 182.

[17] *Ibid.*, p. 207.

and processes, is that the idea of civil society is capable of producing the idea of the *state*, which finally embodies, in theory and in practice, society's universalising capacity, an achievement which is the rationally conceived end of human history. And, in appropriate historical circumstances, such as a 'constitutional monarchy', the idea of the 'state' could become a fact. One thing was certain. The surpassing of civil society in the 'state' could not be achieved in the form of democracy, if that meant a system in which the masses (*der Pöbel*) would, in some sense, govern.

6.13 The consequences of Hegel's depreciation of 'civil society' in relation to 'the state' have been profound and long-lasting. In the hands of Karl Marx, misled perhaps by the unfortunate German translation of Ferguson's 'civil society' as *bürgerliche Gesellschaft* (bourgeois society),[18] it became the *casus belli* of revolution, the end of humanity's pre-history. At the same time, the development of Hegel's 'universal class', in the form of the modern paternalist civil service, with its universalising function in the service of the public interest, rapidly became a feature of liberal democracy, even in the most bourgeois of liberal democracies. But the contempt for, or at least distrust of, the messy business of democratic 'politics', particularly politics of the Anglo-American variety, continued to affect the political development of several European countries until well into the twentieth century.[19] And Hegel's troubled spirit may be with us yet again, in the third and latest life-form of 'civil society' and in its conceptual cousin, the sinister new concept of 'governance'.

6.14 It was in the last two decades of the twentieth century that the idea of 'civil society' was suddenly and mysteriously resurrected or reincarnated. The third life of civil society has already generated its own book-mountain. There is some agreement to the effect that the idea had two spiritual parents: a decline of confidence in the business of institutional politics in liberal democracies; and a tactic of anti-state dissent in late-stage communist countries.[20] But there is a splendid range of disparate views about what 'civil society' is and is for. *Civil Society 1.* For some, particularly for ever-optimistic Americans, it is the arena for

[18] It seems that civil society's latest avatar has been re-branded in German as *Zivilgesellschaft.*

[19] For further discussion of this aspect, see ch. 7 below, at §§ 7.50ff.

[20] The most memorable case of this phenomenon was the role of trade unions in the revolutionary social transformation of Poland, but the idea of 'anti-politics' had for some time been an aspect of the polemics of dissidence in Eastern Europe.

the revival of Fergusonian community, civility and republican virtue as a therapeutic response to institutional corruption.[21] *Civil Society 2.* For others, apparently including the European Commission, it is a neo-syndicalist assertion of the countervailing power of non-state organised interests, mediating between the particularism of the individual and the institutional universality of the state.[22] *Civil Society 3.* For others again, it is the embodiment of a Habermasian *public sphere* in which the differentiated voices of society speak to each other and collectively constitute the consciousness of their sociality and perhaps even of their humanity.[23] *Civil Society 4.* For the apostles of universal democracy, it is the means by which societies whose social development has been delayed or disabled can artificially construct the social sub-structure without which democratic institutions cannot function successfully. And the same principle might be applicable to the democratising of international society itself.[24]

6.15 The spiritual connection between such ideas and the idea of 'governance' is subtle. The word 'governance' in the English language (derived from the Old French *gouvernance*) is older than the word 'government'. It referred to any form of control – of a parent over a child, a natural force, a king's power over a kingdom. John Fortescue's *The Governance of England* (written in the 1460s, first printed in 1714) was

[21] 'The idea of civil society is the idea of society which has a life of its own which is separate from the state, and largely autonomous from it, which lies beyond the boundaries of the family and the clan, and beyond the locality.' E. Shils, 'The virtue of civility' (revised version of an essay originally published in 1991), in E. Shils, *The Virtue of Civility. Selected Essays on Liberalism, Tradition, and Civil Society* (Indianapolis, Liberty Fund; 1997), pp. 320–55, at pp. 320–1.

[22] Syndicalism was a movement, especially in pre-fascist Italy, which sought to take power over (or, in its anarcho-syndicalist version, to replace) the power of the state by using the social power of corporate entities (*sindacati*), especially trade unions. Hegel had approved of the non-governmental collective entity (*Korporation*) as a means of partial universalising within Hegelian civil society.

[23] 'A viable civil society as a kind of third force between the state and the economy, on the one hand, and the private sphere, on the other, seems to require some effective sense of community and of there actually being a community to which people are committed.' K. Nielson, 'Reconceptualizing civil society for now', in *Toward a Global Civil Society* (ed. M. Walzer; Providence, Berghahn Books; 1995), pp. 41–67, at p. 56.

[24] Governments and intergovernmental organisations have adopted this idea as an article of faith. National and international non-governmental organisations have been incidental beneficiaries to the extent that their claim to be self-appointed and self-defined institutions of national and international 'civil society' is recognised by governments and intergovernmental organisations.

the first constitutional treatise written in the English language.[25] It was an instruction manual for a king on the art of wise governance of the kingdom. In *The Governance* and also in his better-known *De Laudibus Legum Angliae* (In Praise of the Laws of England), written for the instruction of the then Prince of Wales and first printed in 1537, Fortescue had explained that the King of England is 'not only regal but also political',[26] that he has *dominium politicum et regale.*[27] This meant that the English polity was to be regarded as a monarchy which was, in some sense, also a republic.[28] The King 'is not able to change the laws without the assent of his subjects nor to burden an unwilling people with strange impositions [taxes]'; 'for a king of this sort is set up for the protection of the law, the subjects, and their bodies and goods, and he has power to this end issuing from the people, so that it is not permissible for him to rule his people with any other power'.[29]

6.16 In *The Governance* Fortescue took up, with remarkable acuity, what would prove to be one of the great perennial themes of English constitutional history, a theme which has traditionally been known as the problem of 'influence behind the throne',[30] a theme which is raised yet again, six centuries later, by the new ideas of 'civil society' and 'governance' and in a political world full of focus groups, lobbyists, special interest groups and non-governmental organisations of dubious representative legitimacy and with purposes which may or may not be for the common good.

6.17 Fortescue devoted much attention to the problem of the composition of the King's Council, the embryo-form of cabinet government.

[25] Sir John Fortescue (*c.*1394–*c.*1476) was briefly Chief Justice of the King's Bench. He went into exile with the Prince of Wales and his mother (Margaret of Anjou, wife of King Henry VI, who had been deposed in 1461) but was later reconciled with King Edward IV (reigned 1461–83) and became a member of his Council.

[26] J. Fortescue, *De laudibus legum Angliae*, in J. Fortescue, *On The Laws and Governance of England* (ed. S. Lockwood; Cambridge, Cambridge University Press; 1997), ch. 1.

[27] J. Fortescue, *The Governance of England* (ed. C. Plummer; Oxford, Clarendon Press; 1885), ch. 1.

[28] Both Voltaire and Montesquieu would come to the same conclusion in their observations on the English constitution. See further in ch. 7 below, at § 7.31, fn. 30.

[29] J. Fortescue, *De laudibus* (fn. 26 above), chs 9 and 13, pp. 17, 21–2.

[30] There is, perhaps, a connection with the German phenomenon, discussed by Weber, of *Räte von Haus aus* (counsel from beyond the court), a controversial practice of German kings. M. Weber, 'Bureaucracy' (part 3, ch. 6 of *Wirtschaft und Gesellschaft*), in *From Max Weber: Essays in Sociology* (eds H. Gerth and C. Wright Mills; London, Routledge; 1948/1991), pp. 196–244, at p. 236.

The Council must be carefully composed, including some commoners, and it must be possible to know who is advising the King. In a paper of 1470, he referred to the bad practice whereby 'our kings have been ruled by private Counsellors, such as have offered their service and counsel and were not chosen thereto'.[31] Four centuries later, John Stuart Mill raised the problem yet again, borrowing a phrase from Jeremy Bentham: 'sinister interests . . . that is, interests conflicting more or less with the general good of the community'. 'One of the greatest dangers, therefore, of democracy, as of all other forms of government, lies in the sinister interest of the holders of power.'[32] Should we recognise the fact that there may even be such a thing as 'the interest of a ruling class'?[33]

The lure of anti-politics

6.18 We may, indeed, wonder what it is that attracts the direct successors of the medieval kings, the ruling classes of the European Union and of its member states and of international unsociety, and the ruling class of the capitalist economy, to the new ideas of 'civil society' and 'governance' and to a re-branding of liberal democracy and capitalism which is also a dangerous reconceiving of essential features of liberal democracy and capitalism. In whose interest would such a thing be?[34]

6.19 In Plato's *Protagoras*, Protagoras says that Hermes asked Zeus, no less, whether he should distribute the gifts of wise government only to the few, as special skills are given to doctors and lawyers and other experts, or to all alike. Zeus answered: 'Let all have their share.'[35] From

[31] J. Fortescue, *The Governance* (fn. 27 above), pp. 301, 346.

[32] J. S. Mill, *Considerations on Representative Government* (1861) (London, Dent (Everyman's Library); 1910), ch. 6, pp. 248, 254.

[33] *Ibid.*, p. 249. John Locke said that if the Prince had 'a distinct and separate Interest from the good of the Community' then the people would not be 'a Society of Rational Creatures' but would have to be seen as 'an Herd of inferiour Creatures, under the Dominion of a Master, who keeps them, and works them for his own Pleasure and Profit'. *Two Treatises on Government* (1689) (ed. P. Laslett; Cambridge, Cambridge University Press; 1960), II, § 163, p. 423.

[34] *Cui bono?* (who would profit from it?). Cicero, who used the phrase in the Second Philippic, attributed it to the judge Lucius Cassius.

[35] Plato, *Protagoras*, 322c–d (tr. W. Guthrie), in *The Collected Dialogues of Plato* (eds E. Hamilton and H. Cairns; Princeton, Princeton University Press; 1961), p. 320. Protagoras goes on to say: 'Thus it is, Socrates, and from this cause, that in a debate involving skill in building,

long and bitter experience, we may wonder whether Zeus underestimated the problem of *politics* in government, the problem of reconciling the governing skills of the few and the chaotic desires and opinions of the many, and the problem of *competition* in business, that is, the problem of reconciling the ruthless order and the formless disorder of the market-place.

6.20 Business and government are systems of social power in which the few (corporate management; politicians and civil servants) organise the social activity of the many. As systems of social power they both have two natural tendencies which, at first sight, seem contradictory. They seek to maximise their power but they also seek to achieve steady-state systems.[36] But the contradiction is only apparent. It is easier to exercise social power in a system which is protected from external disturbance. It is the cunning of the law that it not only creates the structural possibilities of business and government (the corporation, the contract, elections, the police and countless others), and also controls the exercise of the social power which they exercise, but also regulates in favourable ways the general social environment within which they function. The law creates a steady-state within which business and government exercise their freedom-under-the-law. The exercise of that freedom

or in any other craft, the Athenians, like other men, believe that few are capable of giving advice . . . But when the subject of their counsel involves political wisdom, which must always follow the path of justice and moderation, they listen to every man's opinion, for they think that everyone must share in this kind of virtue; otherwise the state could not exist.' (*Ibid.*, 322e–323a, p. 320).

[36] It was Adam Smith who noted the counter-intuitive fact that businessmen dislike competition. 'People of the same trade seldom meet together, even for merriment and diversion, but the conversation ends in a conspiracy against the publick, or in some contrivance to raise prices.' *An Inquiry into the Nature and Causes of the Wealth of Nations* (1776), (ed. K. Sutherland; Oxford, Oxford University Press (The World's Classics); 1993), bk I, ch. 10.2, p. 129. It was de Tocqueville who noted the natural conservatism of 'commerce'. 'I know of nothing more opposite to revolutionary attitudes than commercial ones. Commerce is naturally adverse to all the violent passions; it loves to temporize, takes delight in compromise, and studiously avoids irritation. It is patient, insinuating, flexible, and never has recourse to extreme measures until obliged by the most absolute necessity.' *Democracy in America* (fn. 3 above), II, ch. 20, p. 254. It was J. S. Mill who noted that bureaucracy tends to stifle vitality, aiming to reduce government so far as possible to a manageable routine. *Representative Government* (fn. 32 above), ch. 6, pp. 246ff. It was Max Weber who uncovered a link between modern capitalism and modern bureaucracy, both requiring a controlled and orderly world. 'Parlament und Regierung in neugeordneten Deutschland', in *Gesammelte Politische Schriften* (ed. J. Winckelmann; Tübingen, J. C. B. Mohr; 1971), pp. 306–443, at p. 322. It might be instructive to reread *mutatis mutandis* Weber's analysis of the state of political Germany in 1918 as if it were written about the state of the European Union today.

takes place in arenas (the market, politics) where all kinds of social activity (including so-called 'competition' and 'public opinion', respectively) determine actual outcomes of the exercise of social power within the framework supplied by the law.

6.21 In recent times we have witnessed several developments which are tending to cause the social systems of business and government to converge. (1) The domination of the political system by the economic system is a natural result of the eighteenth-century move to conceive of a nation and its wealth as a coherent social system. What came to be called 'economics' was originally called, and might some day again be called, 'political economy'. (2) The ideas encapsulated in the slogans 'the end of ideology' (after 1945) and more recently 'the end of politics' and, still more recently, 'the end of history' are reflections of a change in the theory and practice of government, as the governing class (politicians and civil servants) struggle to behave as general and neutral politico-economic managers of immensely complex systems in an immensely unstable world, a world where law does not yet provide a safe and satisfactory environment for business or for government. (3) Wider social developments (including consumerism, environmentalism and globalisation) have asserted the social responsibility of the owners and managers of businesses. The governing class of business has joined hands with the governing class of government in what is more and more conceived as a shared social activity of large-scale politico-economic management.[37]

6.22 These tendencies have generated consequences which are structural changes and not merely incidental effects. Popular capitalism has seen workers become shareholders in their own employing corporations and shareholding has been extended to the mass of the people. The arena of business is now not merely the market-place but society as a whole.

[37] Already in 1796, Thomas Jefferson saw a similar threat to the operation of the American constitutional system. 'The main body of our citizens, however, remain true to their republican principles . . . Against us are the Executive, the Judiciary, two out of three branches of the Legislature, all the officers of government, all who want to be officers, all timid men who prefer the calm of despotism to the boisterous sea of liberty, British merchants and Americans trading on British capital, speculators and holders in the banks and public funds, a contrivance invented for the purposes of corruption, and for assimilating us in all things to the rotten as well as the sound parts of the English model . . . We have only to awake and snap the Lilliputian cords with which they have been entangling us during the first sleep which succeeded our labors.' Letter to Phillip Mazzei, 24 April 1796.

Some people even use the same word – 'stakeholder' – to refer to those with a specific interest in the functioning of a given business corporation and those who participate in the political process. 'Corporate governance' is an attempt to normalise the politicisation of business. At the same time, the managerialising of government has meant that governments have come to see that the primary condition for the maximising and the retaining of social power is a satisfactory relationship to mass consciousness and to 'special interests'. The co-opting of *Civil Society 2* by governments (politicians and bureaucrats) and the re-imagining of the function of government as 'governance' are an instinctive response by governments to what they suppose to be their new existential situation. And the co-opting of civil society has been accompanied by the co-opting by governments of the idea of fundamental rights, the last environmental threat to their social control.[38] They are phenomena which were not unforeseen.

6.23 In the passionate final chapters of his book on democracy, Alexis de Tocqueville said that 'the gradual weakening of the individual in relation to society at large may be traced to a thousand things'.[39] 'After having thus successively taken each member of the community in its powerful grasp and fashioned him at will, the supreme power then extends its arm over the whole community... The will of man is not shattered, but softened, bent, and guided; men are seldom forced by it to act, but they are constantly restrained from acting. Such a power does not destroy; it does not tyrannize, but it compresses, enervates, extinguishes, and stupefies a people, till each nation is reduced to nothing

[38] The scandalous decades-long mismanagement of the problem of fundamental rights in the European Union, including now the fiasco of a 'Charter of Fundamental Rights', concocted by or on behalf of the governments and institutions of the EU, and proclaimed by them as environmentally friendly in Nice in December 2000, is part of a much wider story of the decay of the idea of fundamental rights as they have been appropriated and instrumentalised by governments since 1950. We may recall the words of Alexander Hamilton in no. 1 of the Federalist Papers. '[A] dangerous ambition more often lurks behind the specious mask of zeal for the rights of the people than under the forbidding appearance of zeal for the firmness and efficiency of government. History will teach us that the former has been found a much more certain road to the introduction of despotism than the latter, and that of those men who have overturned the liberties of republics, the greatest number have begun their career by paying an obsequious court to the people, commencing demagogues and ending tyrants.' A. Hamilton, J. Madison, and J. Jay, *The Federalist Papers* (1788) (New York, The New American Library of World Literature; 1961), p. 35. See further in *Eunomia*, §§ 15.60ff.

[39] *Democracy in America* (fn. 3 above), IV, ch. 5, p. 304.

better than a flock of timid and industrious animals, of which the government is the shepherd.'[40]

6.24 The New Totalitarianism with a human face is thus a politico-economic phenomenon which involves a re-branding of business and democracy as democratic business and businesslike democracy.

6.25 When, following the managerial revolution,[41] businessmen became managers and when, in the unsocial extra-national sphere, in the European Union and international unsociety, politicians and bureaucrats converged, and became bureaucratised politicians and politicised bureaucrats,[42] it was only to be expected that, sooner or later, they would try to find ways to escape from the entropy of the market-place and of the forum into a world of 'governance', a world of self-determining order, and into a world of 'civil society' where politics could be made unpolitical.[43] Self-governance by industrial and commercial corporations in the name of what they suppose to be ethics is a contradiction of capitalism. Governance by governments in collusion with something which they call civil society is a death-wish of democracy.

The government of Europe

6.26 The European Union is the world's first purpose-built economic-political society in which the relative dominance of the economic aspect has determined the formation, and the gross malformation, of the political aspect. As a median social formation, it is an eloquent precedent

[40] *Ibid.*, p. 319.

[41] The seminal works on the bureaucratising of business (as management of the corporation came to be separated from ownership of the corporation) are J. Burnham, *The Managerial Revolution or What is Happening in the World Now* (London, Putnam; 1942); and J. K. Galbraith, *The New Industrial State* (London, Hamish Hamilton; 1967).

[42] *Politische Beamte* (political official) and *Berufspolitiker* (professional politician) were terms used by Max Weber in a lecture published as one of his last writings in 1919 under the title *Politik als Beruf* (Politics as a Vocation): M. Weber, *Gesammelte Politische Schriften* (fn. 36 above), pp. 505–60, at pp. 519, 521; H. Gerth and C. Wright Mills (eds.), *From Max Weber* (fn. 30 above), pp. 77–128, at pp. 90, 92. In that lecture he analysed the evolving relationship between politics and bureaucracy. He had devoted much effort and much anguish to the emergence of a 'new despotism' involving a sort of collusion between politicians and bureaucrats.

[43] This word is borrowed from Thomas Mann's survey of what he saw as the distasteful realities of democratic politics: *Betrachtungen eines Unpolitischen* (Berlin, Fischer Verlag; 1922). *Reflections of a Nonpolitical Man* (tr. W. Morris; New York, F. Ungar; *c.* 1983).

for the re-forming of national societies as economic-political societies and for the forming of international society, the society of all societies, in which the dominance of the economic aspect is already determining the formation, and the malformation, of its political aspect.

6.27 Even if all the Union institutions observed the Commission's Principles of Good Governance with scrupulous piety, nothing would have changed in the constitutional wasteland of European integration. Principles of Good Governance would do nothing whatsoever 'to enhance democracy in Europe and to increase the legitimacy of the institutions'.[44] On the contrary, we may recall Adam Ferguson's warning. The more government perfects itself, the more it tends to alienate itself from the people.[45] Even if the problem is seen as the need to make a new 'partnership between the different levels of governance in Europe', that project would require something immeasurably more radical than further ineffectual efforts to mobilise the acquiescence or half-hearted co-operation of the long-suffering people and peoples of Europe, efforts to get them to tolerate the institutions of European integration if they cannot be made to love them.

6.28 The failure of European integration is not an institutional failure. The New Byzantium of Eunarchia already has ten times more ingeniously devised institutions than any sane society could possibly tolerate. Nor is the redeeming of European integration a matter of the neurotic manipulation of the powers and relationships of institutions through ever more complex and subtle formulas. The New Scholasticism, of treaties not of treatises, is a tragi-comic psychodrama of the public sphere.[46] And now the New Rome, through what is called 'enlargement',[47] plans to extend its frontier (*limes*) to include all of Central and Eastern Europe. Bulimia plus bureaucracy is a reliable recipe for the decline and fall of empires.[48]

[44] See fn. 6 above. [45] See fn. 16 above.

[46] 'A bureaucracy always tends to become a pedantocracy.' J. S. Mill, *Representative Government* (fn. 32 above), p. 246.

[47] We may recall that, after the publication in 1883 of J. R. Seeley's *The Expansion of England*, that phrase came to be used as an emollient label for British imperialism.

[48] Hobbes lists 'the insatiable appetite, or *Bulimia*, of enlarging Dominion' as one of the diseases to which commonwealths are subject. *Leviathan*, ch. 29. In a bipolar form, it may be accompanied by what we may call *Anorexia nervosa*, lack of appetite for the messy business of politics.

6.29 The failure of European integration is a failure of Europe's ideal self-constituting, a failure in Europe's idea of itself. And the failure in Europe's ideal constitution is not difficult to explain.[49]

6.30 Thanks to a well-founded fear of federalism, which would reduce proud and ancient nations to the status of German *Länder* or Spanish autonomous regions (*regiones autónomas*), the European Union has seemed to be condemned to see itself as an *external constitutional system* which nevertheless takes effect with ultimate legal authority *within* the constitutional systems of the member states. Such a conception is, and would always be, intolerable as the foundational theory of any society.

6.31 But there is a fear which is more inhibiting even than the fear of federalism, a fear which has distorted the mind-world of European integration into a diseased form of social psychology. It is the fear of supra-constitutionality, a paralysing fear caused by the unbearable thought that the Union system might be regarded as a constitutional order which is superior to the national constitutional orders.[50] The condition of psychic denial produced by the fear of constitutionality leads those who are its victims to assert four things. (1) The Union constitutional system is essentially subordinate to each of the constitutional systems of the member states. (2) The constitutional authority of the Union system is derived from a continuing act of delegation from the national constitutions, since the member states, individually and collectively, can at any time alter the terms of the delegation or even terminate it.[51] (3) The Union constitutional order is separate from, external to, and not integrated into the constitutional orders of the member states. (4) Union law is not in itself an everyday source of law in the member states but applies

[49] For discussion of the three interlocking dimensions of a society's self-constituting, see *Eunomia*, ch. 6. In its *ideal* constitution a society constitutes itself in the form of ideas. In its *real* constitution society constitutes itself through the day-to-day social struggle of actual human beings. In its *legal* constitution society reconciles its ideal and its real self-constituting in the form of law.

[50] See L. Favoreu, 'Souveraineté et supraconstitutionnalité', in 67 *Pouvoirs. Revue française d'études constitutionnelles et politiques* (1993) (special number on 'La souveraineté'), pp. 71–7; G. Vedel, 'Souveraineté et supraconstitutionnalité', same journal, pp. 79–97.

[51] Locke thought otherwise. 'To conclude, The *Power that every individual gave the Society*, when he entered into it, can never revert to the Individuals again, as long as the Society lasts, but will always remain in the Community; because without this, there can be no Community, no Common-wealth, which is contrary to the original Agreement [i.e., the contract to form the society].' J. Locke, *Two Treatises* (fn. 33 above), II, § 243, p. 477.

indirectly, by transmission and imperceptible transformation through an imaginary screen consisting of a national constitutional norm, such as the general constitutional rule on the effect of international agreements within the domestic constitutional order. (5) Accordingly, the so-called 'sovereignty' of the member states is unaffected by their participation in the constitutional system of the Union.[52] This fantasy of an inviolable and inviolate national constitutionalism is a lie, an ignoble lie, and a fraud on the people of Europe.[53]

6.32 As in international society so also in the society of the European Union, the reality has overtaken the fantasy. The sharing of sovereign powers between states is now a major structural feature of international society. It is *the* major structural feature of the European Union, where the member states have shared almost all their basic sovereign rights with the Union. Ultimate legislative, executive and judicial authority is shared with Union institutions. The treaty-making power and rights of active and passive diplomatic representation are shared with the Union. The legal regulation of external trade is shared. Citizenship and the right to control movement into and out of national territory are shared. Adjacent sea-areas are shared. In the Euro-currency aspect of Economic and Monetary Union, the sovereign right to issue and manage a currency is shared. Sooner or later, EMU will be extended to include fiscal policy

[52] There is a sort of pathos in the long struggle of the French superior courts to square the circle of the internality of an external source of law in the light of the unforgiving terms of Article 55 of the French Constitution. For a striking instance, relating to treaties in general, but perhaps also applicable to EU law in particular, see *Sarran et Levacher*, decision of the Conseil d'Etat of 30 October 1998, in 1998 *L'actualité juridique. Droit administratif*, at p. 1,039 (discussed by C. Richards, in 25 *European Law Review* (2000), pp. 192–9). One can only wonder, with grudging admiration, at the defiant minimalism of the formula used to define European integration in the new (Maastricht) Article 88 of the French Constitution: 'the member states have freely chosen . . . to exercise certain of their powers in common'. In Germany, the other most original of the original member states, the Maastricht decision of the Federal Constitutional Court (BVerfGE 89, 155) is a sad symbol of a failure to surrender constitutionally to an order which, in its complexity and its sophistication, the Germans have done so much to create. The Court took the view that the Union was merely an inter-state institution (*zwischenstaatliche Einrichtung*) which is 'independent and separate' (*selbständig und unabhängig*) from the individual member states and which is legitimated on a continuing basis by the parliaments of the member states, with the European Parliament as an additional source of legitimation.

[53] 'How, then, said I, might we contrive one of those opportune falsehoods of which we were just now speaking, so as by one noble lie to persuade if possible the rulers themselves, but failing that the rest of the city?' Plato, *The Republic*, bk III, 414b–c, in *The Collected Dialogues* (fn. 35 above), p. 658.

and so, in due course, will take power over the commanding heights of general economic policy. And, when the new defence system of the Union becomes clearer, it may involve a collective control of the deployment of armed forces abroad.

6.33 The highly charged medieval discussion of 'sovereignty', and its lively post-medieval sequel, served various purposes at various periods of European history: structuring the feud between the Pope and the Holy Roman Emperor and their struggle with the self-determining new kingdoms and other new forms of polity; fuelling the arrogance and the ambitions of the new ruling classes of the new absolutisms; inspiring and energising those who sought to overthrow old regimes or to win national independence. But the evolution of the reality of social organisation across the human world has made the idea of 'sovereignty' into an anachronism and an illusion, inappropriate as a theoretical explanation of the totalising structure of society. If the word must still be used, then it must now be understood as a collective noun which conveniently identifies a bundle of the most general internal and external powers of a society's constitutional organs ('sovereign rights') rather than the iconic name of some indivisible supernatural monad.[54] And it is precisely in the European Union that this new conception of social reality is most clearly evidenced.

[54] Rigaudière suggests that, prior to its reconceiving by Jean Bodin (*Six Livres de la République*, 1576), sovereignty was 'principally defined as a bundle [*faisceau*] of specific rights' rather than as 'a global power, a "pure essence" from which the state derives its form' and hence that there could be a sharing of such 'royal rights' or 'rights of sovereignty' ('L'invention de la souveraineté', in *Pouvoirs* (fn. 50 above), pp. 5–20, at pp. 16, 17). Bodin certainly claimed that before him 'no jurist or political philosopher has in fact attempted to define [sovereignty]' (*Six Books of the Commonwealth* (tr. M. J. Tooley; Oxford, Basil Blackwell; no date), I, 8, p. 25). Hobbes would follow Bodin in asserting that 'the Rights, which make the Essence of Sovereignty' are 'incommunicable and inseparable' (Hobbes, *Leviathan*, ch. 18).

But the wonderful luxuriance of medieval thought on the problem of the theoretical basis of society, after the re-emergence in Western Europe of Greek and Roman ideas in the twelfth-century renaissance, contains an intense and complex dialectic of opposing conceptions on every aspect of that problem (the sovereignty of the people and the sovereignty of the law, the divine right of kings *versus* the concession of monarchy by the people, the society of all human beings *versus* the self-contained polity, social contract *versus* natural sociability as the foundational basis of society, natural law and natural right *versus* positive law as the will of the people or of the monarch, government above the law or government under the law). No consensus ever emerged from the intellectual struggle among these and many other competing ideas, but they provided the raw material from which emerged, from the sixteenth century onwards, the ingenious resolution of older ideas contained in the much more consensual theories of liberal democracy which are our inheritance today.

6.34 The true social reality of the European Union is, and always has been, something quite different from its self-denying, self-distorting and self-disabling myth. *The European Union is a union of European societies whose legal constitutions are integrated in the legal constitution of the Union.*

6.35 Such a conception of European Union has a whole series of profound implications.

(1) The European Union is a European *society*, a society of the societies of the member states of the Union. Constitutional institutions can only be legitimated within a society which transcends them. The institutions of the European Union are doubly legitimated, within Union society and within the societies of the member states. Where there is law, there must be society. *Ubi ius, ibi societas.*[55]

(2) European Union society is a society whose ideal is Fergusonian *civil society*. 'That is the most happy state, which is most beloved by its subjects; and they are the most happy men, whose hearts are engaged to a community, in which they find every object of generosity and zeal, and a scope to the exercise of every talent, and of every virtuous disposition.'[56]

(3) The Union's legal constitution is the legal effect of an unwritten *social contract* made by the societies of the member states which is evidenced by, but not confined to, the Union treaties. It follows that each member state owes social and legal obligations to all the other member states in respect of the legal authority of the Union legal constitution. From this it follows also that a member state may not modify unilaterally its relationship to that legal authority.

(4) The constitutional organs of the member states are also constitutional organs of the European Union. The institutions of the European Union are also constitutional organs of the member states. The constitutional system of the Union contains and is contained by the constitutional systems of the member states. It is both internal and external. It is not an hierarchical superior above the national systems but a lateral co-ordination of the national systems.

(5) The *distribution of powers* among the constitutional organs of the Union, including the institutions of the Union and the constitutional organs of the member states, is determined in accordance with the social

[55] For the view that the same principle applies at the universal level, to the international society of the whole human race, see ch. 10 below, and *Eunomia*, ch. 1.

[56] A. Ferguson, *History of Civil Society* (fn. 12 above), p. 59.

contract of the Union and in accordance with the state of its legal constitution at any given time.

(6) The general will of each of the member states contributes to the formation of the *general will of the European Union.* But, thanks to its own political and legal systems, the general will of the Union is distinct from, and not merely an aggregation of, the general wills of the member states.

(7) The *common interest of the European Union* is distinct from, and not merely an aggregation of, the common interest of each of its member states. The common interest of the Union is an integral part of the common interest of each of its member states.

(8) The European Union is an *international legal person*, alongside the international legal persons which are its member states. It asserts the common interest of the Union within international society.

(9) *Europe's ideals*, its values and aspirations, including the ideals of liberal democracy and economic liberalism, animate the societies of the member states and are the priceless but costly inheritance of centuries of intense social experience. They are now the inheritance of the European Union. They must animate and determine every aspect of its activity and its future development.

(10) The animating spirit of the European Union's self-constituting as a society may be expressed in the form of *six theses of Europe's ideal future.*[57]

(i) *Europe is always a potentiality, never an actuality.*
European society is a living organism, a permanent process of human self-transforming, from what it sees that it has been, through what it sees that it is, to what it sees that it can be. What we are can always be transformed into what we could be.

(ii) *Europe accepts responsibility for its ever-present past.*
European society has a past which contains terrible darkness and wonderful light, an inspiration and a warning. We cannot escape our past. Our unique past allows us and requires us to make a better future.

[57] 'I understand, he said. You mean the city whose establishment we have described whose home is in the ideal. For I think that it can be found nowhere on earth. Well, said I, perhaps there is a pattern of it laid up in heaven for him who wishes to contemplate it and so beholding it constitute himself its citizen.' Plato, *The Republic*, bk IX, 592a–b, in *The Collected Dialogues* (fn. 35 above), p. 819.

(iii) *Europe accepts its unique responsibility for the future of the world.* Europe has made the world as it is. We have unique intellectual and practical experience in the making and management of human society. The natural focus of Europe's concern for the human future is the whole of the human world.

(iv) *European society is more than the sum of its institutions.* A society is a self-constituting of human beings. Social institutions are a means, necessary but not sufficient, by which we make possible our survival and our well-being as human beings. European society is a member of international society, the society of all societies, the society of all-humanity.

(v) *Europe recognises its constitutive ideals.* An ideal is an imperious *idea* of the better and an insatiable *desire* to make things better. Our ideals lead us to seek to constitute ourselves, as individual human beings and as societies, in such a way as to become better. They are a destination which we always seek and never reach. Our ideals are a permanent denial of the evil and the madness and the self-inflicted suffering which plague the human world.

(vi) *Europe makes itself by choosing to become what it could be.* Europe can choose to be the instrument of the actualising of the ideal at the level of all-humanity. Such is Europe's permanent potentiality, its greatest destiny, its ideal future. If we do this in the pursuit of our highest ideals, then it is possible that the human future, not merely the European future, could be better than the human past. We may be at the end of humanity's pre-history, the beginning of a new kind of human history, the history of a humanity which, at last, chooses to become what it could be.

New Europe

6.36 A European Union which is seen, at last, as a new and unique form of integration of the legal constitutions of its member states within a new and unique form of European society is a great achievement in the overcoming of the worst, and a surpassing of the best, in European history. It is a society to which we might even wish to belong.

7

The crisis of European constitutionalism

Reflections on a half-revolution

Constitutional psychology: France, Great Britain – Constitutional psychology: Germany – Half-revolution – The presence of the past – Ideas and illusions – Making the future

The creation of the European Communities was a diplomatic and constitutional coup d'état *within European history, a revolutionary re-constituting from outside of European societies which had long, complex and disparate histories of their own self-constituting. Departing from radically different national starting-points and moving towards an unknown destination, it was an inherently hazardous enterprise.*

The different national constitutional psychologies of its member states were not accidents of history but specific distillations of intense national social experience and of the self-conceiving of the different national societies within the self-contemplating of their separate public minds.

European integration also intruded into the separate development of shared idea-structures of national self-constituting, especially those of liberal democracy and capitalism, and into shared idea-structures of the co-existence of the European societies, especially those of diplomacy and war.

The latest revolution in Europe has the familiar hall-marks of revolution – confusion of motives, clash of interests, a dynamic of social change which is beyond the control of those who made the revolution and of those who must deal with its consequences. It is a troubling precedent for revolutionary social transformation at the global level, the level of all-humanity.

> The task confronting the lawgiver, and all who seek to set up a constitution of a particular kind, is not only, or even mainly, to set it up, but rather to keep it going.
>
> Aristotle, *The Politics*, VI.5 (tr. T. A. Sinclair; Harmondsworth, Penguin; 1962)

Constitutional psychology: France, Great Britain

7.1 Europe is a forest of symbols. It is the name of a place, the name of a past, the name of a subjectivity. For those of us who live within the European symbol-forest, our imagination is hardly powerful enough to see Europe as a totality, to objectify our passionate subjectivity. Those who see us from outside see our extraordinary achievements – all the good we have done, all the evil we have done – and they must wonder what the word Europe symbolises, what possible totality could integrate such a place, such a past, such a subjectivity.

7.2 And, indeed, one of our extraordinary achievements, for better and for worse, has been our self-exteriorisation. Is there any human life anywhere untouched by Europe, any place untransformed, any history unchanged, any human mind unmodified by whatever it is that the word Europe symbolises? To know its self, Europe must look also into the obscure mirror of all that is not-Europe.

7.3 In the Preface to the 1869 edition of his History of France, Jules Michelet describes in famous words how and why he undertook that work.

'[France] had annals, but not a history. Eminent men had studied it particularly from the political point of view. No one had entered into the infinite detail of the diverse developments of its activity . . . No one had yet seen it in the living unity of the natural and geographic elements which have constituted it. I was the first to see it as a soul and a person.'[1]

'There was a great light, and I saw France.'[2]

7.4 Were he living at this hour, we would beg Michelet to see, not France now, but Europe, to see Europe as a soul and as a person. Under the great light of all that we have lived through in the twentieth century, we would beg him urgently, desperately to tell us: how should we Europeans imagine our totality? How should we constitute ourselves as practical subjectivity? And he would certainly have told Europe what he told France – that we Europeans have made ourselves, we have constituted ourselves, subliminally, as it were, nonchalantly. And now we are called upon to constitute ourselves consciously, purposively. And it may be a task too much for us Europeans, as France's self-constituting

[1] J. Michelet, *Histoire de la France* (Paris; no date; preface of 1869), I, p. i. (Present author's translations, here and below.)

[2] *Ibid.*, p. i.

seemed, to Michelet in his darker moments, to be almost too big a task for the people of France.

'I derived from history itself a great and too little noticed fact. That is the powerful *work of itself on itself*, by which France, through its own progress, continually transforms its raw elements.'[3]

'Thus each people goes, making itself, engendering itself, grinding, amalgamating elements which no doubt remain in an obscure and confused state, but which are small in comparison with what was the long work of the great soul.'[4]

'France has made France . . . *Man is his own Prometheus*.'[5]

7.5 It was at a time of extraordinary French *travail de soi sur soi* in 1789–91 that Edmund Burke was caused to look across the Channel and to reflect on the nature of the self-constituting of nations. He was appalled by the way in which the French nation was destroying its historic self by its own efforts, by what he saw as a sort of rationalistic folly. Like Michelet, Burke was inspired to find eloquent words to express the mysterious, unspeakable essence of nation-making – of nations in general, and of the British nation in particular. In so doing, he would express a deep and perennial aspect of British social psychology – an aspect which the British have brought to their participation in the European Union.

7.6 'The science of constructing a commonwealth, or renovating it, or reforming it, is, like every other experimental science, not to be taught a priori. Nor is it a short experience that can instruct us in that practical science, because the real effects of moral causes are not always immediate; . . . In states there are often some obscure and almost latent causes, things which appear at first view of little moment, on which a very great part of its prosperity or adversity may most essentially depend.'[6]

'It is with infinite caution that any man ought to venture upon pulling down an edifice, which has answered in any tolerable degree for ages the common purposes of society, or on building it up again, without having models and patterns of approved utility before his eyes.'[7]

'You will observe, that from Magna Charta to the Declaration of Right [the Bill of Rights of 1688/9], it has been the uniform policy of our

[3] *Ibid.*, p. vii (emphasis in original). The phrase which Michelet emphasised is *travail de soi sur soi* in French.

[4] *Ibid.*, p. vii. [5] *Ibid.*, p. viii (emphasis in original).

[6] E. Burke, *Reflections on the Revolution in France* (1790) (London, Dent (Everyman's Library); 1910), p. 58.

[7] *Ibid.*, p. 59.

constitution to claim and assert our liberties, as an entailed inheritance derived to us from our forefathers, and to be transmitted to posterity... This policy appears to me to be the result of profound reflection; or rather the happy effect of following nature, which is wisdom without reflection, and above it...'[8]

7.7 With those two phrases we reach the deepest waters of British constitutional psychology. *The happy effect of following nature. Wisdom without reflection.*

'[Our political system] moves on through the varied tenor of perpetual decay, fall, renovation, and progression. Thus, by preservation of nature in the conduct of the state, in what we improve, we are never wholly new; in what we retain, we are never obsolete... In this choice of inheritance [as our philosophical analogy] we have given to our frame of polity the image of a relation of blood; binding up the constitution of our country with our dearest domestic ties; adopting our fundamental laws into the bosom of our family affections; keeping inseparable, and cherishing with the warmth of all their combined and mutually reflected charities, our state, our hearths, our sepulchres, and our altars.'[9]

7.8 That was Edmund Burke, somewhat carried away by his own eloquence, in his *Reflections on the Revolution in France* (1790). His words help us to begin to establish a deep-structural parallel with what Michelet was saying, and also a great deep-structural contrast. And his words enable us to establish a parallel and a contrast with Hegel, and German constitutional psychology. To talk about these things is to talk about constitutional psychology, but one could as well echo Montesquieu and speak of 'the spirit of the constitutions' of France, Germany and Britain. Our great and urgent task now is to look further, to find the spirit of the constitution of Europe.[10]

7.9 In an early writing of 1802, Hegel diagnosed the problem of Germany: '*Deutschland ist kein Staat mehr.*'[11] England, France, Spain,

[8] *Ibid.*, p. 31. [9] *Ibid.*, p. 32.

[10] 'Better is it to say that the government most conformable to nature is that which best agrees with the humour and disposition of the people in whose favour it is established.' C. de Montesquieu, *The Spirit of the Laws* (1748) (tr. T. Nugent; New York, Hafner Publishing Co.; 1949), bk I.3, p. 6.

[11] 'Germany is no longer a state.' G. W. F. Hegel, *Die Verfassung Deutschlands*, in *Sämtliche Werke* (ed. G. Lasson; Leipzig, Verlag von Felix Meiner; 1923), v, p. 3. The full text was not published until 1893. The circumstances of its composition, over a number of years, are described in G. W. F. Hegel, *Politische Schriften* (Frankfurt-am-Main, Suhrkamp Verlag;

and others, were states, but somehow Germany had disintegrated and had thereby suffered culturally, economically, and politically. In 1802 Hegel had not yet developed the vast intellectual system which would propose a unified meaning for all human history. But it is significant that the German problem presented itself to him as one of unification or, perhaps, reunification. How could the centuries-old multiplicity of Germany be surpassed, so as to achieve the unity of the great European monarchies? It was a challenge worthy of the dialectic of World History, a challenge of *Aufhebung*, to create a German unity-in-multiplicity, a unity-in-multiplicity which was of world-historical significance but which was also uniquely German.[12]

7.10 Hereafter it will be suggested that Hegel's 1802 essay, *Die Verfassung Deutschlands* (The Constitution or, perhaps, Constituting of Germany), with its focus on enforced unification (or, perhaps, reunification), contains not only the seeds of subsequent German history but

1966), *Nachwort* by J. Habermas, pp. 347–8. The whole essay is written in terms of *Staat*, with minimal references to *Volk* and *Nation*. One of Hegel's last writings was an essay on the British Reform Bill (which would become the Reform Act 1832). Hegel gloomily predicted that the transfer of power to 'the people' was sowing the seeds of revolution, since the English monarchy was not powerful enough to arbitrate between the people and traditional privileged classes (G. W. F. Hegel, *Über die englische Reformbill*, in *Politische Schriften* (above), pp. 277–321). Habermas (at p. 368) says that the worried pessimism of Hegel's last political writings reflects his concern that France and England, rather than Prussia, might represent the true historical reality. Marcuse quotes R. Haym, who called the essay a document of fear and anxiety. 'Here, too, Hegel's philosophy ends in doubt and resignation.' H. Marcuse, *Reason and Revolution – Hegel and the Rise of Social Theory* (London, Routledge; 1941), pp. 247–8. Compare the words attributed by Herodotus (fifth century BCE) to a visiting Persian Prince: 'Whatever the despot does, he does with knowledge; but the people have not even that; how can they have knowledge, who have neither learnt nor for themselves seen what is best, but ever rush headlong and drive blindly onward, like a river in spate? Let those stand for democracy who wish ill to Persia; but let us choose a company of the best men [?Hegel's universal class] and invest these with power. For we ourselves shall be of their company; and where we have the best men, there 'tis like that we shall have the best counsels.' Herodotus, *Histories* (tr. A. D. Godley; London, William Heinemann (Loeb Classical Library); 1921), III.81, p. 107. And Aristotle (fourth century BCE) speaks of an 'elective tyranny' which, he says, is a form of despotism acquiesced in by its subjects (*Politics* (tr. T. A. Sinclair; Harmondsworth, Penguin), III. 14, p. 136).

[12] 'It follows, therefore, that the constitution of any given nation depends in general on the character and development of its self-consciousness, . . . The proposal to give a constitution – even one more or less rational in content – a priori to a nation would be a happy thought overlooking precisely that factor in a constitution which makes it more than an ens rationis. Hence every nation has the constitution appropriate to it and suitable for it.' G. W. F. Hegel, *Philosophy of Right* (1821) (tr. T. M. Knox; London, Oxford University Press; 1952), § 274, p. 179.

also the seeds of a European unification which is really a reunification, and the seeds of the present crisis of Europe's reunifying.

7.11 Hegel would find the solution in the idea of the rational state. The state, as a system of rationally organised power, could be an expression of the hidden unity of the German nation and at the same time the means of constituting the German nation. The German state would make the German nation. The German nation would make the German state. The Spirit of the Nation, the *Volksgeist*, would manifest itself in the reality of the rational state. And the rational state was also the culmination of world history, the ultimate manifestation of the *Weltgeist*. All rational states are the same. Each rational state is unique. (Such are the advantages of dialectical thinking!) The natural unity-community of the Greek *polis* was unrealisable in the modern world. The gothic naturalism of the British constitution was deplorable. The revolutionary populism of French republicanism was self-destroying. For Hegel, humanity now had before it the possibility of a form of social organisation which was universal and particular, with the infinite particularity of nations actualised in the universality of the rational state.

7.12 We may treat these three constitutional perspectives as paradigmatic, and give them labels. The Michelet perspective is *nation*. Nation is the central complex of French constitutional psychology. The Burkeian perspective is *society*. Society is the central complex of British constitutional psychology. The Hegelian perspective is *state*. State is the central complex of German constitutional psychology. Society, nation and state haunt the whole process of European reunification. The European Union can only be a product of European social subjectivity, and yet the European Union is, subjectively, neither society nor nation nor state.

7.13 What Michelet, Burke and Hegel had in common was the spirit of the age, the age of revolution, a new condition of European consciousness which, we now know, contained in embryo all the *grandeurs et misères* of subsequent European history. The European eighteenth century closed not only in revolution, and the spirit of revolution. It closed in an unstable union of rationality and subjectivity. It is as if there had been a child of a most unlikely marriage, of Voltaire and Rousseau. Not such an unlikely marriage, perhaps, as each was himself an uncomfortable union of the cold and the passionate, the rationalising and the prophetic. Not only in the fine arts and literature, but also in social organisation, Europe had to find new ways of reconciling individuality and universality. The rationalism of post-medieval Europe could not be unlearned. But the inwardness (*Innerlichkeit*) of a more ancient Europe was reasserting itself, and could no longer be suppressed.

7.14 The intellectual parents of writers such as Michelet, Burke and Hegel were Vico and Herder, pioneers of an historiography which sought to resurrect the inward essence of the past, to create retrospective syntheses of significance, finding universality in great particularity, finding objectivity in pure subjectivity, treating with the greatest respect every form of human self-expression, especially those by which we hear most authentically the voice of the people – poetry, song, myth, fable, custom.

7.15 Herder argued eloquently for a new kind of historical imagination, characterised by such verbs as *sympathisieren, mitfühlen, einfühlen,* inviting the historian, not merely to generalise about past events, but to seek to reconstruct the mentality of a nation and, indeed, of all-humanity.[13] Vico proposed a form of history which was really the history of the human mind, the human mind discovering itself historically. He spoke of early institutions which embody the wisdom of the human race, 'judgment without reflection felt by a whole order, a whole people, a whole nation or the entire human race'.[14] Decades before Burke, he used words almost identical to those used by Burke in the passage quoted earlier.

7.16 The followers of Vico and Herder laid themselves open to the criticism – which has continued to the present day – that they were mere fantasists, retrospective mythologists, shameless mystifiers, agents of reaction. Such was not biographically true in the case of Burke, the

[13] J. G. Herder, *Auch eine Philosophie der Geschichte zur Bildung der Menschheit* (Still Another Philosophy of History for the Education of Mankind) (1774) (München/Wien, C. Hanser Verlag; 1984), pp. 591–689, at p. 612. Herder speaks of *der gemeinschaftliche Geist* (the mind or spirit of a community), *der Gefühl einer Nation* (the feeling of a nation), and of the *Seele, Herz, Tiefe* (soul, heart, depth) of a people or nation, the *Mittelpunkt der Glückseligkeit* (centre of gravity of its happiness) (at pp. 607, 612, 618). For a discussion of Herder's wider intellectual significance, see E. Neff, *The Poetry of History. The Contribution of Literature and Literary Scholarship to the Writing of History since Voltaire* (New York; Columbia University Press; 1947), ch. 2.

[14] *The New Science of Giambattista Vico* (3rd edn, 1744) (tr. T. G. Bergin and M. H. Fish; Ithaca, Cornell University Press; 1970), p. 21. 'There must in the nature of human institutions be a mental language common to all nations, which uniformly grasps the substance of things feasible in human social life and expresses it with as many diverse modifications as these same things have diverse aspects' (p. 25).

supporter of the American rebellious colonists; nor of Michelet, infatuated with the best of the French Revolution; nor even of Hegel, who deplored the *Schwärmerei* of Teutonomania and of the then-fashionable nostalgic medievalism. Their interest in the past was a necessary part of their concern for the future. Revolution is always in part also reaction. And the voices of the revolutionary period were telling us that the future is contained in the past because the future will contain the past.

7.17 We have not needed Freud to teach us that you cannot argue with the unconscious mind, with the reasons of the heart. Society, nation, state are archetypes within the collective constitutional consciousness of Europe, full of Europe's collective past. They have continued to produce dramatic social effects throughout the nineteenth and twentieth centuries, wonderful effects and terrible effects. The master-builders of today's revolutionary reconstituting of Europe must not be allowed to forget a crucial lesson of experience. To ignore the unconscious roots of human social behaviour is to risk creating social instability, or worse.

7.18 We may use the word *society* to identify the totality within which British people believe that they live. Of course, this is not the word that the man- or woman-in-the-street would knowingly use.[15] The truth is that we do not think about such matters very much in abstract terms. And we do not teach our children anything about such matters in school. We do not have what the Americans call Civics classes. In Britain we think so far as necessary, and no further.[16]

7.19 The word society is supposed to symbolise the fact that the British people have very imprecise ideas about the formal, legal nature of the nation, but have a strong view that we, those of us who belong to the society – we, the people – are bound by the most profound and the most substantial bonds of social mutuality.[17] The people in general have

[15] However, a recent British Prime Minister (Margaret Thatcher) initiated a lively, if diffuse, public debate when she said that 'there is no such thing as society' – apparently reflecting the influence of F. Hayek, as, for example, in *The Road to Serfdom* (London, Routledge; 1944), ch. 3. The implication was that individuals, rather than governments, are ultimately responsible for their own well-being.

[16] 'English people seem to me in general to have great difficulty in grasping general and indefinite ideas.' A. de Tocqueville, *Voyages en Angleterre et en Irlande* (ed. J. P. Mayer; Paris, Gallimard; 1957), p. 131 (present author's translation, here and in the following quotations). De Tocqueville, writing in 1835, quotes a conversation with J. S. Mill, who confirmed his view. 'The habits or the nature of our mind do not incline us to general ideas' (p. 132).

[17] De Tocqueville found that the English character contains two apparently contradictory tendencies. 'I cannot understand how the *spirit of association* and the *spirit of exclusion* . . . can

uncertain ideas about the changing territorial extent of their country.[18] Probably the majority do not even know the official title of the country, a title which is simply a bureaucratic invention. Our national anthem is addressed to God and asks that the Queen may long reign over us, whoever 'us' may be. One of our most popular national songs instructs someone or something called 'Britannia' to rule the waves, and boasts and warns that 'Britons', whoever they may be, never will be slaves.

7.20 Tom Paine, an unreliable witness, the British radical who interfered so vigorously in the American and the French Revolutions, expressed the idea in the following characteristic way.

'Some writers have so confounded society with government, as to leave little or no distinction between them; whereas they are not only different, but have different origins. Society is produced by our wants and government by our wickedness; the former promotes our happiness positively by uniting our affections, the latter negatively by restraining our vices... Society in every state is a blessing, but government even in its best state is but a necessary evil... Government, like dress, is the badge of lost innocence; the palaces of kings are built on the ruins of the bowers of paradise.'[19]

7.21 Paine was articulating what is probably the view of very many British people (and, certainly, very many American people) to this day. It is the same idea that lay behind Burke's words quoted earlier, when he said that we bind up 'the constitution of our country with our dearest domestic ties... keeping inseparable... our state, our hearths, our sepulchres, and our altars'. But Paine's words also contain a sub-text of anarchism or misarchism (as Nietzsche called it),[20] which is, and always

exist in such a developed way in the same people, and often be combined in such an intimate way... I am led to think, after reflecting on the matter, that the spirit of individuality is the basis of the English character. Association is a means which intelligence and necessity have suggested to achieve the objectives which individual forces cannot achieve' (p. 144).

18 There are so-called British Islands which are not parts of the United Kingdom (and have a separate status in the European Communities). And the Queen is sovereign of 'her other realms and territories' – some within the British Islands, others elsewhere – in separate right from her title as Queen of the United Kingdom.

19 T. Paine, *Common Sense* (1776), in *Common Sense and Other Political Writings* (ed. N. F. Adkins; New York, Bobbs Merrill Co. (American Heritage Series); 1953), p. 4.

20 F. Nietzsche, *The Genealogy of Morals* (1887), Second Essay (tr. F. Golffing; Garden City NY, Doubleday & Co. (Doubleday Anchor Books); 1956), § 21 p. 211. 'The natural impulse of the English people is to resist authority.' W. Bagehot, *The English Constitution* (1867) (Oxford, Oxford University Press (The World's Classics); 1928), p. 254.

has been, not far below the surface of British (and American) social consciousness.

7.22 It is worth remembering that the two British prophets of liberal democracy – Thomas Hobbes and John Locke – proposed theories of the total social phenomenon, not merely of the nation (still less of the English nation) or the state (still less of the English state). It was Locke, transcending and transmuting Hobbes, who made possible the next phase of the British permanent revolution by popularising the mysterious and paradoxical and powerful idea of self-government, the ideal of a society which governs itself through its system of government, a society of and for the many in which the society-members are their own subjects, a body politic which, to use the ancient metaphor, is like the human body in that it is as much many as it is one.

7.23 It was, on the other hand, the almost-French Rousseau who, in another mysterious and powerful paradox, fused society and government into a single ideal complex, a *corps social*, a one-from-many, a conception of organic social unity which played a part – a different part – both in France's revolutionary self-reconstituting as nation and in Germany's self-reconstituting as state.

7.24 A whole series of profound systematic and legal consequences have flowed from the distinctive constitutional psychology of the British people.

(1) We have no written constitution, because we do not wish to establish public power as systematically separate from all other social power or to give supreme society-making power to the judges.[21]

(2) British society is emotionally, if not formally, a federation. Scotland, Wales and Northern Ireland have distinct organisational systems. But, more generally, we feel ourselves to be a society of societies; we each have a hundred loyalties in addition to our loyalty to the total society. In Britain, politics and religion are team-sports, and team-sports are politics and religion by other means.

[21] Jeremy Bentham, eloquent and energetic apostle of social rationalism in Britain in the first decades of the nineteenth century, drafted a Constitutional Code, codifying what seemed to him the best which could be learned from constitutional experience (especially in England, France and the United States of America). For the text, see *The Works of Jeremy Bentham* (ed. J. Bowring; Edinburgh, Tait; 1838–43), IX. His lead was not followed. Britain adopted a gradualist approach of piecemeal constitutional reform, beginning with the Reform Act 1832. See E. Halévy, *The Growth of Philosophical Radicalism* (tr. M. Morris; London, Faber and Faber; 1928), pt 3, ch. 2.

(3) We have tried to believe in the reality of the representative character of parliament. As Sir Thomas Smith of Cambridge University said, in a book published in 1589 (a century before Locke's *Two Treatises of Government*): 'And the consent of the parliament is taken to be every man's consent.'[22]

(4) Although law has been as important in the making and the imagining of the English polity as it was in ancient Rome, our language has notoriously confused *ius* and *lex* in the one word *law*. For us law is never merely made; it is also found.[23]

(5) We have, until recently, resisted the term *public law*. Public power is subject to the same law, administered by the same courts, as any other social power.[24]

(6) In the absence of a written constitution, the principle of the Rule of Law is not an a priori constitutional principle but simply a generalisation from the behaviour of the courts in relation to the powers of public authorities. It reflects a comforting idea of our law as a means of freedom rather than merely a method of social control.[25]

[22] T. Smith, *De republica anglorum* (ed. L. Alston; Cambridge, Cambridge University Press; 1906), bk II, ch. 1.

[23] So-called (and much criticised) Legal Positivism (as expounded by John Austin in his *Province of Jurisprudence Determined* (1832), following Hobbes and Bentham) was, perhaps, unEnglish in its narrowly and rigidly legislative view of law. See further in ch. 2 § 1 above.

[24] The classic argument against the idea of 'administrative law' is set out in A. V. Dicey, *An Introduction to the Study of the Law of the Constitution* (1885) (ed. E. C. S. Wade; London, The Macmillan Press; 10th edn, 1959), ch. 22, pp. 328ff. Although the terms 'public law' and 'administrative law' are now being used in Britain to refer to law and procedures applied to public authorities, such law is still conceived (at some cost in theoretical coherence) as being part of general law administered by the ordinary courts.

[25] One of the great landmarks of the coming-to-consciousness of the Rule of Law principle was the case of Entick *v.* Carrington (S.T. XIX, 1045; E. N. Williams, *The Eighteenth Century Constitution 1688–1815: Documents and Commentary* (Cambridge, Cambridge University Press; 1970)). The agent of the Secretary of State had entered the plaintiff's premises searching for seditious material. The agent was held liable to pay damages of £300 because he had no legal authority to search. 'No man can set foot upon my ground without my licence, but he is liable to an action in trespass . . . If he admits the fact, he is bound to shew, by way of justification, that some positive law has empowered or excused him.' (Lord Camden in *ibid.*, p. 395).

It is interesting to compare this with the comparable structures in German law: the doctrine of the *Vorbehalt des Gesetzes* (public interference with the freedom of the citizen requires a legal basis); the a priori character of fundamental rights (Article 1.2, *Grundgesetz*); and the right to free development of a person's personality (Article 2.1). See T. Maunz and

(7) We have no fundamental rights. For a thousand years we have spoken of 'the ancient rights and liberties' of the people. No one knows what they are, and no court has ever determined what they are; but the idea has been used, time and again, to tame over-ambitious monarchs, and to dress revolution in the clothes of reaction.[26]

(8) We have never regarded our monarchs as the embodiment of the nation, and, for a thousand years, we have told them that they are 'under the law', in principle if not in practice. This has been made easier by the fact that the English majority of the population have found themselves blessed with monarchs whom they could regard as foreign – Danish, Norman, Welsh, Scottish, Dutch, German.

(9) We have felt no need of an idea of sovereignty to express the unity of the nation. We have, or had, the supremacy of the Queen in parliament – which, until the United Kingdom acceded to membership of the European Communities, was thought to mean that there were no legal limits on the power of the Queen in parliament, and no possibility of judicial review of parliamentary legislation.[27]

(10) So, finally, and very important in the present context, we have no conception of the *state* in the internal sense. There is no 'British state', in the internal sense. Public powers are distributed among a vast constellation of institutions, extending from the Queen in person and a notional legal person called the Crown to the powers of countless forms of indeterminate semi-public agencies.

7.25 It might seem that it would be difficult to organise a modern society in such a vacuum of legal-constitutional order. What we have done is to generate a fantasy constitution to fill the gap. Our fantasy constitution is a monarchy in which all public powers are vested in the monarch, all government is carried out in the name of the monarch, and the rituals of public power are full of numinous monarchical events.

R. Zippelius, *Deutsches Staatsrecht* (München, Verlag C. H. Beck; 28th edn, 1991), 12.III.4, pp. 92ff. Cf. Montesquieu: 'Liberty is a right of doing what the laws permit . . . ' (*Spirit of the Laws* (fn. 10 above), bk XI.3, p. 150).

[26] By the Human Rights Act 1998 certain provisions of the European Convention for the Protection of Human Rights and Fundamental Freedoms (1950) were given legal effect in the United Kingdom. The limited character of that legal effect means that the 'human rights' in question cannot properly be regarded as 'fundamental rights' but rather, perhaps, as 'rights of general application'.

[27] On the supposed sovereignty of the British parliament, see P. Allott, 'The courts and parliament – who whom?', in 38 *Cambridge Law Journal* (1979), pp. 79–117.

7.26 A cold-eyed commentator on our constitution, writing in 1867, said that the whole system depends ultimately on the ignorance of the mass of the British people. Walter Bagehot said that the strength of our constitution lies in the fact that 'efficient' power is exercised behind a 'dignified' facade, the 'theatrical show' as he called it, of a monarchical constitution.[28] In recent years, more than ever, the show-business of monarchy has diverted attention from a vigorously self-presidentialising executive branch of government. But one may doubt whether the British people have ever been deceived by the show or the game of the British constitution. It may well be that it has only been the governing class which has mesmerised itself into treating the appearance as the reality.

7.27 In any event, we are now living through a sort of crisis of constitutional consciousness in Britain. The people have, by and large, ceased to believe, if they ever did believe, in the appearances of the constitution, in the natural authority of those who exercise public power. There is talk of a written constitution, of a bill of rights, even some talk of republicanism. And, by an extraordinary coincidence which is probably not a coincidence, all this is happening at a time when we have become involved in a European Union whose constitutional order seems to the British people to be an alien thing, a negation of their idea of the essential nature of constitutionalism.

7.28 But we must look further into the collective minds of France and Germany before we can face the appearance and the reality of the European Union itself.

7.29 In 1787 the Abbé Sieyès called for the adunation of the people of France in the form of France as nation.[29] It seems that he invented that word in the French language; the word adunation already existed in English (presumably as a survival of Norman French).

'What is a nation? A body of associates living under a common law and represented by the same legislature, etc.' 'What is the will of the nation?

[28] W. Bagehot, *The English Constitution* (1867) (fn. 20 above) pp. 3ff, 235ff. '[W]e have whole classes unable to understand the idea of a constitution' (p. 34). '[O]f all the nations in the world the English are perhaps the least a nation of pure philosophers' (p. 41). In an additional chapter added to the 2nd edition of 1872, Bagehot wondered whether the deferential basis of British society could survive the universalisation of the suffrage and the provision of education to the mass of the people. For an analysis of the continuing role of fantasy in the British constitution, see P. Allott, 'The theory of the British constitution', in H. Gross and R. Harrison (eds.), *Jurisprudence: Cambridge Essays* (Oxford, Oxford University Press; 1992), pp. 173–206.

[29] J.-D. Bredin, *Sieyès – clé de la Révolution française* (Paris, Editions de Fallois; 1988), p. 112.

It is the result of the individual wills, as the nation is the assembling of the individuals.'[30]

7.30 On 17 June 1789 the Tiers Etat decided to call itself the Assemblée Nationale. The Declaration of the Rights of Man and of the Citizen (26 August 1789) declared that 'the essential principle of all sovereignty lies in the Nation'. The constitution of 1791 declared that 'national sovereignty belongs to the people'. At the Battle of Valmy on 20 September 1792, the first engagement of the Revolutionary Wars, the French soldiers rallied to the cry of *Vive la nation!* Already the people were dying for the nation. The new national anthem was conceived in Strasbourg during the same campaign, and the soldiers from Marseille went to Paris singing in the streets: *Allons enfants de la patrie!* When the *Chant du départ* was written in 1794 for the anniversary of the taking of the Bastille, a thousand years of monarchy had been terminated: *La république nous appelle. Patrie. Peuple. Nation. République.* A revolution in four words.

7.31 We can also express the revolutionary essence of the French Revolution in two sentences. France had been a *patrie*, organised as a monarchy. After the Revolution the people of France became a nation organised as a republic. French social consciousness, at its deepest level, had changed. (One might add that, since 1958, it has been possible to detect a revenant of monarchy in the French constitutional machine.) As already suggested, Britain's permanent revolution can be summarised in a single sentence. Permanent revolution has produced a society of the people organised in the form of a republic masquerading as a monarchy.[31]

30 E. Sieyès, *Qu'est-ce que le Tiers état?* (1789) (ed. R. Zapperi; Genève, Librairie Droz; 1970), pp. 126, 204–5 (present author's translation). To understand the way in which a deeply traditional idea had thus been radically reconceived, it is only necessary to recall the words of King Louis XIV: 'In France the nation is not a separate body, it dwells entirely in the person of the King', or the words of King Louis XV (addressing the *parlement* of Paris): 'The rights and interests of the nation, which you dare to make into a body apart from the monarch, are of necessity one with my own, and lie in my hands only.' See P. Goubert, *The Ancien Régime. French Society 1600–1750* (1969) (tr. S. Cox; London, George Weidenfeld & Nicolson; 1973), pp. 3–4.

31 Voltaire had characterised the English constitutional system as 'a unique system of government, in which they have conserved all that is useful in monarchy, and all that is essential in a republic'. *L'Eloge historique de la Raison* (1774), quoted in Voltaire, *Lettres philosophiques* (ed. R. Naves; Paris, Garnier; 1988), p. 214 (present author's translation). De Tocqueville makes an interesting comparison between England and pre-1848 Switzerland: 'Take it all

7.32 Alfred Cobban's provocative phrase – 'the myth of the French Revolution'[32] – was intended to draw attention to the question of what actually changed in the social and economic structure of France at the time of the Revolution – and what were the true causes of that change. Torrents of ink have flowed on those questions. They remain passionately controversial to this day.

7.33 Cobban's answer, like de Tocqueville's, was that not very much changed that was not changing in any case for other reasons. His use of the word 'myth' is misleading, however, if it is taken as denying that there was a profound change of French political consciousness at the time of the Revolution. The question is: what was the nature of that change? 'The Revolution was many things. It was an attempt to reform the government of France . . . But it was also . . . the embodiment of a great idea, the idea of the sovereignty of the people, or nation.'[33]

7.34 The French Revolution was not merely the embodiment of an idea. It was a change of self-identifying consciousness. The adunation which de Sieyès, and many others, sought and achieved was a psychic unification. It was not, as in Germany in 1871, the problem of unifying distinct geographical and political sub-societies. It was not, as in Britain, the unification through socialisation of an indeterminate set of geographic and ethnic identities, and sub-societies. In a secret report, Turgot informed Louis XVI of the state of the nation:

'The [French] nation is a society composed of different orders which are poorly united and of a people whose members have very few bonds and in which, as a consequence, everyone is only concerned with his own interest.'[34]

in all, England seems to be much more republican than the Helvetic Republic.' A. de Tocqueville, *Oeuvres complètes* (14th edn, 1864), VIII (*Mélanges historiques*), pp. 455–7; quoted in A. V. Dicey, *Introduction* (fn. 24 above), pp. 184–7. Walter Bagehot referred to Britain as a disguised republic: 'A Republic has insinuated itself beneath the folds of a Monarchy', *The English Constitution* (fn. 20 above), pp. 44, 258. Condorcet, writing in 1793, was not impressed by the British constitution ('servile and venal'), but held out hope for a reform which would make it worthy of 'a humane and generous nation'. J.-A.-N. de Condorcet, *Des progrès de l'esprit humain* (Paris, Editions Sociales; 1971), p. 256.

32 A. Cobban, 'The myth of the French Revolution', in A. Cobban, *Aspects of the French Revolution* (London, Jonathan Cape; 1968), pp. 90–111. Reprinted in E. Schmitt (ed.), *Die Französische Revolution. Anlässe und Langfristige Ursachen* (Darmstadt, Wissenschaftliche Buchgesellschaft; 1973), pp. 170–94.

33 A. Cobban, *France Since the Revolution and Other Aspects of Modern History* (London, Jonathan Cape; 1970), p. 147.

34 J.-D. Bredin, *Sieyès* (fn. 29 above), p. 54 (present author's translation).

7.35 It was a social unorder which was full of paradox. The peasants were an ubiquitous but socially excluded class, but a class among whom, unusually in Europe, significant numbers owned land. The nobility were much less land-centred than the British or German nobility, more focused on Versailles and Paris, and their peculiar privileges seemed, perhaps for that reason, to be unusually anachronistic and illegitimate. And there was an unsatisfied class in-between, the proto-bourgeoisie, unintegrated, but, as in Britain, beginning to apply their society-transforming energy. And there was another class, the thinking class – the *philosophes* and all those liberated by the free-thinking of the French Enlightenment. It has been suggested that this informal fourth estate, with its feverish exploration of new ideas in every field, was the major political force in France after 1750, filling a vacuum of deliberative political institutions.[35]

7.36 The manoeuvrings of the King, the estates and the people at Versailles and in Paris were a theatrical representation of the dialectical process of French self-surpassing, self-transcending. Turgot's prerevolutionary pessimism had been answered by France's purposive, self-reconstituting. It was nobody's fault in particular – not Robespierre's, not Napoleon's – that the course of that self-constituting would not run smoothly thereafter. But the uniting of the French people in the idea of the French nation – the idea of the hypostatic supra-social nation, uniting in a single idea the cherished soil of France, a thousand years of colourful political history, and the long centuries of sustained high culture – that idea has carried France through two centuries of organisational turbulence (including two empires and five republics), through devastating challenges from outside to her integrity, through her transformation into a modern society based on an exceptionally successful economy.

7.37 To mention the Battle of Valmy is to bring to mind the name of Goethe. Goethe attended the battle at Valmy as a spectator, at considerable physical risk, but in a state of some exaltation. From Valmy he spoke and wrote words which, as he must have guessed, would not be forgotten: 'at this place, on this day begins a new era in the history of the world'.[36]

[35] H. Peyre, 'The influence of eighteenth-century ideas on the French Revolution', in 10 *Journal of the History of Ideas*, pp. 63–87. Reprinted in E. Schmitt, *Die Französische Revolution* (fn. 32 above), pp. 124–51.

[36] R. Friedenthal, *Goethe – His Life and Times* (London, Weidenfeld & Nicolson; 1963), p. 313.

7.38 If Valmy had been the end of the beginning for the new France, it was the beginning of the end for the old Germany. Twenty years of war followed, at the end of which there was a new Germany, a new Europe, a new world, and a hundred years of dramatic human social progress. But Valmy was also the first encounter of the new France with Prussia. It would not be the last. Valmy led to Vienna in 1815, to Versailles in 1871, to Verdun in 1916, to Versailles in 1919, to Vichy in 1940. For Europe, the *via regia* of human progress has also been a *via dolorosa* of human suffering.

7.39 In 1945, after thirty more years of European civil strife, we had another new Germany, another new Europe, and another new world. And there followed, perhaps – it is a matter for delicate judgement – fifty more years of dramatic human progress. And yet we seem more than ever hesitant and confused about what it is we have achieved and what it is that we are creating, in the world and in Europe.

Constitutional psychology: Germany

7.40 When the 1,000-year-old Holy Roman Empire of the German Nation evaporated in 1806, it was the end of an illusion of German unity which had not deceived anyone for a very long time. The true unity of Germany was the idea of Germany, or, perhaps more strictly, a certain idea of Germanness, a possible unity in consciousness. The process of German unification in the period up to 1871 would be the joint product of three forms of self-constituting self-consciousness, which might be identified as: romantic nationalism, hellenic nationalism and Hegelian nationalism. After 1871 there would be a fourth form of unifying self-consciousness, which we may call competitive nationalism.

7.41 Romantic nationalism is a social self-consciousness which articulates its identity in terms of nostalgic subjectivity – Vico-Herder nationalism. In the case of Germany we identify it with such people as the brothers Grimm, Savigny and the Historical School of Jurisprudence, Richard Wagner (as poet-dramatist) – and countless other such backward-looking social manifestations, some of them much less admirable.

7.42 Hellenic nationalism was, in spirit, not really a nationalism so much as a new humanism. But it was a humanism which had a particularly powerful effect in the German mind. We associate it with such names as Herder (again), Goethe, Winckelmann, Lessing, Schiller, von Humboldt. And, of course, Hegel's work is thoroughly imbued with the Hellenic spirit, haunted by the ghosts of Plato and Aristotle.[37] The essential idea was that ancient Athens offered an example to a nation, to the human race, of the possibility of purposive self-improvement.

7.43 A clue to the nature of a nation's constitutional psychology may be found in its attitude to education. In Britain, at least until recently, we have not sought, or have not achieved, high levels of mass education, and, until recently, tertiary education has been provided to only a very small part of the population. The growing involvement of the government and public finance in education was conducted in a grudging paternalist spirit, more or less keeping in step with the extension down the social hierarchy of the right to vote. At the time of the passing of the bitterly contested Education Act of 1870, reference was made to educational standards in Prussia, but what we remember is another slogan in the debate: 'educate your masters'.[38] What the mass of the voting population needed to know has turned out to be: not very much.

7.44 In Germany at the turn of the nineteenth century, education was perceived in a different way. Germany's *travail de soi sur soi* would be a work of national self-improvement, which was only one aspect of human self-improvement. *Bildung.*[39] *Erziehung.*[40] *Humanitätsideal.*[41] Since

[37] H. Plessner discusses a similar phenomenon under the name of Germany's *römische Komplex.* H. Plessner, *Die verspätete Nation* (Stuttgart, W. Kohlhammer Verlag; 1959), ch. 3.

[38] K. Feiling, *A History of England – from the Coming of the English to 1918* (London, Macmillan & Co.; 1952), p. 939.

[39] 'The true purpose of the human being – not that which changing inclination, but that which eternally unchanging reason prescribes for him – is the highest and most proportionate development [*Bildung*] of his powers as a whole. For this development freedom is the first and indispensable condition.' W. von Humboldt, *Ideen zu einem Versuch, die Grenzen der Wirksamkeit des Staats zu bestimmen* (written 1792, published 1851) (Stuttgart, P. Reclam jun.; 1967), p. 22 (present author's translation).

[40] F. Schiller, *Über die ästhetische Erziehung des Menschen* (1795). It is interesting that Goethe, so much a master of the German mind, should have been so little nationalist in spirit, believing in the civilising power of culture in general. 'How can I . . . hate a nation [France] which is among the most cultivated on earth and to which I owe so much of my own cultivation' (1830; quoted in H. Kohn, *The Mind of Germany – the Education of a Nation* (London, Macmillan & Co.; 1961), p. 40). 'National literature has now become a meaningless term. The era of world literature is fast approaching and everyone must strive to hasten its progress' (Goethe to Eckermann, 1827; *ibid.*, p. 42). See also R. Friedenthal, *Goethe* (fn. 36 above), ch. 44.

[41] The word is particularly associated with J. G. Herder, who saw human history as containing the general education of humanity (*allgemeine Bildung der Menschheit*). See A. Gillies,

ancient Greece different European nations had taken on the task of educators of the European mind. Germany could claim, in a Periclean spirit, to be Europe's teacher of teachers in the nineteenth century. Germany set the standards and the ideals of publicly endowed intellectual self-cultivation for Europe and beyond. The character of our universities today still reflects, for better and for worse, the ideals of that German-inspired European High Culture of the nineteenth century.

7.45 But the Ariadne thread of education can lead us into deeper and more troubling regions of Europe's symbol-forest. The question of public education inevitably raises the question of the individual's relation to society, and that leads us back to Hegel and statism.

7.46 Hegel's depreciation of society in relation to state reflected a sort of obsessive aversion on his part to the inwardness and subjectivity which had flooded the European mind in his lifetime. The natural self-ordering of society could be, would be, surpassed by the rational self-constituting of the state. And the individual would find a new sort of fulfilment in organic participation in a self-perfecting state-society. Only in this way could modern society approach the ancient Greek ideal of the natural integration of the individual into a social order which was itself a reflection of a transcendent order.

7.47 These ideas took social effect in Germany in a way which would delay the coming of parliamentary democracy for a century and more. They would inspire the self-perfecting of society through the self-perfecting of the state. And certain of the German sub-societies, not only Prussia, set about the rational reconstituting of society under the control of what Hegel had called the universal class, people specially educated and specially employed to serve the public interest, to universalise society's particularities, to achieve, through the state-machine, through legislation and administration, the amazing dynamic one-from-many of a complex modern society, self-creating and self-regulating, at the expense of the self-creating and self-regulating human individual.

Herder (Oxford, Basil Blackwell; 1945), ch. 8. 'That which is divine in our race is, thus, education (*Bildung*) for humanity (*Humanität*); all great and good men, lawgivers, inventors, philosophers, poets, artists, every noble-minded man, in his own station, in the education (*Erziehung*) of his children, in the observance of his duties . . . has collaborated towards that end' (*ibid.*, p. 106). Goethe and Schiller advised the German people not to seek to be a nation, but to be 'free human beings': 'They hope to make you in vain into a German *nation*; choose to make yourselves free human beings instead.' Quoted in H. Kohn, *The Mind of Germany* (fn. 40 above), p. 35 (present author's translation).

7.48 These forms of national self-constituting had their intellectual parallels elsewhere in Europe, including in Britain and France. To pluck symbols, more or less at random, out of the British symbol-forest: the nostalgism of Ossian and Walter Scott and Pugin and William Morris; the hellenism of Matthew Arnold and Walter Pater; the social rationalism of Bentham and J. S. Mill and Herbert Spencer. Over a large part of Europe – not only in Napoleonic France and in Prussia – society was transformed in the nineteenth century, by rationalistic legislation and administration which was powerfully statist in spirit.

7.49 So what should we say about German uniqueness, German exceptionality, the famous German *Sonderweg*? Perhaps we should simply say that there is no such thing, except in the sense that each of our nations is uniquely self-constituting, each of us is a unique manifestation of general European self-constituting, a particular self within the European self. But what we must say, and insist upon, is that the particular character of Germany's unifying self-constituting, Germany's work on itself, is now of the utmost relevance to Europe's *travail de soi sur soi*, Europe's reunifying.

7.50 The activity of the German mind since 1760 has been prodigious. An English admirer of the German people may be permitted to say – and others have said it – that the German mind has thought too much and felt too much, and sometimes it has confused the two. The German mind has been too intelligent and too sensitive. It is, perhaps, only in the perfection of German music that the German mind has found the ideal resolution of thought and feeling. The superabundance of the German mind and heart led to certain phenomena which temporarily separated it from other parts of Europe, especially France and Britain. And we must now face the problem of Germany after 1871.

7.51 In the troubled minds of Max Weber and Thomas Mann, to take two representative examples from among so many troubled *maîtres à penser* of the German spirit, we can, as fellow Europeans, watch with anguish the playing-out of the German existential drama.

7.52 In Britain and the United States, Weber's work has been treated with respect, at least by academic specialists, but its melancholy rationalism is profoundly distasteful to the practico-optimistic Anglo-American mentality. We would rather not even suppose heuristically, let alone believe affectively, that the essence of the state is its monopoly of legitimate violence. And coldly systematic conceptions of law, legitimacy, rationalisation, bureaucratisation, tradition, religion, authority, charisma – and the other flora and fauna of the bleak Weberian mindscape – are too psychically distasteful to serve as ultimate constituents of progressive social analysis.[42] We are familiar enough with the social phenomena which are represented by such conceptions, in our own constitutional history and social psychology, but their rationalisation takes a quite different form in Anglo-American self-contemplating. Even Weber's conception of nation contains a sub-text which would trouble not only Anglo-American but also French sensibility.

'[A] nation is a community of sentiment which would adequately manifest itself in a state of its own; and hence, a nation is a community which normally tends to produce a state of its own.'[43]

7.53 Thomas Mann, the master of ambivalence, published in 1918 his *Reflections of an Unpolitical Man*, 1,600 pages of unfocused disgust at the current way of the world, with its threat of something, essentially Anglo-American, which he refers to obsessively as 'democracy', that is to say, the rule of 'politics'.[44] Popular democracy was unGerman, infecting national life with parliaments and parties and politics. But the Bismarckian *Machtreich* was also unGerman. The true self-rule of the German *Volk* was the rule of order and decency and freedom. '*Freiheit, Pflicht und abermals Freiheit, das ist Deutschland*.'[45]

[42] For an illuminating account of what Weber owed to a specifically German tradition of legal philosophy (especially Ihering, who had spoken of the state as 'the sole owner of . . . coercive force'), see S. P. Turner and R. A. Factor, *Max Weber: the Lawyer as Social Thinker* (London, Routledge; 1994), esp. ch. 5, at p. 103. The German psycho-masochistic gloom was fuelled in the 1920s by the popular success of Oswald Spengler's *Der Untergang des Abendlandes* (*The Decline of the West*) (published in 1918), predicting a bad end for European civilisation, and of Hermann Hesse's novel *Demian* (1919), which looked to the replacement of corrupt European civilisation by 'a new order of humanity' based on absolute personal authenticity. In England, on the other hand, J. B. Bury's *The Idea of Progress: an Inquiry into its Origins and Growth* (1920), celebrating the triumph of post-religious European humanism, gave historiographic reinforcement to Anglo-American social optimism in difficult times.

[43] *From Max Weber: Essays in Sociology* (trs and eds H. Gerth and C. Wright Mills; New York, Oxford University Press; 1958), p. 176.

[44] T. Mann, *Betrachtungen eines Unpolitischen* (Berlin; Fischer Verlag; 1922), p. 287.

[45] 'Freedom, duty and again freedom, that is Germany' (*ibid.*, p. 258). The unidentified antagonist against which the *Betrachtungen* are directed is his own brother Heinrich. Heinrich said that the essay was 'from the political point of view a catastrophe': U. Naumann, *Klaus Mann* (Hamburg, Rowohlt; 1984), p. 14. On the background, and on Mann's existential dispute with his brother, see R. Karst, *Thomas Mann oder der Deutsche Zwiespalt* (Wien-München-Zürich, Verlag Fritz Molden; 1970), pp. 79ff. On the relentless ambivalence of Mann's politics, Germanness and sexuality, see a convincing account in A. Heilbut, *Thomas*

7.54 In the mental struggle of Weber and Mann with the interlocking ideas of the German nation and the German state – the search for Germany as *âme et personne* – we can see the foreshadowing of what was to follow.

7.55 In the period 1871 to 1914, the idea of the nationhood of France and Britain agitated the minds of Germany's ruling class, including the economic ruling class. Bismarck's violently imposed German power-state re-imagined itself as a great nation, and a potential world power – in competition with a France and a Britain whose appearance of world-power was already becoming a terminal illusion.

7.56 Competitive nationalism was not Germany's invention and was not confined to Germany.[46] It is like a latent virus in the European spirit, a socio-psychic pathology waiting to overwhelm, in times of social stress, all normal and healthy forms of social self-constituting. Its effect in Germany was that Germany become a state-nation: a society organised through its public realm, but now projecting its subjectivity in the form of nation. A dynamic, rapidly developing society, which had been organised as a state, was re-energised by passionate national subjectivity.[47]

Mann: Eros and Literature (London, Macmillan; 1996). 'What is conservatism? The erotic irony of the intellect' (quoted by Heilbut, *ibid.*, p. 296, from the *Betrachtungen*).

[46] The literature on nationalism is voluminous, and still growing rapidly. On the Franco-German mutual nationalising, see P.-A. Taguieff, 'Le nationalisme des "nationalistes": un problème pour l'histoire des idées politiques en France', in *Théories du Nationalisme* (eds G. Delanoi and P-A. Taguieff; Paris, Editions Kimé; 1991), pp. 47–124; and P. Birnbaum, 'Nationalisme à la française', in *ibid.*, pp. 125–38. See also L. Dumont, *German Ideology: From France to Germany and Back* (Chicago, University of Chicago Press; 1994).

[47] An interesting comparison is with the purposive making of the 'nation' of the United States of America. See S. M. Lipset, *The First New Nation* (Garden City, NY, Doubleday & Co. (Anchor Books); 1967), esp. ch. 2; M. Jensen, *The New Nation: A History of the United States during the Confederation 1781–1789* (1950), esp. ch. 4: 'It is the business of Americans to select the wisdom of all nations, as the basis of her constitutions, to avoid their errours, to prevent the introduction of foreign vices and corruptions and check the career of her own, to promote virtue and patriotism, to embellish and improve the sciences, to diffuse an uniformity and purity of language, to add superior dignity to this infant Empire and to human nature' (Noah Webster – who would later compile a dictionary – writing in 1783; quoted at p. 105). It has been suggested that the Declaration of Independence did not acquire its status within American self-consciousness until, perhaps, 1812. See G. Wills, *Inventing America – Jefferson's Declaration of Independence* (New York, Random House (Vintage Books); 1979), esp. pt 5. For the thesis that, even before the Declaration, the US existed as a self-conscious nation (at least in the sense of a distinct political consciousness), see N. M. Butler, *Building the American Nation: An Essay in Interpretation* (New York, Charles Scribner's Sons; 1926), esp. pp. 35ff.

7.57 National socialism was its natural political manifestation – nationalist and statist. And the madness of the Third Reich was the natural perversion of national socialism. The confusion of rationality and subjectivity, that hazardous legacy of the late eighteenth century, had at last produced, at the turn of the twentieth century, its most extreme malformation, full of life-threatening contradictions.

7.58 Personal inwardness (*Innerlichkeit*) and social absolutism. National feeling and its dark shadow, xenophobia. Pietism and *Realpolitik*. Feverish creativity and the wish for death. *Wissenschaft* and *Schwärmerei*. Pure reason haunted by unreason. And, throughout, alongside the monolithic Germany of *Blut und Eisen*, there remained the ancient Germany of *Blut und Boden, gemütlich* Germany, *Heimat* Germany, *Gemeinschaft* Germany and the Germany of local diversity and of German–German rivalry.

7.59 Echoing Jules Michelet once again, we must never forget, and it is a matter of profound importance for the future development of European Union, that a people's *travail de soi sur soi* is never completed. The Third Reich was not the 'true' Germany, any more than the Terror of the second phase of the French Revolution was the 'true' France, nor Britain's arrogant colonialism the 'true' Britain, nor the 'Manifest Destiny' policy of the United States the 'true' United States.

7.60 Helmuth Plessner has called Germany *die verspätete Nation*, the delayed nation.[48] A main goal of European reunification must be the wholehearted reintegration of the German people into the European family. And the same objective must apply to Europe's other 'delayed nations', including the long-suffering peoples of Central and Eastern Europe who have been, for centuries, the victims of other peoples' games of self-constituting. But the surpassing of the past is never an annihilation of the past. Self-constituting of a nation, as of a human individual, is always a reconstituting of what has gone before. A people, like a person, cannot unlive its past. And what is true of each nation is true of all Europe. Europe's self-reconstituting, since the end of the Roman Empire in the West, has never ceased and will never cease. Europe will be what it was, and what it never has been.

7.61 In 1949 Germany was reconstituted once again as two states, two non-nation-states, a violently caused negation of its self-constituting

[48] H. Plessner, *Die verspätete Nation* (fn. 37 above).

as state-nation. One hundred and forty-seven years after Hegel's essay on the Constitution of Germany, Germany was at last unified rationally, ironically, in the disunity of two states. And the West German state was organized by a written constitution which is the *fine fleur,* the *ne plus ultra,* of democratic rationalism, a pure distillation of long centuries of European constitutionalism. But it is a constitution which strikes us as a product of the mind rather than of the heart, lacking the lyrical quality of the originating constitutional texts of the United States or France. It is a constitution with a past.

7.62 The rigour of the *Grundgesetz* demonstrated its amazing efficacy when the Federal Republic swallowed the Democratic Republic, like Jonah and the Whale, in 1990. Two states became one state, more or less overnight and, reversing the direction of causation envisaged by Max Weber, that state, as in 1871, reanimated the subjectivity of a possible German nation.

Half-revolution

7.63 After so much struggle, so much suffering, one might have thought, in 1945, that Europe deserved a period of constitutional rest and relaxation. Far from it. Europe's manic *travail de soi sur soi* resumed. Many European countries have legally reconstituted themselves in the period since 1945 – some on several occasions – Austria, Belgium, France, Germany, Greece, Italy, Portugal, Spain, the United Kingdom – not to mention the countries of Central and Eastern Europe and the successor states of the Soviet Union. Five years to the day after the end of the War in Europe, the reconstituting mania, the *furor constituendi,* manifested itself in a surprising new form. Europe would seek to reconstitute itself, not as *society, nation,* or *state* but as *economy.*

7.64 But the reconstituting of Europe would begin as a transformation of only one part of Europe. Official Britain's persistent and comprehensible, but tragic, equivocation in relation to Continental Europe is co-ordinate with the equivocal course of US foreign policy. George Washington's admonition to the United States to avoid *foreign entanglements* (leading to spasmodic US involvement and detachment in European and world affairs) echoes British foreign policy, not so much a policy as an indolent habit of mind which has persisted from at least the time when our foreign affairs were managed by the egregious Cardinal

Wolsey in the sixteenth century. These equivocations – British and American – have seemed to be a *felix culpa* – *felix* when it has kept us out of wars, *culpa* when it has actually encouraged hegemonism and other undesirable developments on the Continent and beyond.[49]

7.65 The self reconstituting of part-of-Europe as economy would be practico-organic in character, beginning as an excrescence from a small number of Europe's constituted societies, unfolding, multiplying, self-replicating, through one metamorphosis after another, spreading luxuriantly back into the constituted societies. To make sense of it all would become an unprecedented challenge for constitutional physiologists.

7.66 European Union defies conventional legal-constitutional analysis. It is a Europe seen darkly through a constitutional looking-glass, full of distorted images of familiar constitutional forms. In tentatively identifying three stages of the EU's constitutional development, one cannot ignore the comical aspect of such an analysis.

(1) In a first phase, the Community constitutional system was *a partially external, partially constitutionalized partial economy.* Or, using another form of analysis, the Communities, in their original form, were *a dual functionally limited sub-federal system* ('dual' in the sense that functions of law and government were distributed horizontally between the Communities and the member states by reference to what were called, in those days, *the limits of Community competence*).

[49] British foreign policy has made up in consistency for what it has lacked in imagination. (1) Lord Castlereagh regarded the Holy Alliance as a piece of 'sublime mysticism and nonsense' (H. Temperley and L. Penson, *Foundations of British Foreign Policy (1792–1902)* (Cambridge, Cambridge University Press; 1938), p. 37). (2) 'By the late Proceedings at Vienna, which for all purposes of internal tranquillity, bind up the various States of Germany into a single and undivided Power, a great deal of additional simplicity as well as Strength has been given to this Portion of Europe. In addition to these there remain but few Pieces on the board to complicate the Game of Publick Safety' (Castlereagh, 1820; *ibid.*, p. 59). (3) After some initial agitation at the formation of the *Zollverein*, Britain (through Lord Palmerston) expressed a more sanguine view in 1841. Although the British government had 'never looked with a favourable eye upon the Prussian commercial league there seems some hope that the effect of the commercial union may not prove so injurious to the trade of this country as had been imagined; and at all events, the political consequences which may possibly result from the League, are by no means such as to give rise to uneasiness and apprehension.' Quoted in W. O. Henderson, 'Prussia and the founding of the German *Zollverein*', in O. Büsch and W. Neugebauer (eds.), *Moderne Preussische Geschichte 1649–1947* (Berlin, W. de Gruyter; 1981), p. 1,096. (4) When Briand proposed, and Stresemann showed interest in, a United States of Europe based on an economic union, a committee of the League of Nations Assembly was set up to consider the idea. Britain opposed the idea and the committee ceased work. For Stresemann's comments to journalists, shortly before his death, see K. Wessel (ed.), *Europa – Mutter unserer Welt* (München, Bruckmann; 1970), pp. 265–6.

(2) In a second phase, the Community constitutional system became *an internal-external economy-state* (using *state* in the Hegelian sense, as an organisation of the public realm). A *Wirtschaftsstaat*, one might call it – inventing a German word, if it does not already exist. Or, using the other form of analysis, the Communities, up to and including the period of the Single European Act, became a *dual-binary functionally limited pre-federal system* ('dual-binary' because it had become clear that the Communities and the member states were now systematically connected, both horizontally and vertically, in particular, because of the development of the principles of the 'supremacy' and 'direct effect' of Community law and because there seemed to be no natural limit to the need to unify or harmonise economic law).

(3) In a third phase – coincident with, but not wholly caused by, the wretched Maastricht Treaty – the constitutional system seems now to be a *state-of-states (Staatenstaat) containing an internal-external constitutionalised partial economy, together with an external partial public realm of public realms*. Or, using the other form of analysis, it has become a *triple-binary functionally limited sub-federal and confederal system* ('triple-binary' because there are now three corners to the constitutional triangle – the member states, the Communities and the partially confederal EU).

7.67 Such surreal constitutional discourse is difficult to distil into a single communicable idea. But let us say, provisionally at least, that the European Union is a *statist-capitalist diplomacy-democracy*!

7.68 For the time being, our concern is not with the scientific accuracy of this kind of analysis. Our first concern is aetiological, to try to answer the question: what has caused such an exotic manifestation of European social self-constituting? How is it that the spirit of Europe's constitution has given birth, after thirty centuries of intense, and intensely self-conscious, constitutional experience, to such a wonder of our social nature – a *lusus rei publicae*?

7.69 But our major concern must be diagnostic. The form which European reunification has taken has produced deep wounds in the constitutional psychologies of the participating peoples. To redeem and to perfect Europe's re-unifying is not a matter of institutional reform but of psychic healing. To suppose that the crisis of European constitutionalism can be dealt with by institutional reform is like offering minor surgery to a psychotic. And the metaphor is more than a metaphor. If one defines psychosis as the domination of the patient by a private reality which is life-threatening, then something very close to that is what has happened in Europe. Official Europe – politicians and technocrats – are locked into a private reality, the so-called European Union, which threatens the future stability and prosperity of the people and the peoples of Europe.

7.70 European Union is Europe's half-revolution. Half-revolutions are a familiar phenomenon – Britain in 1688, America in 1781, France in 1789, Russia in 1917, Germany in 1919. The problem with half-revolutions is that they tend to be followed by counter-revolution, chaos or worse.[50] In the first of the Federalist Papers (1787), Alexander Hamilton wrote:

'It has frequently been remarked that it seems to have been reserved to the people of this country, by their conduct and example, to decide the important question, whether societies of men are really capable or not of establishing good government from reflection and choice, or whether they are forever destined to depend for their political constitutions on accident and force.'[51]

7.71 Hamilton was arguing for the completion of America's half-revolution. In Europe today, it is for us Europeans now to discover whether we are able, through reflection and choice, to complete Europe's revolutionary self-reconstituting, to redeem and perfect what has already been achieved, to take further Europe's own work upon itself, to rediscover and reconstitute European society. Given all that has happened in Europe since Edmund Burke reflected on Europe's last general revolution, our reflection must contain much new hard-earned wisdom,

[50] We may recall Cicero's comment on the assassination of the *dictator* Julius Caesar. ''Twas a fine deed, but half done!' Cicero, *Letters to Atticus* (letter of 22 April 44 BCE) (ed. and tr. D. R. Shackleton Bailey; Cambridge, Harvard University Press (Loeb Classical Library); 1999), p. 165. (Cicero's comment is in Greek in the original, as if quoted from a Greek play; 'half done' translates the Greek *atelous*.) Those who had killed Caesar on 15 March 44 (the *liberatores*, as Cicero called them) had not prepared any plans for the restoration of the Republic and chaos followed in 'our unhappy or rather non-existent commonwealth' (*miseram seu nullam potius rem publicam*) (letter of 26 April, p. 173). In due course Caesar's great-nephew and adopted son Octavius ('the boy', as Cicero called him) would succeed in transforming the Republic into an Empire. We may not wish to associate another of Cicero's prescient epigrams with our own sadness at the state of the European Union. 'It is clear that after the removal of the tyrant the tyranny remains' (*sublato enim tyranno tyrannida manere video*) (letter of 28 or 29 April, p. 181).

[51] A. Hamilton, J. Madison, J. Jay, *The Federalist Papers* (New York, New American Library of World Literature; 1961), p. 33.

and our choice must have the happy effect of following a European nature which has become more than ever problematic for itself.

7.72 The constitution of a society is a constituting, a process over time, a process of change, of accumulated effects produced by a succession of causes. And it is a process in three dimensions, a process at the level of ideas, of events and of law. A society's self-constituting is the making of three constitutions: the *ideal constitution* – at the level of theories, values, purposes, ideals; the *real* constitution – at the level of the actual day-to-day interactive exercise of social power – political, social, and economic; and the *legal* constitution – through which society transforms into the specific form of law the endless series of outcomes which come from the interaction between its real and ideal self-constituting, and so takes power over its future.[52] A society imagines what it might be, struggles to decide what it shall be, and becomes what it has chosen to become.

7.73 The German people – to cite one example – were organised as a state-nation after 1871, not because the *Zollverein* had, by some natural process, taken on the character of a state.[53] Germany became a state-nation because Bismarck, acting in the real constitution (including the use of threats and force) instigated a new legal constitution (the constitution of the North German Confederation transformed into the Reich Constitution of 1871), and the self-contemplating of the ideal constitution fused the ideas of *German state* and *German nation* (*Staat* and *Volk*). German society had reconstituted itself *really, legally* and *ideally.*

7.74 In considering the constitutional psychologies of Britain, France and Germany, it has already been suggested that the disunited unity of Europe may have deep roots in the ideal self-constituting of the people and the peoples of Europe, and hence that the bizarre form of society-constituting process known as European Union may be a distorted effect of such an ideal cause.

7.75 A sort of self-induced constitutional depression has settled over the people and the peoples of Europe. The peoples of Europe must find a new idea of themselves and a new ideal of their self-re-constituting.

52 On the three-dimensional nature of social self-constituting, see *Eunomia*, ch. 9.

53 It is interesting that in 1867 Bismarck caused the creation of a bicameral legislature for the *Zollverein* – with a directly elected *Zollparlament* with competence for tariff legislation, commercial and navigational negotiations, and the regulation of some indirect taxes and excise duties. A. Craig, *Germany 1866-1945* (Oxford, Oxford University Press; 1978), p. 15.

That idea and that ideal will be found by bringing into fruitful conjunction two great streams of European consciousness: on the one hand, *the spirit of the constitutions* of the peoples of Europe; on the other hand, *the transcendental unity* of European society. The redeeming of European reunifying will be a dialectic in which Europe's superordinate social totality negates, and is negated by, its subordinate social totalities. Europe must become for-itself *a society of societies, a nation of nations, a state of states.* Giambattista Vico would have called such an effort *un ricorso,* a recovering of the past-in-the-future of the European mind.[54] To use the language of Michelet, it means a bringing to consciousness of the *soul and person of Europe – la grande âme de l'Europe,* something which, for centuries, has been repressed and suppressed. It means finding the *formula naturae* of European society – to borrow a splendid idea attributed to that most learned Roman, Varro.[55] To use and abuse three more or less Kantian terms of art, we must seek to form the *idea of reason* of the *possibility* of Europe's *transcendental apperception of its unity.*[56] In the terms of the present author's Social Idealism, it means that we must now propose to European society a *theory* of European society.[57] We shall, in Aristotelian–Nietzschean terms, be inviting European society to choose to become what it is.[58]

The presence of the past

7.76 The European mind must discover Europe's future in Europe's past. And this means that it must make an effort, at last, to understand the source of Europe's disunity. Europe's future must be found in, and in the negation of, Europe's past.

[54] G. Vico, *The New Science* (fn. 14 above), bks IV and V; translators' introduction, p. 1.

[55] *Ibid.*, p. 347.

[56] In a way which foreshadows much later ideas of theory-as-mental-model, Kant uses the concept of the 'idea of reason' to explain the practical effect of social contract theory: 'It is in fact merely an *idea of reason,* which nonetheless has undoubted practical reality; for it can oblige every legislator to frame his laws in such a way that they could have been produced by the united will of a whole nation, and to regard each subject, in so far as he can claim citizenship, as if he had consented within the general will.' I. Kant, 'On the common saying: "This may be true in theory, but it does not apply in practice"', in *Kant's Political Writings* (tr. H. Nisbet, ed. H. Reiss; Cambridge, Cambridge University Press; 1970), p. 79.

[57] On the idea of a society's *theory,* see *Eunomia,* §§ 2.45, 2.49.

[58] See K. Ansell-Pearson, *Nietzsche contra Rousseau – a Study of Nietzsche's Moral and Political Thought* (Cambridge, Cambridge University Press; 1991), pp. 106 et seq.

7.77 To speak of *history* is to speak of our accumulating social self-consciousness. A re-formed history of Europe will be a reforming of European self-consciousness – an *Umformung*, a *metanoia*, a transformation of our self-identifying and self-imagining. European reunifying requires an historiography of our unity which is as powerful as the historiography of our particularism.[59]

7.78 A substantial difficulty in the way of any such enterprise is that European historiography long since became a problem for itself. The past is another country, ceaselessly explored, but mapped in accordance with many radically different principles of historical cartography, from the most historicist (finding law-like patterns in the infinity of human events and human intentions) to the most piecemeal. Worse still, the past haunts the present as the object of an unending struggle to take ideological possession of its equivocal significance. It is not possible to escape these problems, but it is also not possible to evade the responsibility constantly to re-imagine the present and the future by constantly re-imagining the past, a past which must, in some sense, contain the genetic programme of the present and the future.

7.79 The present condition of Europe is the product of an exceptionally well-documented past which may be seen as the scene of the three-way interaction of ideas, action and law which, it has been suggested above, are the characteristic dimensions of social self-constituting. But the European past seems to contain a number of notorious turning-points at which, we are inclined to say, if the turn had been in another direction, subsequent European history would have been fundamentally different. If these structural moments of European social self-constituting had been otherwise, the need for, and the form of, European Union would have been fundamentally different.

7.80 The ambition of Julius Caesar and the subsequent reconstituting of a Roman Republic into a multi-national Empire. Constantine's removal of the seat of Empire from Rome to Constantinople and the assimilation of non-European traditions of monarchism and religion. The creation of a separate (Holy Roman) Empire in the west through the cunning of a pope and of a king of the Franks. The division of Charlemagne's inheritance among his three sons, including the legal-constitutional

[59] For an initiative in this direction, in a form accessible to the wider public, see F. Delouche and others, *Histoire de l'Europe* (Paris, Hachette; 1992) (and in other languages); revised and enlarged edition, 1996. On the nature of historiography, see further in ch. 11 below.

separation of the west Franks from the east Franks (leading to the separate self-constituting of France and Germany). The organisation of the Roman Church as a City of God, with many of the attributes of a City of Man. The competitive imperialism of Pope and (western) Emperor (throughout the Middle Ages). The reassimilation of Graeco-Roman culture and its reconciliation with Christian culture (in the Carolingian renaissance of the ninth century, in the renaissance of the twelfth century, leading to the founding of the universities, and the renaissance of the fifteenth century). Opposition to the legal-constitutional pretensions of the Papacy and to the behavioural imperfections of the Roman Church (from the fourteenth century, leading to the religious and national self-determination of the Reformation in the sixteenth century).

7.81 Each of these decisive turning-points in the history of Europe's disunited unity is a triune point – at which ideas, action and law seem to interact with exceptional clarity and force. They are the tectonic events, the phase-shifts, the mutations of European self-constituting. The one unequivocal lesson that we can learn from them is that there has been no natural and inevitable progression from the Athens of Solon to Economic and Monetary Union, that there has never been a settled point-of-balance in the endless uniting and separating forces of European history.

7.82 If one closes the focus and tries to find patterns in the long centuries which have passed between these structural turning-points, the same conclusion becomes still clearer. To reconceive European history as a history of Europe's unity-in-diversity, we must adopt an unconventional periodisation of that history. *Tribal Europe* from the fifth to the eleventh centuries. *Multinational Europe* from 1100 to 1500. *Social Europe* from 1500 to 1800. *Inter-statal Europe* from 1800 to the present day.

7.83 The expression *tribal Europe* (fifth–eleventh centuries) calls to mind the accidental character of the ethnic composition of each of our supposedly specific nations. And it reminds us of what we Europeans are most like: we are most like an extended family, a large family, more or less closely related, full of interesting and rather difficult members.

7.84 In Britain, at the time of the Norman occupation of 1066, we had become a mongrel mixture of Celts, Jutes, Saxons, Angles and frenchified and non-frenchified Scandinavians. And we found that we had a language which was a Germanic dialect, primarily the east Frisian dialect of German, which would eventually come to dominate and assimilate the Norman French of the latest (and last) occupying class. And if we were cousins of those tribes who would come to identify themselves as Germans, those tribes were cousins, or closer, of the tribes who would come to identify themselves as French. And the proto-Germans would get rid of the Slav tribes from what would one day become the territory of the German Democratic Republic. And the proto-French would go beyond the Somme and then beyond the Loire and frenchify the survivors of the Romanisation of Gaul, and so link up with the Lombards who had moved from northern Europe to become the proto-Italians in conjunction with the aboriginal Romanised tribes of Italy, including tribes in southern Italy who had been colonised by the Greeks . . . and so on and on.

7.85 The expression *multinational Europe* (1100–1500) reminds us that it took manic efforts on the part of kings and their servants, and the spilling of much blood, to make these motley tribes believe that they were a *nation*, genetically and/or generically distinct from neighbouring nations, to separate the royal property of one so-called nation from another, to combine highly effective subordinate social systems (feudal estates, the dioceses of bishops, city-states, free towns) into centralised power-systems. When French kings were kings of England and English kings were also kings of France, what was England, what was France? British kings continued to bear the title 'King of France' long after they had ceased to control any part of France. Multinational Europe also reminds us that it is only ideologically motivated historiography that has monopolised the historical imagination of the people with its stories of the antics of kings and emperors and soldiers, whereas the central social activity was, as it always had been, economic, that is, the transformation of labour and desire into goods and services to which different economic agents attach differential but commensurable value. It is the international character of trade in the High Middle Ages, the cosmopolitanism of the towns, and the development of an international business consciousness which should attract our attention and admiration, as it should have attracted the gratitude and not merely the greed of the holders of ultimate political power.

7.86 The expression *social Europe* (1500–1800) reminds us of a very striking thing, the most important pattern of all – that, after 1453 (the sack of Constantinople and the end of the eastern (Byzantine) empire), the people of Europe rediscovered the most important kind of European unity, a unity of consciousness in the very period which is conventionally presented as the period during which Europe decomposed into a modified state of nature wherein the leading politico-military actors were conceived as being 'in the posture of gladiators' (to borrow an expression used by Hobbes) in relation to each other.

7.87 Social Europe saw a great new flowering of a shared European consciousness, a consciousness which had been preserved, almost miraculously, in unbroken succession from ancient Greece and Rome. Even in the darkest days of tribal Europe, when the lamp of civilised society burned low, the light of the mind burned steadily in the monasteries, those common organisations of the spirit, to be handed on to their intellectual heirs, the universities, in the twelfth century. It was the Church of Rome which had carried a most significant part of the intellectual, social and even political legacy of the ancient world through tribal Europe into multinational Europe. And then, in the period of social Europe, the European spirit manifested itself luxuriantly in the fine arts, music, literature, the law and social institutions, philosophy, humanistic scholarship, the natural sciences, technology, agriculture. Social Europe was a European Union of the Mind, a single market of consciousness, with free movement of artists and intellectuals, of intellectual capital, of the products of hand and brain. Renaissance humanism, the scientific revolution, the enlightenment of the eighteenth century, Romanticism, the industrial revolution, the political revolutions after 1776 – they were all the work of the wonderful unity-in-diversity of the European mind.

7.88 Social Europe also reminds us that, ever since the period of tribal Europe, we Europeans have been capable of layered loyalty – loyalty to family, village, guild and other social corporations, town, estate, province, nation, the Pope, the Emperor – loyalty to our religion, to Europe (in relation to non-Europe), to the City of God as well as the City of Man. Each loyalty has seemed perfectly compatible with all the others. Some of us, from ancient Greece onwards, have even claimed to be cosmopolitans, members of the international society of the whole human race, the society of all societies. As Europeans acquired an ever-increasing sense of their own individuality during the period of social Europe, that new personal self-awareness included an ever-increasing awareness of the complex and multiple and ever-changing social parameters of our personal identity, the social subjectivity of our personal subjectivity.

7.89 And *social Europe* reminds us that, even among the degenerate controllers of the public realms of the nations, there were signs of practical socialising. We think of Hugo de Groot (Grotius) as the prophet of universal international law. But he, and his great Spanish predecessors, can also be seen in their specifically European context, as voices in a new politico-military wilderness, the voice of old Europe recalling the integrity of old Europe's values, values of sociality and rationality, in the face of the terrible challenges of a new political world in Europe, of a new-old world outside Europe.

7.90 So what changed after 1800, to make *inter-statal Europe*, the Europe of the triumphant Public Realms? What made Hegel's essay of 1802 on the reconstituting of Germany so prophetic? What has led so many Europeans to believe that inter-statal Europe is Europe's natural and settled state? How is it that the European mind has produced the European Union that we know, a misbegotten and anachronistic product of inter-statal Europe, of one uncharacteristic phase of European history, standing in the way of a true European reunifying, of another self-surpassing achievement of the great and ancient tradition of Europe's unity-in-diversity?

7.91 We can offer a rudimentary explanation of the complex historical process by which such a thing came about. We can begin to find our way into the heart of Europe's darkness. What we find is that the European Union is a product of a particular developmental process in the most dynamic European societies, a process which enabled the *state* (in its internal sense) to acquire an ideal, real and legal hegemony over the other totalising complexes of society (especially *society* and *nation* and *economy*) and to acquire an external hegemony over all other transnational phenomena (the internal *state* externalised to become the *state* of so-called international relations and international law).

7.92 But the social hegemony of statism has passed its apogee, and all the totalising social concepts are undergoing radical reconceiving. We will be obliged to conclude that the European Union, in its present and potential state, is an exotic relic of a fading social order, like the late-medieval Church of Rome or the latter-day Holy Roman Empire.

7.93 Alexis de Tocqueville's discussions of the American and French Revolutions are among the greatest achievements of human self-contemplating. Among his many powerful and prophetic insights was the idea that the new kind of democracy had within it the seeds of totalitarianism, to use a modern word which he did not use. He quotes a warning uttered by Thomas Jefferson in a letter to James Madison in 1789: 'The tyranny of the legislature is really the danger most to be feared, and will continue to be so for many years to come. The tyranny of the executive power will come in its turn, but at a more distant period.'[60]

7.94 De Tocqueville said that, as the number of public officials increases, 'they form a nation within each nation' and that governments would come more and more to act 'as if they thought themselves responsible for the actions and private condition of their subjects . . . [while] private individuals grow more and more apt to look upon the supreme power in the same light'.[61]

7.95 And so it happened: the controllers of the public realm came to be a nation within each nation, a social class with its own class-interests, and then, as they began to identify with each other transnationally, a transnational class with its own class-interests. And the European Union is the product of their ideals and their ambitions. European Union is the partial integrating *of* the public realms of Europe *by* the controllers of the public realms of Europe. (The *public realm* is that part of the total social process of a society which consists in the exercise of those social powers which have been conferred by society to serve the *public interest* of that society.)

Ideas and illusions

7.96 The form of the constituting of the European Union has been determined and profoundly distorted by certain peculiar characteristics of the minds of the controllers of the public realms, idea-complexes that we may call *technocratic fallacies.*

[60] A. de Tocqueville, *Democracy in America* (tr. H. Reeve; New York, Schocken Books; 1961), I, p. 318.

[61] *Ibid.*, II, pp. 323–4, 336–7. Aristotle had foreseen the tyrannical potentiality of democracy. In what he called a monarchical democracy, the people become monarchical, one ruler composed of many persons. 'Hence such a democracy is the exact counterpart of tyranny among monarchies; its general character is exactly the same. Both lord it over the better class of citizen and the resolutions of the one are the directives of the other; the tyrant's flatterer is the people's demagogue, each exercising influence in his sphere, flatterers on tyrants, demagogues on this type of popular body. They are able to do this primarily because they bring every question before the popular assembly, whose decrees can supersede the written laws. This greatly enhances their personal power because, while the people rule over all, *they* rule over the people's opinion, since the majority follow their lead.' Aristotle, *The Politics*, IV.4 (tr. T. A. Sinclair; Harmondsworth, Penguin; 1962), p. 160.

7.97 The first fundamental fallacy has been the idea that a constitution is a legally formulated arrangement of institutions. The second is the idea that there is something called the economy which is autonomous in relation to the rest of social phenomena, that *res economica* is systematically separable from *res publica,* and even from *res privata.* The third fallacy is the idea that democracy can be conducted as if it were a species of diplomacy, as if diplomacy can be democracy by other means.

7.98 The life-threatening effects of these fallacies can be detected in the deep-structure of the European Union system and, with the conclusion of the deplorable Treaty on European Union in 1992, the constitutional situation has become worse rather than better.[62] At the heart of the system remains the fantasy of the Diplomatic General Will, the idea that the controllers of the public realms of the member states are able to represent the totality of the national interests of the participating peoples, and hence that the public interest of the EU – which is expressed in the law of the EU – is nothing more than the aggregate of the public interests of the member states, mediated through the collective willing of the public-realm controllers. The underlying supposition is that the infinitely complex and intense social phenomenon known as *politics,* which is at the heart of the process of will-formation in a democracy, can be transmuted and subsumed in a bargaining process among the controllers of the respective public realms, spuriously legitimated by mobilising the ante hoc or post hoc consent of this or that institution within the member states.

7.99 At the heart of the system remains also the fantasy of the Aggregate Economy, the idea that an EU economy and market can be made by the legal and administrative co-ordination of the national economies and markets, and hence the idea that the economic public interest of the EU – which is expressed in its economic and monetary policy, and in economic legislation, and in the interpretation and application of economic legislation – can be treated as being the aggregate of the

[62] The Maastricht Treaty introduced into the EC Treaty technocratic fantasies in providing separate legal-constitutional regimes for so-called *Economic Policy* and so-called *Monetary Policy* and in arbitrarily legislating certain transient capitalist dogmas, with collective punishments for recalcitrant member states. And it provided a new non-EC (intergovernmental) system for so-called *Common Foreign and Security Policy, Police and Judicial Co-operation in Criminal Matters* and *Justice and Home Affairs* (this last aspect being more or less reintegrated into the EC system by the Treaty of Amsterdam of 1997).

economic public interests of the member states. The underlying supposition is that the organising of the infinitely complex and intense social phenomenon of interactive (public and private) *economic decision-making* of a capitalist social system can be transmuted and subsumed into the routine interactive decision-making of government ministers, diplomats, national and international administrators, and national and international judges.

7.100 Such ideas directly conflict with other ideas whose social power we have come to understand through many centuries of European social philosophising and through the last two centuries of intense lived social experience. They run directly counter to the constitutional psychologies of the people and peoples of Europe which have been discussed above. They are ideas which wholly misconceive the nature of the self-constituting (ideal, real and legal) of our societies. They are ideas which come from the shared consciousness of a rootless class, the class of technocrats, whose job it is to manage the public realms of our societies abstractly and instrumentally and professionally, rather than through moral and political and emotional commitment. Such people have been allowed to determine the revolutionary reconstituting of European society.

7.101 Against such ideas we must insist on other ideas. The self-constituting of a society is the social self-constituting of human consciousness. What is called the *economy* of a society is simply that part of such self-constituting which is the socialising of human effort and human desire. So-called *democracy* is that part of such self-constituting which is the socialising of the human will. The self-constituting of the most dynamic form of society, that is to say, democratic-capitalist society, is an inextricable integrating of consciousness, effort, desire and will.

7.102 To unravel the historical process by which technocratic fallacies came to dominate and to impede the process of Europe's reunifying requires an understanding of the developmental relationship between the *real constituting* of our societies, during the period which we have called inter-statal Europe, and the *idealisation* of that process in the idea-complexes known as *democracy, capitalism* and *the state* (in its internal and external manifestations).

7.103 It was no coincidence that Jean-Jacques Rousseau and Adam Smith both proposed, almost simultaneously, new ways of imagining the real-constitution processes which would later be ideally constituted in the social theories which came to be known as *democracy* and *capitalism.*

And it was no coincidence that they did so at the very time when our societies had brought to full consciousness such powerful ways of imagining their social totality. The ideal-real-legal interaction of the two – democracy-capitalism/society-nation-state – has been the story of the amazing development of our societies over the last two centuries. Rousseau's *general will* and Smith's *invisible hand* were metaphors of wonderful explanatory power, but they were far more than metaphors – and they were close analogues of each other.[63] Their hypothesis was that it is possible to aggregate human action socially, to aggregate the infinite particularity of human willing and human effort – and, most wonderfully of all, such aggregating can produce what we may call *surplus social effect*, an output that is much more than the sum of the inputs. They had apparently constructed ideally an engine of unlimited social progress, ensuring ever-increasing human well-being through the universalised forms of *law* and *wealth*.

7.104 It turned out that democracy and capitalism involved a wholesale transformation of society, a re-constituting of society. The nineteenth century found a new instrument for social self-reconstituting, a *novum organum* which was a very old instrument reconceived, namely, the public realm of society, the *res publica*. The ancient public realm, which had been the personal property of kings and of one self-serving oligarchy after another, became the means of revolutionary social transformation. The public realm provided a superstructure within which society could be reconstituted, redistributing all forms of social power, including economic power (especially property-power), political power (especially over the legislative process), and psychic power (over the

[63] '[T]he rulers well know that the General Will is always on the side which is most favourable to the public interest, that is to say, most equitable; so that it is needful only to act justly, to be certain of following the General Will.' J.-J. Rousseau, *Discourse on Political Economy*, in *The Social Contract and Discourses* (tr. G. D. H. Cole; London, J. M. Dent & Sons; 1973), pp. 296–7. 'As every individual, therefore, endeavours as much as he can both to employ his capital in the support of domestic industry, and so to direct that industry that its produce may be of the greatest value; every individual necessarily labours to render the annual revenue of the society as great as he can. He generally, indeed, neither intends to promote the public interest, nor knows how much he is promoting it . . . and he is in this, as in many other cases, led by an invisible hand to promote an end which was no part of his intention.' A. Smith, *An Inquiry into the Nature and Causes of the Wealth of Nations* (1776), bk IV, ch. 2. On what German writers call respectively *das Problem J.-J. Rousseau* (individualist or collectivist?) and *das Problem Adam Smith* (is a Smithian-capitalist economy natural or artificial?), see E. Cassirer, *The Question of Jean-Jacques Rousseau* (tr. P. Gay; Bloomington, Indiana University Press; 1954), and J. Viner, 'Adam Smith and laissez faire', in *The Long View and the Short* (Glencoe, The Free Press; 1958), pp. 213–45.

contents of the public mind).[64] The public-realm superstructure came to be referred to as the *state*, another *ancien régime* form reformed.[65]

7.105 The ancient constitutional psychologies adjusted themselves to these developments, seeing the superstructural public realm as the self-governing of *society* as the republican will of the *nation*, as the self-constituting of a people as *state*. (In Germany and Japan in the period up to 1914, it proved possible for the constitutional needs of capitalism to be met by technocratic rather than by democratic forms. And we see now in various countries outside Europe a form of social transformation which might be called *state capitalism*.)

7.106 The superstructural public realms recognised each other externally – *recognition* even became a technical term of international law – so that, regardless of the status of the state internally within the different societies and of the extreme practical inequality among the states, they could treat each other as so-called sovereign equals, since each seemed to be performing a similar social-structural function. The *status in statu*, to adapt Metternich's formula, could also be a *status ex statu*.[66] Their more romantic apologists could even suppose that the states together formed a sort of inter-statal *society*.[67] And it was soon found that the age-old ruling-class game known as *diplomacy* could still be played according to the old rules, as a game among the controllers of the new public realms. And the age-old aspiration known as *international law* could continue to perform its old-regime function, marginally controlling the external activity of the new state-machines, reconciling piecemeal their so-called *interests*.

7.107 The immense increase in the aggregate energy of the new-regime societies gave great force to what has been referred to above as competitive nationalism. There was a new way of increasing the relative power of the social totality – not by war, colonisation or annexation, but by increasing the organisational efficiency of society, and by increasing its aggregate wealth. The most dynamic new-regime societies had

[64] The 'public mind' is the collective consciousness of a society which functions in the same way as the consciousness of individual human beings from which it emerges and to which it returns to modify the contents of individual consciousness. The nature and the role of the public mind are considered in ch. 4 above.

[65] Once again, it is de Tocqueville who offers a fascinating exploration of the origins, in *ancien régime* France, of such a repositioning of 'the state'. A. de Tocqueville, *The Old Regime and the French Revolution* (1856) (tr. S. Gilbert; Garden City, Doubleday Anchor Books; 1955), pt 3, ch. 3.

[66] See text at fn. 70 below.

[67] H. Bull, *The Anarchical Society: a Study of Order in World Politics* (London, Macmillan; 1977).

become vast wealth-machines. The pursuit of external power through wealth is the continuation of war by other means. The peoples of Europe were conscripted into a set of competing *levées en masse* in time of war and a set of permanent working armies in time of peace (with reserve armies of (unemployed) labour, to borrow Marx's metaphor). The two so-called World Wars of the twentieth century were wars made by the controllers of the national wealth-machines, by the nations within our nations. Europe's social progress was bought at the expense of Europe's social unity. And the consequence was a twentieth century whose first half was spent in war among the new competing *state wealth-machines*, and whose second half has been spent in a feverish collective effort by the controllers of the public realms to overcome their past, by seeking to create a self-transcending *status ex statu*, the European Union.

7.108 The making of the European Union, as an external hegemonic public realm, reflects the social hegemony which the national public realms had accumulated over the last two centuries, the self-creating of the state as intra-societal superpower. That process had reached its natural limit with the development of the *mixed economy* after 1929. Not content with having made capitalism possible by providing its necessary political, social, economic and legal conditions, the public realm became a master of the so-called *economy*, that is to say, the socialising of human effort and desire. The public realm became a direct economic actor (especially through state-owned enterprises), and it became the manager of all managers (in the management of the macro-economy) and through fine-tuning of the micro-economy (anti-trust law, consumer protection, etc.).

7.109 After 1945, the public realms, which had caused such indescribable suffering and destruction, rehabilitated themselves by organising yet another reconstituting of our societies. And it was from that reconstituting that the European Economic Community was born, a superstructural reconstituting through the forming of a communal external capitalist *economy*. It was, ironically, the beginning of the end of statist hegemonism. The European Community dawned in the dusk of the world which had made it.[68]

7.110 Over recent decades we have begun to reconstitute ourselves ideally, that is to say, in terms of the ideas by which we organise our

[68] The Austrian dissent to the classical and neo-classical economic orthodoxy had been reasserted in the 1930s with the work of Ludwig Mises and Friedrich von Hayek. Joseph Schumpeter's *History of Economic Analysis* had been published in 1954.

lives. Our *societies* are changing, as we renegotiate the terms and conditions of our sociality. The public mind can no longer be managed by the controllers of the public realm. Our *nations* are being reconceived, as the people reconsider the various sources of their personal identity. The nature and the function of the *state* (in the internal sense) is now an open question, following extensive redistribution of the economic and administrative functions of government. The process known as *globalisation* has put in question the system of management of transnational phenomena through inter-statal activity. *Democracy*, as an idea and an ideal, is being tested against its practical manifestations. *Capitalism*, as an idea and an ideal, is being tested against its practical effects.

7.111 It is the equivocal achievement of the European Community that it has succeeded in surviving from one new age into another. To redeem it and to perfect European Union will require an unprecedented effort of our long-accumulated constitutional wisdom.

Making the future

7.112 What, then, must we do?[69]

7.113 We must first dispose of three courses of action which, strangely and embarrassingly, are precisely the three courses of action which are available at the present time.

(1) The first is *nuclear fusion* (or 'enhanced co-operation'), the prussianisation of the European Union, that is to say, the final rationalisation of the Community system, among a limited number of European states, so that it becomes a supplementary state-system, welded onto the national constitutional systems, an endogenous communal constitutional exo-skeleton (i.e. secreted out from the national systems but shared externally among them all), in which the constitutional problems of dual legal supremacy and dual democratic legitimacy would at last be faced and resolved. Official Germany has seemed to support this line of action,

[69] In his pre-revolutionary tract of 1886, Tolstoy said: 'In the matter with which I am engaged, what I had always thought has been confirmed, namely, that practice inevitably follows theory and, I will not say justifies it, but cannot be different, and that if I have understood a matter about which I have thought, I cannot do it otherwise than as I understand it.' He also said: 'What constitutes the chief public evil the people suffer from – not in our country alone – is the Government . . . ' L. Tolstoy, *What Then Must We Do?* (tr. A. Maude; Bideford, Green Books; 1991), pp. 107, 163.

but ambivalently, in so far as it has ceased, at least for the time being, to speak, or to speak openly, of the unavoidability of *political union* as a concomitant of economic and monetary union.

(2) The second course of action is *inertial evolution*, the gradual intensification of the system, supported, again ambivalently, by official France. It sees the development of the Union as having a natural momentum, a sort of steerable self-evolution, from customs union to common market to single market to economic and monetary union, and beyond – each step seeming to be a more or less logical and ineluctable progression from what has gone before, even at the price of the ever-increasing incoherence of the total constitutional system (the EU plus member states).

(3) The third course of action is *polyvalent diffusion*, apparently favoured by official Britain. It is the concertisation of the European Union, under the slogan *Forward to the Nineteenth Century*, leading to an intrinsically external diplomatico-institutional system, or rather an incoherent set of external systems of unresolved constitutional character, but containing a repertory of useful forms of potential collective action.

7.114 Nothing more need be said about the mutually incompatible second and third solutions. They are technocratic distortions of the constitutional psychologies of the two peoples – for France, the claim to represent externally the natural social integrity of the people-as-nation through the rationalistic authority of the controllers of the public realm; for Britain, the claim to represent externally competing and unresolved social interests through the self-determining activity of the controllers of the public realm.

7.115 But more must be said about the first solution, given the exceptional influence which the German government will have over the future of the European enterprise and given the evident rationality of such an approach. It is a solution which is also an emanation from the complex constitutional psychology of the German people, as it has developed over the last two centuries, the powerful mixture of the psychology of *state* and the psychology of *nation*, the first being the necessary guarantee of the safety and well-being of the second.

7.116 The history of the twentieth century in Europe compels all of us, including the German people, to think as lucidly and frankly as possible about these matters. To that end, we may call to mind three things which may stand symbolically for many others.

(1) At the time of the creation of the *Zollverein* in 1834, Austria found itself in much the same situation as Britain 120 years later. It did not want to be inside, but could it remain outside? Metternich wrote a Memorandum for the Emperor, saying that, within the German Confederation, Prussia was creating a sort of *state-within-a-state.*

'In the German Confederation there is arising a smaller subsidiary union, a *status in statu* in the full sense of the term, which only too soon accustoms itself to achieve its own ends by its own machinery in the first place and will only pay attention to the objects and the machinery of the Confederation in so far as they are compatible with the former.'[70]

(2) In 1916, the German government set up a working-group to consider the necessary conditions for the establishment of a Customs and Economic Community with the countries of Central Europe (a *Zoll- und Wirtschaftsgemeinschaft*), designed to keep those countries out of the grip of Russia, but avoiding their direct annexation by Germany. The German word *Gemeinschaft* is a word with an interesting history, unlike (at least until recently) the corresponding words (*community* and *communauté*) in English and French.[71]

[70] Quoted in W. O. Henderson, ' Prussia and the founding of the German *Zollverein*' (fn. 49 above), p. 1,094.

[71] For an account of these discussions, see W. J. Mommsen, *Max Weber und die Deutsche Politik: 1890–1920* (1959) (Tübingen, J. C. B. Mohr; 2nd edn, 1974), pp. 223ff. The idea of such a union had been mentioned in the September Programme (of war aims) of 8 September 1914 which had called for 'the establishment of a Central European Customs and Economic Union under German leadership' (p. 236). In an aide-mémoire to the Austro-Hungarian government in November 1915, the German government proposed a customs union (*Zollbundniss*) for the unification (*Verschmelzung*) of the whole area into an economic unity (*Einheit*) (p. 232). One may say that the German government was trying to reconcile four policy objectives: (1) to free the Central European countries from Russian control; (2) to constitute those countries as a buffer between Germany and Russia; (3) to increase Germany's status as a European power; (4) to provide economic opportunities for German business. The idea of an economic union was considered as a politically more acceptable way of meeting the demands of the German right and the military for direct annexation (a *Hegemonialstellung des Deutschen Reiches . . . primäir durch indirekte Methoden,* in the words of K. Riezler, p. 223).

The German word *Gemeinschaft* is associated, in particular, with the name of F. Tönnies: *Gemeinschaft und Gesellschaft* (1887); *Fundamental Concepts of Sociology: Gemeinschaft und Gesellschaft* (tr. C. P. Loomis; New York; 1940). The epistemological status of Tönnies' distinction has caused much confusion (to which he contributed). It is best regarded as not being prescriptive or judgemental, or a rationalisation of empirical phenomena, but as something akin to what Weber would call an ideal-type, a heuristic which helps us to situate and compare empirical phenomena. Broadly speaking, *Gemeinschaft* is the idea of a more natural, instinctive type of community, whereas *Gesellschaft* is the idea of a more artificial negotiated society. But the distinction was caught up in the problem of German national

(3) In his biography of Thomas Mann, the German author Klaus Harpprecht has drawn attention to something which Mann wrote in 1947: 'in just fifty years . . . [Germany] will, in spite of everything, have all of non-Russian Europe in its pocket, as Hitler could already have had everything if only he had not been so impossible'.[72] Harpprecht himself comments that this is 'a prophecy that one reads half a century later with something of a shiver'.

7.117 We must surely pay particular respect to the constitutional psychologies of those peoples of Europe who have only recently recovered their identity and their dignity as nations and states after centuries of abuse and oppression. And there is a much wider consideration. An imposed prussianising of part of Europe, accompanied by various kinds of inertial and entropic reconstituting of the rest, including a sort of collective neo-colonialism in Central and Eastern Europe, will mean the division of Europe, a disunifying of Europe. Europe will become an incoherent collection of sub-unions lacking any historical, ethnic, psychic – or even geographical – reason to exist. Their members may not even be geographically contiguous to each other. The sad unity-in-disunity of the Holy Roman Empire after 1648 will have been negated, but by a disunity-in-unity which could do to Europe the damage which that system did to Germany. A bizarre and tragic outcome of thirty centuries of European self-constituting!

7.118 It follows from all the above that the self-constituting of a society is an interaction between consciousness and history. History produces the practical and psychic circumstances which are constantly re-formed by the work of consciousness.[73] Half-revolutions, which carry

self-consciousness after 1871. Was the German nation the coming-to-consciousness of a natural community or the imposition of an artificial society upon rich and proud German diversity? Thus the distinction came to play a role similar to Hegel's distinction between *state* and *civil society* (a distinction which was, however, clearly capable of having both rationalising and prescriptive significance).

In English, it is only recently that the word *community* has come to have a special significance (apart from its use in the title *European Community*), in connection with a communitarian variant within Liberalism. See generally F. Dallmayr, *From Contract to Community: Political Theory at the Crossroads* (New York, M. Dekker; 1978); D. Bell, *Communitarianism and its Critics* (Oxford, Oxford University Press; 1993).

[72] K. Harpprecht, *Thomas Mann: Eine Biographie* (Reinbeck, Rowohlt Verlag; 1995) p. 1,663.

[73] 'Very fitly is man compared to a tree, whose roots are his thoughts, whose branches and leaves his words, the fruit whereof are his works.' R. Allott, *Wits Theater of the Little World* (London, N. Ling; 1599), dedication.

within them the potentiality of their own negation, occur when the products of historical consciousness are not adequately re-formed in the consciousness of the people, in the public mind of society.

7.119 The democratic legitimating of constitutional forms is not achieved by formalistic manipulation of intricate sub-systems, such as the tragi-comic Article 189b (now renumbered as 251) of the EC Treaty. Democratic legitimation is the interiorisation by the people of the *necessity* of particular social forms, forms which produce life-determining social products (legal, political, economic, administrative, psychic). It follows that European integration, if it is to survive and prosper as a revolutionary transforming of European society, must be an interiorisation in the consciousness of the people and the peoples of Europe of the necessity of new social forms of European society. *Necessity* in this context means that the social forms of European society must be seen as a necessary part of the self-identifying of the people and the peoples of Europe and a necessary part of their socialising, that is to say, of their social self-constituting with a view to their survival and prospering in the actual historical circumstance of Europe and of the human world in general.

7.120 The European Union, in its present form, is an *anarche*. It lacks an *arche*, an ultimate principle of its ordering. It lacks a coherent idea of its actuality, an ideal of its potentiality. It is not a Mortal God, to borrow another image from Thomas Hobbes, in the name of which the people and the peoples of Europe can find a further identity, to which they can attach their loyalty, serve a common purpose, and define their opportunities and their responsibilities in relation to the human world in general.

7.121 The first step must be the reintegration of Europe's reunifying into the historical consciousness of Europe, into the ever-maturing constitutional psychologies of the people and the peoples of Europe. It has been the purpose of the present study to make a contribution to that process. European integration must be understood in the light of thirty centuries of Europe's self-conscious self-constituting, of all that we have thought and all that we have done, the good and the evil and the indifferent, to organize our communal living.

7.122 The second step must be the bringing back to consciousness of a public mind of Europe, of a collective consciousness which can process the concepts, the ideals, the values, the purposes, the policies, the priorities, the hopes and the fears of the people and the peoples of Europe – that never-ending dialectical process of collective self-contemplating, self-correcting, self-perfecting which is the work of the public mind of a society. The work of the public mind is logically and practically prior to the process known as *politics*, the process by which a society struggles to determine the public interest and hence to determine its collective willing and acting, above all by the making of law.

7.123 But it is not possible to organise a modern dynamic society without both a dynamic public mind and a dynamic politics. The superstructure of conspiring public realms must be surpassed by a supreme structure of self-conceiving European society.

7.124 The third step in the salvation of Europe's re-unifying must be the instituting, at long last, of a transcendental debate in the public mind of Europe about the idea and the ideal of European integration. Such a debate must include, as a primary constituent, discussion of the relationship of that idea and that ideal to the ideas and ideals which animate our other loyalties, especially loyalty to the very many nations and subnations (the peoples) of Europe, each of which has a peculiar history and a peculiar self-consciousness. That history and that self-consciousness have been characterised by a variety of vigorous *emotions:* pride, patriotism, altruism, courage – and their dark shadows. To make a society strong and, still more, to remake strong societies, a substantial emotional investment must come from the people and the peoples whose lives are changed thereby. Without such an investment the reunified European society will never engage anything approaching the passionate mutuality of *society*, the profound self-identifying of *nation*, or the rational self-perfecting of *state.*

7.125 It is a strange and sad fact that this European revolution, which could have been the latest and the greatest, has inspired no excitement whatsoever in the public mind, even in the minds of the young, especially in the minds of the young. Hegel said of the French and German Enlightenments: 'All thinking beings shared in the jubilation of the epoch.'[74] The English poet Wordsworth said, of the period of the French Revolution: 'Bliss was it in that dawn to be alive. But to be young was very Heaven!'[75]

[74] G. W. F. Hegel. *The Philosophy of History* (tr. I. Sibree; New York, Dover Publications; 1956), p. 447.

[75] W. Wordsworth, *The Prelude*, bk XI.

7.126 One of Edmund Burke's many memorable sayings is: 'To make us love our country, our country ought to be lovely.'[76] Somehow we have to awaken *l'âme et la personne de l'Europe* from its sad, self-induced sleep. A proud and self-confident and lovable Europe – a unique civilisation among the great ancient civilisations of the world – could, once more, yet again, energise itself, take a role of leadership and responsibility, a substantial microcosm in the great reconstituting of the macrocosm of all-humanity, a reconstituting which has already begun, and which will dominate the present century.

7.127 The only power over power is the power of ideas. We, the people of Europe, must consider how we can use the power of ideas to actualise the unique potentiality of Europe, to find a life-giving concept of European Union, so that Europe may play its proper part in the making of a new and better human world. *Seid umschlungen, Millionen.*[77]

[76] E. Burke, *Reflections* (fn. 6 above), p. 75.

[77] 'Embrace, you millions.' F. Schiller, *An die Freude* (*Ode to Joy*), line 9.

8

The concept of European Union

Imagining the unimagined

The self and the other: the dilemma of identity – The one and the many: the dilemma of power – Unity of nature, plurality of value: the dilemma of the will – Justice and social justice: the dilemma of order – New citizens, old laws: the dilemma of becoming – Making the economic constitution – The precession effect – The macro–micro fault-line – European Union as European society

The European Union lacks an idea of itself. It is an unimagined community. In seeking to transcend a set of national societies, its potential development and even its survival are threatened if it cannot generate a self-consciousness within the public minds of its constituent societies and in the private minds of the human beings whose social self-constituting it determines.

The process of European integration has been dominated by two of the paradigmatic forms of social self-constituting. It has been the dialectical product of real-world struggles conducted, in particular, by the national governments and by the controllers of the national economies. It has been the product of obsessive traditions of state-centred law and administration. It has been weakly determined by values, purposes and ideals, the forms of a society's ideal self-constituting.

Above all, the European Union has still not been able to resolve and transcend the contradictory categories of democracy and diplomacy by installing an idea of the common interest of all-Europe within and beyond all conceptions of national interest. The value, the purpose and the ideal of common interest is a necessary part of the forming of the idea of a common identity and a common destiny.

8.1 We, human beings and human societies, become what we think we are. If we have conflicting ideas of what we are, we become a puzzle to ourselves and to others. If we have no clear idea of what we are, we become what circumstances make us. Conceptual dissonance and conceptual drift have been characteristics of the life-story of the three societies (called European Communities) which are now contained in a society called the European Union. A member of a select but ominous class of international social systems which also includes the Holy Roman Empire[1] and the League of Nations,[2] the European Union is a paradoxical social form, namely, an *unimagined community*.[3] And, inadequately imagined, Europe's latest half-revolution may yet become a member of another unfortunate social class – the class of *failed revolutions*.[4]

[1] The Holy Roman Empire was 'neither holy nor Roman nor an empire'. Voltaire, *Essai sur les moeurs et l'esprit des nations* (*c.*1756), ch. 70 (Paris, Editions Garnier Frères; 1963), I, p. 683. The shadowy Empire (*Reich*) evaporated when Francis II resigned the imperial title in 1806 and declared himself Emperor of Austria, after sixteen German states had left the Empire to join the Napoleon-inspired Confederation of the Rhine. In his own lively constitutional imagination, Napoleon, who crowned himself in 1804 as 'Emperor of the French' (taking the crown from the hands of the Pope), was the true successor of the Frankish King Charlemagne, who had been crowned by the Pope as Emperor in the year 800, and whose kingdom had been divided following his death. The East Frankish (German) King, Otto I, invaded Italy, took the title King of Italy, and in 962 (the traditional date of the founding of the Holy Roman Empire) was crowned as Emperor in Rome by the Pope. The Empire came to be called 'Roman' under his son, Otto II, 'Holy' in the twelfth century, and 'of the German Nation' in the fifteenth century. The ghost of the old Empire returned in 1871 when, after the Prussian army had occupied Paris, the newly unified Germany was proclaimed, in the Palace of Versailles, as a new German Empire, with the King of Prussia taking the title of Emperor (without being crowned as such). The last German Emperor abdicated in 1918.

[2] There is a fine example of semantic *mésentente cordiale* in the fact that the English *league of nations* (with indistinct echoes of the inter-city alliances of ancient Greece or the Hansa) was also the French *société des nations* (with overtones of the then-fashionable Durkheim and Duguit and ideas of social solidarity).

[3] Benedict Anderson, in *Imagined Communities. Reflections on the Origin and Spread of Nationalism* (London, Verso; 1983/1991), refrained from imposing any general structural theory on his examination of the way in which societies, always and everywhere, have used a remarkable armoury of imaginative and mind-manipulating techniques to establish subjective social identity. A general inference from his study is that it evidently requires much skill and effort to make and maintain the subjective identity of a society.

[4] Europe's failed revolutions of the twentieth century (Russian, German and Italian) have deeply depressed the European spirit, by seeming to prove finally the lesson of 1792 that fundamental social change, born of a marriage of ideas and violence, must lead to chaos, corruption, terror and reaction. For bitter accounts of one such revolution by former believers, see A. Koestler and others, *The God that Failed. Six Studies in Communism* (London, Hamish Hamilton; 1950). 'The Soviet Union has deceived our fondest hopes and shown us tragically in what treacherous quicksand an honest revolution can founder.' A. Gide, in *ibid.*, p. 198.

8.2 To re-imagine European Union is to help the people and the peoples of Europe to choose to become what they are capable of being. We must create the constitutive idea and the revolutionary ideal of 'European Union' – to sustain, justify, control, surpass and perfect the half-revolutionary institutional structure currently known as 'the European Union'.[5]

The self and the other – the dilemma of identity

8.3 For self-imagining human beings and self-imagining human societies, the self is an other. The self makes itself as it comes to know itself as an other. And, for the self, the other is a self. The self comes to know itself as a self as it comes to know the other as another self. Each self and every other are mutually self-constituting. Such an abstract (Fichtean-Hegelian)[6] conception of the making of human identity is applicable, not least, to the history of Europe – a 3,000-year drama of the self-constituting of countless selves in relation to countless others. European Union is the latest chapter, but presumably not the last chapter, in that interesting story. A putative European public mind (European social consciousness) is constituting a putative European self, which is not merely a multiple *self* formed from the far-from-putative selves of the subordinate societies of Europe, but also a single *other*, a self in its own right, recognised by the far-from-putative public minds of those societies and by the private minds of their members.

8.4 Idealised (and controversially identified and explained) large-scale cultural patterns of shared psychic experience have dominated an accumulating pan-European self-consciousness, forming a shared cultural heritage, forming a communal psychic self, at least within the minds of an internationalised elite – the intellectual and artistic glory that was ancient Greece; the republican-military grandeur of ancient

[5] This distinction based on the presence or absence of the definite article 'the' – in English and those other languages which permit of such a contrast – expresses the fact that a society is not merely a systematic structure of social power but also a structure-system of ideas (a theory) about social power, the latter being represented by abstract words, that is to say, in the formula of medieval philosophy, by words of 'the second intention', words expressing ideas about ideas (cf. the distinction between 'law' and 'the law').

[6] 'They [more than one consciousness] *recognize* themselves as *mutually recognizing* each other.' G. W. F. Hegel, *Phenomenology of Spirit* (1807), § 184 (tr. A. V. Miller; Oxford, Oxford University Press; 1977), p. 112.

Rome; the ambiguous hegemony of the medieval Roman Church; the revival of a Byzantine version of Roman law; the Italian-led cultural revolution from 1250 to 1520; the global projection of Europeanism, led by Spain and Portugal; the multinational politico-religious revolution of the sixteenth century; the multinational scientific and philosophical revolution of the seventeenth century; the French-led cult of *savoir-vivre* in the eighteenth century; the multinational eighteenth-century Enlightenment; the socio-economic revolution after 1770 led by Britain and France; German-led nineteenth-century academic intellectualism (the human sciences) and rationalistic public administration; the new global projection of Europeanism in nineteenth-century imperialism; the new scientific revolution after 1860.

8.5 Cultural diversity, cultural competition and cultural exchange have been intensely enriching within European consciousness. We recall the universities of the Middle Ages, with teachers and students from all over Europe. And we think of the cultural travelling of individuals, a 'grand tourism', a 'free movement' of lively minds. Such cultural transnationalism affected the thinking of those whose thinking had important effects on European consciousness in general, and hence on the course of European history. Cultural travelling, like other forms of travel, could have both positive and negative effects on those who travelled, mind-broadening and mind-narrowing, often generating an unstable mental syndrome which we might call xenophobophilia. Cultural travellers might admire and detest foreign manners and ideas, sometimes both at the same time, sometimes at different stages of the traveller's personal intellectual development.[7]

8.6 Like Babylonian and then Aramaic in the ancient world of South-western Asia, a succession of pragmatically determined international languages – Greek, Latin, French, English – enabled elite to speak to

[7] England was a particularly puzzling and irritating phenomenon for Continental observers, a strange mixture of barbarous manners and advanced thinking. For a vivid account of French xenophobophilia, see J. Texte, *Jean-Jacques Rousseau and the Cosmopolitan Spirit in Literature. A Study of the Literary Relations between France and England during the 18th Century* (tr. J. W. Matthews; London, Duckworth & Co.; 1899). Voltaire's complex and tendentious account of his impressions of England, centring on the effect of the phenomenon of 'liberty' on all aspects of public life in England, was given, soon after his return to France, in his *Lettres philosophiques* (1734). In *La culture et la civilisation britanniques devant l'opinion française au XVIIIe siècle de la paix d'Utrecht aux* Lettres philosophiques *de Voltaire 1713–1734* (Philadelphia, 1948), G. Bonno has suggested that other French observers had anticipated Voltaire's impressions of England.

elite across Europe's political and linguistic frontiers, and across the span of historical time. Heroic efforts of creative Enlightenment philology managed to assemble most of the many European languages into language-families, derived from an 'Indo-European' hypothetical *Ur*-language, but linguistic diversity has been a permanent source of diversity of identity. It is commonly supposed that the character of a given language expresses the character of a given people, reinforcing the idea of a Lamarckian, if not Darwinian, biological basis for intensely individualised identities. The legally imposed formal multilingualism of the European Union affirms an historically determined heterogeneity which history also negates.

8.7 Above all, throughout Europe's three millennia, there has been a fusing of the contemplative and creative consciousness of individual Europeans into the European collective consciousness, the transcendent European public mind. *Contemplative* consciousness reflects on the most general questions which present themselves to the human mind – religious, philosophical and scientific questions. Such questions present themselves as universal in character, calling for universal answers. Although different nations have contributed in distinctive ways to the making of the reflexive European public mind, that diversity has been an enriching of a common project which overrides differences of time and place. To understand the universal and perennial character of collective European philosophical consciousness,[8] we need only call to mind a particular philosophical tradition – say, the (idealist) tradition which links Parmenides, Pythagoras, Plato, Aristotle, Zeno, Aquinas, Descartes, Spinoza, Kant, Fichte and Hegel; or the (sceptical/ empiricist) tradition which links Protagoras, Aristotle, Carneades, William of Ockham, Montaigne, Bacon, Hobbes, Locke, Berkeley, Hume, Kant and Hegel. And the same could be demonstrated still more cogently in the case of religious or scientific consciousness.

8.8 The work of Europe's *creative* consciousness has also been the rich product of artists travelling through time and across political and cultural frontiers. We may think of the development of oil-painting in Europe from a powerful union of Byzantine, Flemish and Italian skills

[8] Hegel took the view that all philosophies are part of one philosophy, the accumulating 'self-knowledge of Mind'. 'They never have passed away, but all are affirmatively contained as elements in a whole.' G. W. F. Hegel, *Lectures on the History of Philosophy* (1831) (tr. E. S. Haldane; London, Kegan Paul; 1892), pp. 55, 37.

and traditions. We may think of the development of European music as a high art-form, formed from a union of skills and traditions from all over Europe, if especially from Italy, France, Germany and Austria. We may think of European architecture, especially medieval Gothic architecture and then the revival of Graeco-Roman architecture, flowing out from France and Italy to provide a communal style of habitat for our communal living. We may think of the development of the play and the novel and the film as high art-forms, to which writers from so many parts of Europe contributed, forms of collective self-contemplating which may be seen as a continuation of philosophy by other (and more accessible) means.

8.9 Finally, there have always been external *others* to help to constitute the European *self.* Ancient Greece could not fail to be exceptionally conscious of the ancient civilisations which had preceded it, some of which co-existed with it. Ancient Rome, at least as its history is traditionally told, was never allowed to forget the other surviving civilisations and the countless unRomanised and non-European 'tribes' which were a permanent, and ultimately disastrous, physical and psychic challenge to its very self-conscious self. Medieval Christendom found a formidable *other* in Islam, which seemed to be a challenge both to Christianity as a religion and to Christendom as a social formation.

8.10 As later medieval travellers ventured further from mainland Europe, in particular to India and China, it became necessary to re-imagine Europe's place in a physical and cultural world which far surpassed it. As European colonisers moved through the rest of the world, a New World, it became necessary to re-imagine the nature and the responsibility of Europeanism as an exportable cultural phenomenon. As most of the rest of the human world developed socially and politically, largely under European influence as a sort of Greater Europe or Europe-in-exile, it became necessary, most recently, to co-exist with global social phenomena which have seemed to pose a life-threatening challenge, physical and economic and cultural, to old Europe as a whole.

8.11 We may conclude that the magnetic attraction of a shared European subjectivity has thus always been in dialectical opposition to the attraction of a particularising subjectivity – a European self at work as a self, and not merely as an other, within the self-constituting of individual Europeans. But there are two seriously complicating factors when such a thing comes to take its place in the self-constituting of European

Union. (1) It is a shared subjectivity largely confined to the minds of society-members who have pan-European intellectual horizons – so that it cannot simply be assumed to be present, actually or potentially, in the minds of other sections of the population. (2) It is a shared subjectivity which has always been used and abused within another dialectic of social self-constituting, namely, that of *the one and the many*, the game of social power, where it has been *invoked* in order to promote resistance to a Europe-threatening other, internal or external, and where it has been *denied* in order to evoke loyalty to some particularising conformation of social power.

The one and the many – the dilemma of power

8.12 Every society is a permanent reconciling of its unity and its multiplicity. Society transforms the natural power of its members (human beings and subordinate societies) into social power, through social structures and systems. Society-members retain their individual capacity to will and act, but society, by means of such structures and systems, may cause their willing and acting to serve the common interest of society. The many of society are one, in so far as they will and act in society's common interest. The one of society is many, since it can only actualise the common interest through its members, human beings and subordinate societies of human beings with all their own particular interests.

8.13 Edward Gibbon said that history is 'little more than the register of the crimes, follies, and misfortunes of mankind'.[9] It is certainly true that any account of European history must include a pathetic story of every form of social pathology, the 'internal diseases' of society identified by Thomas Hobbes, writing during the disorderly reordering of England in the seventeenth century, not least 'the insatiable appetite of enlarging Dominion' which he called *bulimia*.[10] But, on the other hand,

[9] E. Gibbon, *The History of the Decline and Fall of the Roman Empire*, I (1776), ch. 3 (ed. D. Womersley; London, Allen Lane; 1994), p. 102.

[10] T. Hobbes, *Leviathan* (1651) (London, J. M. Dent & Sons (Everyman's Library); 1914), ch. 29, p. 177. Evelyn Waugh, describing the history of an imaginary European country, says that it had suffered 'every conceivable ill the body politic is heir to. Dynastic wars, foreign invasion, disputed successions, revolting colonies, endemic syphilis, impoverished soil, masonic intrigues, revolutions, restorations, cabals, juntas, pronunciamentos, liberations, constitutions, *coups d'état*, dictatorships, assassinations, agrarian reforms, popular elections, foreign intervention, repudiation of loans, inflations of currency, trade unions,

an Olympian observer of Europe's long history, seeing it as a whole in accelerated form, would be struck by the frenzy of ever-changing forms of polity by means of which Europe has sought to reconcile its unity and its multiplicity. Within such a perspective, the apparent novelty and specificity of the European Union would seem like yet another baroque variation on a very familiar theme. The European Union is a waking dream of the bulimic political imagination, offering governmental dominion over fifteen countries and 365 million people, with the prospect of much more to come. Beyond the European Union there remains only the dream of all politico-bulimic dreams, a dream which is no longer merely a dream – global governmental dominion over everyone everywhere.

8.14 'The variety of Bodies Politique is almost infinite.'[11] For twenty-seven centuries, successive ruling cliques have shown remarkable skill and imagination in making the social forms that they have used to organise social power and in making the theories necessary to establish and to sustain a particular organisation of social power. Political metaphysics and social poetry[12] are the raw materials from which the infinite variety of polities may be formed, sustaining intricate legal structures of power with subtle superstructures of ideas, to form an inexhaustible supply of different permutations of the unity-from-multiplicity/multiplicity-in-unity which is a society. Constitutional intelligence of a high order, with the clarity of mind which ruthless self-interest inspires, has been used by princes of all kinds, wise and worthless and everything between, and by the clever and the shameless courtiers and ministers and bureaucrats and clerics and intellectuals who have served and advised them.

8.15 The European Union is a society which contains an extreme multiplicity of subordinate societies, from the government-managed state-societies through non-governmental societies of all kinds, including industrial and commercial corporations, to individual families. The European Union is also a society in which law has been the main means

massacres, arson, atheism, secret societies . . . Out of [this history] emerged the present republic of Neutralia, a typical modern state.' E. Waugh, *Scott-King's Modern Europe* (London, Chapman & Hall; 1947), p. 4.

[11] T. Hobbes, *Leviathan* (fn. 10 above), p. 120.

[12] The term 'social poetry' is particularly associated with the names of Giambattista Vico (1668–1744), for whom historiography is the reconstructing of the story of the social self-constructing of human consciousness, and Georges Sorel (1847–1922), for whom social consciousness is both a weapon and the target of revolutionary social change.

of social self-constituting, making use of the constitutive potentiality of two other realms of law – international and national – to form its own constitutive legal realm. The One of its own legal order is a Many of the three legal orders which it contains.

8.16 The layering of polities within a superstructure of law has been a perennial characteristic of European political history. The transformation of the Roman polity from Republic to Empire, during the principate of Julius Caesar's great-nephew, Caesar Augustus (63 BCE–14 CE), was also the forging of a new kind of empire, in which the imperial power would respect the cultural, and hence legal, diversity of the colonised peoples while superimposing a common law: civil law governing relations among Roman citizens; *ius gentium* for relations with and among non-citizens; natural law, as an ideal of meta-cultural and perennial law-about-law. In this, as in countless other ways, the Church of Rome respected the Roman imperial precedent. The legislative, executive, and judicial system of the Church was superimposed on the internal systems of all the Christian countries of Europe, using charismatic spiritual authority and the threat of supernatural sanctions to enforce an hegemony which went far beyond matters of faith and conscience. The Emperor Constantine's fourth-century creation of a dual Roman Empire – eastern and western – left the Church as the sole form of supranational integration in Western Europe when the western empire faded away in the late fifth century. With the establishment of a new Frankish 'Roman Empire' in the ninth and tenth centuries,[13] the Church took the hazardous step of encouraging a rival form of supranational European integration.

8.17 The relationship between the imperialised Pope and the sacralised Holy Roman Emperor would be the focus of permanent struggle, intellectual and legal and even physical, at least until the disintegration of Christendom after the sixteenth-century Reformation and the religious disintegration of the Empire finally enacted in the Peace of Westphalia (1648).[14] For six centuries, this struggle produced a flood of ideas about the source and conditions of authority in society, a ferment which would

[13] See fn. 1 above.

[14] Even the most obvious solution – the 'two cities' or 'two swords' view, with the Pope as emperor of a spiritual realm and the Emperor as master of a secular realm – left a rich fund of less soluble structural problems, prefiguring the constitutional puzzles of the European Union. Is the Emperor, like the Pope, an agent of God on earth in his own right or is he subject to the spiritual authority of the Pope? Can two 'sovereignties' co-exist? Which trumps

make possible the intense development of general social and legal philosophy in the following centuries, including the development of what would come to be called liberal democracy.

8.18 The three layers of positive law[15] in Romanised Christendom (the law of nations, canon or Church law, national law)[16] were joined by a fourth layer – imperial law – within the realm of the Holy Roman Empire. In institutional terms at least, the Empire rested with a relatively light hand on its constituent members, which were themselves both very numerous and very disparate in character. The Empire was more Many than One. And some of its constituent members were more equal than others, either because their sovereigns were electors, participating in the appointment of a new Emperor, or simply because of their greater political or ecclesiastical or economic or military power. Paradoxically and ominously, the existence of the Empire can be seen as having contributed much to the prolonged fragmentation of a major part of Western Europe.

8.19 From the ninth century, the legal and cultural unifying of England and France followed parallel courses. The unifying of Italy and Germany took a very different course. That discrepancy has had a decisive effect on the whole of European history – from the Treaty of Verdun (843), dividing Charlemagne's Frankish kingdom in a way which would lead to the separate development of France (the West Franks) and Germany (the East Franks), to the Battle of Verdun (1916), where the young of France and Germany would die in bloody, muddy agony. And

which, if they are in conflict? Are the non-spiritual (so-called 'temporal') possessions of the Pope subject to the authority of the Emperor? Are bishops, exercising great power within the separate secular realms, the exclusive appointees of the Pope or must they be approved by the local monarch? What are the limits of the legal competence of the Church authorities, within the separate national systems, and of Church (canon) law in relation to national law?

15 In the influential model proposed by Thomas Aquinas in the thirteenth century, there are three layers of *higher* law (i.e., of *ius* which is not *positum*): eternal law (the divinely ordained order of the Universe); divine law (the ultimate law for human beings: the will of God made known through faith and revelation); natural law (reason's normative intimation of eternal law).

16 In many countries, national law also included elements of Roman (Byzantine) imperial law, after the 'reception' of Roman law beginning in the twelfth century. In all countries, national law also included a mosaic of local custom which was gradually transcended by a national 'common' law (at first judge-made and partially codified, later also legislated). Within what came to be known as 'feudal' societies, each society was constituted as a more or less integrated legal hierarchy, with a vertical distribution of legal powers and responsibilities, and corresponding judicial institutions and remedies.

European history would contain another decisive discrepancy. For ten centuries, a macro-level world of intergovernmental conflict and competition, a realm full of a wild and perverted form of rationality, the realm of war and diplomacy, would co-exist with the steady systematic rationality of Europe's economic and cultural development. The most recent effect of this dual discrepancy at the heart of European history is known as the European Union.

8.20 So far as the forming of the tenuous One of England (later Great Britain, later the United Kingdom) is concerned, it is an interesting irony that a man who has some claim to be regarded as the first King of England may well have been its best. He is the only English or British monarch on whom tradition has conferred the epithet *Great.* Alfred (*c.*849–99), who had been king of Wessex (the West Saxons), was both a general and an intellectual, an English Marcus Aurelius. He led the struggle to recover control of England from Danish invaders, thereby making possible the reuniting of a country which had come to be divided into a number of ill-defined kingdoms after the sudden departure of the Roman occupiers in the fourth century and the immigration of Germanic peoples in the fifth century. He also sponsored and participated actively in a cultural renaissance, echoing that associated with Charlemagne in Continental Europe,[17] translating Roman and ecclesiastical literature from Latin into Anglo-Saxon (a German dialect, as one might say), the proto-English language.

8.21 It is another irony that, from the eleventh to the fifteenth century, English history is inseparable, at least at the governmental level, from the history of France. England and France helped to make each other as self-conscious nations. A duke of Normandy (illegitimate son of a first cousin of an English king) used force to assert a claim to the throne of England (1066), killing the English king in battle. After an English king became the second husband of the widow of the French king in his capacity as duke of Aquitaine (1152), there was created a sort of Anglo–French dual monarchy, covering a large part of south-west France, including the wine-producing area around Bordeaux. In 1337, an English king used force to assert a claim to the throne of France, initiating a campaign of violence (the Hundred Years War) which, at

[17] Alcuin, from York in the English kingdom of Northumbria, had been a leading figure in the Carolingian intellectual renaissance.

one time, placed one quarter of France under the control of the English king. The English were finally excluded from France, with the exception of Calais, in 1453.[18]

8.22 The struggle at the intergovernmental level between England and France,[19] especially as mythologised in the plays of William Shakespeare or in the story of Jeanne d'Arc, became an integral part of the self–other identifying of the English and the French. Traces of a fantasy-psychology of intimate enmity remain to this day, as the two countries find themselves intergovernmentally reconnected in the European Union. But the intentions of the English government in the Hundred Years War were also strategic and economic, and the contemporaneous remaking of society took very different forms in the two countries. The Many of France, many polities of many kinds under the more or less formal authority of the King of France, would be made into a One under centralising monarchs, from Louis IX in the twelfth century to Louis XIII and Louis XIV in the seventeenth century.

8.23 Although there were a number of strong and creative monarchs in England, not least the Tudors in the sixteenth century, English unification was a more complex process, involving an interaction between law and economics. An almost mystical belief in the social significance of law, reminiscent of the ethos of republican Rome, was combined with an assertion of the economic imperative of society-constituting which united baronial landowners with aggressive urban merchants against kings who needed money for their incessant wars and who could be used to produce the necessary legally based (and property-based) conditions of social stability (the King's Peace). The institutional detachment of the Church in England from the Church of Rome in the sixteenth century was merely the end of a long process,[20] but it contributed much more

[18] Calais remained under English control until 1558. The formal title of the kings of England (later, of Great Britain) continued to include the words 'and of France' until the eighteenth century.

[19] England and France were not allies in war from the Siege of Acre in 1191 to the Crimean War in 1854.

[20] In 1395 'twelve conclusions' containing the radical proposals of John Wyclif (*c.*1330–84) for the reform of the Roman Church were attached by his followers to the doors of St Paul's Cathedral and Westminster Abbey. The proposals were close to those which would form the basis of the sixteenth-century German Reformation programme. But *renovatio* ('reform') had been for centuries a *Leitmotiv* of vigorous debate within the Church. Luther acknowledged his debt to Wyclif and to the man he called 'Holy Johannes Hus' (*c.*1371–1415; condemned by the Church as a heretic and burned to death). Hus learned of Wyclif's work through what might be called the Bohemian connection, following the marriage of the sister of King Wenceslaus of Bohemia to England's King Richard II in 1382.

than mere symbolism to the establishment of England as a self-contained polity.[21]

8.24 A new One of Germany was finally made in 1870 from a luxuriant Many, but not including an Austria whose people and government had been intimately involved, politically and culturally, with the polities which were included in the new German state-society, not least in the context of the thousand-year Holy Roman Empire of the German Nation. The Germanic tribes described by the Roman historian Tacitus (*c.*55–*c.*120), tribes which had filled much of non-Roman Northern and Eastern Europe, were too extensive and too diverse to generate either a natural selfhood or a natural polity. In the sixteenth century, Martin Luther's appeals to 'the German nation' and to his 'beloved Germans' and his call for the use of the German language in prayer and liturgy and religious and secular writing were acts of dialectical negation, directed against the hegemony of non-Germany, especially Italy and Rome, rather than a call to nationalism in a political sense. And the post-Reformation religious divisions within a possible German nation, and especially the Thirty Years War (1618–48), not only set back the formation of an integrated polity but, perhaps, contributed to the relative isolation of Germany from social developments taking place in other parts of Europe, at least until the remarkable flowering of German culture from about 1760.

8.25 The political unification of Germany (in 1870) might be seen, in three respects, as a by-product of the French Revolution. (1) Its political structure was formed by a series of steps which began with Napoleon's rationalising of the colourful patchwork of minor south German states, making possible the Confederation of the Rhine (1806), which was followed by Metternich's Austria-dominated, but more or less ineffective, German Confederation (1815), and by the Prussian-dominated *Zollverein* (customs union) which lasted until the formation of the Prussian-dominated North German Confederation (1866), and which has encouraged the idea that economic union can lead to political union (at least if there is someone with the intelligence and determination of a Bismarck to energise the process). (2) The reconstituting of German

[21] There is a fine irony in the mirror symmetry between the wording of the Act of Parliament known as the Act of Supremacy 1559, which terminated the legal authority of the Church of Rome in England, and the wording of section 2 of the European Communities Act 1972, which introduced the legal authority of the European Communities into the United Kingdom.

society after 1815 profited from the extraordinary transformatory energy of Napoleonism, which had transformed the unfocused spirit of the Revolution into a concentrated spirit of rationalistic and paternalistic social reformism. Napoleonic enlightened absolutism was an algorithm which could be used not only to overcome the irrational proliferation of German polities but also to reorganise the internal systems of society to serve a notion of the common interest determined by servants of a rationalised Hegelian 'state'. (3) The metaphysical-mystical hypostasis of the *nation* which had served to carry the ancient idea of France from the old regime of personal monarchy into a new regime of constitutional monarchy could be used as a reservoir for long repressed feelings of collective German identity, an idea of Germany which was much more than merely the idea of a shared language or shared high culture. The One of the Germany made by Bismarck's Prussia was much more than the sum of its many discordant parts.

8.26 The future of the Many-in-One of European Union cannot escape the wonderfully turbulent past of the countless integrations and disintegrations and reintegrations which are the history of the One-and-Many of Europe. In ancient Athens, the people were more than, and prior to, the 'democratic' polity which was also their embodiment. In republican Rome, the One of the *populus* was not merely a collection of human beings but 'an assemblage of people in large numbers associated in an agreement with respect to justice and a partnership for the common good'.[22] In the Roman Church, the Church was, and is, the faithful, and also something which transcends the faithful. In the Holy Roman Empire, the Union's participating governments were masters of the totality when they acted together in the Council and they were subjects of the Union when they acted individually under the law of the Union. In the United States of America, the horizontal relationship of the constituent states had to be transformed by a sort of treaty-constitution into a vertical relationship between the Union and the individual citizens, a relationship which both contains and transcends the constituent states.[23] In a human society, the One is always also a Many in order that the Many can also be a One.

[22] '*coetus multitudinis iuris consensu et utilitatis communione sociatus*'. Cicero, *De re publica*, I. 25 (tr. C. W. Keyes; Cambridge, MA; Harvard University Press; 1988), p. 65.

[23] 'It was generally agreed that the objects of the Union could not be secured by any system founded on the principle of a confederation of sovereign States. A voluntary observance of the federal law by all the members could never be hoped for... Hence was embraced

Unity of nature, plurality of value – the dilemma of the will

8.27 Every society has an ever-evolving theory of itself which contains an ever-changing harmony of ideas set against an ever-changing counterpoint of discordant ideas. Social harmony and social discord at the level of ideas flows between the public mind of society and the private minds of society-members, in a process of permanent mutual psychic conditioning. The theory of a society is an evolutionary product of its process of social self-understanding and self-judging.

8.28 A particular society is a shared inheritance of acquired mental characteristics. Ideas form a republic into which we are born, in which we live, which we modify by our very existence, and which we leave as an inheritance to the generations which follow us. We are citizens of the republic of ideas in our capacity as human beings, sharing in the ideas which flow from our evolved physiology, from instinct and necessity, our phylogenic *species-consciousness*. And we share in the ideas formed in the public minds of the countless societies to which we belong, ontogenic *social consciousness*. And we contribute to social consciousness the ideas formed in our private minds, in the many layers of our own ontogenic *personal consciousness*, including the inarticulate but active layers of physiological consciousness, the inexpressible but active layers of our personal unconscious consciousness, and the expressible layers of the social consciousness which we have internalised, and which we can re-externalise to modify social consciousness.

8.29 Species-consciousness – social consciousness – private consciousness – interpersonal consciousness. These elementary structures reflect the dual species-characteristic of human beings as thinking beings and as social beings. And they account for the fact that there are not only shared ideas but also conflicts of ideas. We live together through the sharing of ideas and through the conflict of ideas. Human social co-existence and human social progress are made possible by the sharing and the conflict of ideas. And the extraordinary fact is that this multiple layering of human consciousness manifests itself not only in the personal consciousness of human individuals but also in the public

the alternative of a government which instead of operating on the States, should operate without their intervention on the individuals composing them . . . ' J. Madison, letter to T. Jefferson (24 October 1787), in J. P. Boyd *et al.* (eds.), *The Papers of Thomas Jefferson* (Princeton, Princeton University Press; 1950–), XII, p. 271.

minds of whole societies. As human beings who happen to be Europeans, we are fellow-citizens of a single republic of ideas, rich with an inheritance formed from the social consciousness of the countless societies, and forms of society, which Europe has generated. And we are citizens of the particular republics of ideas to which we particularly belong, including our own natal nation and our own natal family, each with its own special inheritance of socially produced ideas. And each of us is a unique repository of a personal consciousness which contains those special inheritances in a unique form, the republic of ideas which is the private mind of each European.

8.30 The United States of America was constituted as a society from the fittest ideas which had survived from the long history of European social philosophy, as those ideas presented themselves to minds formed by the tradition of English legal history and by the Anglo–Scottish Enlightenment of the eighteenth century,[24] and as those ideas could be made applicable to the agriculture-based society of colonial America.[25] The European Union is the attempt to constitute a society from the surviving ideas of perennial social philosophy, as those ideas are understood in the late-twentieth century, in minds enlightened and burdened by two more centuries of the most intense human social experience, including the ambiguous and still-disputed inheritance of the French Revolution,[26]

[24] 'This was the object of the Declaration of Independence. Not to find out new principles, or new arguments, never before thought of... but to place before mankind the common sense of the subject... Neither aiming at originality of principle or sentiment... it was intended to be an expression of the American mind... All its authority rests on the harmonizing sentiments of the day, whether expressed in conversation, in letters, printed essays, or in the elementary books of public right, as Aristotle, Cicero, Locke, Sidney &c.' T. Jefferson, in a letter to H. Lee (8 May 1825), in *Thomas Jefferson. Writings* (New York, Literary Classics of the U.S.; Cambridge, Cambridge University Press; 1984), p. 1,501. *The Federalist Papers* (1787–8), a theoretical and polemical analysis of the federal solution by three participants in the reconstituting of the Union (Hamilton, Madison, Jay), was described by Jefferson as 'the best commentary on the principles of government which ever was written'. Letter to J. Madison (18 November 1788), in Jefferson's *Papers* (fn. 23 above), XIV, p. 188.

[25] 'I think our governments will remain virtuous for many centuries; as long as they are chiefly agricultural; and this will be as long as there shall be vacant lands in any part of America. When they get piled up upon one another in large cities, as in Europe, they will become corrupt as in Europe.' T. Jefferson, in a letter to J. Madison (20 December 1787), in Jefferson's *Papers* (fn. 23 above), XII, p. 442. There is a substantial and disputatious literature on the economic bases of the American Revolution.

[26] For a lucid overview of the continuing controversy among historians about the socio-economic basis of the French Revolution, see G. C. Comninel, *Rethinking the French Revolution. Marxism and the Revisionist Challenge* (London, New York, Verso Books; 1987).

and, not least, Europe's twentieth-century experience, about which the public mind of Europe has not even the beginning of a shared theory for understanding and judging that experience.

8.31 Values are ideas which act as the algorithms of human behaviour. An input of circumstance may produce an output of behaviour and, if that process of production involves the application of ideas, those ideas are values. Values are the motive force of the will. Even if, as David Hume insisted, ideas can never move us to action,[27] they are certainly the way in which we present choices of action to ourselves before we act, and justify our action after we have acted. To re-form an idea of Hegel's: *theory* and *practice* form a *syllogism of action* of which the middle term is *value*. The history of Europe is the sum total of all the actions taken by Europeans and, therefore, the history of Europe is the enactment of the values which have been involved in the choices, the acts of will, which have made those actions. The history of Europe is the product of the consciousness of all Europeans, of the sharing of ideas and the conflict of ideas in European consciousness, at every level from human species-consciousness to the biological consciousness of each individual European.

8.32 European experience since 1789 has made the values which were expressed in the making of the United States only partly relevant for the European mind as it makes European Union, whatever may be their continuing relevance for the American mind.[28] The process of development of the social consciousness of Old Europe has separated itself from the development of the social consciousness of New Europe across the Atlantic Ocean. In particular, the story of the operation of the syllogism of action in Europe contains a special, and dramatic, chapter relating to the making of three particular concepts of social totality. *Society. Nation. State.* The *union* of European Union and the constituent *communities* of the European Union are concepts of social totality which cannot avoid forming a relationship, of affirmation or negation or transcendence, with *society, nation* and *state.*

8.33 These concepts of social totality are *paratheses.* That is to say, they are produced by the mind in order to act as a shared presence in public and private consciousness. A parathesis is an idea acting as a

[27] D. Hume, *A Treatise of Human Nature* (1739–40) (ed. D. G. C. Mcnabb; London, W. Collins & Co.; 1962) bk II, III. iii.

[28] For 'American mind', see the opinion of Thomas Jefferson, at fn. 24 above.

social force.[29] Typically, it generates a particular kind of mental entity (*ens rationis*), namely an *hypostasis*, producing effects in consciousness analogous to the effects produced by what the mind conceives of as material objects or forces.[30] The particular parathetic hypostases of *society, nation* and *state* have the notable characteristic that they act as abundant repositories of social value. They are not merely theoretical and practical but also highly *affective.* They can generate powerful emotions of many kinds, not least of attachment and hatred, causing and justifying even death in the public interest. They are powerful terms in the syllogism of social action.

8.34 It has been suggested above that the paratheses of society, nation, and state are epitomes, in a single idea and a single word, of the historically produced constitutional psychology of, respectively, England, France and Germany,[31] No doubt one might find the same, or comparable, ideas acting as concepts of social totality in the constitutional psychology of other societies which are or may be members of the European Union. Such ideas express a worldview, determining not only a society's understanding of itself but also of its conceptual status in relation to other societies. And it is an understanding which is reflected not only in its own willing and acting as a society but also in what it expects and demands from the willing and acting of society-members, up to and including the sacrifice of their lives for the society.

8.35 The central focus of the parathesis s*ociety* is an idea of the common wealth, the common interest and the common destiny of the society and its members. The central focus of the parathesis *nation* is an idea of the common identity, the unity, and the common destiny of the society and its members. The central focus of the parathesis *state* is an idea of a shared social order under law, a mutuality of service between society and its members. The legal system of each society reflects such large-scale ideas. They determine, and are determined by, what Montesquieu called 'the spirit of the laws'. They determine the distribution of public-realm power, including the ultimate terms and conditions of its exercise,

[29] This use of the word *parathesis* is proposed as a novelty, an extension of its meaning in classical Greek (a setting-out for the purposes of comparison).

[30] *Hypostasis* (that is, an immaterial thing which is treated as if it had substance) is a word with a complex history, including its use as an element in a Christian theology of the three-in-one God. See C. Stead, *Philosophy in Christian Antiquity* (Cambridge, Cambridge University Press; 1994), ch. 14.

[31] Ch. 7 above.

its purposes, the bases of its control and accountability. The values – high values and everyday values – which the legal system enacts and enforces are direct or indirect deductions from such ideas. Consciousness, not only of the public mind but also in the private minds of the society-members, is powerfully conditioned by such ideas and such values, so that, as Montesquieu recommended, the spirit of the laws and the spirit of the nation should be in conformity with each other.[32]

8.36 It is a major challenge to the making of the idea of European Union that the spirits of the laws of the different member societies are the product of radically different historical circumstances, of radically different constitutional psychologies, of radically different value-filled worldviews. And yet the European Union, as an institutional system, is a system which has been constructed on the basis of law, which has created its own distinctive legal system, and which, in its everyday social life, is dominated by law.

Justice and social justice – the dilemma of order

8.37 No society is an island. Every society, including the European Union, exists in relation to an *inner space* which contains not only human individuals, with their own minds and projects, but also subordinate societies – families and collective entities of all kinds – each a self-constituting in and through its own social consciousness. And every society, including the European Union, exists in relation to an *outer space* which contains all other human beings, with their own minds and projects, and all other societies, up to and including the society of all-humanity, the society of all societies, all of them a self-constituting in and through their own social consciousness.

8.38 As a system of order, every society, including the European Union, implies an order which transcends its own order. The rules of a game imply the rules of games. The conventions of a map imply the conventions of map-making. The form of a sonata implies sonata-form. The pattern of a painting implies the pattern of vision. The syntax of speech implies the order of language. The rationality of thinking implies

[32] He quotes with approval a saying of Solon (the law-giver of Athens, seventh–sixth century BCE) which the makers of the European Union might well bear in mind : 'I have given them the best [laws] they were able to bear.' Baron de Montesquieu, *The Spirit of the Laws* (1748) (tr. T. Nugent; London, Collier Macmillan; 1949), ch. 19, p. 305.

the order of the mind. The order of a given society implies the self-ordering of human co-existence.

8.39 The fact that we are *able* habitually and constantly to connect the *actual* and the *ideal* as a seemingly inseparable duality in the functioning of our minds is, no doubt, a product of our biological evolution. But the fact that we are *conscious* of that connection, and of its practical potentialities, is, certainly, a product of the reflexive self-contemplating activity known as philosophy and, within the social consciousness of Europe, a product of the particular form which that philosophy took in ancient Greece and of the hazard-filled story of the survival of that philosophy into the medieval and modern world. It has meant that European social consciousness has been filled with a permanent and vigorous dialectic in which the actual is constantly subjected to the possibility of its surpassing by the ideal. The uniquely and relentlessly progressive character of European civilisation, in principle if not always in practice, is the most striking effect of the enacting in social consciousness of this particular European form of self-contemplating human consciousness.

8.40 As considered above, in relation to what has been identified as 'the dilemma of the will', the social order of a society produces and processes its values in a way which generates a unique value-content within its social consciousness. But each society also develops its own relationship to that which it conceives as the transcendental, that is, the ideal order which transcends it. Within European social history, there have been a number of such transcendental worldviews. Mythology. Religion (Greek and Roman polytheism, with elements of monotheism). Metaphysical philosophy (Socrates-Plato-Aristotle). Religion again (Christianity). Philosophical theology (Aquinas). Baconian natural philosophy (science). Humanist natural law (Grotius, Wolff). Cartesian rationalism. Social idealism (Hobbes, Rousseau, Kant). Philosophical empiricism (Locke). Empiricist idealism (Kant, Hegel). Social positivism (Comte). Historicism (Hegel, Marx, Ranke). Biological naturalism (Spencer, Freud, sociobiology).

8.41 The pursuit of the ideal, a higher-order explanation and justification of human order of all kinds, is evidently a human species-characteristic. More problematic is the question of whether the above list, more or less in chronological order, is the history of human self-perfecting. We, wiser or more experienced than the *philosophes* of the eighteenth-century Enlightenment (especially Vico and Condorcet) or the nineteenth-century positivists (especially Comte), can see that such developments are neither inevitable at the level of ideas nor necessarily effective in the improvement of social practice. Who, having known the European twentieth century, could say that the death of God and the rise of human naturalism have instituted the kingdom of heaven on earth?

8.42 The European mind has traditionally expressed the dialectical potentiality of law in the concept of *justice*. Actualising the ideal of justice in the social justice generated by the legal system of a given society at a given time, a society nevertheless retains the supra-societal transcendental ideal of justice as both a critical negation of the actual and a permanent aspiration within the actual. But there has always been (from the Sophists of ancient Greece and Carneades in Hellenistic Greece to Hume and Marx and beyond) a movement of thought which seeks to conventionalise the transcendental and detranscendentalise the ideal, especially by arguing that such ideas, being socially produced, have no claim to priority over any other socially produced ideas.

8.43 One social form which has been used to resolve, for practical purposes, this negation-of-the-negation of the ideal and the actual is the concept of *constitutionalism*, that is to say, the idea that a society may contain its own socially produced transcendental ideal. The ancient and universal idea of the sovereignty of the law, or the 'Rule of Law', was combined with the relatively ancient, and not so universal, idea of the contractual basis of society to produce what came to be called *liberal democracy*, a theory of society in which the ideal is internalised as the pursuit of the common interest, by means of laws which society-members impose on themselves, in accordance with higher-law (law-about-law) principles, including fundamental rights or fundamental principles of legality, which they implicitly accept by participating in the society. It was this particular form of the social integration of the ideal and the actual which came to be known by the complimentary theory-name of constitutionalism, because the legal constitution (written or not) could be regarded as the enacting of an ideal constitution.[33]

8.44 But, in practice, the internalising of the ideal of justice has not suppressed the transcendental potentiality of the ideal of justice. We

[33] For further discussion, see ch. 12 below.

remain capable of judging the actual of a liberal democratic society in terms of an ideal which transcends that society and its theory of its own self-sufficiency. And we evidently remain free, eager even, to judge, by reference to what is presumably a transcendental ideal of justice, societies which are not organised on the basis of a theory of liberal democracy or do not practise it to our satisfaction.

8.45 With the creation of the European Communities, a strange thing happened. Through the process and forms of diplomacy (negotiation/treaties), some of the institutional aspects of constitutionalist societies (parliament, court, executive bodies) were externalised and extrapolated into what was otherwise a social void, that is to say, the 'international' realm. The insouciance of the politicians and technocrats involved would have been remarkable if it had not been characteristic of so many previous attempts at international pseudo-constitutionalism (the League of Nations, the United Nations, the Permanent Court of International Justice, the Permanent Court of Arbitration, the Bretton Woods institutions, the GATT, the Human Rights system of the Council of Europe . . .). Abstracted from the national societies, the national histories, and the national consciousness which give life to such things, the orphan institutions of the European Communities were supposed to survive on their own, gradually forming around themselves the organic social conditions of their own survival.

8.46 Very soon, naïve ideas drawn from a generalised all-purpose theory of 'liberal democracy' were applied to them, and they were found wanting in terms of the ideals of that theory, exhibiting what was called a 'democratic deficit'. The radical but implicit negation of the high values of totalitarian tyranny had evidently been thought to be a philosophically sufficient, sufficiently incontrovertible, and sufficiently substantial transcendental basis for the new enterprise. There was a vague obeisance in the direction of the Rule of Law (Articles 220 and 230 EC (formerly 164 and 173)), but no explicit provision of fundamental rights or of higher-law principles of any kind. Instead, an imperious economic *telos* was installed as the ideal focus of the whole system, and certain rudimentary institutional aspects of a capitalist 'market' were extrapolated and externalised. Justice was equated with social justice, and social justice was equated with economistic justice, the efficient functioning of a 'common market'.

New citizens, old laws – the dilemma of becoming

8.47 Societies are dynamic living organisms, as dynamic as every other life-form, constantly changing over time, undergoing repeated metamorphoses, both systematic and psychological, actual and ideal, growing, flourishing and decaying. To analyse the self-constituting of a society as the product of that society's work on the five 'dilemmas' which have formed the basis of the present study is not merely to offer a new instrument of thinking about society.[34] It is to propose a universal hypothesis about the making and maintaining of social organisation.[35] Every society, including the European Union, is a perpetual struggle to resolve dialectically the dilemmas of *identity, power, will, order* and *becoming*, each of which interacts dialectically with all the others. The constitution of a society is a process not a thing. Every society, including European Union, is a self-producing dialectic of change, a particular history of *becoming* within the universal history of the *becoming* of all living things.[36]

8.48 The unfolding history of European Union is part of a three-in-one historical process: its own history, the histories of its member states, and the history of international society. The past of a society, like the past of a person, determines what the society now is and determines its future possibilities, but the past is not only beyond change and beyond redemption; it is also beyond retrieval. Instead, a society, like a person, must make its own history, the story of its past which acts within present consciousness to condition our choices among the possibilities available to us. European Union is burdened not only with

[34] Francis Bacon called his own new post-Aristotelian method of thinking a 'new instrument' (*novum organum* in Latin, Aristotle's logic having been traditionally known, in Greek, as the *organon* or instrument). René Descartes also proposed a new 'method' of thinking (*Discours de la méthode*, 1637).

[35] 'There was but one course left, therefore . . . to commence a total reconstruction of sciences, arts, and all human knowledge, raised upon the proper foundations.' F. Bacon, *The New Organon* (1620), *Prooemium* (eds. J. Spedding, R. Ellis and D. Heath; London, Longmans & Co.; 1858), IV, p. 8. For further discussion of 'the perennial dilemmas of society', see *Eunomia*, chs 4–6.

[36] Aristotle had the mind of a biologist and hence the application to society of his fine idea of the nature of living things, as systems which are perpetually actualising their potentiality in a process of becoming, was not a metaphor but a necessary corollary of the fact that human societies are composed of human beings as living things.

the burden of the European past but also with the burden of Europe's problematic historiography, the problem of its own idea of its own past.[37]

8.49 European Union causes the multiple pasts of Europe to flow now in a single channel, but the mixing is imperfect because pan-European historiography is in a still less satisfactory state than the national historiographies, and because the separate participating states are continuing to form their own pasts and to form their own ideas of their own pasts.

8.50 In the relentless becoming of a society, *law* acts as a servo-mechanism regulating the process of social change, ensuring stability-in-change, allowing change-in-stability. Law speaks from the past in the present to make the future. Law itself is an unceasing reconciling of the fact of power and the power of ideas. A society's legal constitution is produced by, and helps to produce, its real and ideal constitutions. Max Weber's *Normativität des Faktischen* (normative effect of the actual) is also, one may say, a *Normativität des Idealen* (normative effect of ideas). The self-constituting of a society is a three-in-one process, a three-dimensional self-constituting, as idea, as fact and as law.[38]

8.51 The making of the European Union, as institutional system, has been dominated by its legal constitution, but, as yet another form of social self-constituting in Europe's long history of social self-constituting, the Union is the continuing product of a triple three-dimensional self-constituting – its own, that of international society and that of the 'states' which are its institutional 'members'.[39] It follows that the law of the European Union is performing the function of law at all three levels, a social self-regulating mechanism carrying the European past through the European present to the European future, within the past, the present and the future of its member societies and of the international society of all-humanity, the society of all societies.

[37] For a discussion of the conceptual problems of historiography, see ch. 11 below.

[38] For the hypothesis that the so-called *constitution* of a society is a process of self-constituting in three dimensions (the ideal constitution, the real constitution and the legal constitution), see *Eunomia*, ch. 9.

[39] A 'state' in the international sense is the hypostasis of a society which is managed through a social system known as a 'government' and whose identity as a state is recognised by the governments of other states. In some countries (not the UK or the US), the word 'state' is used internally as an hypostasis of the totality of centralised public power.

Making the economic constitution

8.52 Nowhere is the interaction of idea, fact and law more evident and more significant than in the making of what has come to be called a society's 'economy', its economic self-constituting. On a foundation of the actual social activity of transforming the physical world through the application of physical and mental effort, there has been constructed a superstructure of ideas and law which has come to take possession of every moment and every aspect, physical and mental, of the life of every human being everywhere. The self-constituting of a society is also an ideal, real and legal economic self-constituting. The economy is a product of the mind. It exists nowhere else than in the human mind. It actualises itself through actual human behaviour organised by the actual law-based systems of a particular society.

8.53 The intellectual activity now known as *economics* is a form of social philosophy which – like legal philosophy, psychology, the philosophy of science, the philosophy of history – seeks to explain a particular aspect of human social experience and to justify that explanation as an appropriate basis of human self-knowing.[40] More powerfully and more directly than other forms of sectoral social philosophy, economics, itself a social activity, re-enters the social phenomena which it studies and is liable to have an effect on actual social behaviour. Like such other forms, economics reconstructs sets of social phenomena in the form of systems of ideas and, especially, in the form of *models*.[41] And, like those

[40] It was A. Marshall (1842–1924) who established the intellectual separation of economics from the rest of social philosophy, a development reflected in the use of the word 'economics' as the accepted name of the discipline in place of the earlier 'political economy'. John Ruskin, among others, objected to the 'modern *soi-disant* science of political economy . . . based on the idea that an advantageous code of social action may be determined irrespectively of the influence of social affection'. J. Ruskin, *Unto This Last. Four Essays on the First Principles of Political Economy* (1860) (London, George Allen & Sons; 1862/1910), p. 1.

[41] 'Economics is a science of thinking in terms of models joined to the art of choosing models which are relevant to the contemporary world.' J. M. Keynes, letter to Roy Harrod of 4 July 1938, in D. Moggridge (ed.), *The Collected Writings of John Maynard Keynes* (London, Macmillan for the Royal Economic Society; 1973), XIV, p. 296. Keynes was urging Harrod to repel attempts 'to turn [economics] into a pseudo-natural-science.' 'A system [of ideas] is an imaginary machine invented to connect together in the fancy [imagination] those different movements and effects which are already in reality performed.' A. Smith, *Essays on Philosophical Subjects* (eds. W. P. D. Wightman and J. C. Bryce; Oxford, Clarendon Press; 1980); essay on 'History of Astronomy', pp. 31–105, at p. 66. Cf. Kant's 'idea of reason' and

other forms, economics has its own history, the working-out of a double dialectic of its relationship to changing social reality and its response to the products of its own past. It works on social phenomena as it works on itself.

8.54 The European Union, as an institutional system based on economic ideas and economic systems, has entered into the totality of the history of Europe's socio-economic reality and into the history of Europe's economic philosophy. The idea that it would be possible to create a new kind of society (the European Communities) by creating a new kind of international economic system was the product of a particular stage and state of Europe's economic self-constituting, a particular stage and state of 'capitalism'. The pathology of the present state of European integration has, as a leading symptom, a crisis in its ideal self-constituting as an economy.

8.55 The intimate and indissoluble and problematic connection between ideas, fact and law in the economic field has been apparent since Aristotle linked the property-based household-management of the family and the property-based household-management of society.[42] The contradictory relationship between the ideal and the real and the legal in the economics of capitalism[43] has always been apparent. In the words of Thomas More, writing in the early days of modern capitalism:

'Consequently, when I consider and turn over in my mind the state of all commonwealths flourishing anywhere today, so help me God, I can see nothing else than a kind of conspiracy of the rich, who are aiming at their own interests under the name and title of the commonwealth. They invent and devise all ways and means by which, first, they may keep without fear of loss all that they have amassed by evil practices and, secondly, they may then purchase as cheaply as possible and abuse the toil and labour of all the poor. These devices become law as soon as

Weber's 'ideal-type'. The metaphor of a 'model' is now a commonplace of epistemologies of other intellectual disciplines, e.g., natural science: K. Craik, *The Nature of Explanation*, 1943 (following E. Mach); and sociology: P. Winch, *The Idea of a Social Science and its Relation to Philosophy* (1958).

42 Aristotle, *Politics* (Harmondsworth, Penguin; 1962), I. 3.

43 Capitalism, in the present context, may be considered to have two defining characteristics: the separation of the activity of labour from property in the profits of labour; the determination of the economic value of goods and services by social processes beyond the control of the seller and buyer of the goods or services.

the rich have once decreed their observance in the name of the public – that is, of the poor also!'[44]

8.56 More's theme was taken up by Rousseau, in his deconstruction of the real-world content of the ideal social model known as 'the social contract'.

'You have need of me, because I am rich and you are poor. We will therefore come to an agreement. I will permit you to have the honour of serving me, on condition that you bestow on me the little you have left, in return for the pains I shall take to command you.'[45]

8.57 In the words of Adam Smith, hallowed (and ambiguous) prophet of advanced (*laissez faire*) capitalism.

'Laws and government may be considered ... as a combination of the rich to oppress the poor, and preserve to themselves the inequality of goods which would otherwise be soon destroyed by the attacks of the poor, who if not hindered by the government would soon reduce the others to an equality with themselves by open violence. The government and laws ... tell them they must either continue poor or acquire wealth in the same manner as they have done.'[46]

8.58 Even in third-stage capitalism (so-called *free-market* or *liberal capitalism*), as analysed by one of its hallowed prophets, the role of the legal system in resolving the structural contradiction of capitalism (idealised naturalism *v.* actual artificiality) is fully acknowledged:

44 T. More, *Utopia* (1516), bk II, in *The Complete Works of St Thomas More* (eds. E. Surtz and J. H. Hexter; New Haven, London, Yale University Press; 1965), IV, p. 241. More was Lord Chancellor under King Henry VIII, but was executed for refusing to acknowledge the King as 'supreme head' of 'the Church of England', a refusal made treasonable by Act of Parliament (Act of Supremacy 1534). In the same passage, More anticipated Marxian ideas of 'surplus value' and 'ideology'. 'What is worse, the rich every day extort [*abradunt*] a part of their daily allowance from the poor not only by private fraud but by public law ... and, finally, by making laws, have palmed it off as justice.' K. Kautsky (a leading Marxist theorist who had been, at one time, Engels' secretary) proposed a reading of More as a Marxist *avant la lettre*, in *Thomas More and His Utopia* (1888) (tr. H. J. Stenning; London, A. & C. Black; 1927; republished: New York, Russell & Russell; 1959).

45 J.-J. Rousseau, *A Discourse on Political Economy* (1755), in *The Social Contract and Discourses* (tr. G. D. H. Cole; London, J. M. Dent & Sons (Everyman's Library); 1913/1973), p. 148.

46 A. Smith, *Lectures on Jurisprudence* (lecture of 22 February 1763) (eds. R. L. Meek, D. D. Raphael, P. G. Stein; Oxford, Clarendon Press; 1978), pp. 208–9. 'Civil government, so far as it is instituted for the security of property, is in reality instituted for the defence of the rich against the poor, or of those who have some property against those who have none at all.' A. Smith, *An Inquiry into the Nature and Causes of the Wealth of Nations* (1776), v.i.b. (eds. R. H. Campbell and A. S. Skinner; Oxford, Clarendon Press; 1976), II, p. 715.

'The functioning of competition not only requires adequate organisation of certain institutions like money, markets, and channels of information – some of which can never be provided by private enterprise – but it depends above all on the existence of an appropriate legal system, a legal system designed both to preserve competition and to make it operate as beneficially as possible.'[47]

The precession effect

8.59 A strange feature of social philosophy in general, and economic philosophy in particular, is that they are always out-of-date or premature or both.[48] This *precession effect*, as we may call it,[49] is no doubt a necessary consequence of the dialectical character of social change. The social consciousness of a society, including the European Union, always contains an idea of itself which it has negated, and an idea by which it will be negated.

8.60 We may find evidence of the precession effect in the historical perspective which has been outlined in the present study. (1) The social fragmentation, not to say chaos, which followed the end of the Roman Empire in the west was met by two new forms of *imperialism*[50]

[47] F. Hayek, *The Road to Serfdom* (London, Routledge; 1944), p. 28. He goes on, however, to condemn talk about a supposed 'Middle Way' between 'atomistic' competition and central direction (p. 31). 'For modern rational capitalism has need, not only of the technical means of production, but of a calculable legal system and of administration in terms of formal rules . . . Such a legal system and such administration have been available for economic activity in a comparative state of legal and formalistic perfection only in the Occident.' M. Weber, *The Protestant Ethic and the Spirit of Capitalism* (1905/1921) (tr. T. Parsons; London, George Allen & Unwin; 1930/1976), p. 25.

[48] 'Practical men, who believe themselves to be quite exempt from any intellectual influences, are usually the slaves of some defunct economist . . . for in the field of economic and political philosophy there are not many who are influenced by new theories after they are twenty-five or thirty years of age, so that the ideas which civil servants and politicians and even agitators apply to current events are not likely to be the newest.' J. M. Keynes, *The General Theory of Employment Interest and Money* (London, Macmillan; 1936), pp. 383–4.

[49] *Precession*, as used in mechanics, refers to the behaviour of a rotating body which continues to rotate, but on an altered axis of rotation, after the original axis of its rotation has been affected by an external force (e.g. a spinning-top leaning under the effect of gravity, or a society's institutions continuing to function on the basis of the old ideas which caused them to change their functioning in a particular way).

[50] It seems that an 'emperor', in medieval legal semantics, was simply a ruler who ruled over more than one kingdom but, semiotically, it could not avoid association with the old Roman Empires (east and west).

(the Roman Church and the Holy Roman Empire). (2) The inefficiency[51] and remoteness of imperialism were met by the development of *monarchy*, a form of local imperialism. (3) The inefficiency and the abuses of monarchy[52] were met by the development of *liberal democracy*, in which the metaphysical notion of sovereignty, with its absolutist implications, is retained, in the constitutive ideas of *the sovereignty of the people* and *the sovereignty of the polity* (nation, state). (4) The inefficiency and the life-threatening abuses of competing and conflicting European polities, totalitarian or post-totalitarian or liberal democratic, were met by the *neo-imperialism* of European integration in its original form. (5) The inefficiency and the abuses of democratic pluralism in national societies are now being met by what we may call *post-democracy*, a form of absolutist rationalistic governmental centralism, or collective monarchy, whose primary social function is to provide leadership in economic management.

8.61 Since the eighteenth century the development of economic philosophy has tended to dominate the development of general social philosophy. The naturalising of the idea of society in the work of Hobbes and Locke and Rousseau, suggesting that the present needs of social philosophy could be met by a model which seemed to be universal and perennial in character, was echoed in, and reinforced by, a naturalising of the economy in the work of the French Physiocrats, and then in Smith and Say and Ricardo. The economy was presented as a natural system, and ancient ideas of 'natural law' were given a practical social significance at long last. The self-regulating and value-making 'market' could be seen as the analogue of the self-regulating and law-making 'general will' of society. Society could at last explain itself to itself as being essentially an efficient wealth-producing system.[53]

[51] 'Inefficiency', here and hereafter, means primarily economic inefficiency, as a form of social reality fails to meet the needs of a new actualising of a society's economic potentiality.

[52] The word 'monarchy' (rule by one) expresses the idea that the One of government (*l'état*) is distinct from the Many of society. European monarchs, even those who had originally been Nordic-Germanic elected chieftains in character, were gradually seduced, however petty their kingdom, into pseudo-oriental hieratic ritualism, the most seductive manifestation of which was the court of Louis XIV of France (reigned 1643–1715).

[53] 'The politicians of the ancient world were always talking of morals and virtue; ours speak of nothing but commerce and money.' J.-J. Rousseau, *A Discourse on the Moral Effects of the Arts and Sciences* (1750), in *The Social Contract and Discourses* (fn. 45 above), p. 16. Rousseau was echoing a comment by Montesquieu on English society, in *The Spirit of the Laws*, III.3 (fn. 32 above), p. 21. See C. Larrière, *L'Invention de l'économie au XVIIIe siècle* (Paris, Presses Universitaires de France; 1992).

8.62 The European Communities were created at a time (the 1950s) when economic philosophy happened to be dominated by the idea of *aggregate* economic phenomena. It is another strange feature of the history of economic philosophy that it has been characterised by an oscillation between the *macro* and the *micro* as the central focus of economic model-building.[54] In the period of what came to be called feudalism and of the city-state proto-capitalist economies of Italy and elsewhere (phase 1, in the chronology in § 8.60 above), society was integrated on the basis of property relations and market forces (a micro focus). In the period of the local imperialism of monarchy (phase 2), monarchy served to unite a nation economically through the provision of the law and the institutions necessary for maximising the wealth of the nation (a macro focus, conceptualised in what would come to be called 'mercantilism').

8.63 In the period of the development of liberal democracy (phase 3), Smithian economic philosophy would concentrate on the mysterious aggregative effect (the wealth of the nation) caused by the micro phenomenon of the division of labour. The *laissez faire* of Smith's disciples was the *liberty* of the disciples of Rousseau. In the fourth period, what came to be called 'the Keynesian revolution' reasserted the relevance of aggregate economic phenomena, claiming that post-Smithian economics had failed to produce stable, just or efficient societies, nationally or internationally. Such ideas could be seen as a necessary part of a more general social revolution produced by the turbulent events of the period 1919–45.

8.64 For those, including Jean Monnet, who had experienced those events and who had experienced the successful achievement of Allied co-operative economic management during the Wars, the role of managed economic development in reconstructing Europe and in achieving purposive social progress was not a political dogma but a practical necessity. European integration on a mixed-economy basis (a government-managed European market) was the logical extrapolation of that necessity.

[54] The dispute among economic philosophers about the real or the illusionary nature of economic aggregates (society, economy, market, demand, equilibrium, etc.) is reminiscent of the bitter dispute in medieval philosophy between 'nominalists' and 'realists' about the ontological status of 'universals' (the characteristic contents of an idealist metaphysical universe).

The macro–micro fault-line

8.65 The development of the European Union has been structured on the basis of a series of economic aggregates (customs union, common market, single market, economic and monetary union) which were treated as hypostatic paratheses and were given legally enforceable substance, and which were accompanied by some of the legal-constitutional systems and paratheses associated with liberal democracy. The assumption was that a coherent society at the European level would constitute itself 'functionally', as it was said – that is to say, as a natural by-product or side-effect, as it were, of the economic constitution. Unfortunately, the negating and the surpassing of the Keynesian revolution and the reassertion of the micro-economic focus were more or less contemporaneous with the founding of the European Communities.[55] And the new focus of the economic constitution of advanced capitalist societies has proved to be part of a radical transformation of the political and economic constituting of those societies. Liberal democracy and capitalism were mutually dependent systems of ideas which were successful in managing the vast and turbulent flows of energy associated with industrialisation and urbanisation in one European country after another. Democratic systems made possible the great volume of law and administration required by capitalism. Capitalism made possible an increase in the aggregate wealth of a nation which was capable of being distributed, unequally, among the newly enfranchised citizens/workers/consumers. Post-democracy is also a post-capitalism, a counter-evolutionary absolutism,[56] an integrating of the political and economic orders under a system of pragmatic, rationalistic, managerial oligarchic hegemony, in which law and policy are negotiated, outside

[55] M. Friedman's 'The demand for money: some theoretical and empirical results' was published in 1959 (67 *Journal of Political Economy* (1959), 327–51; republished in M. Friedman, *The Optimum Quantity of Money and Other Essays* (London, Macmillan; 1969), 111–39). J. Muth's 'Rational expectations and the theory of price movements' was published in 1961 (29 *Econometrica* (1961), pp. 315–35; republished in *Rational Expectations and Econometric Practice* (London, George Allen & Unwin; 1981) pp. 3–22).

[56] The intense concern of post-democratic governments with the problem of 'education' was anticipated by A. R. J. Turgot (1727–81), statesman and economic philosopher, who recommended state-controlled education to the French King as the 'intellectual panacea' which would make society into an efficient economic system, changing his subjects into 'young men trained to do their duty by the State; patriotic and law-abiding, not from fear but on rational grounds'. Quoted in A. de Tocqueville, *The Old Regime and the French Revolution* (1856) (tr. S. Gilbert; Garden City, Doubleday & Company; 1955), pp. 160–1.

parliament, among a collection of intermediate representative forms – special interest groups, lobbyists, focus-groups, non-governmental organisations, the controllers of the mass media, and powerful industrial and commercial corporations – under the self-interested leadership of the executive branch of government.[57]

8.66 The contradictions of the European Union as institutional system add up to a structural fault which is at the core of that system and which we are now in a position to identify as its chronic pathology. It is a morbidity which is preventing us from imagining the institutional system of the European Union as a society. It means that its half-revolution may yet prove to be a failed revolution.

8.67 The contradictions of the European Union as institutional system can be expressed as six dialectical tensions which are acting, not as the creative tensions of a healthy and dynamic society, but as destructive tensions. (1) The tension between the *macro* constitutional order of the Union itself and the *micro* constitutional orders of its member states. (2) The tension between the *macro* economic order of the Union's economic constitution (the wealth of the European nation) and the *micro* economic constitutions of its member states (each an economic aggregate in its own eyes in a traditional form of conflict and competition with all the others). (3) The tension between the Council as the *macro* agent of the Union's common interest and the Council as a quasi-diplomatic forum for the reconciling of the *micro* 'national interests' of the member states. (4) The tension between two rival forms of localised imperialism (*macro* and *micro; two cities* or *two swords;* the Thomist *duplex ordo*), in the form of emerging post-democracy at the two levels – the national post-democratic managerial *oligarchy* externalised

[57] Post-democracy may be a fulfilment of the gloomy predictions of Max Weber and of what may have been, at least according to W. Mommsen, his instinctive preference for some combination of rational governmental professionalism and *plebiszitäre Führerdemokratie* (plebiscitory leader-democracy). W. Mommsen, *Max Weber und die deutsche Politik 1890–1920* (Tübingen, J. C. B. Mohr; 1959), pp. 48, 420. On Weber's discussion of the combining of bureaucracy and leadership, see R. Bendix, *Max Weber. An Intellectual Portrait* (Garden City, Doubleday & Company; 1960), pp. 440ff. At the heart of post-democracy is something akin to the spirit of nineteenth-century Prussian bureaucracy. 'The fundamental tendency of all bureaucratic thought is to turn all problems of politics into problems of administration.' K. Mannheim, *Ideology and Utopia. An Introduction to the Sociology of Knowledge* (London, Routledge & Kegan Paul; 1936), p. 105.

as an intergovernmental managerial *poliarchy*, at the level of the European Union. (5) The tension between the imperialist ambition of a *macro* pan-European confederal union and the federalising ambition of a *micro* political union among a limited number of states. (6) The tension between the ambition of the Union to be a single *macro* international actor and the survival of the *micro* 'foreign policies' of its participating governments and their separate foreign diplomatic representation.

European Union as European society

8.68 To overcome these destructive tensions, to turn them into the creative tensions of a dynamic society, it is necessary to bring to consciousness the European society which transcends the European Union as institutional system. It is not possible to have a legal system without the society of which it is the legal system. It is not possible to have an economic system without the society of which it is the economic system. It is not possible to have a political system without the society of which it is the political system. If the European Union already has these systems, it follows that there is already a latent European society which transcends them and of which we can resume the self-conscious self-constituting as idea, as fact, and as law. We can resituate the European Union within the long historical process of Europe's social self-constituting. It has been the purpose of the present study to begin that process.

8.69 Given the function of *law* within the self-constituting of a society, the most urgent task is the re-imagining of the European Union's legal system. Law reconciles the ideal and the real, the power of ideas and the fact of power. Law reconciles the universal and the particular, universalising the particular (law-making) and particularising the universal (law-applying). Law provides detailed resolutions from day to day of the dialectical dilemmas of society – the dilemmas of identity (legal personality), power (the distribution of legal powers), will (the actualising of value in the form of legal relations), order (constitutionalism), and becoming (law-making and law-applying). Our concept of the European Union's legal system must fully and efficiently recognise and actualise its capacity to do these things.

8.70 This means that we must: (1) recognise that the national constitutional orders now form part of a general constitutional order of the European Union;[58] (2) install in the European Union system the controlling idea of the common interest of the Union as overriding the individual common interests of its constituent societies;[59] (3) integrate the urgent problems of social philosophy at the two levels, to re-explain and rejustify the future of European Union, as society and as institutional system, with the problem of the exercise and control of public power at both levels;[60] (4) integrate the philosophical and practical problem of the self-constituting of European society with the philosophical and practical problem of the globalising of human society.[61]

8.71 The crisis facing the European Union is a crisis of social philosophy, a crisis of the ideal self-constituting of a new kind of society and the enactment and enforcement of a new social philosophy in and through a new kind of legal system. European Union, the redeeming parathesis of Europe's higher unity, is not a federation or a confederation, actual or potential, but a state of mind. It is not merely a union of states or governments, but a unity of consciousness. It is a new process of social self-constituting in the dimensions of ideas, of power and of law. European Union, Europe's society, is more like a family, a family with a common identity beyond its countless separate identities, a common destiny beyond its countless separate destinies, a family with an interesting past, not wholly glorious and not wholly shameful, and with much need, at the beginning of a new century, for collective healing, to find a new equilibrium between its past and its future.

[58] This means *inter alia* undoing the decisions of those national constitutional courts which have conceived of the European Union as essentially an emanation from, and inherently subject to, national 'sovereignty'.

[59] This means *inter alia* undoing those decisions of the Court of Justice of the European Communities which have tended to substitute a concept of aggregated or reconciled national interest for the concept of the particularising of a Union common interest.

[60] This means *inter alia* undoing the constitutional concept (reflected in the new Article 88 of the French constitution or the revised version of Article 203 (formerly 146) of the EC Treaty) which treats the EU as essentially the exercise 'in common' of national governmental powers.

[61] See further in ch. 10 below.

9

The conversation that we are

The seven lamps of European unity

Public mind – The conversation – The sacred – The ideal – The imaginary – The real – The social – The suffering – The future

Long before there was a Europe of the European Union, there was a Europe of the European Mind. Europeans have spoken to each other in a permanent conversation across frontiers, the kind of conversation which generates the subjectivity of a community. The future of Europe is not merely the future of the European Union but the future of the European mind. It is possible to identify the constituent elements of Europe's mental unity with which Europeans have designed the architecture of a true European community, a community of unity-in-diversity.

It is possible also to see that Europe's mind is in a pathological state, sclerotic and defeatist in the face of a recent past of which we have reason both to be proud and ashamed, and in the face of a world which has passed beyond Europe's mental and political control.

The European mind can be cured, reasserting an identity in relation to hegemonic powers outside Europe, restoring the social role of the scholar and the intellectual, resuming responsibility for the development of the ideas required for new kinds of social existence in a new kind of human world, asserting a special responsibility for the development of society and law at the global level, the level of all-humanity.

Public mind

9.1 To be is to be thought of as being (Parmenides). To be a self is to think of oneself as a self (Descartes). To think of oneself as a self is to think of oneself as an other for another thinking self (Hegel). To become a self is to make oneself through thinking (Schopenhauer). To be a self is to think of oneself as having made oneself through acting as a self (Heidegger).

9.2 Applying these elementary propositions of idealist philosophy to the self-consciousness of human society, we may say that a human society is a self-constituting, as one society among many, in and through the thinking of many human minds. The self-consciousness of a given human society is the self-consciousness of a society which has made itself in its own mind, its public mind, a mind formed from, and forming, the private minds of the society's members.

9.3 It follows that the self-consciousness of European society is the self-consciousness of a society which has constituted itself, as one society among many, in and through the thinking of the public mind of Europe. Europe's public mind *has* been formed from, and *has* formed, the private minds of Europeans and the public minds of Europe's subordinate societies. Europe's public mind *is* being formed from, and *is* forming, the private minds of Europeans and the public minds of Europe's subordinate societies.

9.4 The history of a society's self is the history of a society's self-consciousness (Dilthey). A society's history of its self forms part of the making of a society's self (Marx).[1] Applying these elementary propositions of idealist historiography to Europe's history, we may say that Europe's history is a history of Europe's self-constituting, but also a history of its consciousness of its self-constituting, the story it tells itself about its self-constituting, and the story it tells itself as an integral part of its self-constituting. We tend to become what we think we have been. To interpret the past is to make the past. To change our interpretation of the past is to change the past. To change the past is to change the present. To change the present is to change the future. In interpreting Europe's past in Europe's continuous present, we are making Europe's future.

9.5 The public mind of a human society, including the public mind of Europe, functions in ways which are directly analogous to the functioning of the mind of the individual human being. Social consciousness flows from and to individual consciousness. An irretrievable social past is stored in a memory which, nevertheless, acts as a cause in society's present. An unknowable unconscious mind nevertheless conditions

[1] This and the preceding one-sentence statements are intended as epitomised summaries. They are not quotations from the writings of the relevant philosopher.

what society knows and how it knows it. A society's public mind is ordered through the self-ordering (rationality) of the private minds of its members. A society's public mind is a self-ordering through norms and values, freedom and responsibility. A society's public mind is formed in a conversation with itself and in conversations with others (society-members and other societies). A society's public mind is haunted by all that surpasses and transcends it, the order of the material world and the mystery of the universe of all-that-is. And there are healthy and unhealthy conditions of the public mind, as there are of the private mind.

9.6 As we understand ourselves, as human beings and as human societies, so we understand our potentialities. The self-contemplating of the human mind, individual and social, is an exploration not only of what we are but also of what we might become. It follows that our idea of the actual state of European society contains within it an idea of what European society might become. It follows also that the present sclerotic and defeatist state of the European public mind is a state which could be overcome, a pathology which could be cured.

The conversation

9.7 Europe's public mind has been formed by a conversation which has continued over a period of twenty-eight centuries.[2] It is a conversation to which Europeans have contributed, at different times and to different degrees, from within the public minds of subordinate societies (Athens, Sparta, Rome, the Roman Church, Arab Spain, Florence, Reformation Germany, England, France, Holland . . .). It has also included an intrinsically transnational conversation (in the Roman Empire, the Roman Church, western monasticism, Byzantium, the Carolingian court, the medieval universities, post-Renaissance royal courts, national academies and institutes with an international perspective, modern

[2] The role of dialogue or conversation in the formation of society is a central idea in the work of H.-G. Gadamer. See especially *Wahrheit und Methode. Grundzüge einer philosophische Hermeneutik* (Tübingen, J. C. B. Mohr; 1965/1975). 'Thus the world is the common ground, trodden by none and accepted by all, uniting all who talk to one another. All kinds of human community are kinds of linguistic community: even more, they form language. For language is by nature the language of conversation; it fully realizes itself only in the process of coming to an understanding.' *Truth and Method* (trs. J. Weinsheimer and D. G. Marshall; London, Sheed & Ward; 1975/1989), p. 446.

universities ...). It has included a conversation stimulated by a succession of interesting, more or less exotic, 'others' – ancient Egypt and Persia and India for the ancient Greeks; ancient Greece, North Africa, and other non-Roman peoples for the Roman Empire; the Arab world and Islam and China for medieval Europe; the 'New World' and various other 'exotic' peoples for post-Renaissance and post-Reformation Europe, the distant colonies for the European imperial powers ...

9.8 The conversation of Europe's public mind has also been remarkable for the cultural displacements of interesting and influential Europeans. We think of Montesquieu and Voltaire and Rousseau in England; of Augustine in Milan; of Aquinas and Hobbes and Freud and Picasso in Paris; of Plato with the Pythagoreans in Sicily; of Voltaire and Maupertuis with Frederick II at Sans-Souci; of Erasmus with Thomas More in London; of Peter the Great and Canaletto and Handel in London; of Diderot with Catherine II in St Petersburg; of Goethe and Byron and Thomas Mann in Italy; of Horace Walpole at Madame du Deffand's *salon* in Paris; of Madame de Staël and Coleridge in Germany; of Luther and Gibbon and Michelangelo in Rome; of Wagner and Proust and Dürer and Turner and Ruskin in Venice; and countless other travels and meetings within the complex geography of the European public mind, a 'single European market' of ideas.

9.9 Europe's conversation with itself produced a specific content of its public mind, that is, a specific culture (in the anthropological sense of the word) and a specific civilisation (in the historical sense of the word). A culture and a civilisation are a specific form of human self-creating, an accumulating reality which grows as it feeds on itself, a *hortus conclusus* of the mind, full of flowers and weeds, growth and decay. The actual state of Europe, spiritual and intellectual and social, is the twenty-first-century harvest of all that has gone before. As archaeologists of the European mind and as architects of Europe's future, we may try to uncover the layers of Europe's cultural self-creating. We might, as a creative hypothesis, identify seven lamps of European unity, the transcendental matrix of Europe's cultural architecture.[3]

[3] In *The Seven Lamps of Architecture* (1849/1855), John Ruskin sought to identify the transcendental principles which distinguish 'architecture', as a product of the higher realms of the human mind, from 'building', the skilful work of human hands. As people have spoken for so long of 'the construction of Europe', so we may now want to imagine the future of Europe's 'architecture'.

The sacred

9.10 We have worshipped many gods. We have worshipped different gods at different places and at different times. We have worshipped the same god under different creeds and different forms of worship. We have fought wars and civil wars in the name of god. We have required faith and worship under legal obligation. We have prohibited faith and worship under criminal penalty. We have persecuted and martyred each other in the name of god. We have reinvented god as a rational being and repudiated god as morbid fantasy. We have doubted god and preached agnosticism. We have denied god and believed in atheism. We have feared god and feared godlessness.

9.11 Until recently, it was normal to believe that 'society has been built and cemented to a great extent on a foundation of religion'.[4] Such has been the case in the making of European society. The popular and literary polytheism of ancient Greece and the superstitious popular and official religion of ancient Rome[5] were transmuted into a monotheism borrowed from the ancient Near East, which was then itself modified under the influence of ancient Greek philosophy (and Hellenistic and Roman versions of that philosophy). Through the spiritual power and the institutional organisation of the Roman Church, through monasticism and the religious orders, and through every form of intellectual and artistic activity, Europe was united by Christianity in a way which is now becoming difficult for us to imagine.

9.12 The separation of western and eastern (Orthodox) Christianity, and the marginalising of non-Roman Christian sects, prefigured the *scandalum magnum* of Christianity – its disintegration, its self-wounding and, perhaps, its final self-destruction. But Christendom lives on in countless ways, not only as a legendary possibility of Europe's social unity, but as a haunting presence in every aspect of our sensibility. It is present in some of the products of the fine arts, of music and of literature which we appreciate the most highly. It is present in some of the ideas and the ideals which we apply to questions of social and moral

[4] J. G. Frazer, *The Belief in Immortality and the Worship of the Dead* (London, Macmillan & Co.; 1913), I, p. 4.

[5] Polybius said that it was superstition 'which maintains the cohesion of the Roman state'. *Histories*, VI.56 (tr. W. R. Paton; London, William Heinemann (Loeb Classical Library); 1923), p. 395.

judgement. It is present in the very language we speak, the images and idioms of everyday discourse.

9.13 The sensibility which is affected by this haunting presence is a European sensibility, a shared mind-world. Within that mind-world we also share a pathetic and persistent sense of a world we have lost, a world which we made and which we have unmade. Religion remains as a more or less vestigial social phenomenon in European society, and as an active presence in the private minds of many individual Europeans. But it co-exists in our collective memory with its dialectical negation, a powerful anti-sacred tradition, which is another all-European tradition, a religion of unreligion, preached with cold conviction by Hume and Voltaire and Feuerbach and Comte and Marx and Nietzsche and Freud, and so many others. The public mind of Europe is confused by the shared memory of the sacred and of its denial. We know that we would not be able to remake a religious world. But we are not yet certain that a post-religious human world is a possible human world.[6]

The ideal

9.14 The invention of philosophy by the ancient Greeks changed the human world, creating a new kind of human potentiality, a potentiality actualised in every subsequent state of European consciousness, in all the subsequent history of the European public mind. By 'philosophy' is here meant a universalising activity of the mind which is neither religion nor natural science, but which shares in the transcendental character of religion and in the meta-cultural character of the natural sciences.

9.15 Plato's conception (with immediate sources in pre-Socratic philosophy, and more distant sources in ancient Greek mythology and mysticism) of a supersensible world, containing universalised versions of aspects of the sensible world (divinised concepts, as it were), gave to the human mind the possibility of constructing an idealised metaphysical version of the universe which could be used not only as a way of

[6] The quotation from Frazer (fn. 4 above) continues: 'and it is impossible to loosen the cement and shake the foundation without endangering the superstructure'. 'To believe in God is to long for His existence.' M. de Unamuno, *The Tragic Sense of Life in Men and Nations* (tr. A. Kerrigan; Princeton, Princeton University Press; 1972), p. 203. In the twentieth century, we may have seen what human society would be like when human beings have ceased to long for God.

interpreting and understanding the actual world (an Archimedean matrix) but also a way of judging the actual world in terms of meta-cultural and meta-temporal values.

9.16 Aristotle's conception of definition (linking all particular instances in a universal conceptual form) and his conceptions of form and substance, essence and existence, and of actuality and potentiality (suggesting that change takes place in something insensible which remains unchanged) offered to the human mind a perfectly practical (barely metaphysical) way of speaking about the actual world in universal terms. These ways of thinking and speaking became the essential key to all the most significant subsequent developments in the making of the European public mind. (The present essay would itself not be possible except as an instance of such a way of thinking and speaking!)

9.17 The infiltrating of such ideas into the early theologising of Christianity, and the ingenious unifying of resurrected Greek philosophy and Christian theology in the work of Thomas Aquinas (in the thirteenth century), and then the uncoupling of re-resurrected Greek philosophy from religion in the context of the fifteenth-century Renaissance, meant that the notion of the idealising of the actual (and the actualising of the ideal) remained as an efficient engine of European self-development until modern times, a self-development which was not only intellectual but also practical, in the ceaseless re-thinking and remaking of European societies.

9.18 As in the case of religion, so also in the case of metaphysical philosophy, the European public mind found within itself the possibility of its dialectical denial, in a powerful tradition extending from ancient Greek materialism and sophism and scepticism to medieval nominalism, up to and including modern positivism and anti-foundational pragmatism. But the haunting presence of the ideal in the present state of the European public mind is much more powerful even than that of the sacred. The whole of academic discourse, the whole of political discourse, the whole of moral discourse, the whole of legal discourse – all the discourse of the public mind is structured around the capacity of the human mind to universalise the particular and to particularise the universal. We speak of 'society' or the 'state', not meaning merely their members or their citizens. We speak of 'justice' and 'social justice', and do not mean only the law or the actual allocation of the benefits and burdens of society. We speak of 'the true' and do not mean only what we think to be true. We speak of 'the good' and do not mean only that which pleases us. (To say these things without implying or inferring their ideal significance requires the specially trained mental effort of certain kinds of professional philosopher.)

9.19 Above all in the twentieth century, professional philosophy conducted a relentless campaign on many fronts to undermine our naïve acceptance of the idea of the ideal and our naïve belief in the possibility of metaphysical philosophy and the philosophy of rationality. We were told that such things were a linguistic illusion, a psychological symptom, a weapon of social power, a mirror of the mind's own functioning, that their truth-claims failed the test of the truth-claims of the natural sciences (verifiability or falsifiability through experiment), that the mind itself was nothing but an epiphenomenon of the physiology of the brain and the nervous system, that philosophy could aspire to be nothing more than a form of social process for the elucidation and pragmatic validation of ideas which prove themselves to be socially well adapted.

9.20 It was a cruel irony that it was in the twentieth century, of all centuries, when unspeakable human suffering was caused by the abusive use of ideas in the service of social power, that we were told that not only the 'death of god' but now also the 'end of philosophy' had deprived us of the capacity to redeem our mind-made world in the name of the ideas and the ideals to which we owed so much of the social and intellectual progress which Europe had produced from within its amazingly productive public mind.

The imaginary

9.21 A delightful feature of Europe's mind-world has been its perennial attachment to one particular form of the ideal, namely, the beautiful. Once again, we owe to the ancient Greeks the idea that the public mind should express itself in public beauty. Still more delightful was the idea that the beautiful order of the universe might be transmitted through the beautiful order of the human mind to re-emerge in things made by the human mind, so that even a human society might become a beautiful place. From the Greek temple to the medieval cathedral to the modern cathedrals of capitalism, from the great public works of Rome to the masterpieces of modern civil engineering, in the palaces and great houses produced by the aesthetic narcissism of the most privileged social classes, we have found ourselves living in a 'built environment' which, amid all the squalor of the real world, contains a permanent tribute to the ideal of beauty, a better potentiality of the human species.

9.22 But it is, perhaps, in the 'thought environment' that the public mind of Europe has produced its most extraordinary transformation of the natural world. All cultures produce a parallel world, a world of the imagination, in which the people live a metaphysical life. The human imagination apparently has no limits. An effect of some extraordinary physical system within the brain, the imagination can imagine the impossible as easily as it can imagine the possible. It can make the real into something imaginary, and the imaginary into something real. It can move mountains and drain the sea, make the true false and the false true. It can abolish time and space, making past time and future time into present time. It can make us conscious of the unknowable content of the unconscious mind, express our unbearable fears and our hopeless hope, making us desire the undesirable and love the unlovable.

9.23 The imagining of a parallel world is a continuation of philosophy by other means.[7] From the Greek tragedies to television soap operas, from Homer to Homer Simpson,[8] we have explored human reality collectively by re-creating it collectively through the power of the imagination. In the visual arts, we have re-created the material world as a world of the mind, holding it at arm's length to study and to evaluate it, to establish our relationship to it, including (especially in 'modern' art) the relationship between the world of our minds and the world of non-mind recreated by mind. In drama and literature, we have made imaginary worlds in our own image and likeness, coherent worlds in which human behaviour is presented experimentally, as in a laboratory, for us to know and judge, as we, wholly immersed in the turbid reality of real reality, are otherwise unable to do. Especially through the novel, and now especially through the film, people have learned what it is to be human, how to be, and how not to be, human, how to think, how to

[7] This idealist aesthetic was expressed most eloquently by Arthur Schopenhauer, for whom the arts surpassed nature by transforming it into a representation of the metaphysically ideal, and for whom music, the highest of the arts, is 'an unconscious exercise in metaphysics in which the mind does not know that it is philosophizing'. *The World as Will and Representation* (tr. E. F. J. Payne; New York, Dover; 1969), I § 52, p. 264. The phrase is in Latin in the original text, presumably presented as a variation on a saying of Leibniz.

[8] The name of a character in a television cartoon series.

feel, how to relate to other people, how to relate to our own personal potentiality.

9.24 In the late twentieth century, it came to seem that the collective imagination might be acquiring absolute power over the public mind. The hegemony of popular culture and mass entertainment over the minds of the mass of the people, the commercialisation of public information and the commodifying of all the works of the mind, including art and literature and even the products of the beleaguered academic mind – such developments have produced a situation in which the public mind is close to being unable to rise above itself and judge its own works, except pragmatically and commercially. More and more, we are coming to be what we imagine that we are – and nothing more. The true, the good and the beautiful – the ideals which have made European civilisation at its best – may be becoming utilitarian measures of immediate pleasure and pain, the greatest pleasure and pain of the greatest number, a final and tragic Benthamising of the European public mind.

The real

9.25 The Baconising of the European public mind has been an exceptional European achievement, reminiscent only of the remarkably sophisticated practical spirit of ancient China, or the universalising and mathematical spirit of ancient India or the early-Islamic Arab world. And it has been an all-European enterprise *par excellence*, the everyday work of an 'invisible college'[9] of co-operating and competing minds in every part of the continent.

9.26 Roger Bacon, *doctor mirabilis*, a product (like his contemporary Aquinas) of the twelfth-century Renaissance, and Francis Bacon, a product of the Italian Renaissance (like his near-contemporary Giordano Bruno and his contemporary Galileo Galilei), may be cited as notably articulate prophets of the scientific revolution, a permanent revolution in the European public mind which continues to the present day. The Ionian philosophers and the materialists had tried to Baconise ancient Greece, and Aristotle, the son of a doctor and himself an occasional empiricist, had brought something of the intellectual spirit of the biologist

[9] For the origin of this idea, see § 1.31 above, fn. 39.

and the physiologist even to his study of social and moral matters. But it would take another eighteen centuries before the public mind of Europe was possessed by the idea that the human mind is capable of re-presenting the real world, the world of non-mind, in a way which gives an extraordinary power to the human mind, a power not only to understand, but also to transform, the real world.[10]

9.27 Natural science is a natural mysticism. Natural science is a new magic. How is it possible that the infinite and unknowable complexity of the order of the universe of all-that-is, in which we participate directly through our bodily senses, can be re-presented by the human mind to itself, in such a way that human beings can have power over the natural world as if they knew the unknowable? Natural science listens humbly as nature speaks to it, but, in return, it requires nature to conform to our understanding of what it has said.[11] How is it that nature seems to recognise itself in the mirror which the human mind holds up to it, in particular in the mirror of mathematics, as if we were speaking to it in a language which it understands? Of one thing we may be reasonably certain – that the mind of a (putative) god would probably not see the order of the universe as the human mind sees it. God's mind is probably not the mind of a mathematician, but it must surely contain a mathematician's mind among others.

9.28 Francis Bacon knew that 'natural philosophy' is, indeed, a form of philosophy, and of a philosophy which tends towards completeness and unity.[12] Isaac Newton himself knew what David Hume would later say, that if 'the Newtonian philosophy be rightly understood', it consists of rational constructions, since we know only the appearances of

[10] The Epicurean (and medieval Christian) sin of *curiositas* had become the great virtue of 'scientific objectivity'. 'Therefore from a closer and purer league between these two faculties, the experimental and the rational (such as has never yet been made), much may be hoped.' F. Bacon, *The New Organon* (1620) (ed. F. H. Anderson; Indianapolis, The Bobbs-Merrill Company; 1960), XCV, p. 93. 'Now the true and lawful goal of the sciences is none other than this: that human life be endowed with new discoveries and new powers.' *Ibid.*, LXXXI, p. 78.

[11] 'Nature to be commanded must be obeyed.' *Ibid.*, III, p. 39.

[12] Bacon has a fine discussion of the question of what role is left for metaphysics in a mental world which would be dominated by physics. *The Advancement of Learning* (fn. 9 above), pp. 91ff. 'So of natural philosophy, the basis is natural history; the stage next the basis is physique; the stage next the vertical point of metaphysique' (p. 95). 'And therefore the speculation was excellent in Parmenides and Plato, although but a speculation in them, that all things by scale did ascend to unity. So then always that knowledge is worthiest which is charged with least multiplicity; which appeareth to be metaphysique . . .' (p. 96).

things and not their 'real nature'.[13] And, in the late nineteenth century, Ernst Mach would make this insight the basis of an exceptionally influential philosophy of science, seeing natural science as a product of human evolution which enables us to make economical (mostly mathematical) models of the natural world to help us to adapt to our natural habitat.[14]

9.29 What we learned in the twentieth century, after two centuries of the wonder-working of science and engineering, is that humanism is not powerful enough to take power over the power of scientism. The mysterious power of scientific ideas and the magic boxes produced by the combination of science and engineering, from computers and genetic engineering to nuclear weapons, overwhelm the puny ideas and the fragile institutions produced by the non-scientific mind. We have also learned a sadder lesson, that the 'attempt to introduce the experimental method of reasoning into moral subjects'[15] has not been successful.

9.30 Enlightenment rationalism and humanism, together with nineteenth-century scientism and progressivism, produced an enterprise, which we may call the Enlightenment project, which undertook a methodical study of every conceivable aspect of human reality, from philology to parapsychology.[16] The enterprise brought into existence a new social class of academic bureaucrats in professionalised universities, alongside the new class of administrative bureaucrats in a professionalised public service. It seemed to offer a new kind of human social

[13] D. Hume, *A Treatise of Human Nature* (1739–40) (ed. D. G. C. Macnabb; London, W. Collins & Co.; 1962), bk I, II. v, p. 110. Newton himself knew that his postulated forces might exist 'not in the physical but only in the mathematical sense'. See J. Hoivel, *The Background to Newton's* Principia. *A Study of Newton's Dynamical Researches in the Years 1664–1684* (Oxford, Clarendon Press; 1965), p. 318.

[14] Albert Einstein said (1916): 'I can say with certainty that the study of Mach and Hume has been directly and indirectly a great help in my work.' Quoted in P. G. Frank, 'Einstein, Mach, and Logical Positivism', in *Albert Einstein. Philosopher-scientist* (ed. P. A. Schilpp; The Library of Living Philosophers, VII; La Salle, IL, Open Court; 1949), pp. 269–86, at p. 272. Later philosophers of science (Craik, Kuhn, Feyerabend) have emphasised the psychological aspects of scientific creativity.

[15] This was the sub-title of David Hume's *Treatise*. 'But it is at least worth while to try if the science of *man* will not admit of the same accuracy which several parts of natural philosophy are found susceptible of.' From an Abstract of the *Treatise* (by Hume, at one time thought to have been written by Adam Smith).

[16] Bacon had called this the *radius reflexus* [reflexive light], 'whereby man beholdeth and contemplateth himself'. *Advancement of Learning* (fn. 9 above), p. 105.

future of rational public decision-making on the basis of ever more rational human self-knowledge. Unfortunately, after two centuries of the Enlightenment Project, we have learned not one single truth about things human. Instead, the clerisy of the universities, at least on the humanities side, have been socially marginalised, like medieval monks, communing with themselves in obscure academic rites. But the naturalism of the 'mind-sciences' (*Geisteswissenschaften*) has seeped into the outside world, spreading the demoralising and dehumanising idea that there may be quasi-scientific causes of human behaviour, individual and social, without being able to identify any such causes with any accuracy at all, let alone with the accuracy of the hypotheses of the natural sciences. And, by the end of the twentieth century, the age-old rampant irrationalism of public life seemed almost to be vindicated, or at least naturalised, by the intellectual self-wounding of the Enlightenment project, and, above all, by the self-wounding and self-abasement of professionalised philosophy.[17]

9.31 In the middle of the nineteenth century, the great philosophical tradition came to an end, like a majestic highway ending in the middle of nowhere. Into the vacuum flowed a whole series of human half-sciences which have had a profound side-effect on the state of the European public mind. An anthropology which began in self-confidence, and ended in self-doubting, left human beings in radical uncertainty about their own human identity.[18] A sociology which seemed destined to be a biology of human society, and ended in methodological confusion, left us more subject than ever to the hegemony of social forces, and hence of social evil.[19] A psychology which seemed destined to be a biology of the human mind, and which also ended in methodological confusion and in a morass of sectarianism, left us more subject than ever to the power of an unconscious mind whose secrets had been half-revealed,

[17] '[T]hat abuse of philosophy, which grew general about the time of Epictetus [*c.*50–*c.*130 CE], in converting it into an occupation or profession'. F. Bacon, *Advancement of Learning* (fn. 9 above), p. 158.

[18] Among those whose influence on the public mind extended beyond the closed world of the academy, we may think of William James, who looked at religious phenomena with the laconic eye of a pragmatist, or James Frazer and his imaginative anthropology of religion.

[19] We may think particularly of Max Weber who managed to communicate to a wide audience his own ambivalent and tortured response to the forces of modern society, at a time when ambivalence was a bad intellectual response to exceptionally powerful and irrational and unambivalent social forces.

and possibly falsely half-revealed.[20] A historiography which claimed at last to be 'scientific' soon lost itself in a maze of hermeneutic and historicist and, latterly, postmodern uncertainty.[21] A 'political economy' (later 'economics') which found itself able to offer mysteriously certain laws of economic phenomena but which also ultimately had to reveal itself as a form of politics by other means.[22]

9.32 It is a strange irony that we ended the twentieth century less certain than ever about what it is to be human, and what it might be. The public mind of Europe has infected itself with a new disease – *acatalepsia*, a surrender to terminal uncertainty about things human.[23] And now triumphalist science is rushing to fill the vacuum of human self-unknowing, with its fraudulent populist promise to solve problems of human consciousness and human sociability through the hypotheses of physiology.

The social

9.33 Socrates made gentle fun of Thrasymachus who had suggested a perfectly reasonable definition of 'justice'.[24] Plato's 'Athenian' wondered

[20] Freud's admirable uncertainty as to whether he was a biologist or a philosopher was not satisfactorily communicated to the general public, who picked up half-digested shreds of his tentative mental model-building, shreds which proved to have profound effects on everyday human behaviour.

[21] We think of Taine: 'The historian may be permitted the privilege of the naturalist; I have observed my subject as one might observe the metamorphosis of an insect.' *Les origines de la France contemporaire. L'ancien régime* (Paris, Hachette; 1876), preface. And we think of Ranke's ambiguous claim that the discipline of history is not only able 'to say what actually happened' but also 'to lift itself . . . from the investigation of particulars to a universal view of events, to a knowledge of the objectively existing relations'. *Geschichte der romanischen und germanischen Völker von 1494–1535* (Leipzig, G. Reimer; 1824), preface.

[22] 'Economics is a science of thinking in terms of models joined to the art of choosing models which are relevant to the contemporary world.' J. M. Keynes, letter to Roy Harrod of 4 July 1938, in *The Collected Writings of John Maynard Keynes* (ed. D. Moggridge; London, Macmillan for the Royal Economic Society; 1973), XIV, p. 296. Keynes was urging Harrod to repel attempts 'to turn [economics] into a pseudo-natural-science'.

[23] This term was proposed by F. Bacon: *The New Organon* (fn. 10 above), CXXVI, p. 115. He hoped, as we may hope, that the disease might be replaced by the benign condition of *eucatalepsia*.

[24] 'This, then, my good sir, is what I understand as the identical principle of justice that obtains in all states – the advantage of the established government. This I presume you will admit holds power and is strong, so that, if one reason rightly, it works out that the just is the same thing everywhere, the advantage of the stronger.' Plato, *The Republic* (tr. P. Shorey), I.338e (Thrasymachus speaking), in *The Collected Dialogues of Plato* (eds E. Hamilton and H. Cairns; Princeton, Princeton University Press; 1961), pp. 588–9.

how we should think about 'law' in society.[25] Aristotle wondered who finally should rule in society,[26] and, indeed, what was the true purpose of society itself.[27] These things are so familiar to us that we easily forget that they are the rootstock of a distinctive European social consciousness, a consciousness which is now being universalised to become a distinctive human consciousness. These three foundational elements – the ethical state, the rule of law, the good life for all – would eventually take their place in the conceptualising and actualising of the highly syncretic (Greek, Roman, Christian, humanist, rationalist) social philosophy of 'liberal democracy', after much delay and many reverses, much conflict and much suffering. It is hard to believe, and painful to recall, that it was only at the end of the twentieth century, twenty-three centuries later, that such ideas finally became the governing ideas in the public mind and the public institutions of all of Europe.

9.34 In the meantime, the social life of Europeans had been carried to levels of collectivisation which the most *dirigiste* of Spartans could not have imagined. The social integration of the Christian order and the feudal order of the Middle Ages, and the social integration of the absolutist monarchies, have been matched and surpassed by the totalitarian order of democratic-capitalist society. The social contract of *democratic* society, under the aegis of 'liberty' and 'equality', gives absolute power to the social institutions which represent the people, and those institutions are not only political but also psychic (education, entertainment, information). The social contract of *capitalist* society, under the aegis of 'freedom' and 'competition', gives absolute power to social systems and forces, including psychic forces, which are conceived of as natural, and naturally beneficial. When democracy and capitalism are combined into a single system, so that democracy provides with perfect efficiency the

[25] 'How should we imagine the rightful position of a written law in society? Should its statutes disclose the lineaments of wise and affectionate parents, or should they wear the semblance of an autocratic despot – issue a menacing order, post it on the walls, and so have done?' Plato, *The Laws* (tr. A. E. Taylor), IX.859 ('the Athenian' speaking), in *ibid.*, p. 1,419.

[26] 'We will begin by enquiring whether it is more advantageous to be ruled by the best men or by the best laws.' '[T]he rule of law is preferable to that of any individual. On the same principle, even if it is better for certain individuals to govern, they should be made only guardians and ministers of the law.' Aristotle, *Politics* (tr. B. Jowett; Oxford, The Clarendon Press; 1905), II.15.3, III.16.3–4, pp. 136, 139.

[27] 'A state exists for the sake of the good life', 'a perfect and self-sufficing life, by which we mean a happy and honourable life'. 'Since the end of individuals and of states is the same, the end of the best man and of the best state must also be the same.' Aristotle, *ibid.*, III.9.6, III.9.13, VII.15, pp. 117, 120, 290–1.

law and administration required by capitalism, then the possibility of rising above the system, in the name of some higher ideal of judgement and purpose, becomes more or less impossible. Democracy-capitalism makes the consciousness by which it must be judged.[28]

9.35 In the meantime also, Europe had spent centuries searching for an appropriate reifiable unifying concept of political society. Europe inherited from the Middle Ages a great diversity of corporate bodies, including professional guilds, dioceses and universities (each a species of *universitas*, or corporate entity). The word 'state' was long used as a generic term for political entities which might also be said to be a 'commonwealth' (*res publica* or *civitas*). After Hegel, the word took on a more specific meaning, as a reified, quasi-platonic Idea of a rationalised polity.[29] The word 'nation' had been used in the medieval universities as a generic term for genetic social groups. With the constitutional transformation in France in which 'sovereignty' was said to have passed to 'the nation', and with the rise of *völkisch* ideology in Germany, the idea of the genetic nation also took on a reified-ideal significance. It is possible to say that, to this day, in the constitutional psychologies of Europe, there is no single ultimate concept of social entity (perhaps, for example: 'state' in Germany; 'nation' in France; 'society' in Britain).

9.36 In the international relations of the diverse forms of European polity, no single reifiable unifying concept of their co-existence was found, or has been found to the present day. With vast practical consequences, a merely horizontal relationship was established, with diplomacy and war as its essential self-ordering systems, and with 'the law of nations' (or 'international law', as Jeremy Bentham proposed to call it, at

[28] 'Laws and government may be considered ... as a combination of the rich to oppress the poor, and preserve to themselves the inequality of goods which would otherwise soon be destroyed by the attacks of the poor, who if not hindered by the government would soon reduce the others to an equality with themselves by open violence. The government and the laws ... tell them they must either continue poor or acquire wealth in the same manner as they have done.' Adam Smith, *Lectures on Jurisprudence* (lecture of 22 February 1763) (eds R. L. Meek, D. D. Raphael, P. G. Stein; Oxford, Clarendon Press; 1978), pp. 208–9. 'Civil government, so far as it is instituted for the security of property, is in reality instituted for the defence of the rich against the poor, or of those who have some property against those who have none at all.' A. Smith, *An Inquiry into the Nature and Causes of the Wealth of Nations* (1776), v.i.b. (eds R. H. Campbell and A. S. Skinner; Oxford, Clarendon Press; 1976), II, p. 715.

[29] In the constitutional systems of Britain and the United States, there is still no reifiable unifying concept of the 'state' in the internal sense, public power being distributed among many constitutional organs and public agencies.

least in the English language), as a modest set of self-imposed principles and rules governing their fragile co-existence.[30] Routine rhetoric and academics might refer to the result as an international system, an international society of states or nation-states, an anarchical society, or the international community. It is a major puzzle of European intellectual history to explain why the most creative social philosophers (especially Locke, Rousseau, Kant, Hegel, Marx) did not extend their core philosophies to embrace a society of societies. Instead, Europe has been haunted by the fact of its terrible disunity and by the ghosts of its past unities.

9.37 Europe's latest self-constituting is haunted by three ghosts – the Roman Empire, the Roman Church, the Holy Roman Empire. They are grey ghosts, if grey is the ambiguous resolution of black and white. The Roman Empire was the Antonines and it was also Diocletian. The Roman Church was Benedict of Nursia and Francis of Assisi and it was also the Holy Office. The Holy Roman Empire was master of Europe's masters and vanity of vanities. The Roman Empire lived on, after its demise in the west, in Byzantium and in the Vatican. The Roman Church lived on, after the disintegration of Christendom, as a world-wide enterprise, a leading religious brand among many other religious brands. The Holy Roman Empire of the German People, after it had evaporated under the pressure of manic Napoleonic post-imperialising, lived on as a possibility of other forms of manic European reimperialising, benign and less benign.

9.38 The ambiguity of Europe's imperial inheritance is no doubt a reason for its ghostly persistence and for its fatal charm. Always there is the tantalising possibility that a European unity could have been imposed successfully and permanently, if only... If only the Christian religion, over-enlargement, economic decline, moral decadence and the invasion of barbarians from the east had not all beset the western Roman Empire at the same time. If only the Papacy and the Empire had found a more sensible *modus vivendi*, and all the popes had been saints, and Italian post-imperial political pluralism had not been so tempting a prey for French and other ambitions, and Wycliffe and Hus and Luther had been more diplomatic. If only the Carolingian empire had not been twice divided (in 840 and 1556), had not become contaminated

[30] The 'state', in the external sense, came to be seen as a society whose public realm is under the control of a 'government' and which is recognised as a state by the governments of other states.

by particularist national ambitions, had been more German or more Spanish or more Austrian. If only . . .

9.39 As we stood, in 1945, among the ruins of the old empires, European and colonial, Europeans were surely entitled to look at what might have been, the counter-factual history of Europe.[31] Surely we could, intelligently, avoid the traumas and the sins of the failed Europeanisms of the past. Surely we could, intelligently, build yet another new New Jerusalem on the firmer foundation of the best of Europeanism. In 1945, the ruling classes who had made the European wars since 1870, the new ruling classes of the political-military-industrial establishment, thought in terms of the politics of economics, because political economy was the source of their personal power and was the language-world they inhabited. Surely it was not they, humble servants of the people, who were ultimately responsible for what had happened. It was from the world of the mind and the spirit, the world of ideas and ideology, that the cause had come, the *causa sine qua non* of so much chaos and suffering – big, over-inflated ideas, historicist ideas, metaphysical ideas, so-called revolutionary ideas, meta-political ideas.[32]

9.40 The new New Jerusalem would be a post-ideal construction, post-philosophical, post-intellectual and post-political. It would not be a people, nation, a state, a super-state, a society, a commonwealth, a republic, a corporation, a body politic, an empire, a federation, a confederation, an international organisation, a union, an order, a movement, or even a polity. Enough of such delusive words! *Faute de mieux*, the New Europe would be a 'community'. The significance of the word would have to be found in all the words that it was not. Echoing Spinoza, we may say that the *negatio* of the word 'community' was its *affirmatio*. In a Sartrean spirit, we may say that its being was in its modest not-nothingness.[33]

[31] 'It was at Rome, on the fifteenth of October, 1764, as I sat musing amidst the ruins of the Capitol, while the barefooted fryars were singing Vespers in the temple of Jupiter, that the idea of writing the decline and fall of the City first started to my mind.' J. Murray (ed.), *The Autobiographies of Edward Gibbon* (London, John Murray; 1896), p. 302.

[32] The post-Marxian excoriation of 'ideology' was, for understandable reasons, taken too far after 1945, not least in K. Popper, *The Open Society and its Enemies* (London, Routledge; 1945), but also in a succession of pragmatist, anti-foundationalist writings which exclude 'big ideas' unless they are generated and validated socially, in and for a particular condition of a given society.

[33] For further discussion of the concept of *Gemeinschaft*, see § 7.116, fn. 71 above.

9.41 Profiting from twenty-six centuries of intense theoretical and practical experience of society-making in Europe, the makers of the 'community' endowed it with the firm foundation of a 'market', since a 'market' is not merely a word or an idea or an illusion. In the mind-world of Smithian-Hegelian-Marxian political economy, a market is the solid structure on which the superstructure of society forms itself. On the basis of a European market, a European social superstructure must form itself, a superstructure of institutions, of law, of ideas, even possibly of ideals. And the superstructure would have a functional rationality, a systematic and transcendental rationality, because it would be formed by practice and necessity, and not merely by the whims and fancies of the mind and the flesh. Who could argue with such hard-earned wisdom?

The suffering

9.42 In the human mind are light and night (Parmenides).[34] The European public mind contains its own particular mixture, in which the wonderful light of sustained self-enlightenment is obscured by the darkness of unending self-inflicted suffering. The Greek tragedians supposed a disease of the mind (*nosos phrenōn*) which causes human beings to bring about their own destruction. We have to wonder whether there is, in the European public mind, some such disease of the mind, whose symptoms are wars, massacres, bloody revolutions, genocide, oppression and exploitation of every kind, publicly inflicted cruelty of every kind, social evil of every kind. Did the gods send such things to give poets something to sing about,[35] or to give something for historians to write about?[36]

9.43 All cultures have sought to resolve the problem of evil. The Greek tragedians (Sophocles, at least) subscribed to the view that suffering could be a way of learning (*pathemata mathemata*). What we had to learn is that the problem of evil is the problem caused by a triangular relationship between the gods, destiny and the individual human

[34] Parmenides, fragment 9, in H. Diels and W. Kranz, *Die Fragmente der Vorsokratiker* (Berlin, Weidmann; 10th edn, 1952).

[35] Homer, *The Odyssey*, bk VIII, lines 579–80.

[36] 'Very true, it seems, is the saying that "War is the father of all things", since at one stroke it has begotten so many historians.' (Lucian of Samosata, 2nd century CE).

being. The gods themselves were not exempt from destiny. And the gods could be an instrument to enforce destiny, or to avert it. A particular self-destructive sin consisted in seeking to surpass the human condition and to defy destiny. In the Judaeo-Christian tradition, the problem of evil (sin) was presented as an inherent human weakness, a revolt against God, which could be overcome through a reconciliation with God through respect for God's law. For the Christian tradition, the prevenient grace of God (God's love of humanity) had been made available through an incarnation of God in a human being, Jesus Christ, who acts as a permanent means of reconciliation with God (humanity's love of God), enabling human beings to do good and avoid evil.

9.44 Christianity would eventually tear itself apart in disagreements about the theory and practice to be derived from these elementary ideas of a supposedly shared religion. Unspeakable human suffering, in religious wars and persecution, flowed from these disagreements. As religion receded as the dominant psychological force in the European public mind, Europeans found other psychic grounds for doing evil to each other and to non-Europeans all over the world. Christianity transformed a national religion of a genetically determined near-eastern people into a religion with universal claims, and those claims were enforced not only through the work of missionaries but also through the behaviour of conquerors and colonisers. The image of Europe and Europeans, in the minds of non-Europeans, became radically equivocal, as the agents of a 'higher' civilisation and as destroyers, doing evil in the name of doing good, including not only 'the good' of the one true religion but also the religion of 'democracy' and 'economic progress' and the religion of 'nationalism'. Europeans were the people of social progress, but they were also the people of the Inquisition and the concentration camp, of the machine-gun and of slavery.

9.45 The human world as it is today is essentially the world that Europeans have made, imposing ideas and systems on indigenous cultures all over the world, directly or through the intermediate power of former colonies, which are themselves outposts of Europeanism in more or less exotic places of exile. A common insight of ancient India, ancient Israel and ancient Greece is that we cannot be responsible for the sins of our ancestors. What we are responsible for is the future, what we will make of the Europeanism which we have inherited, the light and the night.

The future

9.46 There are traditional cultures (China, the Maori, perhaps others) which imagine human beings standing with their faces to the past, which already exists, and with their backs to the future, which is unknowable. The European public mind, despite its rich historiography, has been notable for its obsession with the future. European society has been a long process of self-development, punctuated by remarkable epochs in which the public mind has re-imagined itself, reconceiving human society and human potentiality.[37] There have even been those who have been able to speak of human self-development as a sort of 'education of the human race' or 'the progress of the human spirit' (Augustine, Lessing, Condorcet, Hegel, Comte, Morgan).

9.47 The canker of defeatism which is now present in the public mind of Europe is understandable, given the history of the twentieth century in Europe, and given that the leading role in the drama of human self-creating seems to so many Europeans to have passed from Europe into the hands of others whom we have made as they are, but who have escaped from the force-field of the European public mind. A self-imposed psychological marginalising of Europe has been the product of an obscure sense of moral exhaustion and collective shame. Our first task in changing the future is to change our attitude to the future, which means also changing our attitude to our past.[38]

9.48 We may outline some elements in a possible programme for the reinvigorating of the public mind of Europe.

(1) The European Union has no future except within a restored European public mind, which can provide it with the ideas and the ideals without which a society cannot survive and prosper.

(2) The significance of the European Union, which is a technocratic creation of, and by, a collective European public realm, and which continues to be an unresolved and unsustainable confusion of diplomacy and democracy, must be reconceived within the European public mind.

[37] It is possible to identify a three-century cycle of five European enlightenments. See § 3.18 above, fn. 15.

[38] 'It was lunacy [for Christopher Columbus] to sail the Ocean without knowing one's course, an Ocean on which no one had travelled before, and head for a country whose very existence was in question. By this lunacy he discovered a new world. The future is worse than an Ocean – there is nothing there. It will be what men and circumstances make it.' A. Herzen, *From the Other Shore* (tr. M. Budberg; London, Weidenfeld & Nicolson; 1956), p. 58.

It must not be equated with Europe's future. It has a future within Europe. It is not Europe's future.

(3) There must be a coming-to-consciousness of a new European 'universal' class (Hegel), an invisible college of European intellectuals (F. Bacon), dedicated to the revival of Europe's self-reflection and self-recreating, including the resuming of the great tradition of European philosophy.

(4) The social role of the universities, at least on the side of the humanities, must be reconceived, so that they can perform a function of permanent enlightenment, enabling society to surpass its actual condition and to actualise its potentiality.

(5) Some of Europe's universities must be reconstituted as 'European universities'.

(6) Europe must free itself of its recent psychic dependence on the United States of America. It is an unhealthy cathexis. The United States, in its origin and basic configuration, is a Europe-in-exile. But its public mind has developed in a distinct way, a way which has alienated it radically from the long-term development of the European public mind. Europe shares at least an equal responsibility with the United States for the future of a human world for whose present condition it is primarily responsible.

(7) The European public mind must find within itself the possibility of surpassing the present state of democracy and capitalism, with a view to the rehumanising of socialised humanity in the name of the ideals of justice and social justice.

(8) The European public mind must find within itself the means of remoralising humanity to enable human beings, individually and collectively, to take responsibility for eliminating all forms of social evil, that is to say, evil generated by social systems, or by holders of public power acting in their official capacity.

(9) Europeans must reconceive human society as the means of the collective self-creating and self-perfecting of human beings, with a view to their survival and prospering, as one species among countless species in a natural habitat shared by all.

(10) Europeans must reconceive European society as the society of all the people and peoples of Europe, the society of all European societies.

(11) Europeans must help to ensure that international society is reconceived as the society of all-humanity, the society of all societies,

with international law as the true legal system of a true international society. We must ensure that the evil practices of war and the use of force are finally eliminated from international society by curing holders of public power of their age-old addiction to those practices.

(12) Europeans must ensure that the idea and the ideal of constitutionalism is installed in international society to take power, in the name of the people and the peoples of the world, over an unaccountable global public realm acting in conjunction with an uncontrolled global economy.

9.49 A new future for Europe requires a New Enlightenment.

PART III

International society and its law

Can humanity think of itself as a society under law?

10

The concept of international law

The social function of law – Law and social psychology – Law and justice – Law and the common interest – The international legal system – Customary international law – Treaty-law – The future of the international legal system – The new paradigm

It was a tragic day in the history of humanity when the subtle and complex concept of law was crudely split into two – national law and the law between nations. In earlier times, there had been complex and subtle conceptions of the relationship among various forms of law and even of a common essence of all law. But the brutal managers of the new European polities, monarchies and republics of every degree of conservatism and reformism, chose to see their co-existence as intrinsically unsocial and hence governed by rules of more or less enlightened prudence and pragmatism. And the European worldview was made the worldview of all the world through the world-wide expansion of European power and influence.

In the latter part of the twentieth century, the contradiction between an intensely dynamic development of social relations across national frontiers and the archaic forms and rules of intergovernmental international unsociety became absurd and unbearable.

There could have been another concept of international law. There could be another concept of international law. There can be a conception of law which transcends the frontiers between national legal systems, which sees all legal systems as participating in an international legal system, and which allows international law, as so reconceived, to play the wonderfully creative functions of law in the self-constituting of all forms of society from the society of the family to the society of the whole human race, serving the common interest of all-humanity.

The social function of law

10.1 Law, including international law, has a threefold social function. Law carries the structures and systems of society through time. Law inserts the common interest of society into the behaviour of society-members. Law establishes possible futures for society, in accordance with society's theories, values and purposes.

10.2 Law is a presence of the social past. Law is an organising of the social present. Law is a conditioning of the social future.

10.3 There are eight systematic implications of such an idea of the social function of law in general, and of international law in particular.

(1) Law forms part of the *self-constituting* of a society. A society is a collective self-constituting of human beings as society-members, co-existing with their personal self-constituting as human individuals. International society is the collective self-constituting of all human beings, the society of all societies. International law is the law of international society.

(2) The legal self-constituting of society (the *legal* constitution) co-exists with other means of the self-constituting of society: self-constituting in the form of ideas (the *ideal* constitution) and self-constituting through the everyday willing and acting of society-members (the *real* constitution).

(3) Law is generated, as a third thing with a *distinctive social form*, in the course of the ideal and real self-constituting of society, but law itself conditions those other forms of constituting.

(4) Law is a *universalising* system, reconceiving the infinite particularity of human willing and acting, in the light of the common interest of society.

(5) Law is a *particularising* system, disaggregating the common interest of society so that it may affect the infinite particularity of human willing and acting.

(6) Law requires that society have adequate means for *determining the common interest* of society, in accordance with society's values and purposes. *Politics*, in the widest sense of the word, is the will-forming struggle in the ideal and real constitutions, the struggle to influence the determination of the common interest of society and to influence the making and application of law.

(7) Law requires that society have *theories* which explain and justify law within social consciousness (the public mind) and within individual consciousness (the private mind, including the social consciousness of subordinate societies). Such theories reflect and condition society's values and purposes. They may be customary, religious, or philosophical theories : for example, theories of revealed transcendence, charismatic authority, natural law, sovereignty, constitutionalism, naturalism. They are generated and regenerated in the public mind of society in the course of its ideal and real self-constituting.

(8) Law thus presupposes a *society* whose structures and systems make possible the mutual conditioning of the public mind and the private mind, and the mutual conditioning of the legal and the non-legal. These two reciprocating and reinforcing processes offer a limitless dynamic potentiality for human self-evolving through social self-constituting.

Law and social psychology

10.4 Society and law exist nowhere else than in the human mind. They are products of and in the consciousness of actual human beings. But a society generates a social consciousness, a public mind, which is distinct from the private mind, distinct from the consciousness of actual human individuals. Social consciousness flows from and to individual consciousness, forming part of the self-consciousness of each society-member. The psychology of the public mind is a manifestation of the psychology of the private mind. The constitution of a society and the personality of a human person are both the product of human consciousness. Social psychology is a form, but a modified form, of personal psychology. But social consciousness functions independently from the private consciousness of every society-member, and is retained in forms (the theories, structures and systems of self-constituting society) which are an 'other' in relation to the 'self' of the self-constituting of any particular society-member. Society wills and acts collectively, as the output of systems (including law-making systems) which aggregate the willing and acting of individual human beings. But the intervention of those systems creates a new mind-world, a new form of human reality, a new form of human world. The public mind is society's private mind. The public mind of international society is the private mind of the human species.

10.5 This peculiar relationship, separate but inseparable, between personal and social psychology means that all the systematic functions of personal psychology are present in social psychology, but functioning in a special way. For its own purposes and in its own way, society uses *emotion, memory, rationality* and *morality*. And society's use of these functions affects their functioning in the psychology of individual society-members. Public emotion, especially the emotion of the crowd, flows from and to private emotion. Society's collective memory, its so-called history, flows from and to private memory. Society's collective deliberations, using the self-ordering functions of the human brain, including language and logic, flow from and to our private deliberating. Society's self-regulating in terms of its values and purposes flows from and to our private self-regulating in terms of duty. Beyond the systematic functions of individual psychology, there is the power of unconscious consciousness, the residues of our biological inheritance and of our life-experience which do not function systematically but which intervene in every aspect of our personal self-constituting and must intervene in every aspect of the collective self-constituting of society. Social consciousness is also a collective unconscious.

10.6 For individual human beings, the integrating of the processes of the mind in the moment-to-moment self-constituting of personality is an unceasing struggle. The struggle of self-integrating can lead to crises which may be seen as pathological, in the sense that they threaten the survival or general well-being of the person concerned, or of other persons. Society-members contribute their psychic states to social consciousness, including pathological psychic states. Society-members with exceptional social power may even impose their own psycho-pathology on the society they dominate. So it is that a society may experience episodes of social psycho-pathology, when a society may be said, in crude terms, to go mad, may become alienated, with its potentiality of self-creating distorted by symptoms of self-wounding and self-destroying. Nowhere does social psycho-pathology reveal itself more clearly than in the society of societies, international society, where its symptoms can be human self-wounding and self-destroying on a massive scale.

10.7 Law, as a social phenomenon, corresponds to whatever is the ultimate self-integrating capacity of individual consciousness, that capacity which enables us to pursue our personal survival and prospering in our unique existential situation, in the moment and at the place where our own systematic functioning, as body and mind, intersects with the systematic functioning of all that is not us, that is to say, the natural world and the human world of other people as individuals and as society. I am, therefore I am a legal system for myself. A society also has a unique existential situation, the point in time and space at which it intersects with the existence of the natural world, the existence of other societies, and the existence of its society-members. To exist as a society is to have a legal system with a view to the survival and prospering of the society as a whole and of the human beings who are its members. International society has a legal system with a view to the survival and prospering of international society as a whole, that is to say, the survival and prospering of all subordinate human societies and of all human beings.

Law and justice

10.8 Law is purposive human activity, a particular species of willing and acting, so that it is necessarily action of moral significance, action which is subject to moral duty and gives rise to moral responsibility. Moral duty – the duty to do good and avoid evil – attaches to the participation of *individual human beings* in law-making, law-applying, law-enforcing and law-abiding. The moral situation of *society* is more problematic, since society acts through systems whose aggregative systematic output – surplus social effect, as we may call it – is greater than the sum of the individual human inputs, the surplus being the product, and the purpose, of the systematic process. Law is a surplus social effect of many systems within a society. The apparent consequence is that, since no human individual is responsible for the macro-product of social systems, there can be no moral responsibility for that product, including the macro-product known as law. Apparently, the social actual, and hence the legal actual, is necessarily right. This chain of reasoning, with its machiavellian implications, has been especially characteristic of the conceiving of the relationship among those forms of society which came to be known as 'states'. So-called international relations seemed to be the more or less random aggregating of the aggregate output of the systems of those societies, so that the absence of potential moral responsibility was even more evidently the case between the states than within those states. It seemed also to follow that international law, even more than national law, was morally immune, since it was itself seen as a secondary surplus social effect of the morally immune relations between states, the content of those relations – so-called foreign policy – being itself the morally immune systematic product of the internal national systems.

10.9 *Cui bono*? In whose interest has it been to propagate such ideas? Machiavellism, the overriding of general moral duty by *raison d'état*, was well-intentioned, in the sense that it was designed to define a special kind of moral duty (*virtù*) owed by 'the prince', by those with personal responsibility for government. Its paradoxical character, a morality of immorality, gave it a particular frisson, calculated to shock those with conventional moral ideas, especially the religiously conditioned. But it also gave an impulse of self-justification and self-assertion to those who would have power, not merely over this or that Italian city-state, but over the great centralising monarchies, giving a veneer of moral necessity to the arrogance of their absolutism.

10.10 Machiavellism was also a calculated negation of a long tradition which conceived of values which transcend the power of even the holders of the highest forms of social power. Those ideas – especially ideas of justice and natural law, but also all those philosophies which speak of 'the good' or 'the good life' – were transcendental and aspirational and critical in character, that is to say, they were conceived of as an *ideal* which could not be overridden or even abridged by the merely *actual*, and in relation to which the actual should be oriented and would be judged. The idea of the ideal makes possible a morality of society. It makes possible the idea that society's systems, including the legal system, can have moral purpose at the systematic level, at the level of surplus social effect.

10.11 Within some national societies, an idea of the transcendental was actualised in the development of *constitutionalism*. It was found possible to conceive of a law-above-law which was nevertheless present within the same legal system. Appropriate *theories* were developed (especially social contract theory) to explain and justify the legal system, suggesting that the law itself had purposes, because the formation of society had purposes, and that the law had inherent limits – formal limits (the consent of the people through their representatives) and substantive limits (fundamental rights). In the national societies in question, machiavellism was negated by constitutionalism, and law was conceived as being something other than merely a manifestation of actual relations of social power. *Law* was made to co-exist systematically with its ideal of *justice*. Constitutionalism accompanied, and made possible, the development of an idea of the *public realm*, that is to say, a part of the social process in which legal powers are to be exercised only in the public interest. The holders of public-realm powers are thus immediate and active agents of the common interest of society rather than, as in the case of private-realm power-holders, indirect agents who serve the common interest merely by conforming to the law.

10.12 International society, however, remained a constitution-free zone. On the contrary, the controllers of the national public realms found that they continued to be *ancien régime* free agents, constrained only by natural necessity and the force of the actual, in a form of co-existence which was clearly not a society, with only the most crude of organising systems (diplomacy, war), and with a legal system which, fortunately, seemed to them, and their acolytes, to lack most of the essential characteristics of their national legal systems, not least a transcendental constitutional structure. And international unsociety was evidently also a morality-free zone, in which moral discourse had only a marginal rhetorical or tactical function, and the only recognised ethical imperative was self-judging machiavellian princely virtue. For the controllers of the national public realms and their apologists, an international public realm without law or justice seemed to be a state of nature of the most exciting kind, in which the survival of the fittest is decided by an intoxicating mixture of urbane diplomacy and mass murder.

Law and the common interest

10.13 Common interest is a society's self-interest, a self-interest which may conflict with the self-interest of society-members in their capacity as individual human beings, but which is in their interest in their capacity as society-members. Common interest is not merely an aggregation of particular interests. It is formed at the intersection between the ideal and the real, as society responds to its current and potential situation in the light of its continuing theories, values and purposes. It is an idea of society's enlightened self-interest formed in a society's public mind. A given society may contain conflicting ideas of its theories, values and purposes, conflicting ideas of its current and potential situation, and conflicting ideas about the relationship of the one to the other. Whether it is the whimsical will of a tyrant or direct consultation of the people or anything between, a society contains systematic means for resolving such conflicts, that is to say, *politics* in the widest sense of the word.

10.14 Other social systems are responsible for actualising the common interest, including the dissemination of ideas and information with a view to the conditioning of social consciousness, educational systems with a view to conditioning the minds of the next social generation, action on the part of social institutions of all kinds in furtherance of the common interest. But it is, above all, a function of law to ensure that the willing and acting of society-members, including subordinate societies, serves the common interest. The law is capable of performing this function with wonderful efficiency.

10.15 Law is not, as so often supposed, a system of legal rules. Law is a system of legal relations. A legal system is an infinite number of interlocking legal relations forming a network of infinite density. A legal relation (right, duty, power, freedom, liability, immunity, disability) is a pattern of potentiality into which actual persons and situations may be fitted. It is a *matrix* which identifies persons and situations in an abstract form. It is an *heuristic* which connects aspects of those persons and situations to each other in a particular way, in isolation from the rest of their reality and the rest of social reality. It is an *algorithm* which triggers the operation of other legal relations when actual persons and situations are found to fit its pattern of potentiality.

10.16 Such a network of legal relations constitutes a parallel *legal reality* in which every possible aspect of social reality has a second significance, in which language has a legal meaning, persons have a legal status, natural and human events have a legal character. Actual human beings may be more or less unaware of the legal relations to which they are potentially parties. They may abide by the law, or violate the law, without knowing that they are doing so. And the law itself can never be known for certain. The content of a legal relation is as imprecise as the language in which it is expressed, sharing in the necessary imprecision of all language or purposefully choosing limited precision (with such terms as 'reasonable', 'good faith', 'equal protection', 'due process'). And the abstract form of the content of a legal relation necessarily allows for a wide range of interpretations when the question arises of its application to actual persons and situations, interpretations which may alter with the identity of the interpreter and as a function of the time and context in which the interpretation occurs.

10.17 Notwithstanding the potential character of the legal relation and its limited certainty, and the ignorance of most people for most of the time as to the content of the law, the law gives to society a range of possible futures which society has chosen as futures which would serve the common interest. When a person acts consciously or unconsciously in conformity with the law (exercises a power, claims a right, uses a freedom, carries out a duty . . .), that action, although it may involve a choice on the part of that person and a self-interested choice, actualises society's determination of its common interest. The law-conforming action of all society-members is the self-constituting of a society through law.

The international legal system

10.18 International law is the self-constituting of all-humanity through law. It is the actualising through law of the common interest of international society, the society of all societies. The legal relations of international law organise the potential willing and acting of all human beings and all human societies, including the forms of society conventionally known as 'states'.

10.19 The international legal system contains three systematic levels:

(1) international constitutional law;
(2) international public law;
(3) the laws of the nations.

10.20 *International constitutional law* is what some old writers called the 'necessary' law of nations. It contains the structural legal relations which are intrinsic to the co-existence of all kinds of subordinate societies. It confers on artificial legal persons, including the state-societies, the capacity to act as parties to international legal relations. It determines the systematic relationship between levels (2) and (3), and the horizontal relationship among the many laws of the nations.

10.21 *International public law* is the law of the intergovernment of international society. It is that part of international law which regulates the interaction of the subordinate public realms within the international public realm. The principal participants in the legal relations of international public law are the 'states', represented by their 'governments', that is to say, by the controllers of their respective public realms. 'States' are considered to be those societies whose internal public realms are recognised as capable of participating in the international intergovernment. International constitutional law determines the conditions of that participation and also the participation of other persons, on the basis of legal relations to which they are made parties (for example, intergovernmental institutions, or individuals and non-governmental bodies participating in international public-law bodies).

10.22 *The laws of the nations* are an integral part of the international legal system.

(a) It is international constitutional law which determines the participants in the international legal system (for example, making a particular society into a 'state'), and determines the conditions of their participation.

(b) The geographical and material distribution of constitutional authority among subordinate legal systems cannot be finally determined by those legal systems themselves, but only by a superordinate legal system, namely international constitutional law.

(c) The content of the law of the subordinate systems may be subject to legal relations arising under international constitutional and public law; and those legal relations prevail, as a matter of international constitutional law, over the law of the subordinate systems.

(d) Legal transactions arising under the law of a subordinate system may take effect outside the sphere of the constitutional authority of that system and interact with transactions arising under the law of another system. That interaction may be legally regulated, in the first place, under Private International Law (itself also part of the international legal system), but always subject to any applicable international constitutional or public law. The so-called global economy, for example, is the aggregate product of the actualising of legal relations arising under the laws of the nations (contract law, corporation law, securities law, etc.) and the actualising of legal relations under international constitutional and public law.

10.23 It follows that international public law is a joint product of both international constitutional law and national constitutional law. International constitutional law determines the legal relationship of the subordinate public realms. National constitutional law determines the legal status and powers of each particular state-society and its government. It follows also that the three levels of the international legal system are a hierarchy, with international constitutional law having systematic supremacy, and with international public law dominating the exercise of legal powers within the national public realms, including the powers to make, apply and enforce national law.

10.24 The international legal system, as a systematic totality, thus reconciles the respective common interests of all subordinate societies with the common interest of all human beings in the survival and prospering of the human species, one species among so many in a habitat shared by all.

The making of international law: (1) customary international law

10.25 International law has been made in the form of customary law. Customary law is a form of law which arises out of the ideal and real self-constituting of a society as a particular kind of residue of the past, rather than through a formal law-making process in the present. Society thereby makes law for itself through a tacit legislator which is society itself, universalising its experience of self-ordering.

10.26 Customary law, including customary international law, is the product of a *dialectic of practice*, as opposed to legislation, including international treaty-law, which is the product of a *dialectic of ideas*. Society-members produce the conditions of their orderly social co-existence through the practice of orderly co-existence. Customary law is the presentation of those conditions in the form of law, that is to say, setting the terms of the future co-existence of society-members in the form of legal relations. It follows that the place of *consent* in the making of customary law is subtle. Clearly, it is not the specific consent of the subjects of the law. Customary law is not made by any specific act of will on the part of its subjects. Their assent to customary law (*opinio iuris*) is manifested, in the first place, in their participation in the society whose law it is. Secondly, it is manifested in their participation in the day-to-day struggle of social self-ordering, knowing that some aspect of that self-ordering may come to be universalised as law. Thirdly, it is manifested in their being party to, and relying on, the legal relations flowing from the existing state of customary law.

10.27 Customary law thus shares in the transcendental aspect of constitutionalism, discussed above, at least to the extent that it is systematically independent of the will of current society-members, especially current controllers of the public realm. Customary law may also be said to depend on a form of implicit 'social contract' theory, which finds the authority of the law in the hypothetical 'consent' of the subjects of the law, where consent is postulated as a corollary of their participation in the society in question, including its law-making system. To borrow a Hobbesian play on words, society-members are the 'authors' of customary law because they are the source of its 'authority'. Society-members in a customary law system are also Kantian universal legislators, in the sense that they know that the governing principle of their own willing and acting is liable to be universalised as a governing principle of legal relations applying to all society-members.

10.28 It follows also that there is no merit in that trend in international legal theory which supposes that states, as the subjects of customary international law, consent to its formation as if by some specific act of will, as if their participation were a voluntary act. The abusive use of the ideas of the 'natural liberty' of states, and hence the need for their 'consent' to any abridgement of that liberty, are a cynical misappropriation of some part of the ethos of revolutionary democracy. For the controllers of the public realms of old- and new-regime states, it was good to learn from Vattel (*The Law of Nations*, 1758) that the states were all 'free, independent, and equal', fortunate inhabitants of a Lockeian 'state of nature', so that the making, judging and enforcement of the law was entirely in their hands. It might have been thought that such a voluntary theory of international law had reached its pitiful nadir in the decision of the Permanent Court of International Justice in the so-called Lotus Case (1927).

10.29 But the intellectual decline has continued, reaching new low-points in such ideas as: (1) the idea that the formation of new rules of customary international law requires some actual assenting state of mind on the part of states, as if governments, let alone states, had determinable states of mind; (2) the idea that states might unilaterally exclude themselves from the application of a new rule of customary international law, or even, when they first become members of international society, from the application of pre-existing rules; (3) the idea that certain rules of customary international law function as a minimal form of higher law (*ius cogens*), merely because the states choose to regard them as being immune from their power to override them.

10.30 The dialectic of practice which makes customary law includes ideas, but ideas as a form of practice. At any particular time, society's struggle of self-ordering takes the form of both a struggle of willing and acting and a struggle about the theories, values, and purposes applicable to such willing and acting, including a struggle about what the law is and what it should be. It is possible to chart the development of international society over the last five centuries as a progressive self-ordering reflected in a corresponding development of customary international law. Each episode can be seen as a stage in a gradual process of international self-ordering at the level of *intergovernment*, that is, the interaction of the controllers of the national public realms.

10.31 *Public Order 1. The Possibility of Universal Law.* Modern international law (from 1500) began with a dialectic of practice which produced a fragile notion of the potentiality of universal international order from profoundly disordering diversity (the New World, the disintegration of Christendom), a dialectic in which powerful actors struggled using the weapons of powerful ideas (Christianity, civilisation, law, reason, natural law, the law of nations, sovereignty, self-preservation and self-interest).

10.32 *Public Order 2. Diplomacy and War.* In the sixteenth century, the centralising monarchies and the multitude of other forms of polity became self-conscious participants in an evolutionary game of survival, in which diplomacy and war were the instruments of competition and co-existence, as each national realm began to identify its self in opposition to the many others, and as it came to seem necessary and possible to imagine a 'law of war and peace', as a compendium of the minimal conditions of co-existence.

10.33 *Public Order 3. The Territorial Polity.* Violent competition in the appropriation of overseas territories and in relation to the control of local and distant sea-areas focused the struggle of ideas on the question of the physical limits of state-power. Physical frontiers, which had been uncertain and unstable, became an integral part of the defining of the selfhood of the polities, and customary international law developed into an externalised feudal law of land-holding and the adjustment of relations between land-owners. The disintegration of Christianity meant that physical frontiers became mental frontiers (*Treaty of Augsburg*, 1555), and the dialectic of ideas within the dialectic of practice, which forms customary international law, came to be dominated by a dialectic of *reason of state*.

10.34 *Public Order 4. The Two Realms.* The idea of the intrinsic independence of the national and international realms was established before the period of seismic internal social change following the French Revolution. The dialectic of ideas soon freed itself from talk about 'natural law' as a universal quasi-legal and quasi-moral regime applying equally to both realms. The law of the co-existence of the 'states' came to be seen as a product of the mutual recognition of their right to determine the conditions of their internal self-ordering. With the development of the subjective identity of the 'nation', with its own personality and its own history, the international realm became derivative and residual in relation to the national realm, with the controllers of the national public realms (governments) now behaving not only as sole agents of the public realms of the states but also as sole representatives of national charisma in the international struggle to survive and prosper, a struggle in which diplomacy and war were still the primary instruments of social control. (It was at the end of the eighteenth century that the word 'diplomacy' came to be used to apply to the conduct of the formal relations between states.) The 'law of nations' or 'international law' (a neologism dating from early in the nineteenth century) was still a secondary socialising phenomenon. It was seen as the rules of the game of the externalised public realms, a pale shadow of national public law. But it was a social phenomenon of growing intellectual and practical substance, developing in complexity and density in step with the development of national public law.

10.35 *Public Order 5. The International Public Realm.* From the latter part of the nineteenth century, there began to appear, in the international realm, *externalised forms of national public realm management.* International institutional processes proliferated as simulacra of national constitutional processes – deliberative, administrative, arbitral. They took on systematic integrity and organic life, each a social system with its own constitutional structure and process, but systematically linked to the national systems, with the social outputs of the external systems flowing back into the national systems as social inputs (leading to legislation and administration and judicial decisions giving effect to decisions of the international systems). In this way, national processes were *communalised externally* to form an informal and rudimentary international public realm of ever-increasing complexity (of organisation) and density (of outputs), and national processes began to be *co-ordinated transnationally* with national decision-making processes coming more and more to be conditioned by products of international decision-making processes. It began to be appropriate to see national public-realm systems as systematically integrated within an international public-realm system which had itself been formed from an external communalising of the national systems. International constitutional law responded by acknowledging the capacity of international institutional systems to participate as such in international legal relations, legal relations with and in their own member-states and non-member-states (*ICJ Advisory Opinion on Reparation for Injuries,* 1948). International public law also expanded rapidly to include the law governing the intergovernmental public realm, including an international administrative law governing the internal and inter-se functioning of the international public-realm systems.

10.36 *Public Order 6. The Possibility of Universal Values.* The management of a public realm of a society reflects the theories, values, and purposes of that society, given that it is itself an integral part not only of the real and legal self-constituting of society but also of its ideal self-constituting. After 1945, the international public realm began to generate theories, values and purposes appropriate to its general nature as a public realm and its particular nature as an international public realm. They are ideas which flow out from and into national social self-constituting, in such a way that it began to be appropriate to see an emerging process of ideal self-constituting even at the global level. As always, that process is inseparable from real self-constituting at the global level, as the controllers of national public realms bring vastly differing actual capacities to the dialectical struggle of idea-formation and law-making at the global level. The dialectical ideal struggle has been a struggle concerning the potential universality of particular ideas: human rights, the rule of law, public order, self-determination, distributive justice, global commons, environmental protection, democracy, public-realm crime. And it is also a struggle as to whether and how far such ideas are appropriate as the content of legal relations, both international public-law relations and legal relations under the laws of the nations as they are co-ordinated by international constitutional and public law. The reciprocating character of law as a social system means that the dialectic of idea-forming and the dialectic of law-making and the dialectic of real-world action have reinforced each other, together conditioning social consciousness, the social consciousness of all subordinate societies and the social consciousness of international society itself.

10.37 The current self-ordering of international society is a palimpsest which includes all six layers of public order, in a cloudy confusion of atavism and progressivism. Customary international law is the legal form of the sedimentary self-ordering of a self-evolving international society.

The making of international law: (2) treaty-law

10.38 Treaties are older than the idea of international law. Wherever polities have co-existed, the possibility of the inter-polity exchange of promises in ritualised form seems to have been present, even if, perhaps especially if, the promising parties do not regard each other as belonging to a single transcendental system of ideas, let alone of law. In the absence of a superordinate idea-system or legal system, the taboo-sanction for treaty-violation is determined by the respective idea-systems of the contracting parties – shame, ostracism, disrepute, reprisal, retorsion, purification, compensation. The social practice of treaty-making has continued from the days of the earliest recorded human history to the present day, more or less in isolation from the troubled development of international law in general. It is as if the controllers of the public realms of polities had treaty-making as an inherited and instinctive mode of behaviour, regardless of their attitude towards international law in general, and regardless of the familiar fact of human experience, that a treaty successfully regulates inter-polity interaction until the day when one or other party chooses otherwise.

10.39 Within the history of national societies, there came a time when the increasing complexity and density of social relations made necessary a transition from customary law to legislation, from slow-motion law-making to instant law-making. The hand of the invisible systemic legislator began to give way to the very visible hand of the institutional legislator. King, council, senate, parliament. Doom, decree, statute. Each society generated appropriate institutional forms. Lacking a legislative institution, international society has appropriated the hallowed institution of the treaty as its institutional legislator. As international society began to increase rapidly in complexity and density from, say, 1815, treaties began to perform a social function closely analogous to legislation in national legal systems. (The *Règlement* on diplomatic representation of 19 March 1815 is a striking early example, but many of the other texts adopted at the Congress of Vienna are legislative in function.)

10.40 In legislation, the dialectic of ideas dominates the dialectic of practice. The dialectic of ideas which is concealed within the dialectic of practice of customary law becomes the dominant form of the dialectic of practice, in the sense that the act of legislating reflects a specific purposive choice of a possible future for the society in question, a specific purposive actualising of the common interest of the society, in accordance with the society's theories and in implementation of its values and purposes. But legislated law is structurally the same as customary law, in the sense that it consists of legal relations, so that behaviour in conformity with legislated law is also necessarily behaviour which serves the common interest of society.

10.41 The idea of the legislative function of treaties in international society necessarily raises two questions: (1) in what sense is the *common interest* of international society as a whole actualised in a treaty among particular members of international society? (2) in what sense is treaty-law subject to a will-forming process of *politics* in international society?

Common interest. A treaty is a disagreement reduced to writing (if one may be permitted to do such violence to the hallowed definition of a contract). But so is legislation. The eventual parties to a treaty enter into negotiation with different ideas of what they want to achieve. Negotiation is a process for finding a third thing which neither party wants but both parties can accept. The making of legislation, at least in a society with an active system of politics, is a similarly dialectical process, by which conflicts of ideas and interests are resolved into a legal form which then re-enters the general social process as a new datum. A treaty is not the end of a process, but the beginning of another process. And so is legislation. The treaty and the law become a datum in the general social process, but it is a datum with a life of its own. The parties to a treaty, like the parties interested in the making of a legislative act, no doubt have different ideas about what has been fixed in the treaty, and different interests in relation to its interpretation and its application to actual persons and events. But their degree of control over their own social situation is limited by the social effectiveness of the treaty or the law. The treaty and the law create a micro-legal system within the general legal system from which they derive their legal effect, and within the society from which they derive their social effect.

10.42 There is a common interest of international society as a whole in the creation of micro-legal systems of treaties, just as there is a common interest of national societies in the creation of the micro-legal systems of legislation. They are an integral part of a society's legal self-constituting, its self-ordering through law. Treaties are a delegation of law-making power. The parties may make law for themselves, their legal capacity to do so deriving from international constitutional law, which may set formal and substantial limitations on that capacity (for example: *ius cogens*, interaction with legal relations under other treaties). But the international legal system is a legal system which still contains a customary form of law, and treaties have a complex and subtle relationship to customary international law.

10.43 Treaty-law has three *meta-legislative effects.*

(1) The first such effect is that treaties are an integral and important part of the *dialectic of practice* which generates customary international law. Within that dialectic, treaties may contribute to the formation of legal relations applying not only to their parties but also to non-parties.

(2) The second meta-legislative effect is that treaties may create a *general legal situation* in which legal relations with non-parties are modified without their specific consent. This is the case where a treaty empowers a party to create a situation (say, a sea-area regime, or a regime of universal criminal jurisdiction, or an arms-control regime, or a use-of-force regime, or an external trade regime) which cannot reasonably be applied on the basis of a discrimination between parties and non-parties. This is especially the case where the international regime falls to be applied within national legal systems, or where the international regime is an aspect of an indivisible conception of international public order. In such a case, the corresponding legal relations of customary international law must be understood as containing the power (of the party) and the liability (of the non-party) to create and to be affected by such a regime. It follows that the ruling of the International Court of Justice in the Nicaragua Case (1992), that the relevant customary international law had not been modified by the existence of the UN Charter, can only be regarded as preposterous.

(3) The general-legal-situation effect is a particular instance of a general effect of treaty-law. Treaty-law breaks the *network of mutuality* which underlies customary international law. A customary legal system is a permanent negotiating of a social contract, the forming and re-forming of a legal basis of social co-existence from day to day, with a necessary and inherent deep-structural mutuality of legal relationships. When, as in the international legal system, the surpassing of customary law by legislation is not a surpassing by and for all members of society, the relationship of the two sources of law cannot be conceived either in terms of a lazy analogy with contract law or by a one-to-one correspondence with their relationship in a national legal system. The existence of treaty-law modifies the legally protected expectations of all members of international society, including non-parties to particular treaties.

10.44 Within the history of national societies, the ever-greater complexity and density of social relations gave rise to the need for delegated legislation, and powers to make legislation are conferred, by legislative act, on persons or bodies other than the primary legislative institution, especially the executive branch of government. Nationally, the volume of delegated legislation soon came to exceed the volume of primary legislation. It is also important to understand that society delegates a law-making function to countless forms of subordinate society, especially industrial and commercial corporations, which are micro-systems of self-legislation and self-government. It is in the common interest of society that such micro-systems should pursue their self-interest under and in conformity with the law of society which actualises the common interest of society as a whole.

10.45 With the development of the international public realm (Public Order 5, above), the need for delegated legislation has been met by conferring legislative powers on international institutional systems. The volume of treaty-law long since exceeded the volume of customary international law. The volume of international delegated legislation probably now rivals the volume of primary treaty-law. And international society, like national societies, includes the activity of countless subordinate societies, other than the state-societies, not least industrial and commercial corporations acting outside the place where they are incorporated. Such societies are systems of delegated self-legislation and self-government under and in conformity with international law and the laws of the nations in which their activities take place.

10.46 Within national systems, it also became necessary to develop forms of para-legislative acts (so-called *soft law*, such as codes of practice, administrative rules, etc.), whose function is to control specifically the law-interpreting and law-applying behaviour of public-realm persons and bodies. They do not give rise to direct legal relations to which the citizen is a party. Rather they modify the application of pre-existing public-realm powers and duties in relation to the citizen. They have been held to give rise to 'legitimate expectations' on the part of the citizen that such powers and duties will be implemented in accordance with the soft-law provisions. Such a thing has now been found to be necessary also in the international public realm. Multilateral and unilateral declarations, resolutions, final acts, memoranda of understanding, statements of principles, programmes, action-plans – all such things have been developed organically to be something other than treaties, giving rise to legitimate expectations about the implementation of legal relations rather than themselves giving rise to legal relations. In those institutional systems where national public law and international public law are now functionally linked in the work of specialised international institutions, such para-legislative acts may especially affect the implementation of legal relations within national legal systems.

10.47 Within national societies, and now within international society, it became necessary also to confer a new kind of legal power on public-realm bodies. All legal powers include a double discretion (whether to exercise the power, what decision to take within the limits of the power). All legal powers include the potentiality of the modification of the legal situation of persons other than the power-holder. But what we may call *administrative-law powers* take these characteristics to a degree which almost gives rise to a difference of kind. Public-realm bodies take power-decisions within broad areas of discretion, sometimes formulated in the most general terms ('necessary in the public interest', 'with a view to the preservation of public order / international peace and security', 'in accordance with equitable principles', 'on a basis of non-discrimination', 'to give effect to the purposes of the present Act / treaty'). Although modern administrative law gives to courts a legal power to define and control the outer limits and the procedural aspects of such discretions, the generality of their scope and the scale of their effects (perhaps, the whole population or all members of international society) give a sort of law-making power to public-realm bodies, including international institutions.

10.48 *Politics.* Politics seeks out public-realm power. Public-realm power seeks to negate politics. The social struggle to control and influence the exercise of public-realm power arises most powerfully in relation to the making of law. The exercise of public-realm power, especially the making of law, is a sustained effort to resolve the struggle of politics into an act which defines and enacts the common interest of society and transcends particular interests. Treaty-law, like all law-making, is a by-product of politics. Treaty-law negates the politics which produces it. In the case of treaty-law-making, however, the role of politics is obscure and complex.

10.49 There are three phases in the making of treaty-law.

(1) *Projection.* The internal political process of each participant generates its input into the negotiation (sometimes referred to as 'instructions to the delegation') and then projects that input externally into the negotiation. The nature of the internal process is specific to each society and its constitutional structure. The process may itself involve complex inter-departmental negotiation within the public realm, and negotiation with parliamentary organs or relevant special interest-groups.

(2) *Negotiation.* Negotiation is dominated by potential treaty-texts, most often prepared in advance, and the crux of the negotiation is a search for 'forms of words' acceptable to all, or the relevant, participants. The passionate and formless world of politics is reborn as a world of words. Matters of great practical consequence, perhaps involving life and death on a great scale, are concentrated into the tiny mass of a few words, in a sort of ritualised trench-warfare, in which big victories are measured in small gains of verbal territory.

(3) *Re-entry.* The treaty-text produced by negotiation is taken back into the internal political process of each participant. In constitutional systems where the executive branch of government and parliament are systematically integrated, the final acceptance of the treaty may be relatively straightforward, politically and legally. Elsewhere, most notoriously in the United States constitutional system, the re-entry stage is a resumption of the projection stage, and the fate of the treaty-text is as uncertain as that of any other executive-branch initiative.

10.50 The Wilsonian new-diplomacy ideal of 'open covenants openly arrived at' has not proved possible, even in the most apparently public of conference-settings. (Of the Paris Peace Conference itself, Harold Nicolson, a member of the British delegation, said: 'few negotiations in history have been so secret, or indeed so occult'.) The crux of a negotiation, as in the most traditional forms of diplomacy, is still located in confidential meetings of restricted groups of participants. A form of negotiation which has become common since 1945, and which may be entitled to be called a new form of diplomacy, is *parliamentary diplomacy* – large-scale conferences in which there is a projection of extra-parliamentary national politics, in the form of open-ended participation by persons and groups other than the representatives of the national and international public realms and where the rituals of diplomatic negotiation are overtaken by free-ranging debate of a broad political character, about ends and means, values and purposes. But, even in this form of negotiation, the last word as to the content of the treaty-law and its re-entry into the national legal systems remains with the controllers of the public realms.

10.51 The making of treaty-law is accordingly anomalous in relation to national constitutional systems, in the sense that it brackets out of the national process a central part of the making of a form of law which is liable to become an important factor in national public-realm decision-making, or even to become part of the substance of national law. This bracketing-out means that normal national constitutional processes, including political accountability for executive-branch action, may apply in a disorderly way, if at all, to treaty-law-making. Treaty-law-making, a substantial and rapidly increasing part of the law-making of the international legal system, continues to share in the unreality of traditional diplomacy, a ghost-filled world of 'power' and 'national interest' and 'foreign policy', the world of war by other means. (It follows that nothing can be said in favour of the existence and the work of the International Law Commission, which manages to combine the unreality of the academy with the unreality of traditional diplomacy.)

The future of the international legal system

10.52 The *aggiornamento* of international society means purposively bringing international society into line with our best ideas and highest expectations about society in general. At the beginning of the twenty-first century, such a thing seems at last to be a reasonable enterprise. It is an enterprise of which the reconceiving of the international legal system is an integral part. It is also an enterprise which faces a series of formidable obstacles which we must identify if we are to overcome them.

10.53 (1) *The degradation of universal values.* The emergence of potentially universal values after 1945 suffered a deformation as the emerging values were subjected to almost instant rationalising, legalising, institutionalising and bureaucratising. That is to say, they were corrupted before they could begin to act as transcendental, ideal, supra-societal, critical forces in relation to the emerging absolute statism of society, including 'democratic' society. They were also systematically corrupted before they could acquire a more clearly universal substance, so that they became vulnerable to charges of cultural relativism and hegemonism. And they were corrupted, finally, in the context of the so-called Cold War which was waged, at the ideal level, as a cynical disputation about general ideas, so that the 'winning' of the Cold War could be presented as a final validation of general ideas. It will not be easy to redeem the idea, the power, and the social function of transcendental values from such relentless degradation.

10.54 (2) *The hegemony of the economic.* In democratic-capitalist societies, experience over the last two centuries of the relationship between the economic development of society and its socio-political development (including the development of the legal system) suggests that there is a definite correlation between the two, but no unequivocal correlation, either in point of time or in substance. Leading cases (the United Kingdom, the United States, Prussia, Japan, the European Union) show significant differences on the most critical of all points, namely, the post-Marxian questions of whether socio-political change is caused by economic development and whether the form of socio-political change is determined by the form of economic development. However, such questions have themselves been overtaken by a form of general social development which has led to the conceptual and practical dominance of economic phenomena over all other social phenomena.

10.55 The economy has become a virtual public realm. The 'economy' here means the socially organised transformation of natural and man-made resources through the application of physical and mental effort. In a capitalist society, private-interest economic activity is seen as activity also in the public interest. The primary function of management of the traditional public realm, where social power is exercised exclusively in the public interest, has gradually come to be, not the service of some common interest of well-being conceived in terms of general values (say, justice or solidarity or happiness or human flourishing), but the maintaining of the conditions required for the well-being of the economy, including, above all, the legal conditions.

10.56 The global economy is the limiting-case economy, as the transformatory activity of the whole human race comes to be socially organised under an international legal system which is, in this context, dominated by the laws of the nations (§ 10.22 above). Functional economic high-values will dominate the development of the global economy, and hence presumably the further development of the international legal system, to an even greater extent than in national societies, so long as there is only a piecemeal international public realm and rudimentary international politics.

10.57 (3) *The poverty of politics.* When politics is seen as a general social process for determining the common interest, then it is possible to make judgements about the way in which politics makes such determinations in particular societies or at particular times. Since early in the nineteenth century, institutionalised politics has been public-opinion-led and ends-oriented. There developed alongside such politics a public decision-making system ('government') which is rationality-led and means-oriented. The merit of a political system might be measured by the degree to which it allows for a rich debate about both ends and means and provides efficient systems for resolving the debate in the form of legal and other action.

10.58 Politics in the most socially developed national systems has recently degenerated into an impoverished debate within narrow dialectical limits, focused particularly on the manipulation of mass-opinion. At the same time, the professional controllers of the public realm (politicians and public servants) have acquired an unprecedented degree of depoliticised pragmatic power, corresponding to the urgency and complexity of the day-to-day problems of the internal and external management of such systems, especially the economic problems. It is the externalised form of this politics-free power that has been pooled in the intergovernmental institutions of the international public realm. And the controllers of the economic virtual public realm, often causing large-scale social effects by their private-interest decision-making, are not accountable through the general public-realm political and legal control-systems, but devote substantial resources to managing the outcomes of those systems. The development of the international system, including the international legal system, is likely to be determined by such national developments. It is not likely that international politics will be better than the best of national politics, even if it ever comes to be better than the worst.

10.59 (4) *The poverty of philosophy.* Who killed philosophy? Was it democracy, with its capacity to process all questions of ends and means in the public forum? Or was it capitalism, with its own internalised high values, interpreted and applied in the market-place? The primary perpetrator was philosophy itself. While societies continued to embody the fruits of old-regime transcendental philosophy in the forms of their social organisation, and continued to enact the fruits of old-regime philosophy in their self-understanding, their high values and their purposes, a new-regime philosophy, strictly an unphilosophy or an anti-philosophy of terminal pragmatism, decreed that old-regime transcendental philosophy is impossible, an illusion, a fraud. It followed that the surpassing of old-regime philosophy on its own terms was impossible, and that the surpassing of existing forms of social organisation and social consciousness was possible only to the extent that such surpassing arose within existing social processes. Democracy and capitalism have taken power over the possibility of their own negating, and hence over their own surpassing, and it is philosophy which has given a spurious charisma to their mental absolutism. Corrupted social consciousness fills the private minds of human beings everywhere with low values generated as systematic by-products of social systems which will soon be, if they are not already, beyond the redeeming power of higher values.

10.60 The reciprocating character of a legal system, formed by and forming the ideal and the real self-constituting of society, means that a legal system cannot be better than the social consciousness that it enacts. If the role of philosophy in human self-surpassing and self-perfecting is not restored, perhaps with the assistance of non-Western participants in global social consciousness, then the development of the international legal system is condemned to be the impoverished product of an impoverished human consciousness.

10.61 (5) *The tyranny of the actual.* The actual seems inevitable because, if it could have been otherwise, it would have been otherwise. From the necessity of the actual it is a short step to the rationality of the actual (Hegel), to believing that what is is right (Pope), in the best possible world (Leibniz). But the human actual, including the social actual, is the product of human choice, that is to say, moral choice. To rationalise or naturalise the human actual is to empty it of its moral content, to neutralise it. It has been an effect, if not the original purpose, of the 'human sciences', over the last century-and-a-half, to rationalise and naturalise the human actual, and so to make the actual seem to be morally neutral. We seek to assign 'causes' to things in the human world, such as slavery or trench-warfare or genocide, knowing that causation is our category for understanding the non-human world. Conversely, we assign personality to reified ideas of particular social systems ('nation' or 'state' or 'class'), so that actuality-making choice is isolated from any particular human moral agent or agents, and then we speak of the 'intention' of such a systematic process, knowing that a process cannot be morally responsible.

10.62 Nowhere has human demoralising been as relentlessly practised as in the international realm, the imaginary realm inhabited by 'states'. It is practised by those who act within that realm and by those who study it. The external aspect of government is still conducted in pursuit of what is still called 'foreign policy' through the means still known as 'diplomacy', old-regime games as anachronistic as real tennis or prize-fighting. And those who study such things still seek to uncover the rules of such games, as if they were studying the behaviour of alien life-forms, as if their bizarre ideas of the human actual were the hypothetical rationalising of some part of the natural world.

10.63 The meaning and the measure of human progress are difficult to establish. A fair general judgement might be that material progress has not been matched by spiritual progress. It also seems right to say that such human progress as there has been, over the last several thousand years, has been due to three strange accidents of evolution, or gifts of God: rationality (the capacity to order our consciousness); morality (the capacity to take responsibility for our future); and imagination (the capacity to create a reality-for-ourselves). Using these capacities, we found within ourselves another capacity, the capacity to form the idea of the ideal – the idea of a better human future which we can choose to make actual. The ideal has been the anti-entropic and anti-inertial moving-force of human progress, of human self-surpassing and self-perfecting. To overcome the tyranny of the actual, to overcome the ignorant and infantile belief that the actual idea and the actual practice of the self-organising of humanity are necessary and inevitable, we need only to recall and recover our extraordinary power constantly to reconceive the ideal, in order yet again to choose to make it actual.

The new paradigm

10.64 The new paradigm of the international legal system is a new ideal of human self-constituting. It has three leading characteristics. (1) The international legal system is a system for disaggregating the common interest of all-humanity, rather than merely a system for aggregating the self-determined interests of so-called states. (2) The international legal system contains all legal phenomena everywhere, overcoming the artificial separation of the national and the international realms, and removing the anomalous exclusion of non-governmental transnational events and transactions. (3) The international legal system, like any legal system, implies and requires an idea of a society whose legal system it is, a society with its own self-consciousness, with its own theories, values and purposes, and with its own systems for choosing its future, including the system of politics.

10.65 The idea of international society, the society of the whole human race and the society of all societies, takes its place at last, centuries late, within human self-consciousness, and international law finds its place at last, centuries late, within the self-constituting of international society, that is to say, as an essential part of the self-creating and the self-perfecting of the human species.

11

International law and the idea of history

Law's histories – The third memory – The third memory and international law – The lure of historicism – The making of the past – From human history to human law – Human memory

The future of the human world will be a product of its present state. The present state of the human world is a product of its past states. In our continuous present we tell and retell the story of our past. But the writing of history is a dangerous occupation. In seeming to tell us what we have been, it seems to tell us what we are, and so to tell us what we can be and even what we will be. The fact that we cannot see what we have been except through the eyes of what we are means that we are always in the process of making the past. It means also that the writing of history is also a history of the writing of history. Past historiography is part of the history of the past.

A central temptation of historiography is to claim that it is a human science, uncovering the nature of human nature and human nature's laws. Human existence and human behaviour are facts as much as any other fact of the material universe, so surely there must be the possibility of discovering a human ontology at least as soundly based as the consensual ontology of the natural sciences and a human metaphysics at least as soundly based as the consensual metaphysics of the physical sciences. We have reason to believe, in the light of the long history of historiography, that such a claim is unjustified. The laws of human nature exceed the hypothetical power of the human mind.

International history, the history of all-humanity, is a limiting case of the dangers of historiography, if it seems or claims to tell all-humanity what it is and what it might be. Instead, we should want to use historiography as a form of 'teaching by example', showing us what human beings are capable of, the good and the evil that humans do, and reminding us of our responsibility to choose a better human future, to constitute a better form of human sociality, imposing on ourselves as a species the laws necessary to make that better human future.

Law's histories

11.1 International law, like any other legal system, is a bridge between the social past and the social future through the social present. But international law has a unique fourfold relationship to the past. It is the law of a social system which is the product of many pasts, the pasts of all human societies. It is a universalising of the pre-existing values not merely of one particular society, but of all human societies. It is a form of law which is generated by a law-making process which transforms past events involving all human beings into present legal relations affecting all human beings. It is a product of the past that conditions the future not merely of one particular society, but of all human societies. Law is a real presence of the social past. International law is a real presence of the human past. Law is an actual potentiality of the social future. International law is an actual potentiality of the human future.[1]

11.2 Like any legal system, international law has its own history, a history which is both intrinsic and extrinsic. It has an *intrinsic* history of the development of its structures and systems (personality, law-making, treaty, arbitration, permanent diplomacy, intergovernmental institution), a history of its legal substance (law of the sea, diplomatic law, humanitarian law, human rights law), and a history of its idea of itself (legal philosophy). It has an *extrinsic* history of its relationship to all other social phenomena, other social structures and systems (custom, religion, morality, subordinate legal systems), and of its relationship to the phenomena of general history, to the things that historians write about (war and peace, the rise and fall of empires, revolutions, socio-economic change, the psychology of world-historical individuals, the development of ideas and ideologies).

[1] 'Real presence' and 'actual potentiality', with their Aristotelian overtones, express the strange fact that law, like a work of art or a genetic programme, is something which acts as a timeless cause, producing pre-determined effects as and when conditions in present time require it to do so, and which will continue to do so in the future. 'Present' time is the moral present, the moment of moral and legal choice, when choosing the future presents itself as a necessity.

11.3 Like any legal system, international law's idea of itself has internal and external perspectives. Its *internal* perspective is its significance seen from the perspective of participants in the system as they act as participants in the system. Such a perspective is, in the first place, a logically necessary consciousness: that is to say, to participate in the system is necessarily to participate in its idea of itself; to play a game is to play the rules of the game. Secondly, it is an observable significance, that is to say, an idea which an outside observer may infer from the behaviour of participants acting as such. And, thirdly, it is a psychological significance, actually present in the consciousness of participants. Needless to say, neither the validity nor the efficacy of international law, no more than of any other legal system, depends on anything more than a hypothetical minimum of actual awareness of the system's theory of itself on the part of those currently participating in the system. The validity and efficacy of the system are rather an effect of the first (logical) aspect of the internal perspective.

11.4 The *external* perspective of a legal system's idea of itself is its idea of its significance in relation to other social phenomena, other natural phenomena, other aspects of human consciousness, both individual and social consciousness. It is a function of social consciousness to generate theories[2] about a society's structures and systems which explain them and justify them, ideas which create an internal perspective of the society's idea of itself. The external perspective of a legal system's idea of itself is part of the internal perspective of a society's idea of itself. A democratic-capitalist society or a theocratic society or a totalitarian society has appropriate theories of the presence of law within that society. The external aspect of international law's idea of itself is part of the internal aspect of international society's idea of itself.

11.5 These five aspects of the significance of international law as a legal system (its particular relationship to the past, its intrinsic and extrinsic histories, the internal and external perspectives of its idea of itself) are in constant motion in relation to each other, as they are in any legal system. At any given moment in time, a society's social consciousness must contain some sort of integration of its ideas about its

[2] A special meaning is given to the word 'theory' in *Eunomia*, § 2.45. A *theory* is a society's explanation of itself to itself.

legal system, a functional integration, sufficient to enable the society to continue to function as a society. Such integration may be imposed by those who control social consciousness as part of a general social theory which it is within their legal and practical power to impose. Or else such integration may be the subject of ceaseless renegotiation as part of society's general social process, its day-to-day self-constituting, its real constitution.[3] Experience shows that a society's effective functional integration at the level of social consciousness is compatible with high levels of uncertainty, confusion and dispute about all five aspects of the theory of its legal system.

11.6 After five centuries of the intrinsic and extrinsic history of international law, five centuries of the negotiating of an idea of itself and an idea of its place within international society, there is still no effective functional integration of a theory of international law within a theory of international society. To diagnose the causes of that state of affairs is a formidable challenge for the international historian, seeking to recover the past of international society and the past of international law. It is a task made no easier by the fact that there are high levels of uncertainty, confusion and dispute about the very idea of the 'past' and even about the very idea of the recovery of the past in the form of 'history'. Since the earliest recorded history, the human past has not been a thing but an idea. The idea of history is an idea with its own history. International history, the history of all-humanity, is a limiting case of the idea of history. International law, with its unique relationship to the history of all-humanity, is a limiting case of the relationship of all legal systems to the past. At the beginning of the twenty-first century, the public mind of all-humanity may at last be capable of taking stock of the place within the history of all-humanity of the legal system of international society, the society of all societies.[4] As a prolegomenon to the study of the history of the place of international law in international society, its intrinsic and extrinsic history, it is first necessary to consider the notorious problems connected with the idea of the recovery of the past.

[3] For the three dimensions (ideal, real and legal) of the self-constituting of a society, see *Eunomia*, ch. 9. The real constitution is the social struggle to give effect to the ideal constitution, including through the making of law (the legal constitution). The three constitutions determine each other dialectically.

[4] Such a theory is proposed in *Eunomia*, centred on the ideas of society (the collective self-constituting of human beings in consciousness) and law (the self-ordering of a society).

The third memory

11.7 History is public memory. It is the remembering of the public mind.[5] Like the memory of the private mind, history is as much a forgetting as an unforgetting. The human past is mostly lost beyond recall, as dead as the human beings who made it. Social consciousness contains no algorithm for determining what will be remembered and what will be forgotten. The public past, like the private past, simply haunts us like a dream. Like a dream, the unforgotten past is full of familiar and unfamiliar faces and places, full of meaning and meaninglessness, full of the anxiety of an actor, involved and responsible, and full of the gaze of the spectator, detached and powerless, but lacking the continuity and coherence and seamless density of our lived experience, and lacking the integrating focus of our moral and practical responsibility for what happens next. We are what we were, as individuals and societies, but we have very imperfect knowledge of what we have been.

11.8 As compared with the remembering of our private minds, history has the further strange characteristic that it is a remembering of things that we did not experience.[6] They may be things done by people with whom we feel a particular affinity – our ancestors, our nation, our co-religionists, those who have made a social reality which we regard as our social reality. Or they may be things done by people who seem to be alien, exotic perhaps, things done by people and in circumstances with which we seem to share no common feeling or common interest beyond the fact that they have been done by people who are also human beings. A dream of a past which is not our own, history nevertheless becomes our own, and ceases to be a dream, when we live in the reality which it has formed. We are what our societies have been, and we cannot escape the presence of the social past. And we cannot escape society's idea of its past. It is as if each human being possesses a second memory as a member of all the societies to which we belong, a social memory as active as our personal memory, but still less under our personal control. And the social past and the social memory which we share and cannot escape must include the past and the memory of the social co-existence of the human species, the history of all-humanity.

[5] The 'public mind' is the consciousness or 'mind politic' of a society. See ch. 4 above.

[6] Thucydides was the first of countless generals and politicians who have recounted their own experience, which becomes the second-hand experience of the reader.

11.9 A bolder speculation is the idea that there is a faculty of memory of the human species itself, a species-memory, a biological memory, a phylogenetic memory, which we may here identify as a *third memory.* The idea is that, beyond the consciously accumulated public memory of the human species re-presented to itself in the form of 'history', some part of the experience of the human species has been accumulated in the inheritance of all human beings. The idea has taken three successive forms: (1) the idea of human nature; (2) the idea of human species characteristics as an evolutionary residue; and (3) the idea of a collective unconscious within the human mind.

11.10 The significance of the idea of a third memory, in whichever form, is that it implies that the human past is not merely a collection of contingencies acting as causes and effects of each other, but must be seen as subject to pre-conditioned or pre-programmed parameters which transcend the willing and acting of actual human beings. It suggests that there is a hidden necessity which sets limits on the apparent freedom of human behaviour, a human constant in the midst of an infinity of human variables. It suggests that the phenomena of history are epiphenomena of a reality which is as permanent as events are transient. It suggests that our understanding of that necessity, however imperfect, offers an explanatory matrix for interpreting the past. Such an idea would also permit us to believe that the future will be much like the past, at least at some fundamental level, and even that we may project our idea of the past into an idea of the future on some basis which is more sound than mere speculation or wish-fulfilment or self-interest. Among other things, it would tend to reinforce the idea that the international future will merely be a continuation of the international past.

11.11 (1) The idea of a human nature came naturally to the universalising mind of the philosophers of ancient Greece. Their vivid awareness of human diversity led them to look for evidence of human uniformities. Their initiation into what we call natural science, especially the science of biology, taught them that natural uniformity is as fundamental as natural diversity, that there are types of animals as well as particular animals. Their epistemology led them to find universals in the particular, to define a definition as a universalising of every particular to which it is referable. Their metaphysics led them to look for a reality manifesting itself in appearances, an order which is present in all instances of ordering. It was not merely an easy step, but a necessary step, to suppose that there is a human uniformity, a human universal, a human reality, a humanity of which each human being is an instance.[7]

11.12 To postulate the common identity of humanity is only the beginning of a task, and a passionate struggle, to identify the content of that humanity. The effort to distinguish the natural in the human identity and the human situation from the contingent, the conventional, the transient and the illusory has been the mainspring of philosophy, not only social and ethical philosophy but also epistemology itself, insofar as philosophy's study of itself is the study of human consciousness itself. To do philosophy is to think universally. To philosophise about things human is to universalise the nature of human beings.

11.13 The belief in an ultimate uniformity in things human is the necessary, if usually unspoken, premise of the 'human sciences', as they have developed over the last two centuries. They are customarily supposed to depend on a particular methodological foundation which is customarily supposed to be a borrowing from the method of the natural sciences. But what they have copied from the natural sciences, for better and for worse, is rather the scientist's foundational belief in the uniformity of nature.[8] And that belief, we may say, is itself inspired by the Pythagorean insight, a semi-mystical wonder at the universality of mathematics, a universality of the universe which includes the universality of the natural world, and the universality of the human world as part of the natural world.

11.14 (2) The idea of universal human characteristics as an evolutionary residue seems to be a necessary corollary of Darwinian evolutionary theory. It is a central postulate of evolutionary biology that biological change is retained at the level of the species, and hence that individual species-members carry the characteristics of the species in addition to the unique characteristics of their individuality.[9] Once again, to postulate such a thing is only the beginning of a task and a struggle to

[7] The Aristotelian human animal, with biological characteristics, took on, with the Stoics, the purely philosophical species-characteristic of *humanitas* (humanness).

[8] Durkheim expressed trenchantly the naturalistic goal which had inspired the founding fathers of social science (Hume, Saint-Simon, Comte, Mill): 'All that [sociology] asks is that the principle of causality be applied to social phenomena . . . not as a rational necessity but only as an empirical postulate.' E. Durkheim, *The Rules of Sociological Method* (1895) (eds and trs S. A. Solovay and J. H. Mueller; Chicago, University of Chicago Press; 8th edn, 1938), p. 141.

[9] Darwin considered the biological heredity of the human species in *The Descent of Man and Selection in Relation to Sex* (1871). He argued that an instinctive moral sense in man is an evolutionary product. See also A. Flew, *Evolutionary Ethics* (London, Macmillan; 1967) and

identify the distribution of universal and particular biological characteristics in the human animal. A very great deal turns on the chosen distribution. Our species-characteristics may seem like a fate, an inevitability or, at least, an excuse. To overcome our species-characteristics through the use of some other aspect of our potentiality – overcoming instinct through the use of reason, to use a hallowed formula – is considered to be an application of exceptional energy, an anti-entropic act, if we assume that to submit to our species-characteristics requires no special application of energy, that it comes naturally to us, as we say. If we assume that, say, aggression and predation are part of our evolutionary residue, then to behave co-operatively and altruistically may seem like supererogatory acts of virtue.

11.15 A bolder speculation has been the idea that human species-characteristics have been retained at the social level.[10] Sociobiology has its point of departure in the idea that the human animal is biologically a social animal, and hence that part of our evolutionary residue is expressed in our social behaviour. It would follow from this that, at the social level also, our species-characteristics have some determining effect on the form and functioning of human societies and on the interacting of human societies. Once again, it would seem to follow that if societies do what comes naturally – say, if they compete and conflict to the point of mutual self-destruction – then that is not surprising in itself, and hence that, on the contrary, if societies live peacefully and co-operatively, then that is an overcoming of a sort of fate or necessity, a display of heroic virtue, another triumph of reason over instinct.[11] Of course, it might equally be possible to suppose that socially positive behaviour – such as the protection of 'human rights'[12] – is explicable in biological terms.

K. Lorenz, *Behind the Mirror. A Search for a Natural History of Human Knowledge* (tr. R. Taylor; New York, Harcourt Brace Jovanovich; 1977).

[10] E. O. Wilson, *Sociobiology – the New Synthesis* (Cambridge, MA, The Belknap Press of Harvard University Press; 1975).

[11] Much has been written on the biological bases of aggression, and its relevance to understanding the conflictual behaviour of states. See J. Groebel and R. A. Hinde (eds.), *Aggression and War. Their Biological and Social Bases* (Cambridge, Cambridge University Press; 1989) (with bibliography).

[12] E. O. Wilson, *On Human Nature* (Cambridge, London, Harvard University Press; 1978), pp. 198–9. 'I suggest we will want to give [the idea of universal human rights] primary status not because it is a divine ordinance, or through obedience to an abstract principle of unknown extraneous origin, but because we are mammals . . . I suggest that this is the true origin of the universal rights movement and that an understanding of its raw biological causation will be more compelling than any rationalization contrived by culture to reinforce

11.16 Once again, the problem is that it is impossible to resolve conflicts between competing hypotheses about the content of the evolutionary residue at the social level, and yet different hypotheses lead to dramatically different deductions, and hence judgements, about actual social behaviour. For example, to believe that warfare is or is not biologically natural is liable to have significant effects on the decisions and judgements we make and hence on the behaviour of human beings in relation to each other. A choice of hypothesis is, in such a case, literally a matter of life and death.

11.17 But there is a more profound problem raised by hypotheses which locate an evolutionary residue in the present human condition. It is more than arguable that the development of human consciousness, itself a product of biological evolution, has not only terminated human participation in the process of natural species-selection but has also enabled the human species to override, as it were, its biological inheritance. Human physiology is, no doubt, a biological inheritance, but that part of physiology which makes possible human consciousness has enabled human beings to behave in ways which have no necessary relationship to any biological necessity.[13] It is, of course, possible to imagine biological explanations for the most bizarre, and seemingly the most unfunctional, of human behaviour, from torture to tree-worship to playing computer-games, but such an explanation would be too speculative and generalised to form a basis for rational decision-making.

11.18 (3) It is an ancient speculation that there is an unconscious part of the human consciousness which has some sort of power over the conscious part of the mind, and over which the conscious mind has little control, and hence that the unconscious mind has an uncontrollable power over human behaviour, including human behaviour which is rationally selected.[14] Since society is a product of the human mind,

and euphemize it.' See also G. E. Pugh, *The Biological Origin of Human Values* (New York, Basic Books; 1977), speculating that 'primary values' (including, say, justice) may be a biological inheritance at the root of moral and social values.

[13] R. Dawkins, *The Selfish Gene* (Oxford, Oxford University Press; 1976). Dawkins postulates a unit of cultural inheritance (a meme) which acts in ways analogous to the gene as a unit of biological inheritance. In *The Extended Phenotype – the Long Reach of the Gene* (Oxford, Oxford University Press; 1982), Dawkins considers evolutionary theory at the level of the genetic totality (phenotype) of an organism, an idea with useful implications, if only heuristic, for understanding social phenomena.

[14] See L. L. Whyte, *The Unconscious Before Freud* (New York, Basic Books; 1960).

or rather of human minds interacting, it is certainly not rash to speculate that social consciousness reproduces all aspects of the individual mind, including the unconscious mind, and hence that the activity of a society will also be affected by the power of the unconscious mind.

11.19 A more daring speculation is the idea that the unconscious mind of each human being participates in some sort of collective unconscious which is, in some way, shared with all other human beings. Such an idea has been proposed in two distinct forms: either as a system which has developed within human consciousness and which conditions the current content of social consciousness,[15] or as a human species-characteristic which causes an underlying uniformity in the distinct cultural manifestations of different societies.[16] The idea of a species-consciousness gives rise to an obvious and fundamental problem – how can it be reconciled with generally accepted notions of genetics which exclude the inheritance of characteristics acquired in the course of the life-experience of the organism, except to the extent that a gene-mutation occurring in a particular organism is transmitted to its own progeny or a mutated genetic form establishes itself as a separate species?[17]

[15] '[A] collective mind, in which mental processes occur just as they do in the mind of the individual'. S. Freud, *Totem and Taboo – Some Points of Agreement between the Mental Lives of Savages and Neurotics* (1912/1913) (tr. J. Strachey; London, Routledge & Kegan Paul; 1950), p. 195. Sociology is 'applied psychology' (*New Lectures*, 1921/1933). Freud also believed that the mind contains an 'archaic heritage', a phrase borrowed from G. Le Bon: *La psychologie des foules* (1895), which includes not only the individual super-ego but also collective mental phenomena that are at the root of 'civilised' social phenomena.

For Ricoeur, Freud's genetic models of shared consciousness 'will have to be understood not only as tools meant to co-ordinate ontogenesis and phylogenesis, but as instruments of interpretation meant to subordinate every history – that of mores, of beliefs, of institutions – to the history of desire in its great debate with authority'. P. Ricoeur, *Freud and Philosophy. An Essay in Interpretation* (tr. D. Savage; New Haven, London, Yale University Press; 1970), p. 179. See also R. Bocock, *Freud and Modern Society. An Outline and Analysis of Freud's Sociology* (London, Thomas Nelson & Sons; 1976).

[16] 'My thesis, then, is as follows: In addition to our immediate consciousness ... there exists a second psychic system of a collective, universal, and impersonal nature which is identical in all individuals. This collective unconscious does not develop individually, but is inherited.' C. G. Jung, *The Archetypes and the Collective Unconscious* (Princeton, Princeton University Press; 2nd edn, 1968), p. 43.

[17] J.-B. Lamarck (1744–1829) proposed that species-members may transmit to their offspring characteristics acquired during the life-experience of the species. For a discussion of writers who have proposed various forms of human Lamarckism (including the supersession of one race by another (higher) race), see P. J. Bowler, *Theories of Human Evolution. A Century of Debate 1844–1944* (Oxford, Basil Blackwell; 1986/1987), esp. ch. 9.

11.20 A society is an inheritance of acquired characteristics, formed by biology but transcending biology. In the second memory which is a society's history, collective consciousness, including its unconscious strata, is retained and remade and handed on. It is the shared consciousness of human beings who share in the species-memory of their biological inheritance and who make what they can of that inheritance by the social activity which it makes possible.

The third memory and international law

11.21 The extrinsic history of international law is the story of its relationship to a social past which is an unsocial past, to a rudimentary second memory which is full of the contents of species-memory, full of the outward signs of the unconscious consciousness of humanity's biological inheritance. In default of a history of the self-making of all-humanity through social activity, it is the idea of a natural human history, a third memory which is a species-memory, which has had a decisive effect in the making of international law's idea of itself.

11.22 Such human naturalism has had a particularly powerful effect at three crucial moments[18] in the history of international law – (1) in the appeal to 'natural law' within the internal perspective of international law's idea of itself; (2) in the postulating, within the external perspective of international law's idea of itself, of a 'state of nature' as the original, and perhaps continuing, state of co-existence of human societies; and (3) in the 'realist' rejection, within the extrinsic history of international law, of the efficacy, or even possibility, of international law as the law of an international society.

11.23 (1) The idea of *natural law* is founded on the idea that law-abidingness is part of human nature and that patterns of law-abiding can

Freud was well aware of the Lamarckian difficulty, but treated it as irrelevant. The never-resolved problem of the epistemic status of his ideas left him free to suggest that he was dealing with phenomena at a different level from that of mere biology. Jung believed that he had overcome the problem by assimilating the 'archetypes' of the collective unconscious to human instincts. The archetypes merely make possible the cultural forms in which they are represented. 'The representations themselves are not inherited, only the form, and in that respect they correspond in every way to the instincts which are also determined in form only.' (C. G. Jung, *The Archetypes* (fn. 16 above), p. 79).

[18] 'Moment' is here used in approximately the Hegelian sense: *das Moment* (a determinative element in a social structure or a determinative development in a social system), as opposed to *der Moment* (a moment in time).

be uncovered by human reason in contemplating humanity's situation as part of nature.[19] Such ideas suggest as a corollary that such patterns might be allowed to have the same kind of social effect as 'law' which is imposed socially ('positive law') and so become a sort of 'natural law', a paradoxical formula implying a law without a law-giver. As a further corollary, it was suggested that natural law could, and would necessarily, apply to the law-givers themselves to regulate their co-existence, since there was no law-giver to impose law on the law-givers.

11.24 The term 'natural law' carried two alternative metaphorical resonances. It could evoke an association of ideas with 'laws of nature', a formulation which is now more or less obsolete but which was used to refer to the wonderful orderliness of a Platonic-Aristotelian universe, and later a Newtonian universe, which seemed to be a perfectly law-abiding, or at least a mathematics-abiding, universe. In this perspective, the content of international law, as a special case of natural law, might be determined by universalising human law-abiding experience. In another perspective, the idea of natural law was associated with the idea of human rationality, so that its content, and by further derivation the content of international law, could be determined by necessary deduction from the most general principles of human order. These two strains of natural law – universalising and particularising – dissolved into cloudy confusion when international law's idea of itself began to develop vigorously after, say, the year 1500, an effort full of intellectual seriousness and moral commitment but taking the unfortunate form of a mingling of the unity-from-diversity of the Roman law of nations with the particularity-from-universality of medieval scholasticism.

11.25 It is difficult to judge whether such an enterprise contributed to the cause of establishing the rule of law in international society, or set it back by several centuries. It is arguable that Grotius, in particular, past-master of the use of ironic empiricism and ambivalent rationalism in a sublime cause, lent unintended assistance to the cause of those who could use the motley residues of history to reach very different conclusions and who would use the equivocal power of reason to deduce

[19] In the most cogent presentation of the idea of natural law, Thomas Aquinas found the sources of natural law in the 'natural inclinations' of human beings, and in the specifically human characteristic of reason, which enables us to know and to seek the good. Natural law is a participation in eternal law, which is 'the ideal of divine wisdom considered as directing all actions and movements'.

very different diagnoses and prescriptions. Paradoxically, the idea of natural law, as a law whose validity and efficacy does not depend on the authority of a law-giver, would serve another historical function in making possible the idea of constitutionalism within the idea of itself of liberal democracy. Having failed to establish itself above and beyond national legal systems, the idea of constitutionalism was internalised as a sort of natural law of liberal democratic societies, particularised and actualised in such derived concepts as fundamental rights and the rule of law. The limiting case of that internalising has been the United States of America. Trapped between a philosophical pragmatism which struggles against transcendentalism as if it were a sin of the mind and an oppressive presence of religion which is not allowed to be an established religion, the public mind of the United States developed constitutionalism as a secular religion, with 'rights' as a form of grace leading to instant justification and salvation.

11.26 The laborious effort has now begun, centuries too late, to create an idea of constitutionalism appropriate for international society.[20]

11.27 (2) The strange idea of a pre-societal state of nature was remarkably successful in assisting in the great social transformations of certain societies in the seventeenth and eighteenth centuries. The epistemic status of the idea was always known to be dubious, and any possible basis in historical fact was firmly disclaimed, long before anthropology suggested that it was more than unlikely that humanity had ever been in such a condition.[21] Also, the state of natural freedom was found, somewhat surprisingly, to contain a sort of resurrected natural law, based on ideas about human nature, and even, in John Locke's version, a sort of prefiguring of an ideal British constitution.

11.28 Epistemically dubious, historical only in form and suspiciously convenient in its content, the idea of the state of nature made possible the creation-myth of social contract theory, a theory about the origin of human society in general. Social contract theory was always seen to rest

[20] For a discussion of constitutionalism in an international context, see ch. 12 below.

[21] The propagators of social contract theory were well aware of its dubious epistemic status. Its powerful intellectual and social effect was best explained by Kant: 'It is in fact merely an idea of reason, which nonetheless has undoubted practical reality; for it can oblige every legislator to frame his laws in such a way that they could have been produced by the united will of a whole nation.' I. Kant, 'On the common saying: "This may be true in theory, but it does not apply in practice"' (1793), *Kant's Political Writings* (ed. H. Reiss; Cambridge, Cambridge University Press; 1970), pp. 61–92, at p. 79.

on a paradox – that people in the state of nature freely choose to give up their natural freedom for the unfreedom of society. It is a paradox which echoes a paradox of theodicy: why would a perfect god create an imperfect universe? Social-contract philosophers rightly devoted little attention to this obvious problem. The important historical question is: why did such a plainly paradoxical theory establish itself in the social consciousness of societies in the seventeenth and eighteenth centuries? The answer must be that it was a theory which fitted the nature of a deep-structural social transformation, as the displacement of social power in favour of a newly dominant social class needed a displacement of old theories about the source of ultimate social authority – whether God, the King or tradition. Social contract theory made it possible to suppose that a society is made by and for its members, that they are the authors of all social authority, that they are the law-givers of the law to which they are all subject. In other words, the paradox of social contract theory made possible the foundational paradox of liberal democracy, and its noble lie, that the people are their own subjects.[22]

11.29 However, beyond the sphere of the national societies a strange thing happened. The idea of the pre-societal state of nature was commonly used to characterise the essential nature of inter-societal relationships, but it was not used as the basis of a creation-theory of a contractual international society. International pre-society was left with a vestigial law of nature, of increasingly dubious epistemic status, and with a sort of pre-legal system, which came to be known as international law, containing, like Locke's state of nature, shadows and echoes of the familiar furniture of societal legal systems. Why was the society-forming surpassing of the myth-theoretical inter-societal state of nature not postulated as a theory of an international society? Why was the ancient idea of a natural society of all human beings simply side-lined in international social consciousness? Why did Hobbes, Locke, Rousseau, Hegel and Marx abstain from extrapolating their society-forming theories to the level of international society?[23] Once again, the answer must be that a class which dominated the relevant area of social consciousness felt

[22] Theologically, we might say that the paradox of an imperfect world made by a perfect god has generated the efficient paradox that human beings have self-perfecting as the divinely ordained purpose of their existing.

[23] Locke spoke of the 'great and natural community' of mankind, but said that 'the corruption and viciousness of degenerate men' made necessary 'smaller and divided associations' (*Two Treatises on Government* (1689), II, § 128). And Rousseau said that 'the establishment of

no need to transform the theoretical content of social consciousness beyond the limits of national society. To be more specific, an old-regime ruling-class managed to retain its dominance over international social consciousness, long after it had lost dominance over social consciousness within some national societies.

11.30 The urgent effort has now begun, centuries late, to find within international social consciousness an appropriate theory of the nature and purpose of international society, the society of all societies.

11.31 (3) The *realist rejection* of international law as the true law of an international society is as old as the idea of a law between nations and as new as yesterday's newspaper. It comes in many forms, but at its root is a negation of two kinds of idealism. (a) It essentialises and personifies social entities (state, nation, people, government, class ...), supposing that they are not constructs in consciousness but virtual things and virtual persons, treating them as if they had their own will, their own power, their own interests, their own history. (b) It takes a particular view of human nature and a particular view of human history, extrapolating that view to the condition and behaviour of such social entities. It is a view of human nature which sees human beings, and hence personified social entities, as essentially self-seeking, and a view of human history which sees no ground for postulating idealistic hypotheses about the actual or potential motivation of social entities or of those who dominate them. In a realist worldview, international law cannot be anything more than a random aggregated product of the prudential calculation by collectivities of their own self-interest.

11.32 Realism is a default-theory of international society, a theory that requires no anti-entropic intellectual effort to believe it, or to get

little republics makes us dream of the great one'. J.-J. Rousseau, *The Social Contract and other Discourses* (ed. G. D. H. Cole; London, J. M. Dent & Sons (Everyman's Library); 1913), pp. 160–1. The quotation is from a chapter called 'The General Society of the Human Race' which Rousseau omitted from the published version of *The Social Contract.* He was a 'realist' in the matter of international relations. The general will cannot operate in a state of nature. 'As for what is commonly called international law, because its laws lack any sanction, they are unquestionably mere illusions, even feebler than the law of nature.' See S. Hoffmann and D. P. Fidler (eds), *Rousseau on International Relations* (Oxford, Clarendon Press; 1991). The most surprising failure is that of Hegel, whose locating of the end of history in the development of the state seems a perverse limitation of a philosophy that should surely culminate in the history of the human race as the actualising of the 'world mind'. For a discussion of Hegel's failure, see J. Plamenatz, *Man and Society* (London, Longmans; 1963), II, pp. 266–7.

others to believe it. It is a first-cousin to philosophical pragmatism, that default-theory of unphilosophy which proclaims the rationality of the actual. Historically, it has meant that a relentless *machiavellian counterpoint* has accompanied all efforts to insert the common interest of all-humanity into the self-interest of subordinate societies and into the self-interest of those who dominate them.[24] And it has meant that a *Vattelian two-world model* of the human world has established itself within the second memory of humanity, its social memory, a two-worldism which sees national and international social phenomena as parallel and unintegrated, two political realms, two moral realms, a divided human world with two kinds of history, national and international.[25]

11.33 In a two-world worldview, the world of all-humanity is regarded as secondary and derivative. At the end of the twentieth century, a formidable challenge has been recognised, centuries late: to integrate the world of all-humanity with all its subordinate worlds, to integrate the legal system of international society with all subordinate legal systems, to integrate the history of all subordinate societies in the history of the society of all societies, that is to say, human history.

The lure of historicism

11.34 Personal memory. Social memory. Species-memory. From the earliest days of recorded human history, it has been suggested that human history itself has a pattern which is latent in the human past and

[24] 'Realism is a theory that divides the globe into two different domains. There is the domain inside the state which is often seen as progressive, where politics operates and where society can evolve; and there is a domain outside the state or between states which is not seen as progressive but as static . . . Realism assumes that states are all locked into their own survival and into the pursuit of their own interests.' 'Realism vs cosmopolitanism – a debate between B. Buzan and D. Held', in 24 *Review of International Studies* (1998), pp. 387–98, at p. 387 (Buzan). See also B. Frankel (ed.), *Realism: Restatements and Renewal* (Ilford, Frank Cass & Co.; 1996).

[25] It was the supremely influential Vattel who argued that the coming of the 'nation' or 'state' had overtaken all talk about a universal society of the human race. 'Such a society [state or nation] has its own affairs and interests . . . and it becomes a moral person having an understanding and a will peculiar to itself, and susceptible at once of rights and obligations'; 'it devolves henceforth upon that body, the State, and upon its rulers, to fulfil the duties of humanity towards outsiders'. E. de Vattel, *The Law of Nations or the Principles of Natural Law applied to the Conduct and to the Affairs of Nations and Sovereigns* (1758) (tr. C. G. Fenwick; Washington; 1916), pp. 3, 6. See further in ch. 14 below.

which is liable to shape the pattern of the human future.[26] If we were inclined to believe in such a thing, we would have to regard it as a fourth form of human memory, history's memory.

11.35 Human history has repeatedly been found to contain different kinds of pattern at the universal level and at the level of 'civilisations' and empires and nations – cyclical patterns, patterns of recurrence, linear patterns of decline or progress. Such ideas have proved to be remarkably resilient, resisting both the arguments of principle and of harsh reality which have been set against them. In the twentieth century, they took on a new lease of life at the supra-national level, generating lively interest in the general public, an interest fuelled by despair at the apparently terminal self-destroying of 'Western civilisation', by the apparently apocalyptic potentiality of the 'Cold War', or by the revolutionary implications, and conflictual possibilities, of 'globalisation': for example: Spengler, Toynbee, Kennedy, Huntington . . .

11.36 The word *historicism* came into common usage in the English language with the publication in 1957 of K. Popper's *The Poverty of Historicism.* Popper gave the impression that he had invented the word, or at least a new meaning for the word,[27] and he wrote as if the ultimate historicist sinners were Hegel and Marx.[28] In fact, a much more complex idea of *Historismus* had long been identified in German historiography as an important product of the Enlightenment, full of promise and full of danger.[29]

[26] It was Hesiod (eighth century BCE) who initiated a historiography based on a progression of 'ages', beginning with a 'golden' age.

[27] 'This approach . . . I call "historicism" . . . I mean by "historicism" an approach to the social sciences which assumes that *historical prediction* is their principal aim, and which assumes that this aim is attainable by discovering the "rhythms" or the "patterns", the "laws" or the "trends" that underlie the evolution of history.' K. Popper, *The Poverty of Historicism* (London, Routledge & Kegan Paul; 1957), p. 3.

[28] The book is dedicated to the 'countless men and women . . . who fell victim to the fascist and communist belief in Inexorable Laws of Historical Destiny'. At Marx's funeral, Engels said that Marx had 'discovered the law of evolution in human history'.

[29] For a full account of the history of the word, see G. Iggers, *The German Conception of History – The National Tradition of Historical Thought from Herder to the Present* (Middletown, Wesleyan University Press; 1968/1983), pp. 295–8. Meinecke called historicism 'one of the greatest mental revolutions that Western thought has experienced'. F. Meinecke, *Die Entstehung des Historismus* (München/Berlin, Verlag R. Oldenbourg; 1936), p. 1 (present author's translation). He traces its source in eighteenth-century historiography, beginning with Shaftesbury. Hegel and Marx are not included in his history of historicism. He identifies the work of Ranke as the 'high-point' (*Gipfel*) of that history. Bury said that this

11.37 It had always been recognised that history-writing cannot share in the methods of the natural sciences. There is no possibility of conducting control-experiments, let alone a restaging of the past, altering this or that variable – supposing that Caesar had not crossed the Rubicon or Adolf Hitler had been the happy child of a comfortable bourgeois family.[30] It was also accepted in the nineteenth century that history-writing was an essentially different activity from the other mind-sciences (*Geisteswissenschaften*), especially sociology. Leopold von Ranke insisted that the basis of history-writing must be the value-free presentation of historical facts in their absolute individuality, and he became the mastermind of professionalised academic historiography throughout Europe. But he also saw the job of the historian as being one of abstraction and generalisation, universalising the particular, finding the *allgemeine Einflüsse* (universal forces) at work under the surface of historical reality. It is that aspect of historiography which gave rise to philosophical and even political problems.[31] As it acquired the prestige of high professionalism, history-writing took on also a prophetic character, in the sense of revealing a form of knowledge obtainable by no other means, namely, knowledge of the inner development of human social life, its organic processes. Historians were offering a *metaphysics of history*, as one might

'transformation' of historical studies was 'itself a great event in the history of the world'. J. B. Bury, *An Inaugural Lecture* (as Regius Professor of Modern History at Cambridge University) (Cambridge, Cambridge University Press; 1903), pp. 7–8. For a less optimistic view, see C. Menger, *Die Irrtümer des Historismus in der deutschen Nationalökonomie* (Wien, A. Hölder; 1884; Aalen, Scientia Verlag; 1966); K. Heussi, *Die Krisis des Historismus* (Tübingen, Mohr; 1932).

[30] Cf. Blaise Pascal (1623–62): 'Cleopatra's nose: if it had been shorter the whole face of the earth would have been different.' *Pensées* (tr. A. Krailsheimer; London, Penguin; 1966), II. 162, p. 148. J. B. Bury wrote an essay entitled 'Cleopatra's Nose' (1916), on the world-historical consequences of contingent facts, such as the love of the Roman general Antony (83–30 BCE) for the Egyptian queen Cleopatra (69–30 BCE). H. Temperley (ed.), *Selected Essays of J. B. Bury* (Cambridge; University Press; 1930), pp. 60–9.

[31] 'The strict presentation of the facts . . . is undoubtedly the supreme law. After this, it seems to me, comes the unity and progress of events.' 'I believe rather that the discipline of history – at its highest – is itself called upon, and is able, to lift itself in its own fashion from the investigation and observation of particulars to a universal view of events, to a knowledge of the objectively existing relatedness.' L. von Ranke, *Histories of the Latin and Germanic Nations 1494–1514* (1824), preface. Quoted in F. Stern (ed.), *The Varieties of History from Voltaire to the Present* (New York, Meridian Books; 1956), pp. 57, 59. These words come immediately after Ranke's most celebrated (and misleading, even as to his own method) dictum: that history's task is simply to say what actually happened: *Ich will nur sagen wie es eigentlich gewesen ist.*

say, and a great deal depended on the social entity whose unique metaphysical development was revealed in the presentation of its history.

11.38 From the middle of the eighteenth century, this form of historicism proved a powerful force in the making of middle-level history, especially in writing the history of the nation and, in the nineteenth century, of the state.[32] It contributed much to competitive and conflictual nationalism and statism as phenomena of international social consciousness, and much also to the internal and external hypostasising of the 'state'.[33] German historians, and their epigones in other countries, carried diplomatic history – the story of the interacting of states and nations – to the level of a high art and thereby contributed much to re-enforcing in social consciousness the two-world worldview discussed above. Value-free at the level of fine detail, it bestowed a naturalistic and even an ethical value on its favoured social forms. Having explicitly eschewed naturalistic historical determinism, the historicism of the professional historians could be found, in the end, in the same *galère* as that form of historicism which was Popper's target and which even now shows no signs of succumbing to its intellectual wounds.

11.39 Historicists of all kinds tell the people something the people apparently want to be told – that there is a way of understanding the past that allows us to look into the future. When metaphysical historicism takes on the character of historical determinism, it is liable to exercise the fascinating power of the prophet over the public mind. The rise and fall of civilisations, of empires, of great powers, or – *ne plus ultra* – the

[32] Vico, Herder and Fichte were the dominant figures in making history serve in forming the self-consciousness of a nation. Hegel and Ranke and Meinecke were the dominant figures in making history serve in forming the self-consciousness of the nation as state. For the role of the ideas of society, nation and state in, respectively, British, French and German self-consciousness, see ch. 7 above.

[33] 'Pay great attention to the full significance of these entities! So many separate earthly and intellectual communities, evoked by genius and moral energy, comprehended in continuous development advancing towards the Ideal by an inner impulse amid the confusions of this world, each in its own way. Examine them closely, these heavenly bodies, in their paths, their alteration, their system!' L. von Ranke, *A Dialogue on Politics* (1836), quoted in F. Meinecke, *Machiavellism. The Doctrine of Raison d'état and its Place in Modern History* (tr. D. Scott; New Haven, Yale University Press; 1957), p. 378. Ranke's *Dialogue* is reproduced as an appendix to T. H. von Laue, *Leopold Ranke: The Formative Years* (Princeton, Princeton University Press; 1950). Meinecke's own book was a sustained naturalising of the 'state' phenomenon. 'That part of action prompted by raison d'état which willingly obeys the power impulse belongs to the realm of nature. One does this, one must do it, because there is in operation here an elemental force which can never be completely stifled, and without which moreover . . . States would never have arisen' (p. 5).

so-called 'end of history'[34] – all of these, insofar as people believe them, are liable to be more disempowering and dispiriting than liberating. But historical determinism and astrology will remain popular as long as people need the consoling idea that the future is not wholly unknowable and not wholly in our unreliable hands.

The making of the past

11.40 The past, like the future, is in our unreliable hands. From the moment when Thucydides distinguished his own work from what had gone before, the enterprise of history has been problematic.[35] The problem is, as it always has been, twofold: history-writing excludes, from the little that is unforgotten, that which it does not include;[36] and history is not merely a mirror of the past (Lucian of Samosata) or a picture of the past (Raleigh), but an interpretation of the past, not a reflection-of but a reflection-on.[37] History makes a past. There are as many pasts contained in the past as there are those who write its story.

11.41 Like the fine arts and literature, history-writing, in all the discord and confusion of its method and its witness, seems as if it must

[34] Especially powerful in both directions have been the idea of the fulfilment of the process of history in a particular theologico-social situation (Augustine, Bossuet); the idea of the fulfilment of history in a particular intellectual-social situation in which religion and metaphysics are finally overcome (Condorcet, Comte); the idea of history reaching a fulfilment of self-ordering in a particular social formation (Hegel) or in the overcoming of a particular social formation (Marx).

More difficult to take seriously is the idea of history reaching its fulfilment in social formations labelled 'democracy' and 'capitalism'. In F. Fukuyama, *The End of History and the Last Man* (New York, The Free Press; 1992), the author took inspiration from a Hegel seen in the distorting lens of the work of A. Kojève: *Introduction à la lecture de Hegel* (lectures delivered in 1933–9) (Paris, Gallimard; 1947/1976); A. Kojève, *Introduction to the Reading of Hegel* (tr. J. H. Nichols, ed. A. Bloom; New York, Basic Books; 1969).

[35] 'The way most men deal with traditions... is to receive them all alike as they are delivered, without applying any critical test whatever... The absence of romance in my history will, I fear, detract somewhat from its interest; but if it be judged useful by those inquirers who desire an exact knowledge of the past as an aid to the interpretation of the future, which in the course of human things must resemble if it does not reflect it, I shall be content. In fine, I have written my work, not an essay which is to win the approval of the moment, but as a possession for all time.' Thucydides, *The Peloponnesian War* in *Versions of History* (tr. R. Cawley, ed. D. R. Kelley; New Haven, London, Yale University Press; 1991), pp. 33, 34–5.

[36] 'Such is the unity of all history that anyone who endeavours to tell a piece of it must feel that his first sentence tears a seamless web.' F. W. Maitland, quoted in B. Southgate, *History: What and Why? Ancient, Modern, and Postmodern Perspectives* (London, New York, Routledge; 1996), p. 113.

[37] *Ein schaffender Spiegel* (a creating or fashioning mirror), in Meinecke's formula.

be classed as a form of play, if we define play as an activity which is not biologically necessary and which has an inherent purpose (the rules of the game) but not an ulterior purpose. And yet history-writing can have social effects so significant that they give it a social function, an ulterior purpose, which may far surpass its inherent intellectual purpose.

11.42 The success of history-writing is judged, like any other social activity, in terms of its intention, its performance and its effects. The intensity of the conceptual debate about the writing of history, which continues to the present day, reflects the historian's understanding of the social significance of history-writing. To defend one's own idea of history-writing is to defend the history that one writes. For a historian to modify a society's idea of its own past is to succeed in justifying that historian's own idea of history.

11.43 The most socially successful history-writing (Thucydides, Livy, Bede, Gibbon, Michelet, Ranke . . .) changes not only a society's idea of itself but also that society's idea of history-writing, not only a society's idea of its own past but also its idea of the activity of recovering the past. It changes history and the idea of history. As in the case of the human individual, a society's relationship to its own past can be a major factor in its psychic state of health. A society's memory of its past, like our own personal memory of our past, powerfully affects actual states of mind and actual behaviour. At the level of individual consciousness, great controversy has surrounded particular efforts in the twentieth century to explain the effects of past psychic states, and to alter the latter by adjusting the subject's idea of the former. At the level of social consciousness, it is worth speculating that, whatever the merits of those particular efforts, parallel phenomena, and hence parallel problems and possibilities, arise. It would be possible to find evidence of memory-behaviour in the social consciousness of particular societies – repression of aspects of the past, displacement of ideas of the past, obsessional fixation on aspects of the past – which has been either beneficial and creative or else morbid and self-destructive in its effects on the public mind of those societies.[38] The pathology of a society may include a morbid relationship to its own past.

[38] For such manifestations in individual psychology, see, in particular, A. Freud, *The Ego and the Mechanisms of Defence* (1936) (tr. C. Baines; New York, International Universities Press; 1946). For the relevance of Freudian psychology to the understanding of history, see P. Gay, *Freud for Historians* (Oxford, New York, Oxford University Press; 1985).

11.44 The second-level debate about the writing of history has been a debate about the proper purpose, and hence the proper method, of writing history. A spectator of that debate, self-appointed arbiter, is inclined to conclude that the many purposes and methods of history-writing cannot be resolved into a 'proper' purpose and a 'proper' method, however vehemently particular historians may insist on so doing. It seems rather that socially effective history-writing serves different social purposes in different circumstances. Societies find the history-writing they need, as they need it.

(1) *Self-knowing history.* History-writing is self-discovering. Human beings are naturally interested in the behaviour of other human beings. Such interest is not merely curiosity. Our idea of our self is a reflection of our idea of other selves. History as self-knowing has taken three main forms – retrospective journalism,[39] self-naturalising[40] and hermeneutics.[41] We are what we seem to have been.

[39] Herodotus (fifth century BCE), 'the father of history' (Cicero), may also be seen as the father of retrospective journalism. '[H]is unfailing, unflagging spirit of enquiry prompted an endless succession of spicy, wonder-loving anecdotes which make him the outstanding entertainer among Greek and Roman historians'. M. Grant, *Greek and Roman Historians. Information and Misinformation* (London, Routledge; 1995), p. 6.

[40] 'The historian may be permitted the privilege of the naturalist; I have observed my subject as one might observe the metamorphosis of an insect.' H. Taine, *Ancien régime* (1876), preface; present author's translation. Taine also notoriously said: 'After the assembling of the facts, the search for causes.' On the troublesome idea of causation in history, see P. Gardiner, *The Nature of Historical Explanation* (London, Oxford University Press; 1952), with a discussion of Taine's maxim (111.2).

There is a laconic tradition of British historiography which denies that historiography is problematic. 'I don't believe in the philosophy of history.' W. Stubbs, Regius Professor of Modern History, Oxford University, 1866–84. '[History] is . . . simply a science, no less and no more.' J. B. Bury, *Inaugural Lecture* (fn. 29 above), p. 42. When Ranke's *eigentlich gewesen* dictum is taken fully to heart, 'there will no longer be divers schools of history'. (This led G. M. Trevelyan, who succeeded Bury at Cambridge, to defend, in *Clio, a Muse* (1913), a more romantic view of history-writing, as 'art added to scholarship'. Some of their successors have joined in the debate with slim volumes containing personal reflections on their respective 'ideas of history': Carr, Butterfield, Elton, Oakeshott . . .) For other examples, see Southgate, *History: What and Why?* (fn. 36 above), pp. 2–3. See generally J. Hale, *The Evolution of British Historiography* (London, Macmillan; 1967).

[41] From W. Dilthey to H.-G. Gadamer, there has been a self-conscious hermeneutic tradition of German historiography, seeking to re-create past states of subjectivity, through empathic understanding (*Verstehen*). 'The interpreter is absolutely simultaneous with the actor.' History-writing is 'moving to one's place in the continuing tradition' (Gadamer).

Under the influence of B. Croce, an idealist historiography was promoted by R. G. Collingwood. 'All history is the history of thought.' 'Historical knowledge is the knowledge of what mind has done in the past, and at the same time it is the redoing of this, the

(2) *Self-judging history.* History is philosophy teaching by example.[42] Self-judging history sees the past in the perspective of value. To contemplate the grandeur and the misery of human history cannot leave us indifferent. We judge ourselves in judging the behaviour of those whose values we have inherited.[43]

(3) *Self-ordering history.* Historians impose form on the formless past. The patterns and categories in which we understand the past become the patterns and categories in which we perceive the present and imagine the future. We are liable to become what we think we have been.[44]

perpetuation of past acts into the present.' *The Idea of History* (Oxford, Oxford University Press; 1946), pp. 215, 218.

Drawing on both traditions, there is a group of mildly hermeneutic historians of ideas, centred at Cambridge University, aiming at the elusive target of determining what speculative writers thought that they were saying, and what their contemporaries understood them to be saying. See J. Tully (ed.), *Meaning and Context. Quentin Skinner and His Critics* (Princeton, Princeton University Press; 1988). See also R. Rorty, J. B. Schneewind and Q. Skinner (eds.), *Philosophy in History. Essays in the Historiography of Philosophy* (Cambridge, Cambridge University Press; 1984), especially Rorty's scintillating essay, 'The historiography of philosophy: four genres', pp. 49–75.

42 Dionysius of Halicarnassus (*De arte rhetorica*). History is *magistra vitae* (Cicero). 'What makes the study of history wholesome and profitable is this, that you behold the lessons of every kind of experience set forth as on a conspicuous monument; from these you may choose for yourself and for your own state what to imitate, from these mark for avoidance what is shameful in the conception and shameful in the result.' Livy, *Ab urbe condita* (tr. B. O. Foster), in D. R. Kelley, *Versions of History* (fn. 35 above), pp. 71–2.

43 The value-perspective may be religious, moral or political, but its motivating force is always the Marxian ambition not merely to interpret the world but to change it. It is an anti-hermeneutic position in the sense that it sees the past as the actualising in public consciousness of what M. Foucault called 'relations of power, not relations of meaning'. In his own work, Foucault, using the metaphors of archaeology and genealogy, saw history-writing as the methodical uncovering of past states of public consciousness as if they were a chain of events. His highly engaged history-writing should be seen as quite separate from the post-structuralist/postmodern movement which is better seen as a reduction to the absurd of hermeneutics. See I. Goldstein (ed.), *Foucault and the Writing of History* (Oxford, Blackwell; 1994); D. Attridge (ed.), *Post-structuralism and the Question of History* (Cambridge, Cambridge University Press; 1987). For Nietzsche's conception of 'genealogy' as the process by which 'value' is created, philosophy being a contemplation of that process, and for a discussion of Nietzsche's 'will to power' as a 'will to joy', where power and joy are not seen as ends but as determinative characteristics of willing, see G. Deleuze, *Nietzsche and Philosophy* (tr. H. Tomlinson; London, The Athlone Press; 1983).

44 History-writing determines structures of consciousness even at the stage when it chooses its focus: the universal level (e.g., Augustine, Vico, Hegel, Marx); the level of civilisations (e.g., Livy, Gibbon, Petrie, Toynbee, Spengler); the level of the race or the nation or the people or the state (e.g., Herder, Hegel, Ranke, Gobineau, Meinecke). *Staatengeschichte* has conditioned the minds and fed the vanity of the war-making class. A reaction against it has been the writing of close-focus social history, such as that associated with the French

(4) *Self-creating history.* In history a society finds an idea-of-itself in the past in order to project an idea-of-itself into the future. Society looks into the mirror of its past and sees its future. We will be what we imagine we have been.[45]

From human history to human law

11.45 Humanity has no history, only histories. Universal history has been a small part of history-writing. An idea of the past of humanity as a whole has played a negligible part in forming the social consciousness of human beings in general. Such universal history-writing as there has been has most often been historicist in intention, and hence in method, ranging across the histories of different times and different places to find support for some predetermined idea of human existence.

11.46 The social consciousness of humanity is filled with an absence and a presence. The *absence* is the absence of a history of its histories, the absence of what we have called second memory, a society's present consciousness of its own past. The *presence* is a consequence of that absence. To form an idea of itself, humanity must resort to its third memory, the continuing presence of our species-past, rudimentary and disputed ideas about human nature, about an international state of nature, about a species which has not actualised the self-evolved species-transforming potentialities of socialisation at the level of the whole species.[46]

journal *Annales: économies, sociétés, civilisations*, and *Alltagsgeschichte* (Everyday History) in Germany, or the work of G. D. H. Cole, E. P. Thompson and P. Laslett in England.

45 For the struggle of German historians with the problem of the writing of recent German history, see C. S. Maier, *The Unmasterable Past: History, Holocaust, and German National Identity* (Cambridge, MA, Harvard University Press; 1988/1997). Maier quotes M. Stürmer: 'Loss of orientation and the search for identity are brothers. But anyone who believes that this has no effect on politics and the future ignores the fact that in a land without history whoever supplies memory, shapes concepts, and interprets the past will win the future' (p. 44).

For an annotated bibliography on the role of history in the making of social self-consciousness, see I. Irwin-Zarecka, *Frames of Remembrance. The Dynamics of Collective Memory* (New Brunswick, NJ, Transaction Publishers; 1994), pp. 193ff.

46 This was Kant's despairing counsel. 'Since men neither pursue their aims purely by instinct, as the animals do, nor act in accordance with any integral prearranged plan like rational cosmopolitans, it would appear that no law-governed history of mankind is possible (as it would be, for example, with bees or beavers) . . . The only way out for the philosopher, since he cannot assume that mankind follows any rational *purpose of its own* in its collective actions, is for him to attempt to discover a *purpose in nature* behind this senseless course

11.47 When certain national societies 'took off' economically and developed new social institutions to manage the ever-more populous and ever-more dynamic national societies, the interrelationship of those societies remained in a primitive, old-regime condition. The intellectual development of the national societies matched their socio-economic development, not least in the writing of national and cultural history. History-writing, in all the functional forms noted above, played a part in forming, reforming and remaking society. The role of the law was clearly understood, as intermediary between the past and the future, as a survival from the past full of the potentiality for making the future. Legal history – national, cultural, and cross-cultural – was seen as an integral part of general history. Legal history played an important part in the dynamic self-re-imagining of national societies.

11.48 In the twenty-first century, the coming-to-consciousness of the international society of all-humanity will generate the forms of history-writing which will perform the social functions of history-writing at the level of all-humanity, presenting to humanity an idea of itself in the dimension of its past – self-knowing, self-judging, self-ordering, self-creating. To imagine the presence in international society of the social force of history is to imagine a human world in which history can serve as a human being's fourth memory. Personal memory. Social memory. Species-memory.

Human memory

11.49 International legal history is a necessary part of the history of international society. The writing of the *intrinsic* history of international law – the history of the law itself – will re-form our consciousness of the identity, the functioning, and the potentiality of international law as law. The writing of the *extrinsic* history of international law – its relationship to the history of other social phenomena – will re-form our consciousness of the role of international law in the forming, re-forming and remaking of international society. In particular, it will remake international law's *idea-of-itself*, both the *external* perspective of that idea (the theory of its functional relationship to the behaviour that it conditions)

of human events . . . ' 'Idea for a universal history with a cosmopolitan purpose', in *Kant's Political Writings* (fn. 21 above), pp. 41–2.

and the *internal* perspective (the logic of its validity for those whose behaviour it conditions).

11.50 The more we know of how we have made ourselves what we are, the better we are able to imagine a new kind of human being inhabiting a new kind of human society in a new kind of human world. In the public mind of a humanity which sees itself at last in the mirror of its own memory, in a human society empowered by human history, international law will at last perform the true function of all law, as an instrument of humanity's self-transforming and self-perfecting, taking a road not yet travelled by the human species as a whole, the road from *kratos* to *ethos*.[47]

[47] At least at one stage of his intellectual development, Meinecke (from whom this phrase is borrowed) believed that the antinomy of power and morality could only be resolved through the enlightened self-developing of the state *(raison d'état*, or *virtù* in the machiavellian sense). *Machiavellism* (fn. 33 above), p. 5. Experience of the long twentieth century has taught us that such an idea is the most dangerous and disabling of errors.

12

Intergovernmental societies and the idea of constitutionalism

The challenge of intergovernmental public power – Constitutionalism as social theory – International societies and social theory – The presence of the past – The genealogy of constitutionalism – The genetics of constitutionalism – The naturally artificial – Three mythologies and a heresy – The generic principles of constitutionalism – The constitutionalising of intergovernmental organisations: *captor captus*

The idea of constitutionalism is the idea that all public power is subject to the law, that all public power is delegated by the law, that the exercise of public power is accountable before the law. The revolutionary transformation of international society includes the insertion of the idea of constitutionalism into its theoretical structure, into the pure and practical theories of international society.

The idea of constitutionalism is a golden thread running through the better history of the human race, a perennial and universal possibility in humanity's social self-constituting, a meta-cultural and meta-temporal theoretical potentiality. It is an idea which has had intimate and essential connections with the perennial and universal phenomenon of religion, allowing us to see religion as a spiritual constitutionalism. It is an idea which has had intimate and essential connections with the idea of social self-constituting, with the intrinsic hegemony of that which, in a society, transcends the self-constituting of individual society-members. It is an idea which has had an intimate and necessary connection with the most abstract conception of law *as a meta-physical and meta-personal and meta-social phenomenon.*

As the fabric of international society becomes ever more dense and complex, as the cross-frontier socialising of human beings develops in dynamic intensity, the idea of constitutionalism is emerging as a necessary and natural control on the ever-increasing accumulation of communal governmental power, which is gradually reproducing at the global-level phenomena of public power, which are closely analogous to those which have developed over recent centuries at the national level and to which national systems have had to respond with ever more sophisticated systems of social and legal control.

The challenge of intergovernmental public power

12.1 Wherever and whenever public power is exercised, there arises the challenge of its explanation and justification. Why is public power being exercised by this person or these persons? What are the conditions governing the exercise of public power accepted by those exercising that power and by those affected by its exercise? The posing of such questions, and the answers given to them in a particular society at a particular time, are a product of historical circumstances, including the historically produced state of social consciousness in that society. Intergovernmental organisations are a particular systematic form in which public power is exercised in the contemporary world. They cannot avoid the challenge of the explanation and justification of public power.

12.2 The public power exercised by governments participating in an intergovernmental organisation is an externalising of their public power. It is for the social consciousness of the society within which a given government is constituted to explain and justify the externalising of that power within the context of the social consciousness of that society. Within that context, the explanation and justification of the externalised power of particular governments participating in a given intergovernmental organisation may accordingly differ, as a function of the state of the particular social consciousness of the different societies.

12.3 This situation gives rise to a special and especially difficult challenge in the case of intergovernmental organisations. How can the collective exercise of public power in the systematic processes of an intergovernmental organisation be explained and justified in the context of the social consciousness of international society?

12.4 The present study is based on the premises that, like the exercise of any other form of public power, the collective exercise of public power in intergovernmental organisations must be explained and justified, and that, as in the case of any other form of public power, the conditions governing the collective exercise of public power in an intergovernmental organisation must be acceptable not only to those exercising that power but also to those affected by its exercise. It is the purpose of the present study to suggest that the exercise of public power in intergovernmental organisations may be explained and justified at the level of international society in terms of a theory of constitutionalism. It is a theory of public power which has been historically produced within the social consciousness of countless societies over long periods of time. It is a theory which is capable of transcending the theoretical diversity of the explanations and justifications of public power of particular societies at the present time.

Constitutionalism as social theory

12.5 Constitutionalism is a *theory*, that is to say, a mental ordering of the reality within which a particular society constitutes itself.[1] It is an explanatory and justificatory theory of a society's self-constituting. The defining characteristic of constitutionalism as a theory is that society makes an *idea* of its own self-constituting into an *ideal* of its self-constituting, and incorporates that *ideal* into the *theory* of its self-constituting. The idea is projected from the actual to form an ideal and, as an ideal, is reintroduced into the actual. For a society which adopts constitutionalism as its theory, constitutionalism enables and requires the society to organise and direct its own self-constituting in accordance with its transcendental idea of itself.

12.6 Within the *pure theory* of such a society,[2] constitutionalism is the way in which the society contemplates and articulates the actuality

[1] For the concept of a society's *theory*, see *Eunomia*, esp. §§ 2.45ff. '[A]s force is always on the side of the governed, the governors have nothing to support them but opinion. It is therefore, on opinion only that government is founded.' D. Hume (1711–76), 'Of the first principles of government', in *Essays Moral, Political, and Literary* (eds. T. H. Green and T. H. Grose; London, Longmans, Green; 1907), I, no. 4, p. 110. 'For a society is not made up merely of the mass of individuals who compose it, the ground which they occupy, the things which they use and the movements which they perform, but above all is the idea which it forms of itself.' E. Durkheim, *The Elementary Forms of the Religious Life* (1912) (tr. J. Swain; London, George Allen & Unwin; 1915/1976), p. 422.

[2] For the concepts of pure theory and practical theory, see *Eunomia*, §§ 2.52ff. The distinction is related to Aristotle's distinction between speculative reason and practical reason (*Politics*, VII.14) or, as he puts it in bk I.vii of the *Nicomachean Ethics*, the difference between the thinking of the geometer and the thinking of the carpenter. In Eunomian terms, *practical* theory consists of the ideas which are present in actual social behaviour (ideas as practice), *pure* theory is the theory of practical theory (ideas about ideas). *Transcendental* theory is a society's epistemology, its understanding of the source of truth and value, its theory of theory. All three forms of theory are actualised as particular social phenomena in particular societies.

and the potentiality of its own self-constituting. It is what the society says to itself about what it is and why, and what it might choose to be. It dominates the society's *ideal self-constituting*, as the society debates within itself the nature and significance of its idea and ideal of constitutionalism.[3] It is formed by, and forms, its *social consciousness*, that is, the consciousness of its *public mind*.[4] It dominates each aspect of the society's dynamic process of self-constituting – the forming of its unique identity, the integrating of its willing, the unifying of its values, the relating of its order to the order of that which lies beyond it, its persistence through the passage of time.[5]

12.7 Within the *practical theory* of such a society, constitutionalism means that the society's self-transcending idea and ideal of its self-constituting is made into an integral and functional part of the day-to-day process of its *real* and *legal self-constituting*. The ideal is present in the actual. Society *enacts* as practical theory its pure theory of constitutionalism. A major part of the day-to-day social process of such a society consists of political debate and political struggle about the interpretation and application of its own theory of constitutionalism, *politics*

[3] For the three dimensions of a society's self-constituting, see *Eunomia*, §§ 9.6ff. A society constitutes itself *ideally* in the form of ideas, *really* through the day-to-day exercise of social power by society-members, and *legally* in the form of law.

'[T]he real constitution (*wirkliche Verfassung*) of a country exists only in the true actual power-relations which are present in the country; written constitutions thus only have worth and durability if they are an exact expression of the real power-relations in the society.' F. Lassalle, 'Über Verfassungswesen' ('On the nature of the constitution') (1863), in *Gesammelte Reden und Schriften* (ed. E. Bernstein; Berlin, P. Cassirer; 1919), II, pp. 24–61, at p. 60 (present author's translation). Lassalle, a follower of Hegel and, less faithfully, of Marx, and the founder of the General Union of German Workers (the first political party of the working class), contrasted the real constitution with the written (or legal) constitution, the former but not the latter (in the Germany of the 1860s) being the expression of the real power of nobles, great land-owners, industrialists, bankers and major capitalists.

In the Eunomian framework, the other forms of social self-constituting do not merely express the state of the real constitution. All three forms develop in dialectical relation to each other. The constitution is a permanent process, not a thing. 'The laws reach but a very little way. Constitute Government how you please, infinitely the greater part of it must depend upon the exercise of powers which are left at large to the prudence and uprightness of Ministers of State . . . Without them, your Commonwealth is no better than a scheme on paper; and not a living, active, effective constitution.' E. Burke, *Thoughts on the Cause of our Present Discontents* (1770), in *The Writings and Speeches of Edmund Burke* (ed. P. Langford; Oxford, Clarendon Press; 1981), II, pp. 251–322, at p. 277.

[4] For the concept of *social consciousness (public mind)*, see *Eunomia*, §§ 2.42ff and ch. 4 above.

[5] For these five *perennial dilemmas* of a society's self-creating, that is to say, oppositions which a society resolves dialectically, see *Eunomia*, §§ 4.10ff. On dialectical thinking, see fn. 9 below.

being the leading institutional form of that debate and struggle. Society's own idea of its potentiality is actualised in the course of its becoming.[6]

12.8 To illustrate its specific character as the theory of particular societies, constitutionalism may be contrasted with other pure and practical social theories of particular societies, especially absolutism and theocracy.

12.9 *Absolutism* excludes, from the self-constituting of a society which adopts it as its practical theory, any systematic appeal from the actual to the ideal, so that the willing and acting of the holders of social power is validated in practice by, and is understood to be validated in theory by, the fact of that willing and acting. The actual is the ideal.

12.10 *Theocracy* places the focus of a society's self-transcending in something which is conceptually and systematically external to that society, so that the willing and acting of the holders of social power is explained and justified, in practice and theory, by reference to ideas whose source and validity are not themselves explicable and justifiable by reference to the society's own idea of itself formed in the historical process of that society. The ideal is other than the actual.

12.11 In addition to its role within the theory of particular societies, constitutionalism is also a category within *social philosophy*. Social philosophy is the self-contemplating of human beings in their capacity as social beings. Constitutionalism, as the theory of particular societies, was historically produced within the development of those societies. As a matter of social philosophy, we are able to abstract a particular theory, such as constitutionalism, from its historical and social contexts, and to use our abstraction of the idea in our understanding of the actuality and potentiality of societies in general, and hence in our understanding of the actuality and potentiality of particular societies.

12.12 As social philosophers, we may choose to undertake a specific society-transcending function, namely, to think about the self-constituting of societies in such a way that our thinking is not intended to form part of the ideal self-constituting of any particular society, including the societies to which we, as particular human beings, happen to belong. Such a thing is a possible ideal of the personal self-constituting of the philosopher. But even the mind of the social philosopher is socially produced. And social philosophy, when it is communicated, enters the

[6] The Aristotelian echo is intended here also. Aristotle, bringing to philosophy the mind of the biologist, universalised the wonderful mystery of organic life that is the negating of a present state of development by something which is, however, contained in the present state.

public mind of particular societies, and is liable to modify their ideal self-constituting. It may affect the pure and practical theories of their self-constituting and so may even affect the actual social process of their real and legal self-constituting. The potential world-changing effect of philosophy is no reason to abandon the project of philosophy. But it imposes a particular kind of moral responsibility on the philosopher.[7]

International societies and social theory

12.13 An intergovernmental organisation is a *society*.[8] It is a collective self-constituting of human beings. It is also a *society of societies*, if it has states as its society-members, since states are themselves societies. The activity of human beings within the society of the intergovernmental organisation includes not only willing and acting on behalf of the organisation itself, especially by its own employees, but also willing and acting on behalf of the society-members of the organisation. Finally, an intergovernmental organisation is itself a *society-member*, in the sense that it participates in international society, the society of all societies, the collective self-constituting of all-humanity.

12.14 As a society, a society of societies, and a society-member, an intergovernmental organisation is thus an *intermediate society*, intermediate between the self-constituting of all-humanity and more particular levels of social self-constituting. Intermediate societies *contained within* other societies are a common social phenomenon. The societies known as 'states', in the current stage of international social development, are themselves full of intermediate societies – the constituent states of a federation, constitutional organs, political parties, industrial and commercial corporations and countless others. And even such intermediate societies, contained within societies, themselves often *contain* other societies.

[7] For further discussion of the moral responsibility of the philosopher, see ch. 1 above.

[8] For the concept of *society*, see *Eunomia*, ch. 1. Society is the collective self-constituting of human beings for their survival and prospering. The Eunomian concept of society is related to Aristotle's conception of *koinonia* (variously translated as community, association, partnership): 'Every state [*polis*] is a community [*koinonia*] of some kind, and every community is established with a view to some good; for mankind always act in order to obtain that which they think good.' *The Politics* (tr. B. Jowett; Oxford, Clarendon Press; 1905), I.1, p. 25. Aristotle links the idea with the idea of friendship: '. . . friendship [*philia*] appears to be the bond of the state'; 'friendship is essentially a partnership [*koinonia*]'. *Nicomachean Ethics* (tr. H. Rackham; Cambridge, MA, Harvard University Press (Loeb Classical Library); 1926), VIII. 1, IX. 12, pp. 453, 573.

12.15 The specificity of intergovernmental organisations as international societies thus arises from their particular intermediate situation between the superordinate international society, on the one hand, and the subordinate state-societies, on the other. We may classify them as *superordinate intermediate societies*. The particular challenge which intergovernmental organisations pose for the social philosopher is a function of three facts. (1) The societies which are their society-members (the states) bring to the ideal self-constituting of the organisation their own social theories, an array of social theories which are intrinsically, and perhaps profoundly, heterogeneous, since each social theory is the unique product of the particular history of the particular society. (2) Those theories are also theories of a different form of society (state-society), not inherently applicable to a superordinate level of international society. (3) The superordinate international society itself has only the most rudimentary theories of its own self-constituting and hence of its constitutional relationship to its subordinate societies. Like its real and legal self-constituting, the ideal self-constituting of international society is at a primitive stage of development, by comparison with even the least complex of national societies, let alone the most complex.

12.16 On the other hand, thinking about the self-constituting of intergovernmental organisations is assisted by the fact that they are societies which are established purposively *ex nihilo*, by specific legal-constitutive behaviour, and by the fact that their day-to-day functioning is generally more transparent and less complex than, for example, that of the state-societies which participate in their self-constituting.

12.17 In four respects, the social-philosophical category of constitutionalism is a particularly useful heuristic matrix for the study of intergovernmental organisations as international societies, given the social-theoretical diversity of their society-members.

(1) The category of constitutionalism identifies a form of social theory which postulates a society whose self-constituting is self-contained, in the sense that its idea of itself is not necessarily dependent on some other religious or philosophical theory external to the society. (2) It identifies a form of theory which, when applied as the theory of a given society, accepts and even promotes social diversity within that society at the level of general ideas, even including the possibility of competing theories of religion and philosophy, and competing ideas about fundamental

social and political purposes and values (normally institutionalised in the form of political parties). (3) It identifies a form of theory which privileges the *legal* self-constituting of a society as the principal means of resolving the struggle of ideas and power which are the ideal and real self-constituting of the society. Intergovernmental organisations are characteristically and predominantly *legal* in their formation, form and functioning. (4) Constitutionalism is a theory whose central focus is the problem of the relationship between the source of the authority of political power and the practical control of its exercise, which is, incidentally, one possible definition of the social-philosophical problem of 'legitimacy'. Intergovernmental organisations are a new manifestation of that age-old problem.

12.18 There is a still more general reason for considering intergovernmental organisations in the light of the category of constitutionalism. The human individual and the human species are the particular and the universal poles of human self-constituting. The particular and the universal of human self-constituting are resolved dialectically in the many-in-one of the countless forms of human society. Intergovernmental organisations in their present form have been produced in the course of international history, especially the history of the last 150 years, as a specific new form of the further universalising of subordinate social forms, as an extrapolation from the subordinate societies rather than as an intrapolation from international society. It is important to know whether the characteristic features of the category of constitutionalism, if and to the extent that they apply to intergovernmental organisations, might be universalised still further to apply to the ultimate form of human society, the international society of the whole human species, the society of all societies. We need to know whether the category of constitutionalism could be applied to international society, not only as a theory within social philosophy but also as the theory adopted by international society itself as the theory, pure and practical, of its own self-constituting.

12.19 The particular characteristics of intergovernmental organisations mean that the challenge which they pose for the social philosopher is of exceptional interest and significance. In studying the theory of the self-constituting of intergovernmental organisations, we may be able to see with unusual clarity the dynamic potentiality of the socialising of all-humanity within its inadequate actuality.

The presence of the past

12.20 Eighteenth-century rationalists and nineteenth-century positivists convinced themselves that the study of human history reveals a line of progress in human enlightenment, leading from the *Urdummheit* (primal stupidity) of pre-theistic religion through the relative *Dummheit* of theistic religion, to the primitive rationality of metaphysics, and thence to the triumph of rationality in science, natural and human. After two more centuries of unusually enlightening human experience, we are less inclined to take such an optimistic view, or even to regard such a view as, in principle, optimistic. We are now more inclined to wonder at the intelligence and sophistication of earlier complex cultures, and to acknowledge the humbling fact that they articulated with extraordinary clarity the problems of human existence which remain problems to the present day. It seems that the problems of human existence are never solved, only worked on once more. Revenants of Confucius and Lao Tze, Aristotle and Averroes, Machiavelli and Voltaire, not to mention the Buddha and Jesus Christ and Muhammad, would find that they could re-enter with very little difficulty the continuing dialogue of the human mind with itself. We might hope that they would take the consoling view that the human species is still a young species, that 5,000 years are as a day in the long process of human self-evolving.

12.21 We are more inclined now to see that religion and philosophy and science are distinctive, if related, manifestations of human self-consciousness, and that they can co-exist, competitively and also co-operatively, in the forming of social consciousness. We can, as individuals and societies, choose to favour one at the expense of the others, to reject one or more as worthless or harmful. As historians and as social philosophers, we cannot ignore the power which they have exercised, and are still exercising, over the making of human history, over the future of the human species.

12.22 There is a second dramatic aspect to our new-found humility in relation to the human past. The present is the presence of the past. We are now able to see that all our social institutions are inheritances, each the particular product of a particular succession of events which occurred within the general history of human socialising, and in one or more of its particular sub-histories. We see now that both the capacities and the limitations of our social institutions, social good and social evil, are by-products and side-effects of that history and those histories.

Above all, we see now that all our ideas have been historically produced – our ideas of God and gods, our ideas of nation and gender and race, our ideas of the true and the good and the beautiful, our ideas of society and law, our ideas of international society and international law, our ideas about our own humanity, our ideas about the past and the future, our ideas about ideas. All of them might have been otherwise. All of them are not otherwise. Social consciousness forms itself organically, by accretion and transformation. New ideas grow in the compost of old ideas.

12.23 It follows also that old ideas contain the possibility of new ideas. The ideas we have contain the ideas that we might have. The present state of human consciousness contains the possibility of new states of consciousness which are ours to explore and ours to choose.

The genealogy of constitutionalism

12.24 At the level of all-humanity, social consciousness is formed from the flow of consciousness within and between the public minds of countless subordinate societies over thousands of years, as they constitute themselves in consciousness, as they form their self-consciousness in the light of the self-constituting of other societies. Nowhere is this more true than in the evolution of the idea of constitutionalism. The past of the idea of constitutionalism is a past which extends over several millennia and many cultures, and includes not only the turbulent development of social consciousness within particular societies but also the flow of consciousness among all the most dynamic cultures, ancient and modern. So deep are its roots in human social experience, in all times and all places, we might well wonder whether it is a manifestation of some part of the genetic programme of human socialising, a species-characteristic and not merely a contingent by-product of history.

12.25 The future of the idea of constitutionalism, as a possible idea within our ideas of international society and international law, is thus a present potentiality which we have inherited from an exceptionally long and an exceptionally rich past. As an historically produced social phenomenon, constitutionalism has taken countless different forms, as the theory, pure and practical, of countless different societies. Its deep-structural unity lies in the fact that it offers to a society the most valuable prize of all, that is to say, a practically effective idea of the order of its own self-ordering. In an unusually clear example of the dialectical development of social consciousness, the idea of constitutionalism allows a society to reconcile the ideal with the actual by negating and incorporating its idea of the transcendental.[9] For each society, it presents in one mental structure its own theory of the idea and the ideal of law. The history of constitutionalism is the history of the struggle of countless societies with the problem of the idea and the ideal of law.

12.26 It is a striking fact of history that there seems to have been a parallel development in the idea and the ideal of law in otherwise disparate cultures. It is a mental phenomenon whose history can be plotted over time in particular cultures but which cannot be isolated from their general history, because it has always been closely connected with other aspects of social and economic development. In particular, it seems that, in periods of exceptional social and economic change, and especially in periods of great social disorder, societies have been led to reconsider the foundations of their social order, including its transcendental parameters. That reconsideration has been an integral part of the social struggle, as contending parties sought to enlist competing versions of transcendental ideas into their own idea of a better society. Such an appeal could be used as a weapon either of reaction or of revolution, an unchanging standard of judgement by reference to which it could be argued that the present state of society was either a betrayal of society's ancient ideals or else a denial of the true potentiality of those ideals.

12.27 The fact that all sides in revolutionary social struggle refer to the idea of the social-transcendental, but struggle passionately about its meaning and its relevance to the current social situation, has created a particular difficulty for historians, generating secondary disputes, among historians themselves, about both those things. It is also particularly difficult to avoid anachronism in making our historical judgements about such matters, given that we happen to know how things turned out, how the struggles were resolved in the further development of the ideal, real and legal self-constituting of the societies in question.

12.28 As we enter the new century, social philosophy must make the effort to form a reliable view of such processes, because the perennial

[9] Hegel's dialectical logic, which has a place on the human intellectual genome close to the dynamic epistemology of Socrates/Plato and the metaphysical biologism of Aristotle, resolves dissonances at all epistemic levels into something which 'apprehends the unity of terms (propositions) in their opposition – the affirmative which is involved in their disintegration and in their transition'. *Hegel's Logic* (part 1 of the *Encyclopaedia of the Philosophical Sciences*; 1830) (tr. W. Wallace; Oxford, Clarendon Press; 1973/1975), § 82, p. 119. For Hegel, dialectic is 'the very nature and essence of everything predicated by mere understanding' (p. 116).

problem of human social self-constituting now presents itself as its limiting case, at the level of all-humanity, where oppositions of social theory, including transcendental oppositions of philosophy and religion, will have to be resolved in some new idea and ideal of law. Revolutionary social change is now present at the level of all-humanity, and that social change puts in question, among many other things, the nature and function of intergovernmental organisations, as superordinate intermediate societies, a relatively new form of human self-socialising, which may or may not contain the emerging pattern of still more developed forms. The international social struggle at the level of ideas, the ideal self-constituting of international society, calls for the contribution and the courage of a new breed of international social philosopher.

12.29 International social philosophy must consider urgently whether the idea of constitutionalism might realise its ultimate genetic destiny as the *practical theory* of the ultimate society, international society, reconciling and overcoming the passionate pure-theoretical diversity, historical and religious and philosophical, of its countless subordinate societies within the revolutionary self-reconstituting of all-humanity.

The genetics of constitutionalism

12.30 Historically, the various forms of constitutionalism have been a manifestation of the ideas which particular societies have formed of the relationship between the theory of their own social order and one (or more than one) of four more general theories: (1) divine order; (2) the sovereignty of law; (3) natural cosmic order; (4) natural social order.

12.31 Constitutionalism has been used to establish (1) an idea of a very human social order which is seen, paradoxically, as the controlling presence of *divine order*. It has been used to establish (2) the idea of the authority of everyday law-making and law-enforcing as the controlling presence of the *sovereignty of law*. It has been used to establish (3) the idea of a very particular and artificial human social order which is seen, paradoxically, as the controlling presence of *natural cosmic order*. It has been used to establish (4) the idea of the particular and artificial order of a given society as the controlling presence of *natural social order*.

12.32 Or, to put the four germ-ideas in a single genetic programme, we may say that constitutionalism postulates an idea and an ideal of law which is (1) less than the Will of God and (4) more than the General Will, something which is (2) more than the Rule of Law and (3) less than Natural Law. Such is the evolved charismatic power of the idea of constitutionalism, and the potentiality of its future power.

(1) Divine order

12.33 In *La cité antique*, Fustel de Coulanges set an extreme benchmark in relation to which all subsequent opinions may be situated.

'Among the Greeks and Romans, as among the Hindus, law was at first part of religion.'[10] 'The law among the ancients was holy, and in the time of royalty it was the queen of kings. In the time of the republic it was the queen of the people.'[11]

12.34 *Religion* may be 'what the individual does with his own solitariness', as Whitehead said,[12] or it may be a product of 'man's need to make his helplessness tolerable', in the words of Freud.[13] Or, on the contrary, it may be a society's 'collective ideal', as Durkheim suggested,[14] or 'the dream-thinking of a people'[15]or 'collective desire personified'.[16] It may be a crude weapon of power in the hands of the ruling class, as Polybius and many others have suggested,[17] or it may be the self-serving

[10] N. D. Fustel de Coulanges, *The Ancient City. A Study on the Religion, Laws, and Institutions of Greece and Rome* (1864) (Baltimore, London, Johns Hopkins University Press; 1980), p. 178. Compare Frazer's assertion: 'society has been built and cemented to a great extent on a foundation of religion, and it is impossible to loosen the cement and shake the foundation without endangering the superstructure'. J. Frazer, *The Belief in Immortality and the Worship of the Dead* (London, Macmillan; 1913), I, p. 4. Many of Fustel's main contentions have been disputed by classicists and anthropologists, but his book can still be read with pleasure and profit as a lively intellectual catalyst.

[11] Fustel de Coulanges, *Ancient City* (fn. 10 above), p. 182.

[12] A. N. Whitehead, *Religion in the Making* (Cambridge, Cambridge University Press; 1926), p. 16.

[13] S. Freud, *The Future of an Illusion* (1927) (London, Penguin (The Pelican Freud Library); 1985), XII, p. 198.

[14] E. Durkheim, *The Elementary Forms of the Religious Life* (fn. 1 above), p. 423.

[15] E. Dodds, *The Greeks and the Irrational* (Berkeley, University of California Press; 1951), p. 104, citing, as sources of this idea, Harrison, Rivers, Lévy-Bruhl and Kluckhohn (p. 122, fn. 5).

[16] E. Doutté, quoted and discussed in G. Murray, *Five Stages of Greek Religion* (London, Watts & Co.; 1935), pp. 26ff.

[17] 'I believe that it is the very thing which among other peoples is an object of reproach, I mean superstition, which maintains the cohesion of the Roman state . . . My own opinion at least is that they have adopted this course for the sake of the common people.' Polybius, *Histories* (tr. W. Paton; London, William Heinemann (Loeb Classical Library); 1923), VI.56, p. 395.

ideology, or at least the dominant mentality, of an ascending social class, as Tawney and Weber argued.[18]

12.35 Whether religion is seen rather as the internalising of social consciousness or as the externalising of individual consciousness, social imposition or individual expression, religion as a social phenomenon is a fusion of pure theory and practical theory. The puzzling human disposition known as 'belief' may be defined as assent to a set of ideas (pure theory) manifested as a corresponding modification in the believer's willing and acting (practical theory).[19] Religion manifests itself not only as a system of ideas but also in ritual forms of modified behaviour, ranging from individual acts of piety in front of a shrine, altar, or image to complex public ceremonies, and complex social structures and systems of overwhelming social power.

12.36 Religion places a focus of ultimate reality beyond the limits of the society within which it manifests itself. But the constitutive consequences of this constitutional transcendentalism have varied from society to society. (1) Religion may be fully integrated in society's structures and systems, as in ancient Egypt,[20] ancient India[21] and ancient Israel.[22] (2) Religion may be invoked as the ultimate source of public authority,

[18] 'It is not wholly fanciful to suggest that ... Calvin did for the *bourgeoisie* of the sixteenth century what Marx did for the proletariat of the nineteenth ... [He] taught them to feel that they were a chosen people, made them conscious of their great destiny in the Providential plan and resolute to realize it.' R. H. Tawney, *Religion and the Rise of Capitalism. A Historical Study* (London, John Murray; 1926), pp. 111–12.

[19] This definition takes up the idea that belief is not merely a primitive or degenerate epistemic form, but is rather another way of knowing and being. 'Our word "credo" is, sound for sound, the Vedic *çraddhā*, and *çraddhā* means "to set one's heart on"... Man, say the wise Upanishads, is altogether desire (*kāma*): as is his desire so is his insight (*kratu*), as is his insight so is his deed (*karma*).' J. Harrison, *Themis. A Study of the Social Origins of Greek Religion* (London, Merlin Press; 1963), p. 83. Harrison is apparently referring to a passage in the *Brihad Āranyaka* which continues as follows: 'Where one's mind is attached – the inner self goes thereto with action, being attached to it alone.' A. Embree (ed.), *The Hindu Tradition* (New York, Vintage Books; 1966), p. 63.

[20] Whether or not its physical remains reflect the true nature of ancient Egyptian society as a whole, that society seems to have been the limiting case of a complex theocratic society, with the pharaoh-king being appointed by the Sun God, himself a living god.

[21] The ancient Vedic religion of India is entitled to be regarded as the limiting case of religion, the *summa* of all religions, integrating universalist theology, philosophy, social theory and law within a structure of ideas which links the making and nature of the universe to the ordering of everyday life. It is a necessary implication of such a religion that 'the Lord of Heaven' is also 'the King of Earthly Kings'. *Athava Veda*, in Embree, *The Hindu Tradition* (fn. 19 above), p. 44.

[22] 'By me kings reign and princes decree justice.' Proverbs, 8. 15.

as in ancient Mesopotamia[23] and ancient China.[24] (3) Religion may be an integral part of the society's self-identifying, conditioning but not determining society's structures and systems, as in ancient Greece[25] and ancient Rome.[26]

12.37 The constitutive paradigms of religion have persisted throughout human history. They are present in the contemporary world, even if only in vestigial form in those societies which have a legally constituted separation of religion and political authority. But the part they have played in the genesis of the idea of constitutionalism lies in an important logical corollary that they contain in their deep-structure.

[23] Even Hammurapi (autocratic Babylonian king of a forcibly unified Mesopotamia; 1792–1750 BCE) prefaced his law-code with the words: 'When Marduk [chief of the gods] commanded me to give justice to the people of the land and to let (them) have (good) governance, I set forth truth and justice throughout the land (and) prospered the people.' G. Driver and J. Miles, *The Babylonian Laws* (Oxford, Clarendon Press; 1952), II, p. 13. 'In no other antique society did religion occupy such a prominent position . . . The fact that the Sumerian society crystallized around temples had deep and lasting consequences. In theory, for instance, the land never ceased to belong to the gods, and the mighty Assyrian monarchs whose empire extended from the Nile to the Caspian Sea were the humble servants of their god Assur, just as the governors of Lagash, who ruled over a few square miles of Sumer, were those of their god Ningirsu.' G. Roux, *Ancient Iraq* (London, George Allen & Unwin; 1964), pp. 85–6. According to Roux, the 'Sumerian model' dominated Assyro-Babylonian civilisation of the second and first millennia BCE (after the disappearance of the separate kingdom of Sumer, and other subordinate polities, in about 2000 BCE).

[24] 'The implications of the phrase *T'ien-tzu* [Son of Heaven] have exercised a profound effect on the Chinese concept of sovereignty. In so far as he is regarded as Heaven's descendant, a sovereign is responsible for the conduct of the worship of *T'ien* [Heaven], just as every dutiful son attends to the placation of his deceased ancestors' souls.' M. Loewe, *Imperial China. The Historical Background to the Modern Age* (London, George Allen & Unwin; 1966), p. 74. Loewe is here speaking of the pre-imperial age (before 221 BCE) and, indeed, the time before Confucius (551–479 BCE). See further in D. Keighley (ed.), *The Origins of Chinese Civilization* (Berkeley, University of California Press; 1983).

[25] 'Now in the contest between city and tribe, the Olympian gods had one great negative advantage. They were not tribal or local, and all other gods were. They were by this time international . . . They were ready to be made "Poliouchoi", "City-holders", of any particular city, still more the "Hellânioi", patrons of all Hellas [Greece].' Murray, *Five Stages of Greek Religion* (fn. 16 above), p. 67. The original religions of Greece had included a familiar mixture of myth, magic, taboo and ritual on the pattern of the early stages in the development of religion generally. The propagation by Homer and Hesiod (before seventh century BCE) of the Olympian gods, under the chief god Zeus but themselves ruled by super-divine powers of fate and necessity, also prepared the way for the philosophy-religion initiated in fifth-century BCE Athens. See H. Kitto, *The Greeks* (Harmondsworth, Penguin; 1951), pp. 196ff.

[26] The part played by religion in the social consciousness of Rome is difficult to determine. It manifested itself in pious beliefs and rituals at the level of individual households, in public ceremonies of a superstitious character but of dubious sincerity, and in the literary and rhetorical rehearsing of parts of the Greek Olympian mythology. It seems that law rather than religion was the 'cement' (fn. 10 above) of Roman society from the first days of the monarchy to the last days of the Empire.

Belief in a theory of the transcendental *source* of public power is also a belief in the *subjection* of public power to its transcendental source. An emperor or a king is both empowered and constrained by having the status of Son of Heaven, the Lord's Anointed, King and Priest, *pontifex maximus* (high priest), or God's vicar on Earth, or if royal power is believed to be held 'under God' or 'by the grace of God'.[27]

12.38 Belief in a religious source of public power may be part of the ideal self-constituting of societies, and may be made part of their legal self-constituting. It must be said, however, that all of recorded human history shows that such a belief may also be the source of the most extreme abuses of public power, in the everyday real-constituting of particular societies.

(2) The sovereignty of law

12.39 A second thread in the fabric of the idea of constitutionalism, from the most ancient complex societies to the most complex societies of the present day, is to be found in a legal transcendentalism which is reminiscent of, and sometimes accompanies, socially transcendent religion.

12.40 Indeed, it is tempting to rejoin the thesis of Fustel de Coulanges[28] at an analytical level at least, and to say that religion and law were originally inextricable because a common categorical pattern is to be found at the root of both of them.[29] They both affirm systems of order which transcend the order of individual consciousness. They both imply acceptance of an external control of consciousness, not by force but by the conforming of consciousness to the external system of order. They both recognise the interaction of individual and social consciousness,

[27] James Frazer's *The Golden Bough. A Study in Magic and Religion* (1890/1900) and his *Lectures on the Early History of the Kingship* (1905) bring together very many historical and legendary examples and aspects of the religion of kingship. Of the first Christian Roman Emperor (reigned 306–37), it was said (tendentiously): 'The God of all, the supreme governor of the whole universe, by His own will appointed Constantine . . . to be prince and sovereign . . . he is unique as the one man to whose elevation no mortal may boast of having contributed.' Eusebius, quoted in C. N. Cochrane, *Christianity and Classical Culture. A Study in Thought and Action from Augustus to Augustine* (London, Oxford University Press; 1940), p. 186. For the post-medieval survival of such ideas, see J. N. Figgis, *The Divine Right of Kings* (Cambridge, Cambridge University Press; 1922).

[28] See at fn. 10 above.

[29] This more or less metaphorical echo of the concept of the 'category' found in the Aristotelian and Kantian philosophies is intended to share in their idea that the mind co-operates with non-mind in forming reality, by imposing its own patterns on the phenomena produced by non-mind.

each flowing into the other. They both assume a shared acceptance of such systems of order by others, not only by other faithful and loyal individuals but also by rulers and, indeed, by whole societies.

12.41 Customary law, that is to say, unlegislated law, is a feature common to all societies at some stage in their development, especially and necessarily at the pre-literate stage. It is the law which arises from the day-to-day *real* self-constituting of a society to become the means of its *legal* self-constituting, and so finds its reflection in that *ideal* self-constituting which in turn conditions the making and finding of law.[30]

12.42 It seems that, paradoxically, the *idea* of law, as opposed to the fact and practice of law, and as opposed to the idea of religion, came to the surface of social self-consciousness when law-giving began to co-exist with law-finding, when unlegislated law was supplemented by legislated law. The ancient world knew many events of law-giving – Hammurabi, Manu, Draco, Moses, Lycurgus, Solon, the Twelve Tables of ancient Rome, Ashoka, Justinian – each of which had, or acquired, a legendary status. But the striking fact is that it was claimed, in each case, that the ordained law was designed to supplement and to reinforce unordained law, not to replace it. Even the most powerful law-givers – Hammurapi in Babylon,[31] Ashoka in India,[32] Solon in Athens[33] and

[30] See fn. 3 above.

[31] For a discussion of the status of the Laws of Hammurapi, see Driver and Miles, *The Babylonian Laws* (fn. 23 above), I, pp. 48ff: 'whatever the Laws are, they are not a code in the modern sense of the term; they may rather be compared with the English "Statutes of the Realm". They do not wholly take the place of existing law but are a series of amendments to that law, much in the same way as English statutes amend the common law and sometimes codify it in part.'

It is remarkable how, in the polities of Mesopotamia, the cradle of urban civilisation, so many of the characteristics and problems of national and international social life in the following three millennia were prefigured. See generally C. Maisels, *The Emergence of Civilization. From Hunting and Gathering to Agriculture, Cities, and the State in the Near East* (London, Routledge; 1990), esp. chaps 7–10; J. N. Postgate, *Early Mesopotamia. Society and Economy at the Dawn of History* (London, Routledge; 1992).

[32] 'In the past kings sought to make the people progress in Righteousness but they did not progress . . . Thus I have decided to have them instructed in Righteousness, and to issue ordinances of Righteousness, so that by hearing them the people might conform, advance in the progress of Righteousness, and themselves make great progress.' From the Seventh Pillar Edict of King Ashoka (*c.*269–232 BCE), in Embree, *The Hindu Tradition* (fn. 19 above), p. 116. In his decrees, Ashoka added a Buddhist overtone to the ancient and beautiful Vedic idea of the *moral* order of the universe (*dharma*) of which law, unlegislated and legislated, and the moral conscience of human individuals are particular manifestations.

[33] Aristotle surveys a large number of Greek law-givers in *Politics*, II.12 and describes Solon's laws at length in his *Athenian Constitution*. Athens did not have a written constitution, but it had much constitutional law. The laws of Solon (*c.*640–*c.*548 BCE) contained a mixture

Justinian in the eastern Roman Empire[34] – placed their law-giving in a context which affirmed their own function as agents of a law which pre-existed and transcended them. The new law was set against a background of inherited law the obscurity of whose source (personal or impersonal) was an integral part of its authority, the later law-giving events being designed to borrow the charisma of the old law while correcting and completing it. Law that was made affirmed the dignity of law that was found.

12.43 It was in ancient China that the idea, and not merely the fact, of law first came to dominate the ideal self-constituting, the self-understanding and the self-directing, of a complex society. It was Confucius (K'ung Fu Tzu; 551–479 BCE) who symbolised and formed that social self-consciousness. And it was Confucius who insisted most on his role as a faithful voice of the past rather than as a mere legislator of the future.[35] Again and again, from eighteenth-century Babylon, through fifth-century Athens and republican Rome, to the English Civil War and the French Revolution, a society is compelled to explore the basis of its own order in periods of the greatest social disorder.[36] Such was the historical role of Confucius. At such times, society reconstitutes itself ideally; in reconceiving its past it reorients its future.[37]

12.44 The belief that there is an idea of law which is above and beyond the fact of law was represented in powerful imaginative form in the *Antigone* of Sophocles.[38] It was enacted poignantly in the death of

of what we would call constitutional law and social legislation, proposing a new – and, as it turned out, not very successful – Athenian social contract.

[34] The law-commissioners of the Emperor Justinian (*c.*482–565) had to bring order to a thousand years of intense but disorderly legal experience. 'Instead of a statue cast in a simple mould by the hand of an artist, the works of Justinian represent a tessellated pavement of antique and costly, but too often incoherent fragments.' E. Gibbon, *The History of the Decline and Fall of the Roman Empire*, IV (1788) (ed. D. Womersley; London, Allen Lane, The Penguin Press; 1944), ch. 44, p. 799.

[35] On Confucius, 'a creator through being a transmitter', see Fung Yu-lan, *A History of Chinese Philosophy* (1937) (tr. D. Bodde; Princeton, Princeton University Press; 1952), I, pp. 62ff. On the central concept of *li* (socially accumulated rules of human conduct), see at pp. 66ff. On the effect of *li* as a socialising and civilising force, and on its long-term influence on Chinese society, see Loewe, *Imperial China* (fn. 24 above), pp. 95ff.

[36] 'And when there is good order in the empire, the people do not even discuss it.' Confucius, in Fung Yu-lan, *A History of Chinese Philosophy* (fn. 35 above), p. 59.

[37] Two centuries later, in another period of social disorder, an authoritarian reading of Confucius was given by the Legalist or Legist school, emphasising authority, statecraft and the sovereignty of law. Ibid., pp. 312ff; Loewe, *Imperial China* (fn. 24 above), pp. 78ff.

[38] '*Creon.* And yet you dared, then, to defy the law? *Antigone.* It was not God that gave me such commandments,/ Nor Justice, consort of the Lords of Death,/ That ever laid on men such

Socrates.[39] It was imagined metaphysically in the philosophy of Plato, and it was established by Aristotle in the language of social and moral philosophy.[40] The Romans relied also, in Confucian fashion, on ancestral custom (*mos maiorum*) which could be invoked by reactionary, reformist and revolutionary alike in the unending real-constitutional political struggle.[41] But it was the idea of law which provided the social cement of Roman society – successively monarchy, republic, principate, and empire – a society whose permanent characteristic was ceaseless social change. It was an idea of law which was constantly repaired and refashioned, but never abandoned, until the Roman inheritance was handed on to its various law-obsessed heirs, especially to those other hazardous forms of polity which included many nations and many subcultures – the Church of Rome, the Holy Roman Empire, the European colonial empires, the European Union.

12.45 The Romans established a powerful conceptual distinction between *fas* (divine law and religious custom), *mos* (social custom), *ius* (human law in the broadest sense) and *lex* (legislated law). *Ius* was the

laws as these./ Nor did I hold that in your human edicts/ Lay power to override the laws of God,/ Unwritten yet unshaken – laws that live/ Not from to-day, nor yet from yesterday,/ But always – though none knows how first made known.' Sophocles, *Antigone* (*c.*441 BCE), lines 449–57 (tr. F. Lucas; New York, The Viking Press; 1968), p. 141.

39 'As it is, you will leave this place, when you do, as the victim of a wrong not done by us, the laws, but by your fellow men.' Plato, *Crito* (tr. H. Tredennick), in *The Collected Dialogues of Plato* (eds E. Hamilton and H. Cairns; Princeton, Princeton University Press; 1961), p. 39. The dialogue recreates a conversation with Socrates (*c.*469–399 BCE) while he was in prison, following the judgement of an Athenian people's court which had sentenced him to death. Socrates imagines 'the laws' telling him why he must respect them, rather than seek to escape from prison and evade his punishment.

40 'And the rule of law is preferable to that of any individual. On the same principle, even if it be better for certain individuals to govern, they should be made only guardians and ministers of the law.' *Politics* (fn. 8 above), III.16.3–4, p. 139. 'He who bids the law rule, may be deemed to bid God and Reason alone rule.' Ibid., III.16.5, p. 140.

41 'The Romans believed that they were a conservative people, devoted to the worship of law and order. The advocates of change therefore appealed, not to reform or progress, not to abstract right and abstract justice, but to something called *mos maiorum*. This was not a code of constitutional law, but a vague and emotional concept. It was therefore a subject of partisan interpretation, of debate and of fraud; almost any plea could triumph by an appeal to custom or tradition.' R. Syme, *The Roman Revolution* (Oxford, Oxford University Press; 1939), p. 153. Cicero took the Burkeian evolutionary view of the Roman constitution: 'Now we have further proof of the accuracy of Cato's statement that the foundation of our State (*constitutionem rei publicae*) was the work neither of one period nor of one man.' *De re publica*, II.xx.37 (tr. C. Keyes; Cambridge, MA, Harvard University Press (Loeb Classical Library); 1928), p. 145.

generic idea of human law (in English, *the* law, as opposed to *a* law).[42] The conceptual isolation of such an idea helped to establish it as an active presence in the theory, pure and practical, of countless societies, as something which was distinct both from *justice* and from positive law (*ius positum*), something which is both transcendental in relation to any particular society (and hence capable of being common to all societies) and yet which is formed, in its substance, in the self-constituting of each particular society.

(3) Cosmic order

12.46 In the middle of the first millennium BCE, there occurred three parallel moments[43] of human enlightenment, in China, India and Greece. *Taoism*,[44] *Buddhism*[45] and *Metaphysical Philosophy*.[46] They had two important effects – one general, one particular – on the evolving idea of constitutionalism. The general effect was that society would in future be

[42] Other languages reflect the Roman distinction by having separate words for *ius* and *lex*. They then create a new confusion by using the former word also to refer to 'a right', in the sense of a particular legal relation. 'Human rights' might have been more effective if they had been known as 'human law' (*ius humani generis*). The ancient Greeks did not have a conception corresponding to the Roman *ius*. See C. McIlwain, *Constitutionalism Ancient and Modern* (Ithaca, Cornell University Press; 1940), p. 19. On the absence of an idea of *ius* in the perennial Chinese legal tradition, see J. Escarra, *Le droit chinois* (Pékin, Editions H. Vetch; Paris, Recueil Sirey; 1936), pp. 70ff. According to Escarra, the Chinese did not develop an abstract conception of positive law, since the law was subordinate to socially determined morality and to *li*, and was seen as both transcendental (reflecting the nature of the universe and of society) and casuistic (concerned with the uniqueness of each law-violating situation).

[43] 'Moment' in the Hegelian sense (*Hegel's Logic* (fn. 9 above), § 79, p. 113); not a moment in time (*der Moment*) but, in a sense borrowed from mechanics, a turning-point (*das Moment*) in the development of a thought-process.

[44] The dating of Taoism is not straightforward. The source-book (the *Tao te ching*), if it is itself of the fourth century BCE, may have been a compilation of thought going back at least to the time of Confucius. See E. R. Hughes (tr. and ed.), *Chinese Philosophy in Classical Times* (London, J. M. Dent & Sons (Everyman Library); 1942), p. 144. But see also Fung Yu-lan, *A History of Chinese Philosophy* (fn. 35 above), pp. 170ff.

[45] The Buddha's illumination occurred in *c*.525 BCE. We may say that with Buddhism, the first world-religion, the potentiality of a supra-national and supra-cultural human consciousness was revealed. The spread of Greek metaphysical philosophy beyond Greece may be seen as a further step in that process.

[46] Pythagoras (*c*.570–*c*.480), Parmenides (*c*.515–440), Socrates (469–399). For contemporaneous Chinese thought on the problem of knowledge (so central a problem for these Greek philosophers), see E. R. Hughes, *Chinese Philosophy* (fn. 44 above), pp. 119ff. For contemporaneous thinking in the Hindu tradition on the self-redeeming of the mind, see Embree, *The Hindu Tradition* (fn. 19 above), pp. 180ff.

accompanied by a second image of itself, a reflection not of its actuality but of its potentiality, of what it could be, an alternative reality seen in the light of its highest values. The particular effect was that law would be accompanied by a second image of itself, seen in the light of an order which transcended it, an order of its order, a higher order which might be expressed as *tao*, as *dharma*, or as *justice*.[47]

12.47 The threefold enlightenment was not religious in the sense considered above. It proposed a *cosmology*, not a second reality of gods and the supernatural, but a form of reality which included things natural and human in a single order, even if all three cosmologies proved capable of being translated into religious practice, including practice of the most popular kinds. The new enlightenment proposed an idea of a *transcendental reality* in which humanity was present only as an atom in an infinity, but which might nevertheless be particularised in the most specific programmes of value and action for individual human beings and societies.[48] And it presented itself as a *universalism*, abstracted from the history and consciousness of any particular human society, but capable of being particularised as the theory (transcendental, pure and practical) of particular societies. Each was a *way*, a way of knowing and being, rather than a body of doctrine and practices, but each proved to be an inexhaustible source of derived doctrine and practice.

12.48 This new self-empowering of human consciousness has been charted with particular precision in the case of ancient Greece, because the written materials which survive from that period, such as they are, enact and celebrate the change with remarkable self-consciousness, much self-admiration, and much passionate debate. The process was doubly dialectic. The new way of thinking made possible the negating of its own negating, as philosophical arguments were used to challenge the validity and the value of the new philosophy – a debate which has

[47] Given the relentlessly dialectical character of collective human thought (fn. 9 above), it is no surprise that each of these ideas was itself a surpassing of more ancient ideas.

[48] Buddhists insist on the radical difference between what they see as the two-reality (phenomena-noumena) view of Western idealism and the seamless reality which is both the focus and the process of 'enlightenment'. Sangharakshita, *A Survey of Buddhism, Its Doctrines and Methods through the Ages* (London, Tharpa Publications; 1957/1987), pp. 118ff, discussing the extraordinary complexity of the idea of *dharma*. However, the Plato of the *Republic* was certainly not a dualist (still less Spinoza or Hegel), even if the British empiricists and Kant may have been. The shadows on the wall of the dark cave (*Republic*, bk VII) represent an illusionary reality, to be dissipated by something which is seen as a form of enlightenment, even if it is very different from the Buddhist form.

continued unabated to the present day. And the new thinking was enriched by the old thinking which it negated.

12.49 The road from *mythos* to *logos*, as one writer has described it, from mythical thinking to rational thinking,[49] is not a one-way road. The personalised Olympian gods and the heroes of mythology might be seen as forming a transitional stage on the way from inchoate animism and fatalism to the individuated abstractions which would become the hall-mark of Greek philosophy.[50] But the new individuated abstractions, including those which would so profoundly affect the future of the idea of constitutionalism – Justice, the Good, Law, Nature – carried with them still something of the aura of the individuated gods and heroes.[51] We can watch the process of change. Hesiod (eighth century BCE) speaks of Justice who sits beside the throne of Zeus.[52] Plato (fifth–fourth century BCE) will devote the most influential of his dialogues (*The Republic*) to an exploration of the *idea* of justice as the ideal of human self-perfecting through social self-perfecting in accordance with an ideal of cosmic order. Hesiod tells how Zeus (chief of the gods) married Themis (tribal law) and had three daughters, one of whom was Eunomia. Solon, law-giver and poet (seventh–sixth century BCE), will describe in an elegy

[49] W. Nestle, *Vom Mythos zum Logos* (Stuttgart, Alfred Kröner Verlag; 1940/42). Nestle presents it as a dramatic struggle in ancient Greece, a struggle which Reason never finally won. Among the rationalist avant-garde, Hecataeus found mythology 'funny'. Heraclitus said that praying to a god's image was like speaking to a house instead of to its owner. Xenophanes said that, if an ox could paint a picture, its god would look like an ox. Herodotus (sixth century BCE), the first of a new kind of historian, spoke of the Hellenic race emancipating itself from 'silly nonsense'. References in Dodds, *The Greeks and the Irrational* (fn. 15 above), pp. 179ff; G. Murray, *Five Stages of Greek Religion* (fn. 16 above), p. 39. Thucydides (fifth century BCE) would in turn accuse Herodotus of being still the captive of myth, thereby initiating the great and continuing debate about the nature and function of historiography. See further in ch. 11 above.

[50] J. Harrison, *Themis* (fn. 19 above), pp. 445ff. Subsequent religious history is the history of much travel in both directions. Christianity, a hellenised form of Judaic monotheism socialised under a romanised legal-administrative system, made its central belief the incarnation of the *logos* (God made Man), the demonstration (epiphany) of what human reality would be, if the ideal potential reality were simply and fully actualised as the ideal of everyday personal and social life.

[51] The Greek myths, like the myths of so many other countries, remained as a permanent and substantial presence in Western consciousness, at least until very recent times. Aristotle said, in a private letter: 'the more time I spend on my own, the fonder I have become of myths'. M. Finley, ed., *The Legacy of Greece, A New Appraisal* (Oxford, Oxford University Press; 1984), p. 322.

[52] For the complex and changing significance of the noun *dike* (justice), see H. Lloyd-Jones, *The Justice of Zeus* (Berkeley, University of California Press; 1971), pp. 166–7, fn. 23.

(*Eunomia*) the work he has done for Athens, telling the Athenians of the practical merits of *eunomia* (good social order), which 'straightens crooked judgements' and 'stops the works of factional strife'.[53]

12.50 Within the Western tradition, the effect of the idea of ideal reality has been historically decisive. It has meant that not only individual human beings but also whole societies have been able to imagine and articulate a reality-for-themselves which is a potentiality within actual reality, and which can be chosen to become actual reality. In other words, the idea of the ideal has been at the heart of the *idea* of *progress.* It has been at the root of the *fact* of ceaseless, relentless self-directed *change*, a lyrical counterpoint to all the evil and all the atavism which have also characterised the twin dialectics of theory and practice in the Western tradition.[54]

12.51 Within the Western idealist tradition, the idea of cosmic order also manifested itself (in the third century BCE) in the form which came to be known as *stoicism*, and from it there emerged the idea of *natural law*, the ideal order of law. The idea of natural law would also affect profoundly the evolving idea of constitutionalism.

12.52 The Greeks distinguished between *physis* (nature or, rather, the energising force of the universe and its order) and *nomos* (the law of human society). The idea of natural law is a paradox, a *nomos* which is rooted in *physis.* The paradox is still more apparent in Latin, where the phrase *ius naturale* (natural law) or *ius naturae* (law of nature) manages to combine into a single idea the idea of human 'law' in the broad sense (*ius*)[55] and the idea of 'nature'. The idea of nature was the central stoic idea, closely analogous to the *tao* of philosophical Taoism. Stoicism, like taoism, moralised the idea of the order of the universe by prescribing that the ultimate moral responsibility of human beings is to make their daily life, and indeed their consciousness, conform to the order of nature. The human mind is equipped with a characteristic (*logos*, reason) which enables us to uncover the order of the universe, the *logos* of the *kosmos*

[53] V. Ehrenberg, *From Solon to Socrates. Greek History during the 6th and 5th Centuries B.C.* (London, Methuen & Co.; 1967), p. 61.

[54] Cf. Cicero's unRoman tribute to philosophy – 'O philosophy, thou guide of life, o thou explorer of virtue and expeller of vice! Without thee what could have become not only of me but of the life of man altogether? . . . thou hast discovered law, thou hast been the teacher of morality and order.' Cicero, *Tusculan Disputations* (tr. W. King; London, William Heinemann (Loeb Classical Library); 1937), v.ii.5, p. 429.

[55] See fn. 42 above.

(Chrysippus), because the mind (*nous*) itself participates in that order, the order of nature, the *nous Dios* (the mind of Zeus or God). Since mind and reason are shared by all human beings, it followed, for stoicism as for taoism, that there is an order of obligation which is shared by all human beings on a basis of natural equality.[56]

'True law [*vera lex*] is right reason [*recta ratio*] in agreement with nature [*naturae congruens*]; it is of universal application, unchanging and everlasting ... We cannot be freed from its obligations by senate or people, and we need not look outside ourselves for an expounder or interpreter of it. And there will not be different laws at Rome and at Athens, or different laws now and in the future, but one eternal and unchangeable law will be valid for all nations and all times, and there will be one master and one ruler, that is, God, over us all, for he is the author of this law, its promulgator, and its enforcing judge.'[57]

12.53 To provide everyday law with such a monumental philosophical superstructure – nature, reason, justice, universality, God – was a central strategy in the Roman use of law as the theoretical binding force of an overwhelmingly heterogeneous and unstable society. The same

[56] It followed that all human beings belong to a universal society (*kosmopolis*). In the words of the Roman Emperor who was also a Stoic philosopher, Marcus Aurelius (121–80), writing in Greek: 'If the intellectual capacity is common to us all, common too is the reason [*logos*], which makes us rational creatures. If so, that reason also is common which tells us to do or not to do. If so, law [*nomos*] also is common. If so, we are citizens [*politai*]. If so, we are fellow-members of an organised community. If so, the Universe [*kosmos*] is as it were a state [*polis*]'. *Meditations*, IV.4 (tr. and ed. C. R. Haines; Cambridge, MA, Harvard University Press (Loeb Classical Library); 1916), p. 71. Augustine of Hippo (354–430) spoke of 'mine own kind ... mankind' (*Confessions*, II.iii.5). Alexander (356–323 BCE), the Macedonian warrior-king, had adopted *homonoia* (unity of consciousness) as an ideal of his intensely heterogeneous empire in Greece, Egypt, Persia and Babylon. A source of Stoic cosmopolitanism is in a saying attributed to Socrates and recounted by, among others, Cicero in *Tusculan Disputations* (fn. 54 above), V.xxvii.108, p. 533. When asked which city or state (*civitas*) he belonged to, Socrates said that he was 'a citizen of the world' (*mundanus*, one of the many Latin words which Cicero invented or reinvented to express Greek ideas, in this case the idea of the *kosmopolites*).

[57] Cicero, *De re publica* (fn. 41 above), III.xxii.33, p. 211. '[B]ut out of all the materials of the philosophers' discussions, surely there comes nothing more valuable than the full realization that we are born for Justice, and that right is based, not upon men's opinions, but upon Nature.' 'Now all men have received reason; therefore all men have received Justice.' Cicero, *De legibus* (tr. C. W. Keyes (Cambridge, MA, Harvard University Press (Loeb Classical Library); 1928), I.x.28, I.xi.33, pp. 329, 333. Cicero (106–43 BCE) – practising lawyer, politician, philosopher, polemicist – who had received part of his education from a Stoic teacher, thus managed to bring together various leading aspects of the Greek philosophical inheritance.

strategy was used by Roman Christianity to help to establish the theoretical binding force of an intrinsically universal society. In the second hellenising of Christianity, dominated by Thomas Aquinas in the thirteenth century,[58] natural law was installed as a product of human reason seeking to uncover the 'eternal law' of God's universe, in addition to that part of 'divine law' which had been revealed to believers in the Book of the Bible and the teaching of the Church.[59]

12.54 The social-theoretical effects of the idea of cosmic order would continue to be substantial, not least in the further development of the idea of constitutionalism.

(4) Natural social order

12.55 We have seen that the genealogy of the idea of constitutionalism contains three powerful universalising elements which seem to have a relatively high degree of cultural universality – the idea of a supernatural universal order which can be known through the life-transforming and society-transforming medium of belief; an idea of law which transcends all particular instances of law; an idea of the order of the universe in which the human mind can participate and which can become an ordering principle of individual and social self-ordering.

12.56 The remaining universalising element in the making of the idea of constitutionalism has the highest claim to cultural universality. There cannot be a major religion or any major philosophy which has not treated as a central focus of concern the question of the species-nature of the human species, the problem of what are called *human nature* and the *human condition*. Human self-constituting in consciousness has

[58] The first hellenising was the work of neo-Platonism, of the early Church Councils, and of Clement, Origen and, especially, Augustine of Hippo. Mohammedenism may be seen as a reformation (eighth century) restoring obedience to the Will of God as revealed to and by the Prophet and as recorded in the holy Book of the Koran. The Christian Reformation (fourteenth–sixteenth century) also sought, among other things, to restore Christianity as the unmediated Word of God revealed in the holy Book of the Bible.

[59] In the meantime, natural law had been incorporated formally into the rationalising and codifying of Roman law (including the codes of Justinian, fn. 34 above). Gradually, *ius naturale* took on the character of *lex naturae*, expounded with ever more substantive content, to become, in Aquinas and his followers, a sort of positive law of higher morality. On the medieval development of natural law, see O. Gierke, *Political Theories of the Middle Age* (tr. F. W. Maitland; Cambridge, Cambridge University Press; 1900), pp. 73ff. W. Ullmann, *Principles of Government and Politics in the Middle Ages* (London, Methuen & Co.; 1961), pp. 237ff.

necessarily included a never-ending effort to form a theory of the human self and the self of human society.

'In its (human nature's) reality, it is possible to be good. This is what I mean by saying that it is good. If men do what is not good, it is not the fault of their natural powers.'[60]

'We are not spoken of as good or bad, in respect of our feelings but of our virtues and vices . . . Again, what capacities we have, we have by nature; but it is not nature that makes us good or bad. So, if the virtues are neither feelings nor capacities, it remains that they must be dispositions.'[61]

12.57 It was Aristotle, above all, who ensured that, for the following twenty-three centuries, the human mind would contain as a powerful, and controversial, presence the idea of the naturalness of human society incorporating the natural characteristics of human beings. The reason for this is, no doubt, that Aristotle, although himself a pupil of Plato's, did not derive such an idea as a deduction from any universal metaphysical system but from a feature of his own personality – his own obsession, as we may put it, with the nature of physical reality, especially in its biological aspects. It was an idea which was based on *nature*, not in the sense of ideal universal order, but in the sense of the order which we share with the rest of the living world and the rest of the material world, and hence an idea of nature which is inherently and potentially supra-cultural and supra-temporal. Moving in this different direction, he arrived at a worldview which was as much a mind-made reality (of logic, categories, definitions, abstractions, essences, substances, potentiality, dispositions) as Plato's. But it was a worldview which shared something with that of the contemporary Greek materialist philosophers and scientists and which, following the scientific revolution of our own era, anticipated that other mind-made reality, the reality of the modern natural sciences.

12.58 A contractual model of society was one of the social theories considered by Socrates and the other participants in the discussion in

[60] Mencius (Meng Tzŭ; *c.*371–289), quoted in Fung Yu-lan, *A History of Chinese Philosophy* (fn. 35 above), p. 121. The philosophy associated with the name of Mencius is remarkable in its concern with the connection between individual and social morality which was also a central concern of Plato and Aristotle. For the Heraclitan/Aristotelian naturalism of the so-called Yin-yang school of Chinese philosophy, see *ibid.*, pp. 159ff.

[61] Aristotle, *Nicomachean Ethics* (tr. J. A. K. Thomson: Harmondsworth, Penguin; 1953), II.5, p. 63.

Plato's *Republic*.[62] It was a primary purpose of that dialogue as a whole to show that such a model was wholly inadequate as a theory of human society. But Aristotle rejected the model on quite different grounds from those put forward by Socrates-Plato. Society is not an artificial construction, but a reflection of the species-characteristics of the human animal.

'For what each thing is when fully developed, we call its nature, whether we are speaking of a man, a horse, or a family ... Hence it is evident that the state is a creation of nature, and that man is by nature a political animal.'[63]

'It is clear then that a state is not a mere society, having a common place, established for the prevention of crime and for the sake of exchange. These are conditions without which a state cannot exist; but all of them together do not constitute a state, which is a community of well-being in families and aggregations of families, for the sake of a perfect and self-sufficing life. Hence arise in cities family connections, brotherhoods, common sacrifices, amusements which draw men together. They are created by friendship, for friendship is the motive of society. The end is the good life, and these are the means towards it.'[64]

12.59 Once again, by a quite different route, Aristotle has arrived at a position not wholly remote from Plato's: the idea of the ethical state. That idea, paradoxically, is a special form of contractual theory, a sort of natural social contract, if only in the sense that it postulates the naturalness of a society in which society-members share in, and in the acceptance of, the purpose of society, and hence the implicit terms and conditions of their socialising.[65] It is this idea – of a naturally conditioned social order – which would provide the basis for the flourishing of the idea of constitutionalism in the modern world.

12.60 But the idea of constitutionalism would be in permanent dialectical tension with another powerful idea which would also flourish in the modern world, and which has dominated the development of international society to the present day – the idea of society as an artificial construction constituted by its institutions and by the legally enforced

[62] Theory supported in the discussion by Glaucon: *Republic*, II. 357–67.

[63] Aristotle, *The Politics* (fn. 8 above), I.2, p. 28.

[64] *Ibid.*, III.9, pp. 119–20.

[65] Ancient Chinese ideas of the king as 'son of heaven' and the duty of ancient Indian kings to respect the higher Vedic law meant that the theory of their power was a theory of a sort of metaphysical contract of government.

distribution of social power, an idea which owes much to the experience of Rome.

12.61 Rome, in all its ceaseless constitutional change, was certainly not, and was not conceived of as, a natural society, let alone an ideal society.[66] It was precisely because of its artificiality that law played so great a part in its social self-conceiving.[67] In the absence of a written constitution, it was law (a cloudy mixture of *mos*, *ius* and *lex*) which was used, and abused, to determine the distribution of ultimate social power. In republican Rome (up to 27 BCE), a benevolent version of social theory sustained the idea that power was divided between the people and the senate, with the senate exercising a law-making authority which derived from the ultimate power of the people: *potestas in populo, auctoritas in senatu.*[68] When, in the real constitution (with the coming-to-power of

[66] Greece and Rome are the *Yin* and *Yang* of a certain period of history, as, at other times, Greece and Persia, India and China, the Roman Church and the Holy Roman Empire, the United States and the Soviet Union. The self-admiring self-consciousness of fifth- and fourth-century BCE Greece was itself a transient epiphenomenon rising above chaotic social events, but the charismatic image of Greece, reinforced by the world-dominating success of Alexander the Great, haunted Roman self-consciousness which was obliged to create a story of its own identity (*Romanam condere gentem*, as Virgil said – to construct the Roman race), including an account of Roman history (Livy) which made it at least as remarkable as Greek history and also a legend of the origin of Rome (Virgil's *Aeneid*) in the coming to Italy of one of the Trojan warriors (Aeneas) who had defeated Greece (as told in Homer's *Iliad*).

[67] Greece and Rome are also an example of what we may call the *captor captus* phenomenon, which has occurred on many occasions, where a conqueror is conquered by the culture of the conquered – Greece/Rome, Roman Empire/ Roman Church, Roman Empire/ the barbarian nations of Northern Europe, the Normans/the English. Perhaps the modern European colonial empires were destroyed by an idea (self-determination) which they introduced to the colonised peoples.

The origin of the *captor captus* (the captor captured) metaphor is in the Roman poet Horace (65–8 BCE), *Epistles*, II.1, lines 156–7: 'Graecia capta ferum victorem cepit et artes / Intulit agresti Latio.' ('Captive Greece took captive her fierce conqueror, and introduced her arts into rude Latium [the Latin name for the area of Italy which includes Rome].')

[68] 'Supreme power in the people . . . actual authority in the Senate.' Cicero, *De legibus* (fn. 57 above), III.xii.28, p. 493. In fact, social theory and social reality were always somewhat distant from each other in Rome; fictions and self-serving fantasy served their perennial function of marrying the reality of power to its theory, the real constitution to the ideal constitution. See C. McIlwain, *The Growth of Political Thought in the West. From the Greeks to the End of the Middle Ages* (New York, The Macmillan Company; 1932), pp. 132ff. Cf. R. Syme, *The Roman Revolution* (fn. 41 above), pp. 152ff: 'The realities of Roman politics were overlaid with a double coating of deceit, democratic and aristocratic.' 'Nobody ever sought power for himself and the enslavement of others without invoking *libertas* and such fair names.' 'Fair names' is borrowed from the Roman historian Tacitus (*c*.55–*c*.120): *speciosa nomina.*

Octavian under the grandiose title of Augustus), all political power came to be concentrated in the hands of someone at first called 'the Prince' (*princeps*, the prime member of the senate), the old theory survived for a while, until the first citizen came to be, and to be seen as, an 'Emperor', a mon-arch (single ruler) reminiscent of Egyptian and Persian traditions, uniting *potestas* and *auctoritas* in one person.

12.62 After the collapse of the Roman Empire in the west, the ideal self-constituting of the successor nations was filled with a passionate Roman-style dialectic about the distribution of ultimate legal power. At the highest level the debate was conducted between the head of the Church of Rome (the Pope) and the Emperor of the Franks, who allowed himself to be crowned in Rome by a pope (in the year 800) and whose successors, for 1,000 years, were monarchs of a 'Holy Roman Empire of the German People'. It was a debate which would have the most profound effects on the further development of the idea of constitutionalism. In the thirteenth century, this Roman tradition of constitutionalism, as we may call it, entered into dialectical competition with a revived Aristotelian tradition, as we may call it. From that dialectic there would emerge a succession of new theories about the distribution of *potestas* (government by the people) and *auctoritas* (government of the people). It is a dialectic which must now be raised to the level of the problem of the power and authority of a new type of society – intergovernmental international societies – and the problem of power and authority in the society of all societies, international society.

The naturally artificial[69]

12.63 In England, the medieval dialectic was resolved in a particular, not to say peculiar, way. Thomas Hobbes (1588–1679), geometer of the human psyche, as he might have been pleased to be called, proposed to make a theory of society and government and law on the basis of deductions from realistic axioms about human nature and the human condition. In so doing, he respected one aspect of the Aristotelian tradition and rejected another. And, in so doing, he respected one aspect of the Roman tradition and rejected another. He accepted Aristotle's

[69] There follows an interpretation of historical phenomena of baffling complexity over which turbulent oceans of speculative ink have flowed.

biologism, but rejected the wishful thinking of his practical idealism. He accepted the sovereignty of positive law (*lex*) but rejected the anarchic tendency of *mos* and *ius*. From both traditions he rejected the speculative morass of medieval ideas of limited kingship (*la monarchie tempérée*) – contracts of government, coronation oaths, kings by election, by divine right, or by papal anointing, kings *sub Deo* and/or *sub lege*, kings subject to the *consilium* of leading citizens, kings subject to customary law or the 'ancient liberties of the people', kings subject to the ultimate right of citizens to resist or overthrow tyranny. We post-Marxians may tend to see all such things as a 'coating of deceit' (fn. 68 above), the false consciousness manufactured by the intellectual acolytes of this or that form of entrenched or aspiring social power. For Hobbes, they were simply no basis on which to establish the sovereignty of law. That could only be based on conceptions which transcended all social institutions. He paid ambiguous respect to the ideas of divine order (the ambiguity leading to his being denounced as an atheist) and natural law (which he saw as the law of our biological nature rather than as a mystic communing of human reason with cosmic order). But the sovereignty of law can only be securely founded on consideration of the species-characteristics of the human species. Society is an artificial construction imposed by biological necessity, and law is sovereign because it is the voice of natural necessity.

12.64 To reject Aristotelian biologism and yet to believe in the naturalness of society requires an heroic effort of social metaphysics, an effort which we associate with the name, and the ramshackle social philosophy, of John Locke (1632–1704). A pre-societal natural legal system, the Will of God, social teleology, natural human sociability, pre-societal constitutional sagacity, a constitutionally limited sovereign, sovereign law made and enforced by means of a confusion of separated legal powers, *potestas* restored to the people and *auctoritas* to the legislative assembly, the will of the representative majority, a remote right of popular resistance and revolt – the Lockeian constitutionalist cocktail contained something of everything, something for everybody. It was an ironical, almost comical, product of millennia of passionate theoretical and practical human social experience.[70] Locke's syncretism managed

[70] The third naturalist-metaphysical theory (Jean-Jacques Rousseau; 1712–78) showed no less conceptual ingenuity, fusing power and authority in the idea of the General Will, and adding

to combine something taken from all four elements of the idea of constitutionalism as we have analysed it. God, the idea of law, natural law, natural social order – they were all present, albeit in a somewhat quixotic form.

12.65 The fact that such ideas arose within the ideal self-constituting of England seems to be attributable, among other things, to a particular social phenomenon – that the profession and the practice of the law acquired a status in medieval and post-medieval England which made it a countervailing social power in relation to the monarch and the royal court. The Continental European phenomena of revived Roman law and feudalism took only tenuous hold in medieval England.[71] A Roman obsession with the transcendental society-forming power of law (especially the *ius* of the common law) provided a Roman-style illusion of constitutionalism, punctuated by occasional more or less constitutional *leges*, including the legislative affirmations of *Magna Carta* (1215), which itself makes use of the *ius*-like term *lex terrae* (law of the land). When sixteenth-century monarchs sought to emulate the power and the splendour of Continental monarchs, the idea of law played a major part in the long struggle in the real-constitution to put an end to such ambitions. The fact, and not merely the idea, of law also played a role in the economic transformation which culminated in the development of capitalist society in England.[72]

a daring echo of Platonic idealism, in the idea that society so constituted must be seen, and can only be justified, as an instrument of human enlightenment and self-perfecting.

[71] The Norman-French invasion (1066) modified but did not displace the existing customary law system, its main effect being a partial feudalising of land law. See F. Barlow, *The Feudal Kingdom of England 1042–1216* (London, Longmans; 1955/1961), ch. 1. McIlwain, *Constitutionalism* (fn. 42 above), calls it 'the riddle of our medieval constitution' – was the English monarchy absolutist or constitutionalist? He says that the first use of the English word 'constitution' in the modern sense was in 1610 (p. 27).

[72] 'The first country in modern times to reach a high level of capitalistic development, i.e. England, thus preserved a less rational and less bureaucratic legal system. That capitalism could nevertheless make its way so well in England was largely because the court system and trial procedure amounted until well into the modern age to a denial of justice to the economically weaker groups.' M. Weber, in M. Rheinstein, *Max Weber on Law in Economy and Society* (Cambridge, MA, Harvard University Press; 1954), p. 354. Hegel took the view (*Philosophy of Right*, § 211, comment) that the monstrous confusion of uncodified English law not only made judges into legislators but prevented rational universalising. However, he accepted (*Philosophy of Mind*, § 394) that the fact that the English recognise the rational in the form of individuality rather than universality made for tenacity in the pursuit of individual rights and, perhaps, accounted for 'the conspicuous aptitude of the English for trade'.

Three mythologies and a heresy

12.66 The pure theories sustaining the ideas of Representative Democracy and *Laissez Faire* Economics acquired charismatic power through their practical-theory application in many countries, helping to transform Old Regimes, as it was said, into New Regimes, in the name of something which was given the seductive brand-name of Modernity.[73] At the same time, they became subject to intellectual fall-out from the force-field conventionally referred to as the eighteenth-century Enlightenment in Western Europe, with profound consequences for the further evolution of the perennial and universal idea of constitutionalism. The idea of constitutionalism came to be confused with the idea of democracy.[74] Modernity (democracy and capitalism) came to be seen as the beginning of 'the end of history'. International society was left irredeemably anomalous.

12.67 These developments led to a new kind of absolutism, the absolute power of society, not only the unlimited power of the public realm (through law and administration) over the everyday life of the citizens, but the total power of society over consciousness. The new totalitarianism included the internalising of the transcendental. Democracy and capitalism seem to contain their idea of themselves. They seem to be the cause and effect of their own values and purposes. Whatever remains of the transcendental (in religion or philosophy) is seen merely as a socially tolerated contingency. Constitutionalism, on the other hand, as we have analysed it, depends on a separation between the social actual and the social ideal, the social actual being profoundly affected by the ideal which haunts it as judge of social actuality, mediator of social struggle, attractive force of social progress, interceding between individual and social consciousness in the name of a form of order which transcends both, making the perennial and the universal of human existence into a permanent presence within the transient and the particular. Within the idea of constitutionalism, it is the function of the ideal to be other than the actual.

[73] The capitalising of terms used in this and the next sentence indicates that they stand for ideas which are themselves tendentious socially constructed phenomena.

[74] For an incorporating of the English tradition of constitutional monarchy into the ideal self-constituting of the society of the United States of America, see E. S. Corwin, 'The "higher law" background of American constitutional law', in 42 *Harvard Law Review* (1928–9), pp. 149ff. and 365ff.

12.68 The de-transcendentalising of the social order, in certain countries over recent centuries, was re-enforced by three intelligent but disturbing mythologies – Naturalism, Realism, Pragmatism – by-products of the eighteenth-century Enlightenment. They have had powerful effects on pure and practical social theory in those societies, but their most important effect is at the level of transcendental theory, that is to say, in relation to our understanding of the mental processes through which humanity makes and remakes itself in consciousness, our idea of what we can say about ourselves.[75]

12.69 *Naturalism*, the Anglo-French ideology, as we may call it, is the idea that human phenomena can be assimilated to natural phenomena, and hence, inter alia, that appropriate investigation may discover their *causes*.[76] When this idea is added to the irreversible Marxian enlightenment that socially significant ideas are socially constructed and the Freudian enlightenment that human consciousness is determined or conditioned by its unconscious vector, then humanity's relationship to its own mental products – including its conception of knowledge, values, ideals, the transcendental and, not least, of constitutionalism – is profoundly modified.

12.70 *Realism*, the German ideology, as we may call it, is the idea that an entity produced by human consciousness (an *ens rationis* – people, nation, state, race, market, public opinion) has characteristics analogous to those of entities in the natural world, including its own history, its own potentialities, its own power over human consciousness.[77] Such an idea inevitably tends to disempower human consciousness in relation to its own products, alienating itself from itself, greatly complicating humanity's moral responsibility for its own products.[78]

[75] See fn. 2 above.

[76] The sub-title of D. Hume's *Treatise on Human Nature* (1748) is *An Attempt to Introduce the Experimental Method of Reasoning into Moral Subjects*. The challenge was taken up: by Saint-Simon, who proposed as new intellectual disciplines 'social physiology' and 'political science'; by Comte, who proposed 'social physics' and 'sociology'; by J. S. Mill, who proposed 'moral sciences'. For Hume's friend, Adam Smith, on the other hand, all systems of ideas (including the Newtonian system of the universe, as well as social and moral philosophies) are 'imaginary machines', 'mere inventions of the imagination'. A. Smith, 'The history of astronomy', in *Essays on Philosophical Subjects* (eds W. P. D. Wightman and J. C. Bryce: Oxford, Clarendon Press; 1980), pp. 31–105, at pp. 66, 105.

[77] The dispute between so-called 'realists' and so-called 'nominalists' is as old as philosophy. Sixteen centuries before William of Ockham and twenty-three centuries before Logical Positivism, Diogenes the Cynic said that he could see a table but not tableness (*trapezotes*).

[78] See further in ch. 1 above.

12.71 *Pragmatism*, the American (United States) ideology, as we may call it, is the idea that there is not, and cannot be, a hierarchy of ideas, with 'higher-level' ideas determining the validity, or otherwise controlling the significance, of lower-level ideas.[79] The validity and the significance of ideas can only be determined by the same process by which all socially significant ideas are created and controlled, through social interaction among the makers and users of ideas – even if, in the course of that process, some ideas are proposed and accepted as having a higher-level status (for example: constitutional values, intellectual objectivity, fairness, moral seriousness . . .).[80] Such an unphilosophy or anti-philosophy undermines rather fundamentally the self-confidence of human consciousness in saying anything *about itself*.

12.72 These movements of thought may be characterised as mythologies because, like the pre-philosophical Olympian mythology of pre-classical Greece, they disempower in seeming to empower. They involve a primitive surrender to a fatality which is made by humans but is beyond human control – ancient Greek *moira* or Latin *fortuna* – the state, the market, consensus. In the twentieth century, they have been re-enforced in their social effect by the rise of a new form of magic – science and engineering – whose world-changing power is a product of human consciousness but whose effects are inescapable but are incomprehensible to most people. And they have been assisted by the self-disarming of much of professional philosophy, through those sets of ideas (logical positivism, phenomenology, analytical philosophy, neo-pragmatism) which seem to resign themselves to an idea of philosophy as nothing more than 'talk about talk'.[81]

[79] Contradicting all those foundational systems within the philosophical tradition which purport to have such an effect – logic, epistemology, moral philosophy, transcendentalism of all kinds.

[80] Jürgen Habermas has proposed to reconstruct some sort of foundation for pragmatic discourse from within pragmatic discourse itself. See *The Theory of Communicative Action* (tr. T. McCarthy; vol. I: *Reason and the Rationalization of Society* (London, Heinemann; 1984; republished, Cambridge, Polity; 1994); vol. II: *Lifeworld and System: A Critique of Functional Reason* (Cambridge, Polity; 1987)). The German title of vol. I is more accurate: *Handlungsrationalität und gesellschaftliche Rationalisierung* (Action-rationality and Social Rationalising). The task is to find a foundation for 'argumentative speech' in 'good reasons or grounds'. See D. Ingram, *Habermas and the Dialectic of Reason* (New Haven, Yale University Press; 1987), esp. ch. 4.

[81] A. J. Ayer, 'Philosophy and Language', in *Clarity is not Enough. Essays in Criticism of Linguistic Philosophy* (ed. H. D. Lewis; London, George Allen & Unwin; 1963), pp. 401–28, at p. 403. R. Rorty recommends that we should 'see keeping a conversation going as a sufficient

12.73 They have also been joined by an idea which has particular relevance to the significance of the idea of constitutionalism. That idea, which we may associate particularly with the name of Max Weber, suggests that the question of the *legitimacy* of social systems is a matter which can be rationally determined.[82] This is a heresy in relation to the orthodox belief-systems of democracy and capitalism, which contain internal (non-transcendental) grounds of self-identifying and self-judging which function vigorously as *values*, their own totalitarian values, and not merely as rational models of social reality. In relation to the perennial and universal idea and ideal of constitutionalism, the self-justifying of a social system is a matter which is neither rationally determined from outside the system nor determined merely by reference to the internal values of the system.

The generic principles of constitutionalism

12.74 It has been the purpose of the present study to show that, given the perennial and universal character of the idea and ideal of constitutionalism, it is available to *social philosophy*[83] as a way of understanding the self-constituting of those societies which are intergovernmental international organisations, and hence that it is available to form part of the self-creating *theory*[84] of the self-constituting of actual intergovernmental organisations within the self-constituting of the society of the whole human race, the society of all societies.

12.75 Our survey of the genetics and the genealogy of the idea and ideal of constitutionalism has also sought to identify constitutionalism conceptually as something which is seen, from the point of view of a given

aim of philosophy' and 'see wisdom as consisting in the ability to sustain a conversation', abandoning the futile effort, even that of Habermas, to find an epistemological basis for objectivity. R. Rorty, *Philosophy and the Mirror of Nature* (Princeton, Princeton University Press; 1979), p. 378. Such ideas were classified as 'negative dogmatism' by Sextus Empiricus (late second century) in his survey of the various schools of philosophical scepticism.

82 The point of departure is in J.-J. Rousseau: 'How did this change [the substitution of social obligation for natural freedom] come about? I do not know. What can make it legitimate? That question I think I can answer.' *Social Contract* (tr. G. D. H. Cole; London, J. M. Dent & Sons; 1913/1973) I.1, p. 165. Weber's idea of 'legitimacy' is of a justificatory theory of social domination (*Herrschaft*), whereas Rousseau, like Marx, sought to find a way of overcoming theoretically, and hence practically, the dehumanising-through-alienation of the citizen in society. Liberal-democratic theory is not a theory of domination but of *self*-government, whatever the real and legal conditions of actual liberal-democratic societies may be.

83 'Social philosophy' in the sense proposed at § 12.11 above.

84 'Theory' in the sense indicated at fn. 1 above.

society, as transcending the self-creating of that society, but which acts as an immanent force within its own ideal self-constituting. We have suggested that the idea might be specified conceptually in relation to other foundational ideas and ideals of social self-constituting: as something less than the Will of God and more than the General Will, something more than the Rule of Law and less than Natural Law. It remains to specify the structural-systematic implications of constitutionalism as it forms part of the theory of a society, to postulate its social-genetic programme, its inherent social reality-forming potentiality.

12.76 The logical structure of the idea is also a structural metaphysics of the societies in whose theories it is present. Those theories, as the theories of actual societies, not only condition the given society's understanding of its own self-constituting. They also influence the most general organisation of the social structures and systems which distribute and regulate all forms of social power and, in particular, the social power which takes the form of law. We may distil the logical-metaphysical implications of the perennial and universal idea and ideal of constitutionalism into a set of *generic principles.*[85]

Principle of *integration.* Law is an integral part of the total social process of a society, inseparable from the rest of the society's self-constituting.

Principle of *transformation.* Law is dynamic, not a thing but a process of ceaseless social self-transforming.

Principle of *delegation.* All legal power is power delegated by society. To claim to exercise legal power is to acknowledge the source of the power.

Principle of *the intrinsic limitation of power.* All legal power is limited by the terms of its delegation by society.

Principle of *the supremacy of law.* All social power is under the law, since the function of law is to transform social power into the particular form of law.

Principle of *the supremacy of the social interest.* All legal power is power delegated by society in the social interest and hence is to be exercised to serve the social interest.

Principle of *social responsibility.* The exercise of all social power, including legal power, is accountable to society which conferred the power.

[85] For further discussion, see *Eunomia*, ch. 11.

12.77 In the application of each of these principles to intergovernmental organisations, the superordinate society in question is the international society of the whole human race, the society of all societies. By incorporating such principles in their ideal self-constituting, and by actualising them in their real and legal self-constituting, intergovernmental organisations will participate in a perennial and universal tradition of human social self-constituting, a tradition which may at last find its natural fulfilment at the level of the society of all-humanity.

The constitutionalising of intergovernmental organisations: *captor captus*[86]

12.78 Since intergovernmental organisations are international *societies*, they are constituted in the manner of the self-constituting of all societies. Because they are *intergovernmental* societies, they cannot escape the potentiality of the universal and perennial idea and ideal of constitutionalism. To claim to act as a government is to claim to exercise public-realm social power, that is to say, power which is delegated by society to be exercised in the public interest. To claim to exercise public-realm power is to acknowledge the theoretical conditions which are inherent in the power, the conditions which the ideal constitution of the given society imposes in conferring such power, conditions which are contained in that society's theories of its self-constituting, including conditions for justifying all public-realm power and conditions concerning the determination of the public interest. Constitutionalism may be an actual theory, and is always a potential theory, of the ideal self-constituting of any society.

12.79 When a government exercises public-realm power externally, in relation to other governments, including in the forming of intergovernmental societies, it carries with it the constitutional conditions on the exercise of that power. To act as a government externally, on behalf of a given society, is to claim to act as the holder of public-realm powers which have been conferred in the self-constituting of that society.

12.80 The coming-to-consciousness in international society of the idea and ideal of constitutionalism is thus a reintegration of the theoretical coherence of an aspect of the exercise of public-realm power by

[86] See fn. 67 above.

governments, the removal of a self-contradiction in the case of those societies which acknowledge constitutionalism within their own theories, and a self-redeeming in the case of other societies. Needless to say, in either case there are obstacles in the way of a self-reconceiving of intergovernmental societies at the beginning of the twenty-first century. Intergovernmental societies have existed, throughout the twentieth century, in a primitive, old-regime international society, theoretically isolated from national constitutional systems, in a sort of constitutional wasteland or Empty Quarter. They have allowed the controllers of the national public realms to act in relation to each other like unconstitutional monarchs, exercising a combined monarchy limited only by the systematic conditions which they themselves have accepted. In intergovernmental societies in their present form, *auctoritas* and *potestas* are fused, a self-conferred and self-regulated power which is subject to the *consilium* of other social actors, including the people and the peoples of the world and their non-governmental representatives, to a degree varying from small to negligible.

12.81 As more and more of the responsibility of the national public realms is exteriorised and communalised in what we may call international intergovernment, the more urgent becomes the problem of its theoretical justification, in terms of the ideals not merely of this or that subordinate culture, however dominant in the actual self-constituting of international society, but in relation to all the cultures which participate in international society.

12.82 For those who look to a new kind of future for international intergovernment within a new kind of international society, the society of all-humanity, the necessary theoretical revolution must proceed from the starting-point of the perennial and universal idea of constitutionalism, whose outline we have attempted to sketch in the present study, an idea inherently and necessarily suited to be an idea and an ideal within the ideal self-constituting of international society, the society of all societies. The actual form which a theory of constitutionalism will take, within the actual development of international society hereafter, is something which will be determined dialectically in the total process of the self-constituting, ideal and real and legal, of the international society of the twenty-first century.

13

International law and the international *Hofmafia*

Towards a sociology of diplomacy

Representative aristocracy – The Great Game – Public Law – The New Law of Nations – The new aristocracy

The present state of international society is a product of its past states. But who was responsible for making the past of international society? It was a clique of cliques, a conspiracy of one small part of the governing classes of those national societies which used diplomacy and war as the continuation of crude politics by other means.

The externalising of their internal social power somehow managed to override the profound differences of their national social systems, their profoundly different forms and degrees of social development, so that absolutist monarchies and republican city-states, and all intervening social forms, could interact in a game in which they were also the masters of the rules of the game (the so-called law of nations). They even purported to recognise rules about war (the mass murder of human beings and the mass destruction of property).

Still more mysteriously, the game of externalised social power somehow managed to survive revolutionary transformations within some of the national societies, so that an international governmental absolutism continued, unabated and unabashed, while very new social theory and social practice transformed every other aspect of the holding and exercise of public power.

Representative aristocracy

13.1 '[T]he Sieur Clement Venceslas Lothaire, Prince of Metternich-Winneburg-Ochsenhausen, Knight of the Golden Fleece, Grand Cross of the Royal Order of St Stephen, Knight of the Orders of St Andrew, of St Alexander-Newsky, and of St Anne of the First Class, Grand Cordon of the Legion of Honour, Knight of the Order of the Elephant, of the Supreme Order of the Annunciation, of the Black Eagle and the Red Eagle, of the Seraphim, of St Joseph of Tuscany, of St Hubert, of the Golden Eagle of Wurtemberg, of Fidelity of Baden, of St John of Jerusalem, and of several others; Chancellor of the Military Order of Maria-Theresa, Trustee of the Academy of Fine Arts, Chamberlain, Privy Councillor of His Majesty the Emperor of Austria, King of Hungary and Bohemia, his Minister of State, of Conferences, and of Foreign Affairs.'[1]

13.2 The principal Plenipotentiary of the King of France and Navarre to the Congress of Vienna was another self-conscious aristocrat, one who claimed a nobility more ancient and more interesting than that of Metternich. 'The Sieur Charles Maurice de Talleyrand-Périgord, Prince of Talleyrand, Peer of France.' Thus did the relentlessly self-recreating Talleyrand choose to identify himself on this occasion. His list of French and foreign honours ends tantalisingly with 'the Order of the Sun of Persia, etc., etc., etc.' The Plenipotentiaries of His Majesty the King of the United Kingdom of Britain and Ireland included 'the Right Honourable Robert Stewart, Viscount Castlereagh', and 'the Most Excellent and Most Illustrious Lord Arthur Wellesley, Duke, Marquess, and Earl of Wellington, Marquess of Douro, Viscount Wellington of Talavera and of Wellington . . . Duke of Vittoria, Marquis of Torres Vedras, Count of Vimeira in Portugal.' The list of his distinctions also ends with a bathetic 'etc., etc., etc.' The other British Plenipotentiaries were the Earl of Clancarty, Earl Cathcart and Lord Stewart.

13.3 Who were such people? Whom and what did they represent? The *Règlement* on the Precedence of Diplomatic Agents, also adopted at the Congress of Vienna (19 March 1815), provided that only the first class of *Employés Diplomatiques*, namely, Ambassadors, Legates and Nuncios, have *le Caractère représentatif*.[2] The representative character of the plenipotentiaries at the Congress of Vienna was no doubt beyond question as a matter of diplomatic convention, but their representative character as a matter of social fact is a much more complex matter.

[1] Act of the Congress of Vienna, 9 June 1815, list of plenipotentiaries (present author's translation), in C. Parry, *The Consolidated Treaty Series* (Dobbs Ferry, NY, Oceana Publications Inc.; 1969), LXIV, pp. 454–5.

[2] *Ibid.*, pp. 2–3.

13.4 Every human being has a worldview, a view of the world seen from a unique perspective, a reality-for-oneself. The worldview of the inhabitants of a world mapped and measured by the Almanach de Gotha is a consciousness of belonging to a race apart, a chosen people. Metternich, Talleyrand, Castlereagh and Wellington, for all the differences of their social status and life-experience, shared an old-regime aristocratic worldview, a sense of the exceptional rights and responsibilities attaching to their exceptional social status, including especially their natural right and responsibility to determine the lives of whole nations. But they shared also a sense that they were living in the last days of the old social order which they and their kind had dominated. A new order of things (to adopt the Roman formula for revolutionary change) was arising out of the disasters of war and revolution, a new world in which the right to govern the lives of others seemed, as always, a precarious prize to be won in an obscure game of chance, but, thanks to the French Revolution, it had clearly become a new kind of game with new kinds of players. Metternich (1773–1859; Austrian Foreign Minister 1809–48), *magister ludorum* of the Congress of Vienna, who 'swam as happily as a fish in a glittering pool',[3] truculent defender of the old order and suave master of the old diplomacy, nevertheless concluded, as early as 1820, that his life had 'coincided with a terrible time', that he had been born either too soon or too late, condemned to perform the task of shoring up 'crumbling buildings'. 'I should have been born in 1900 and had the twentieth century ahead of me.'[4]

13.5 The Congress of Vienna was the last great party of the old order dancing on its own grave. It epitomised the best and the worst of the old order of international government. It contained the seeds of that form of international government which has dominated human social development from 1815 to the present day, the government of a form of international polity which may soon be surpassed.

13.6 Aristocratic international government had been well adapted to the old social order. Its greatest practitioners – Wolsey, Richelieu, Metternich, Bismarck – were not merely courtiers or diplomatists nor even merely courtier-diplomatists. They were international politicians.

[3] H. Treitschke, quoted in A. Milne, *Metternich* (London, University of London Press; 1975), p. 18.

[4] Quoted in F. Herre, *Metternich. Staatsmann des Friedens* (Köln, Verlag Kiepenhauer & Witsch; 1983), p. 360.

The stage of their political activity and their political ambitions was the great theatre of the world, that is to say, all-Europe and Europe's interests in the rest of the world. It is a mistake to suppose that they were merely conducting the external relations of their respective countries, that they were merely playing the game of diplomacy. They were managing the political and social development of their countries in a market-place of the most intense cultural, political, social and economic competition. The internal and the external realms were in an inseparable continuum, each an aspect of the other. To survive and prosper as a separate national identity and a separate political and economic entity was a particular mode of co-existing with other identities and entities. The inescapable presence of many others was a permanent part of the forming of the tenuous national self.

13.7 Cardinal Wolsey (1471–1530), himself of humble origin, managed to turn himself into a second self of the English king, combining his own shamelessly ambitious and obsessively industrious personality with that of his new-style Renaissance monarch (Henry VIII), a monarch who was himself a monster of dissolute energy, defining himself, and hence the English nation, in competition with monarchs and nations of much greater market-power. But Wolsey had a second power-base and a second horizon of ambition. He was a prince of the Church, with a distant eye on the possibility of himself becoming Pope. Wolsey sought to manage the politics of all-Europe, a Europe full of other ambitious and erratic monarchs and courtiers, not least King Francis I of France and the Emperor Charles V. His manoeuvres and machinations were only sometimes successful, but he was struggling to manage an immensely complex and dynamic international situation, setting patterns of international politics which survive to the present day.[5]

13.8 When power of personality is combined with a powerful ideology, the combination is liable to be much more powerful than mere personal ambition. Cardinal Richelieu (1585–1642) was yet another of the formidable politician-clerics who have played so large a part in the history of European politics. But, unlike Wolsey, he had an all-consuming belief. He believed in France. He devoted the power of his mind and his will to the actualising of his idea of France, an idea embodied in the

[5] See S. J. Gunn, 'Wolsey's foreign policy and the domestic crisis of 1527–8', in *Cardinal Wolsey. Church, State and Art* (eds S. J. Gunn and P. G. Lindley; Cambridge, Cambridge University Press; 1991), pp. 149–77, and the editors' Introduction, pp. 1–53.

absolute sovereignty of the French monarchy. His diplomacy was not the conduct of the external relations of France. It was a continuation of the self-constituting of France by other means. Above all, it was a post-Reformation self-constituting, a struggle to reintegrate a society, and a European society of societies, which had been torn apart by the disintegration of western Christianity.[6]

13.9 It is an irony of the aristocratic old order that such figures of great power may be said to have had a truly representative character. They embodied the internal order of their respective societies, and they embodied the reality of the co-existence of those societies. The old diplomacy used the generic term 'Power' (*puissance*) to reflect the extraordinary diversity of the polities participating in the business of self-constituting through competitive co-existence, ranging from the most pompous monarchies to the most republican of city-states, and including the supra-national institution and agencies of the Church of Rome and the multinational institution of the Holy Roman Empire. International co-existence generated a sort of virtual court of the courts, a court without frontiers, an invisible *Hof* of the *Höfen*, in which cardinals and bishops and ambassadors, resident and ad hoc, and soldiers of fortune of all kinds could mingle with the courtiers of countless national courts of every degree of political significance and insignificance. There were no rules about who could participate in the international court of courts but, as at Versailles or Schönbrunn or Potsdam or St Petersburg, mere presence as part of what we may call the international *Hofmafia*[7] did not confer any automatic degree of power or influence or even of prestige. Within the old aristocracy there was, and still is, an acute sense of delightful and painful inter-familial inequalities. The world of the old diplomacy was no less fiercely realistic about the relative powers of the various Powers.[8]

[6] On the centrality of the religious question in Richelieu's foreign policy, see M. Carmona, *Richelieu. L'ambition et le pouvoir* (Paris, Fayard; 1983), pp. 274–7. On Richelieu's legacy, see *ibid.*, pp. 716ff.

[7] The word *Hofmafia* (court-mafia) is borrowed from A. Wheatcroft, *The Habsburgs. Embodying Empire* (London, Penguin; 1995), p. 248.

[8] 'We cannot . . . have European affairs decided by the Princes of Lippe and Lichtenstein,' said the Prussian representative Hardenburg, when Talleyrand was seeking to insinuate France into the inner council of the leading powers by posing as the champion of the minor powers. Comte de Saint-Aulaire, *Talleyrand* (tr. G. F. Lees and F. J. Stephens; London, Macmillan & Co.; 1937), pp. 263–4.

13.10 The orientalising and medievalising of the French monarchy, culminating in the megalomania of the Palace of Versailles and the crazily fastidious rituals of French court-life, was a reasonable plan of action to consolidate a difficult polity condemned to exist in a geographic and political situation which was, and always would be, precarious. The misfortune was that the idea of France became the most seductive of all courtly brand-images. It misled the rulers and the courtiers of countless other polities into a fantasy-world of micro-Frenchism, managing and mismanaging their randomly accumulated domains from their mini-Versailles. The Reformation had conferred on the lesser monarchs and the princelings of Northern Europe, including the English King, a delightful opportunity for unjust and fortuitous enrichment, at the expense of the Church of Rome, a crude redistribution of wealth perfumed with an odour of hypocritical sanctity. French absolutism was a counter-revolution, undoing the revolutionary potentiality of Renaissance humanism. To the European *Hofmafia* it was a stay of execution and an incitement to self-justification and self-indulgence.

The Great Game

13.11 So long as international society was nothing more than the co-existence of diverse polities competing in their self-constituting, international government necessarily reflected the dominant ideas, philosophical and political, of that self-constituting. The old aristocratic international order was a world still haunted by the medieval world of competitive pomp and ceremony, in which war and diplomacy were the games which kings and their courtiers played. The making of a nation was the making of a brand.[9] Louis XIV was simply the most outrageously successful of the masters of collective illusion, a virtuoso in the personifying of the 'state', that last great masterwork of the medieval courtly imagination. The personifying of the state, in the internal sense, might take the absolutist form proposed by Bodin or the collectivist form proposed by Hobbes, but, in either form, it was a convenient generic conception, consistent with unlimited diversity of actual forms of internal social order, and consistent with extreme inequality in the capacity of

[9] The conferring of pseudo-chivalric orders (the Garter, the Golden Fleece, de l'Esprit, and the countless etc., etc., etc. orders) was, and is, the licensing of a courtly trade-mark.

individual nations to control or even influence the external conditions of their social self-constituting.

13.12 Within the aristocratic old order of Europe, treaties had always been a useful instrument of diplomacy – to tie down the troublesome, to intimidate third parties, to deceive the unwary, to create a temporary illusion of stability, even occasionally to further objectives of common interest (for example, the series of commercial treaties between France and England from the days of Richelieu onwards).[10] The only effective rules of the aristocratic game were unenacted minimum conditions of co-existence, a network of understandings and expectations, rules of international competition, the product of centuries, if not millennia, of chaotic but instructive experience, only sporadically and tenuously conceived of as *legal* rules.

13.13 Such a shared consciousness was a conservative constitutionalism characteristic of an aristocratic ruling class. There was a background consciousness of 'the peace', in the medieval legal sense – *la paix* (justices of the peace, breach of the peace) – and a rudimentary value-system which was neither communitarian nor merely amoral. It was a transnational class-consciousness, a shared commitment to stability as the necessary basis for the continued enjoyment of social privilege, and a shared understanding of the idea of machiavellian princely *virtù*, the normal and necessary self-seeking of, and on behalf of, the first servant of the state (to borrow Frederick the Great's tiresome formula), a combination of pragmatic self-interest and half-remembered notions of chivalry.

13.14 A succession of great crises had threatened to unsettle the unwritten constitution of Europe, beginning with the century-long struggle caused by the Reformation, that is to say, by the disintegration of the supranational social system of the Church of Rome. The great treaty settlements (Westphalia 1648, Utrecht 1713, Vienna 1815) were restabilising events, re-establishing the European constitutional order, the dialectical resolution of stability and change. The central feature of each crisis, and hence of each dialectical reconstituting, was the problem of the relationship between internal politics and external politics. And the same problem and the same task of conservative reconstituting would

[10] Of the treaty of 1786 Talleyrand said: 'it reflects those liberal principles which are appropriate to great nations and from which France . . . would gain the most if they were universally adopted in the commercial world.' G. A. Morlot and J. Happert, *Talleyrand – une mystification historique* (Paris, H. Veyrier; 1991), p. 70.

be manifested in the making of the League of Nations (1919) the United Nations (1945) and the European Union (from 1952).

13.15 The consequences of the French Revolution were remarkably similar to those of the Reformation. The Reformation had been a transformatory event within Europe, as a society of societies, and within each separate society, leading to extremes of both intra-national and international violence. Like the Reformation, the French Revolution, and its Napoleonic sequel, challenged the old constitutional order of Europe not only by the force of arms but also by the force of ideas.[11]

13.16 Already in 1792 the British government analysed the double nature of the challenge, as evidenced by the decree of the French National Convention of 19 November, 'in the expressions of which all England saw the formal declaration of a design to extend universally the new principles of government adopted in France, and to encourage disorder and revolt in all countries, even in those which are natural'.[12] 'England will never consent that France shall arrogate the power of annulling at her pleasure, and under the pretence of a pretended natural right, of which she makes herself the only judge, the political system of Europe, established by solemn treaties, and guaranteed by the consent of all the powers.'[13]

13.17 The revolutionary challenge of the French Revolution was a challenge to the constitutional structure of the old aristocratic

[11] 'The present revolution in France . . . is a revolution of doctrine and theoretic dogma . . . The last revolution of doctrine and theory which has happened in Europe is the Reformation . . . [The effect of the Reformation] was to introduce other interest in all countries than those which arose from their locality and natural circumstances.' E. Burke, *Thoughts on French Affairs* (1791) (London, Dent (Everyman's Library); 1910), p. 288. De Tocqueville took the same view. '[As a result of the Reformation], former interests were superseded by new interests, territorial disputes by conflicts over moral issues, and all the old notions of diplomacy were thrown into the melting-pot – much to the horror and dismay of the professional politicians of the age. Precisely the same thing happened in Europe after 1789. Thus the French Revolution, though ostensibly political in origin, functioned on the lines, and assumed many of the aspects, of a religious revolution.' A. de Tocqueville, *The Old Regime and the French Revolution* (1856) (Garden City, NY, Anchor Books; 1955), p. 71.

[12] H. Temperley and L. Penson, *Foundations of British Foreign Policy 1792–1902* (Cambridge, Cambridge University Press; 1938), p. 4.

[13] *Ibid.*, p. 7. We may recall the reverse situation, namely, Cardinal Mazarin's concern in 1646 that the British monarchy would be replaced by a republic. He instructed the French Ambassador 'to bring into play every sort of contrivance and adopt every kind of expedient . . . to avert so great a calamity'. J. R. Seeley, *The Growth of British Policy* (Cambridge, Cambridge University Press; 1903), pp. 419–21.

international order in the sense that it threatened to unsettle fundamentally and irremediably the two axes or dimensions of that order – the horizontal axis of the international oligarchy of 'the powers' and the vertical axis of the interface between the internal and the international.

Public Law

13.18 In a communication of 19 January 1805 to the Czar of Russia, the British Prime Minister outlined British war aims. At the end of the war it would be necessary 'to form a Treaty to which all the principal Powers of Europe should be Parties, by which their respective Rights and Possessions, as they then have been established, shall be fixed and recognized . . . It should re-establish a general and comprehensive system of Public Law in Europe, and provide, as far as possible, for repressing future attempts to disturb the general tranquillity, and above all, for restraining any projects of Aggrandizement and Ambition similar to those which have produced all the Calamities inflicted on Europe since the disastrous aera of the French Revolution.'[14]

13.19 The strange expression 'Public Law in Europe' was certainly not a reference to international law, in the modern sense. It was a reference to a central structural feature of the old international order, namely, its horizontal axis. The 'Game of Publick Safety' as Castlereagh would call it in a celebrated state-paper of 1820,[15] was the management of international politics on the basis of an oligarchy of 'the powers'. In the same note of 1805, Pitt called for 'the closest Union of Councils and Concert of Measures' to manage the restored Public Law of Europe.[16] Oligarchy in the form of 'union' and 'concert' would reappear in the Council of the League of Nations, the Security Council of the United Nations, and the Council of the European Union. The Vienna constitutional structure met the challenge of the French Revolution to the horizontal aspect of the old aristocratic order of war and diplomacy. There remained the problem of the vertical axis, the relationship of international politics to internal politics.

13.20 The expression 'public law' became a *Leitmotiv* of the Congress of Vienna, daringly appropriated by Talleyrand himself, who had so

[14] Temperley and Penson, *Foundations* (fn. 12 above), p. 18.
[15] *Ibid.*, pp. 48–63, at p. 59. [16] *Ibid.*, p. 11.

recently been a close collaborator of the greatest of the violators of that 'public law'.[17] But whereas the British aristocratic view of constitutional development had been, for a thousand years, a never-ending struggle to incorporate social change into the fabric of social stability, at Vienna the expression began to be confused in the minds of the continental *Hofmafia* with the idea of 'legitimacy', which was something much closer to defending, by force if necessary, the internal political status quo of the old aristocratic constitutional order, a holy alliance to defend the past against the future.[18]

13.21 Lord Castlereagh put into words a perennial British general policy of opposing all general policies in the field of international affairs.

'The principle of one State interfering by force in the internal affairs of another, in order to enforce obedience to the governing authority, is always a question of the greatest possible moral as well as political delicacy . . . [T]o generalize such a principle and to think of reducing it to a System, or to impose it as an obligation, is a Scheme utterly impracticable and objectionable . . . No Country having a Representative System of Government could act upon it, – and the sooner such a Doctrine shall be distinctly abjured as forming in any Degree the Basis of our Alliance, the better.'[19]

'One of the general principles which Her Majesty's Government wish to observe as a guide for their conduct in dealing with the relations between England and other States, is, that changes which foreign Nations may chuse to make in their internal Constitution and form of Government, are to be looked upon as matters with which England had no business to interfere by force of arms, for the purpose of preventing such Nations from having Institutions which they desire. These things are considered in England to be matters of domestic concern, which every Nation ought to be allowed to settle as it likes. But an attempt of one Nation to seize and appropriate to itself territory which belongs

[17] In a famous riposte, Talleyrand (1754–1838), when challenged by the Czar on this very point, said: 'Sire, that is a matter of dates.' Saint-Aulaire (fn. 8 above), pp. 264–5. On another occasion, Talleyrand reproved the Czar for saying that 'The convenience of Europe is law.' 'This language, Sire, is alien to you and your heart disowns it.' Talleyrand insisted that the Congress adopt as a rule that all proposals 'should conform to public law and the experience of Europe' (p. 264).

[18] For Metternich's own explanation of the Holy Alliance, see vol. I of his *Memoirs*, quoted in G. Bertier de Sauvigny, *Metternich* (Paris, Fayard; 1986), p. 277.

[19] Temperley and Penson, *Foundations* (fn. 12 above), p. 61.

to another Nation, is a different matter; because such an attempt leads to a derangement of the existing Balance of Power, and by altering the relative strength of States, may tend to create danger to other Powers; and such attempts therefore, the British Government holds itself at full liberty to resist, upon the universally acknowledged principle of self-defence.'[20]

13.22 This profoundly ambiguous solution to the problem of the vertical axis of international politics became the essence of the Vienna constitutional system: on the one hand, the systemic separation of internal and international politics; on the other hand, a supervisory role for certain powers, acting as managers of international constitutional order. In other words, the new international constitutional order rested on a dialectical negation of a negation: the systemic separation and the practical inseparability of the national and international political orders. The apologists of this new-old order had available to them and their successors a perfectly adapted system of ideas to gain acceptance of the new order, in Vattel's conception of international society as consisting of 'free, equal, and independent' states or nations, 'free persons living together in a state of nature', subject to a legal system deriving from their consent.[21] This noble lie, or opportune falsehood,[22] institutionalises, and thereby seems to justify, the gross real-world inequality of social development and social power of the participants in international society, rather as the corresponding noble lie at the root of liberal democracy institutionalises, and thereby seems to justify, gross social inequalities within national societies.

13.23 It has been customary to praise the intelligence and wisdom of the old-order aristocratic actors at Vienna, the makers of a constitutional order which, as historians have repeatedly said, prevented a general European war for 100 years.[23] From the perspective of the end of the long and tempestuous twentieth century, we might better say that what they achieved was that the old international order of war and

[20] *Ibid.*, p. 136.

[21] E. de Vattel, *The Law of Nations or the Principles of Natural Law applied to the Conduct and to the Affairs of Nations and Sovereigns* (1758) (tr. C. G. Fenwick; Washington, DC, Carnegie Institution; 1916), p. 7.

[22] Plato, *Republic*, III, 414.b.

[23] For a dissenting opinion, see Morlot and Happert, *Talleyrand* (fn. 10 above), p. 809. 'In fact, the Congress of Vienna laid the basis for British hegemony in the Victorian era, the making of the Bismarckian empire, and the decline of France.'

diplomacy would rule the world from its grave for two more centuries; that, for two centuries, the social development of international society would fail to match the social development of national society; that, for two more centuries, international law would continue to be nothing more than the minimal rules of a game of international politics played by an international oligarchy in an unresolved relationship with the game of national politics; and hence that the grossest inequality of national social development would be concealed behind the dishonest façade of the sovereign equality of states. By so ingeniously covering revolutionary instability with a veneer of reactionary stability, they made inevitable the catastrophes of the twentieth century, including Europe's thirty-year civil war, the wasteful absurdity of the Cold War, and the prolonged suffering of countless human beings at the hands of gross abusers of public power, political and economic, national and international.

The New Law of Nations

13.24 The cognitive and conative dissonance concealed within the ingenious Vienna settlement – the defiant voice of the past and the uncertain voice of the future, legitimacy versus public law – was very soon exposed. Metternich called George Canning (1770–1827) 'a malevolent meteor hurled by divine Providence upon Europe'.[24] In his two terms of office as British Foreign Secretary (1807–9 and 1822–7), Canning managed to introduce a new way of talking about international politics. He became the voice of that international political monism, as we might call it, of which William Gladstone (1809–98) and Woodrow Wilson (1856–1924) would be the most notorious apostles. International political monism resolves the problem of the relationship between national and international politics by denying their conceptual separation. National and international politics belong to a single political and moral value-order. Such a view is intended to negate the old-order aristocratic view of war and diplomacy as value-free or value-neutral instruments of national politics on a horizontal plane of oligarchy. Canning, passionate and combative practitioner of national politics, burst onto the international stage speaking of another kind of legitimacy, of what would later

[24] Quoted in H. Nicolson, *Diplomacy* (London, Oxford University Press; 1939), p. 73.

come to be known as national self-determination, a new vertical axis of international politics. He invoked the idea originally as a war-time strategy, to arouse national resistance across Europe to Napoleonic hegemonism.[25] He invoked it to oppose the threat of Prussian domination of Germany.[26] In the case of the independence of the Spanish American provinces, he justified Britain's early recognition as the mere recognition of a fact, of 'their political existence as States'.[27]

13.25 Gladstone took the new rhetoric further.

'Certain it is that a new law of nations is gradually taking hold of the mind, and coming to sway the practice, of the world; a law which recognises independence, which frowns on aggression, which favours the pacific, not the bloody settlement of disputes, which aims at permanent and not temporary adjustment; above all, which recognises, as a tribunal of paramount authority, the general judgment of civilised mankind. It has censured the aggression of France; it will censure, if need arise, the greed of Germany. *Securus judicat orbis terrarum.* It is hard for all nations to go astray. Their ecumenical council sits above the partial passions of those, who are misled by interest, and disturbed by quarrel. The greatest triumph of our time, a triumph in a region loftier than that of electricity or steam, will be the enthronement of this idea of Public Right, as the governing idea of European policy; as the common and precious inheritance of all lands, but superior to the passing opinion of any. The foremost among the nations will be that one, which by its conduct shall gradually engender in the mind of the others a fixed belief that it is just. In the competition for this prize, the bounty of Providence has given us [the British] a place of vantage; and nothing save our own fault or folly can wrest it from our grasp.'[28]

[25] 'I discharged the glorious duty... of recognizing without delay the rights of the Spanish nation.' Temperley and Penson, *Foundations* (fn. 12 above), p. 24. The recognition was of Ferdinand VII as King of Spain in 1808 while Britain was still in a state of war with French-dominated Spain. There followed the successful campaign led by Wellington (the Peninsular War) to restore Spanish independence from France.

[26] '[S]ubjecting to [Prussia]... the neighbouring Countries which are as much entitled as Prussia to the recovery and maintenance of their Independence, is a Project in which there would be as little of Policy as of Justice.' *Ibid.*, pp. 26–7.

[27] *Ibid.*, p. 79.

[28] W. E. Gladstone, 'Germany, France and England', published (anonymously) in the *Edinburgh Review* (October 1870), quoted in H. C. G. Matthew, *Gladstone 1809–1874* (Oxford, Clarendon Press; 1986), pp. 181–2. Twenty years earlier, Gladstone had said that the law of nations was 'a great and noble monument of human wisdom, founded on the combined dictates of

13.26 International political monism has always seemed to non-believers to be merely an advanced stage of hypocrisy. The strange fact was noted that value-based international politics, especially as preached by Canning and Gladstone,[29] seemed to serve British national interests, including the interests of British capitalism, quite as effectively as any old-order pragmatic diplomacy.[30] For most of the managers of the aristocratic old order, hypocritical moralising was worse than an embarrassment; it was a mistake. It gave rise to false expectations, especially in the minds of the masses, and was liable to complicate the management of a world which was still playing the old-order games of war and diplomacy.

13.27 Gladstone's thoughts on the 'new law of nations' were published during the Franco-Prussian War, after the battle of Sedan, when he was trying, by direct and indirect means, to dissuade Bismarck from annexing Alsace and Lorraine.[31] It was above all in the making of Germany, the delayed nation,[32] that there was manifested with awful clarity the perilous legacy of the Congress of Vienna – the survival of the old international order of war and diplomacy within the unresolved relationship between international and national politics.

13.28 Bismarck (1815–98) was the Richelieu of Germany. With the stubborn arrogance of an ancient land-owning family, he pursued a single idea – the making of an all-German state under the domination of Prussia. The manic militarism of Frederick II of Prussia (1712–86), called the Great, had made Prussia into a power capable of acting as one of the leading 'Powers' at the Congress of Vienna. Frederick's obsession with things French, and his distaste for Germany and things German,

sound experience'. J. Morely, *The Life of William Ewart Gladstone* (London, E. Lloyd; 1908), I, p. 274.

29 Canning was a protégé of William Pitt, Prime Minister 1783–1801 and 1804–6, himself the son of the dominant politician of the previous generation, who had led Britain during the Seven Years War (1756–63). Canning knew and admired the young Gladstone, whose father lived in Canning's parliamentary constituency and who, as a schoolboy at Eton, wrote verses in praise of Canning.

30 For Gladstone's combination of realism and moralism in international politics, see R. A. P. Sandiford, 'Gladstone and Europe', in B. L. Kinzer (ed.), *The Gladstonian Turn of Mind* (Toronto, University of Toronto Press; 1985), pp. 177–96.

31 Bismarck did not enjoy Gladstone's preaching and used to refer to him as Professor Gladstone. In old age, on a visit to Kiel (1895), Gladstone met Bismarck, who presented him with an oak-tree which was planted at the Gladstone estate at Hawarden Castle. Watching Kaiser Wilhelm II reviewing the new German fleet at Kiel, Gladstone said: 'This means war.' P. Magnus, *Gladstone. A Biography* (London, John Murray; 1954), p. 429.

32 See H. Plessner, *Die Verspätete Nation* (Stuttgart, W. Kohlhammer Verlag; 1959).

had meant that it was left to others to create an idea of Germany as a potentiality and to actualise that potentiality as a fact. The fact of Prussia and the idea of Germany combined to produce, a century late, a 'power' to rival France and Britain. For Bismarck, as for Richelieu, internal and external politics were, indeed, in an unbroken continuum, with the latter to be used as part of the former, and with the use of force, as it had been for Frederick, acting as a necessary continuation of national politics. For Bismarck, politics was, as he said, the art of the possible, and diplomacy was accordingly the highest art-form of politics. Within such a worldview, even mighty France was nothing more than 'an unavoidable pawn on the chessboard of diplomacy'.[33]

13.29 Under Bismarck's leadership, and in conformity with the Vienna constitutional order, the German ruling class were able to postpone, for a century, the development of post-1789 democratic institutions, choosing instead the intensive rationalising of old-order courtly government, thereby pioneering the development of a new kind of aristocratic mafia, the professional civil service. Early and energetically, Germany joined in the new economic order of the Industrial Revolution and capitalism, even if, at one time, it sought to resist, at least for the time being, the globalising of capitalism (free trade) promoted by British politico-economic hegemonism, using the 'infant industry' argument which would be used again in relation to the economies of developing countries in the modern post-imperial period.[34]

13.30 For Max Weber, Gladstone was the classic example of the ideal-type 'democracy-leader'.[35] For the young Woodrow Wilson, whose grandfathers were British, Gladstone was 'the greatest statesman that ever lived' and he remained an obsessive presence in Wilson's troubled psyche for the rest of his life.[36] Wilson certainly reproduced many of the character-traits of his hero, including a belief in the redeeming power of

[33] H. Kissinger, *Diplomacy* (New York, Simon & Schuster; 1994), p. 125. It is interesting to compare Cavour's management of the unification of Italy, achieved with more diplomacy and less blood and iron. Cavour experienced pangs of anguish concerning the unworthy deeds which international politics requires of international politicians.

[34] F. List's *Nationale System der politischen Ökonomie* was published in 1841.

[35] W. Mommsen, *Max Weber und die deutsche Politik 1890–1920* (Tübingen, J. C. B. Mohr; 1959/1974), p. 433.

[36] E. M. Hugh-Jones, *Woodrow Wilson and American Liberalism* (London, Hodder & Stoughton; 1947), p. 7. For an idiosyncratic psycho-biography of Wilson, see S. Freud and W. C. Bullitt, *Thomas Woodrow Wilson. A Psychological Study* (Boston, Houghton Mifflin; 1966).

ethically based politics, a power which could be extended to the whole world in accordance with a doctrine which came to be called liberal internationalism but which might as well be called liberal imperialism. It has been suggested that Wilson the internationalist was strongly influenced by a fashionable turn-of-the-century set of ideas which saw human social progress as a matter of increasing, and increasingly rational, 'social control'.[37] This social-Darwinist, proto-Weberian ideology resonated also with the characteristically pragmatist behaviourist and social psycho-therapeutic strands in American thinking. Wilson welcomed the advent of the United States to the ranks of the imperial powers, through the acquisition of Cuba and the Philippines in 1898, on the ground that it opened up the possibility of a new kind of civilising mission, bringing democracy, capitalism and Christianity to those peoples who lacked these blessings of civilisation. International politics would no longer be based on mere material interest, but would rather seek to establish a 'spiritual union' among the people of the world.[38] American involvement in international politics in the twentieth century was dominated by a notorious tension between the advice of the first President, in his Farewell Address, to avoid 'foreign entanglements' and an urgent desire to share America's exceptionality with the rest of the world. Isolationism and internationalism have been dialectically resolved in something akin to Britain's nineteenth-century policy, from Castlereagh to Salisbury, of 'splendid isolation', that is to say, disentangled entanglement in international politics.

13.31 It is not wrong to personalise Wilson's participation in the disaster of the Paris Peace Conference (1919).[39] An American president of exceptional thoughtfulness and sensitivity, fuelled by an obsessive, almost pathological, desire to change the world, collided with two

[37] L. E. Ambrosius, *Woodrow Wilson and the American Diplomatic Tradition. The Treaty Fight in Perspective* (Cambridge, Cambridge University Press; 1987), pp. 12ff.

[38] Hugh-Jones, *Woodrow Wilson* (fn. 36 above), p. 183 (speech at Mobile, Alabama, in October 1913).

[39] It is interesting to compare the avalanche of criticism which followed the Versailles settlement, and the manner of its making, with criticisms of the Vienna settlement. In the British House of Commons, one member (J. Lambton) spoke of 'the acts of rapine, and aggression of the club of confederated monarchs at Vienna, who appear to have met, not to watch over the interests of Europe, but as contemners of faith and justice, as the spoliators of Saxony and the oppressors of Norway'. Another (R. B. Sheridan) spoke of the 'crowned scoundrels cutting up Europe like carcass-butchers'. S. M. Alsop, *The Congress Dances 1814–1815* (New York, Simon & Schuster (Pocket Books), 1984), p. 190.

godfathers of the mafia of international politics (Clémenceau, Lloyd George), ruthless manipulators of the Vienna constitutional order, content to institutionalise in a so-called League of Nations the post-Vienna union of councils and concert of measures, if such a thing might be a means, however feeble, of tying down other still more unreliable mafiosi.[40] Wilson's Fourteen Points had been a manifesto of international political monism, seeking to reconcile the vertical and horizontal aspects of international politics, the internal and the external political realms. Little of that manifesto survived the drafting of the Treaty of Versailles and, with the possible exceptions of the provisions on mandates and minorities, the League of Nations Covenant proved to be a work of classic international horizontalism, a grim parody of the Vienna settlement.

The new aristocracy

13.32 In this respect, the Paris settlement was at least prophetic. Twentieth-century international politics has seen the rise of an international ruling class of unprecedented size, power and arrogance. One point of intersection between American internationalism and the self-interest of the old-order ruling class has been the vigorous reproduction on the international plane of institutional forms reminiscent of national constitutional orders. Intergovernmental councils (cabinets of cabinets), deliberative assemblies (normally containing only representatives of governments), courts and tribunals (containing government-appointed members), bureaucratic organisms of every kind. Isolated from their national constitutional orders, unencumbered with any corresponding international constitutional order, such bodies have managed to enjoy what might be called a collective international absolutism, a life-after-death of the pre-revolutionary national *anciens régimes.*

13.33 The new-model international *Hofmafia* includes a *noblesse de cour,*[41] consisting of the national politicians and senior national and

[40] The concept of tying-down has been an obsessive theme of the old order of war and diplomacy and continues to haunt the idea of European Union. 'In my opinion, the third sound principle is this: to strive to cultivate and maintain, nay, to the very uttermost, what is called the Concert of Europe, to keep the powers of Europe in union together. And why? Because keeping all in union together you neutralize and fetter and bind up the selfish aims of each.' W. E. Gladstone (from an election speech in his Midlothian campaign, 1879), quoted in Nicolson, *Diplomacy* (fn. 24 above), p. 71–2.

[41] For the hierarchy of French *ancien régime* court-life, see P. Mansel, *The Court of France 1789–1830* (Cambridge, Cambridge University Press; 1988), ch. 1.

international officials who deliberate in the global public interest in their Olympian conclaves. It includes a *noblesse de robe*, all those public servants (and international lawyers in professional practice) who devote themselves to the well-being of the people of the world, even if the people of the world have little knowledge, and less appreciation, of their work. It includes also what we may call a *noblesse de la plume*, diplomatic historians, academic international lawyers, international commentators and analysts of all kinds, and specialists in a field known as 'international relations'.[42] They provide intellectual sustenance and psychological reassurance to those who bear the burdens of international government.

13.34 The European Union is the greatest achievement of the new international ruling class. It seeks to resolve the perennial tension between the horizontal and vertical aspects of international politics in the most dramatic way possible. It simply fuses the internal and the external, within a system of decision-making which is neither democracy nor diplomacy, under a legal system which is neither national nor international law, regulating an economy which is both integrated and disintegrated, the whole enterprise serving a common interest which is both communal and an ad hoc aggregation of national interests. Furthermore, such a constitutional fusion, a revolution-from-outside for each member state, has the extraordinary characteristic that it is only a partial fusion, with the member states remaining in a classic horizontal relationship as regards aspects of government not included in the Union system. The complex pluralist monism of the EU system, a partial constitutional nuclear fusion, has accordingly not yet produced a commensurately energetic transformation of the external aspect of the Union itself, in its so-called Common Foreign and Security Policy, that is to say, in the form of its own participation in the horizontal international order, in place of, and alongside, the governments of its member states.

13.35 This failure is a symptom of a general indisposition of international society. Since 1945 the international ruling class has been

[42] There is a sect of such specialists ('realists') who treat states as real entities and the national and international realms as intrinsically separate. See B. Frankel (ed.), *Realism: Restatements and Renewal* (Ilford, Frank Cass; 1996) and contributions by various authors on the present state of 'realism' in 24 *Review of International Studies* (October 1998). The origin of such ideas is not scientific but polemical. It is to be found in a revolt in the United States against liberal internationalism (Lippmann, Kennan, Morgenthau).

preparing its own downfall, its own nemesis. It has generated an unsustainable disjunction between the vertical and horizontal components of international society. On the one hand, it has continued, with very little alteration, the old-order twin-track system of war and diplomacy, throughout the period of the Cold War, and then in the impotent inefficiency of its management of the post-Cold War situation. On the other hand, it has used the privilege of its international absolutism to intervene in national society, using the existing governmental systems of horizontal international society (treaties and intergovernmental institutions) to modify collectively and substantially not only the legal self-constituting of national societies (conditional recognition of states, human rights law, law of the sea, international criminal law) but also the substance and functioning of national law and government, in the systems of the functional UN agencies, macro-economic management (the Bretton Woods bodies), trade law (especially GATT/WTO), and environmental law. It has even sought, in a rudimentary way, to affect the international division of labour and distribution of wealth, through the law and practice of so-called 'development' and through the regulation of international investment.

13.36 Metternich, aristocratic rationalist, might well have been happier, as he supposed, in such a twentieth century. But we would be bound to tell him that, in the meantime, we have learned that the international consequences of what Edmund Burke called revolutions of doctrine and theory, such as the Reformation and the French Revolution, cannot be controlled merely by war and diplomacy. The third post-medieval international revolution, through which we are now living, is imposing a new international constitutional structure, a new relationship between the horizontal and vertical axes of international society, between the internal and the external aspects of government. A new kind of international polity and new systems of international government, superseding the ideas of war, foreign policy and diplomacy, will generate new ideas of international law and a new role and a new self-consciousness for those who will take over the determination and management of world public interest from the current successors-in-title of the age-old international *Hofmafia.*

14

International law and international revolution

Reconceiving the world

The people and the peoples of the world must find a way to communicate to the holders of public power – the international Hofmafia *– their moral outrage at the present state of the human world. It is an outrage made almost unbearable by the complacency of those who operate the international system and the conniving of those who rationalise it, as commentators in public discussion or analysts in an academic context.*

Social evil on a national scale *is routinely legitimated and enforced through social theory and social practice, including the legal system, of each national society. National systems contrive to make us see social injustice, and socially caused human suffering of every kind, as incidental and pragmatic effects, however much they may violate our most fundamental values and ideals.*

For 250 years, a perverted, anti-social, anti-human worldview has allowed the holders of public power to treat social injustice and human suffering on a global scale *as if it were beyond human responsibility and beyond the judgement of our most fundamental values and ideals, and the holders of public power have imagined an international legal system which enacts and enforces such a worldview. And the people and the peoples of the world have simply had to acquiesce in and to live with the consequences of this disgraceful perversion of theory and practice.*

It would be possible, and it is necessary and urgent, to destroy the old international unsociety and to create the theory and the practice of a true international society, the society of all societies and the society of all human beings, enacting and enforcing a true international law, the legal system of all legal systems, for the survival and prospering of all-humanity.

We must make a world-wide revolution, a revolution not in the streets but in the mind.[1]

14.1 I want to think aloud about a question which is easy to state but very difficult to answer. Why do we put up with it all? That question reflects a dull pain, an anguish, an anger even, that many people feel in considering the state of the world. It would be uttered as a sentimental question, not expecting an answer, at least not expecting a practical answer. But let us, for a while, treat it as a question to be answered in practical terms.

14.2 Why do we put up with it all? Obviously it is a question which implies three other questions – and it is those implied questions that give rise to all the difficulty. What exactly is it that so troubles us in the state of the world? What is the cause or origin of the things that trouble us? What could and should we do to change those things?

14.3 Let us consider a practical example. You will have heard of the country called Nowhere, but you may not know much about it in detail. Nowhere is an independent sovereign state with a president, a government, a single political party called the Nowhere People's Party, a population of 12 million people, consisting of two ethnic groups – the Nos and the Wheres. The ratio of Nos to Wheres is two-to-one. The Nowhere People's Party is dominated by the Wheres, the smaller ethnic group. The Wheres arrived in the country in the early nineteenth century and soon came to dominate the indigenous No people.

14.4 Nowhere's economy has been a two-product economy – copper and tourism. The copper-mining industry is controlled by a multinational company centred in a country called Globalpower One. The tourism industry is controlled by Where businessmen in co-operation with various foreign interests. The menial labour in tourism is provided by the No people. In recent years Nowhere has been flourishing as an off-shore financial centre, with foreign banks and holding companies establishing offices in the capital, Nowhere City. There has been a consumer boom, with great demand for imported video-tape recorders and cocaine. Next month there is to be a state visit by Madonna Jackson, who is to be given the country's highest honour, for services to Nowenese

[1] Having regard to the nature and intention of this chapter, it has been left in its original form as a lecture, with additional material added in the form of footnotes.

culture. Nowhere's immediate neighbour is No-man's-land, whose population consists almost entirely of No people. No-man's-land is a multiparty state with a Westminster-style parliament. It is a poorer country than Nowhere. It has a long-standing claim to the territory of Nowhere and supports a Nowenese Liberation Army which is seeking to overthrow the regime in Nowhere. The NLA is also supported by a country called Globalpower Two. A sum of money equivalent to one-third of its Gross Domestic Product is spent every year by each country on arms, which are obtained from Globalpower One and Globalpower Two and on the international arms market. Nowhere has a written constitution containing a Declaration of Political and Social Rights. However, the President declared a State of Exception five years ago and the Declaration of Rights was suspended. The President's eldest son is the Chief Justice of the Supreme Court. His second son is Commander-in-Chief of the Nowhere Armed Forces. His youngest son is studying at Harford Business School.

14.5 I do not need to say much more. It is all very familiar. Nowhere is a member of many international organisations. It is also an object of interest to many international organisations, including the UN Security Council, the World Bank, the International Monetary Fund, leading international banks, Amnesty International and the Church of Perpetual Healing, which has missionaries in Nowhere City, in the tourist resorts and in remote villages. The President's sister is an ardent Perpetual Healer. You will not be surprised to hear that deforestation in the north of Nowhere has turned the fertile southern plain of No-man's-land into a virtual desert. Soil erosion in Nowhere is silting up the River Nouse which flows into No-man's-land, threatening a hydro-electric power-station on a tributary of the Nouse.

14.6 You react in one of two ways, when you come across news items about Nowhere and No-man's-land. Either – so what? Or – so why? Those who react with *so what?* believe that the world is as it is, human nature is as it is, and human beings are as they are, corrupt or corruptible, sometimes decent, always long-suffering, patient of the miseries and follies of the world. And societies are as they are, some progressive and some not progressive, some successful and some not successful. So it has always been through all human history, and so, presumably, it will always be. Those who react with *so why?* believe that *human beings are what they could be*, not simply what they have been, and *societies are systems made by human beings for human survival and human prospering,* not for human oppression and human indignity. I suppose that, from now on, I will be speaking to so-why people but hoping to be overheard by so-what people.

14.7 Let us make an abstraction of the world-situation of which Nowhere and No-man's-land are one small part. And we may thereby begin to answer the first of the three subordinate questions – what exactly do we object to in the present world situation? Here is a possible short-list, containing five intolerable things.

(1) Unequal social development. That means that some human beings worry about the colour of the bed-sheets in their holiday-home in Provence or the Caribbean, while other human beings worry about their next meal or the leaking tin-roof of the hut which is their home.
(2) War and armaments. From time to time, human beings murder and maim each other in the public interest, by the dozen and by the million, and bomb each other's villages and cities to rubble. And, all the time, human beings make more and more machines for murdering and destroying in the public interest, and more and more machines to prevent other people from murdering and destroying in the public interest.
(3) Governmental oppression. In very many countries around the world, the ruling class are not servants of the people but enemies of the people, evil and corrupt and negligent and self-serving, torturing people, exploiting people, abusing people. And, in all countries, the people have to struggle to control the vanity and the obsessions of those who want to be their masters.
(4) Physical degradation. On the planet Earth are 5 billion human beings, one species of animal among countless other societies of living things, a species which has taken over the planet, using the Earth's resources, irreversibly transforming the Earth as a physical structure and as a living system.
(5) Spiritual degradation. Human beings everywhere are being drawn into a single mass culture dominated by a crude form of capitalism, a mass culture which is stifling all competing values and all local cultures, a mass culture which is depraving human consciousness.

14.8 You may not like that list. You may worry about other things. You may want to challenge some item on my list, to defend something that I seem to be attacking. You will have noticed that my list of five intolerable things consists of five cliches of so-called global anxiety. We have heard about them all until we are sick and tired of them. The mass media of communication exploit them at regular intervals, enriching their everyday fodder with an occasional healthy supplement of moral fibre – the emaciated survivor of the concentration camp, the family sleeping in the street, the mutilated body, the starving baby, the napalmed countryside, the delirious crowd at the political rally or the rock concert, hooligans on the rampage, riot police with batons and water-cannon, drug addicts killing themselves slowly, dead fish floating on a polluted river, the television set in the mud-hut. Banal images of a reality made banal. So-why made as tedious as so-what.

14.9 And, then again, you may object that, surely, we are not simply putting up with such things. On the contrary, a lot of effort is being devoted to facing up to such things, to alleviating them, even to solving them. There are dozens of organisations and foundations and charities and conferences and good-hearted individuals worrying about each and every one of them. Surely some part of our taxes and some part of our voluntary giving is going to deal with precisely such world social problems. I will add that as a sixth cause of our anger – perhaps the most painful of all.

(6) Social pragmatism. We treat the symptoms of world-wide disorder, because we cannot, or dare not, understand the disease. We see the effects because we cannot, or will not, see the cause.

14.10 So that brings us to the second question. What is the origin or cause of the things we find intolerable? You will say, especially if you are a so-what person, that we cannot comment on the causes of the situation of Nowhere and No-man's-land unless and until we know more of their territories and resources, their cultural characteristics, their history. Each is a sovereign independent state, with its own destiny to work out, its own possibilities, its own constraints. Who are we to know what is the best for them, let alone to do anything to bring about what is best for them?

14.11 I would ask you to notice three things about the two well-known unknown countries I have described, three features of their structural situation. The first is that they are not very independent. The market-price of Nowenese copper is determined in London, where demand is related very directly to the general state of world manufacturing industry at any particular time. Nowenese tourism depends on the international holiday companies which send their packaged tourists to fill the Nowenese hotels which have been built by foreign construction companies, using cement brought halfway round the world in ships controlled by foreign shipping-lines. The off-shore companies established in Nowhere City are there because taxes are low, because few questions are asked, because the climate is pleasant. They may leave as suddenly as they arrived. And the territory of No-man's-land, its physical environment, its climate even, depend on what is done in the territory of Nowhere. And even the minds of the Nowenese people are not their own. Their values and their wants are a function of forces far beyond their control – capitalism, foreign religions, international crime, world popular culture, militarism, materialism.

14.12 Of course, Nowhere is not nowhere. It is everywhere. All the world is more or less Nowhere. Remember that the most economically successful countries in the world maintain their economies and their standard of living by selling goods and services to other countries. There must be other countries willing and able to buy. And even the most successful countries depend on the value of their currency, which depends on international economic relativities, as well as on internal economic realities. And they depend on investment which, particularly if they have a substantial budget deficit, may be foreign investment, created and terminable through decisions made elsewhere. And they depend on technology which may be originated and controlled abroad. And they depend on cultural tides which sweep across the world, shaping human events and human expectations and human anxieties. Every country, from the most prosperous to the least prosperous, is at an intersection of internalities and externalities. Our independence is a function of what we control and what we do not control.

14.13 The second thing to notice about Nowhere and No-man's-land is that their national identities do not coincide with their political identities. The No people in Nowhere feel more kinship with the No people in No-man's-land than with the Where-dominated state of which they are said to be nationals. The No people in No-man's-land feel that Nowhere and its incoming Where people have usurped some part of the No birthright. By the sound of it, they have taken the more valuable part of the traditional No territory, the part which contains the deposits of copper and the best beaches.

14.14 We know that this problem of national identity has been one of the greatest social problems through all human history, giving rise to endless wars, endless struggle and suffering, endless oppression and exploitation. And, of course, it is very much with us today. It is hard to think of a single country in the world which is not significantly affected by one or more problems of national identity, including the United Kingdom of Great Britain and Northern Ireland. The fact is that the political frontiers of the so-called nation-states have evolved under the pressure of forces other than merely those of national identity. And yet it is the political systems of the so-called nation-states which have, somehow, acquired the power to control the social development of all the peoples of the world, to determine the well-being of humanity, to determine the future of humanity.

14.15 The third thing to notice about the structural situation of Nowhere and No-man's-land is that their population consists of human beings. They share with us the species-characteristics of human beings. They think and want and hope and suffer and despair and laugh and weep as human beings. The mothers of their sons who are killed in their wars or their prisons or their hospitals have hearts as tender as the hearts of our mothers. Their children look to the future as our children look to the future. Whether we are so-what people or so-why people, we cannot stop ourselves from feeling sympathy.

14.16 And yet somehow we stop ourselves from feeling responsibility for them. They are aliens. As human beings, we know that we are morally responsible for all that we do, and do not do, to and for other human beings, a responsibility which we cannot think away, a responsibility which we owe to a billion human beings as we owe it to one human being. Every alien is also our neighbour. And yet as citizens, we have somehow been led to believe that we are not socially responsible for them – and that even our moral responsibility is qualified by their social alienation from us.

14.17 I have mentioned three structural features of the situation of two countries which are also structural features of the world situation. They are like geological fault-lines running through the world structure. First, our single human destiny must nevertheless be pursued in isolated state-structures. Second, our national identity may be in conflict with our legal and political identity. Third, we are not able to take responsibility for human beings for whom we know we are responsible. What I want to suggest to you is that there is a direct connection between the things which we find intolerable in the world situation and these three structural faults in the world system. And that direct connection is located nowhere else than in our own minds. It is not a matter of physics or biology or physiology or geography or history. It is a matter of philosophy – that is to say, of human self-conceiving and human self-creating.

14.18 What we have to discover is not how the present world structure came about as a story of historical events, but how the present world structure came to seem natural and inevitable. The question of causation I am considering is the question of what causes certain social and legal situations to be accepted within human consciousness. In particular, what is the origin of the consciousness which makes possible, which legitimates, which naturalises, the way in which we conceive of international society and international law?

14.19 Why do we put up with it all? We put up with it all because our consciousness contains ideas which cause us to put up with it all. Who makes our consciousness? We make our consciousness. And so, if we can change our consciousness of the world, we can change the world. It is as simple as that. That is the revolution I am proposing to you. A reconstruction of our understanding of the world in which we live, a reconceiving of the human world, and thereby a remaking of the human world.

14.20 Let us treat it as a mystery to be solved, how we got into our present state of consciousness about international society and international law. If we treat it as a mystery story, a whodunnit?, I can name one of the guilty parties and I can explain the *modus operandi*. Whodunnit? It was Emmerich de Vattel in his study with an idea. That sounds unlikely. One particular Swiss writer, writing in 1758, making a certain use of certain words. Let me put the evidence before you. I can express the same thing almost as briefly, but in a more abstract form.

14.21 Humanity, having been tempted for a while to conceive of itself as a society, chose instead to conceive of itself as a collection of states. State-societies have undergone a long process of internal social change since the end of the Middle Ages. That process has been conducted on two planes – the plane of history and the plane of philosophy. There has been the plane of historical events, power-struggles, wars and civil wars, revolutions, institutional change, legislative reforms, everyday politics. And there has been the plane of philosophy, as human consciousness has sought ways to express what is and what might be in society, to legitimate what is, to bring about what might be.

14.22 On both planes – of history and philosophy – there have been two developments which have dominated all others in the evolving of the state-societies since the end of the Middle Ages: democratisation and socialisation. Democratisation and socialisation are words to describe two revolutions which have made the state societies we know today. So, returning to the mystery of international society, I can now reformulate the story as follows.

14.23 *International society, having chosen not to conceive of itself as a society, having chosen to conceive of itself as essentially different in kind from the state-societies in their internal aspect, has managed to avoid both forms of social revolution. The social world of humanity has been neither democratised nor socialised because humanity has chosen to regard its international world as an unsocial world.*

14.24 What have democratisation and socialisation meant within the state-societies? Democratisation has meant that societies became able to conceive of themselves as composed of the people, as governed by the people, and as serving the people. Socialisation has meant that societies acquired the capacity to form socially their social purposes.

14.25 The development of the idea of *democracy* was a response to the greatly increasing energy of national societies at the end of the Middle Ages, as their economies and the international economy developed dramatically, as humanity rediscovered the self-ordering capacity of the human mind, and hence the world-transforming possibilities not only of philosophy but also of natural science and technology, and as new areas of the world were visited, offering new possibilities for the application of human energy, individual and social energy.

14.26 The response at the level of philosophy was to take up an old idea, the idea of sovereignty: the idea that a society is structurally a unity, and that that structure depends on an ultimate source of authority, an unwilled will, which is the ultimate source of social self-ordering, the source of law in society. The idea of sovereignty was structurally necessary to turn amorphous national societies into more and more complex self-organising systems. But there was obviously an inherent anti-social danger in sovereignty, an anti-systemic, self-disabling uncertainty. Who was to be the sovereign? How was the sovereign to be controlled? The difficulty was that the sovereign societies, as they developed, generated a particular sub-system which came to be known as *the state*.

14.27 The state came to be conceived as a public realm within society under the authority of the government. The public realm was loosely separated from the private realm, in which individuals remained, as it were, sovereign. But the state could determine for itself the limits of the public realm, by taking control of both physical power and law-making power. The development of democracy at the level of philosophy took place primarily in the development of various theories of social contract and in the ancient idea of constitutionalism. Sovereignty could be retained to provide the systematic structure of society, with its public realm under the government. But sovereignty would be reconceived to contain the idea of self-government. A society was to be a structure of sovereignty, but also a structure of self-government. And that structure came to be expressed in the new-old form of the so-called constitution embodying 'higher law'.

14.28 The development of democracy at the *philosophical* level was, of course, accompanied by dramatic developments at the historical level. Much blood was shed. Many suffered, in their person and their property, in the process of social change. The new philosophy, of democratic constitutionalism, had the effect of increasing the actual power of those who controlled the power of government, who actually controlled the public realm. In other words, the constitution proved to be an excellent means of organising democratic power but it proved incapable by itself of *determining social purpose*, of deciding how the great power of the state-society would be used.

14.29 Society had to find some means, at the philosophical level and at the historical level, to organise, from day to day, social willing and acting. Democracy had to become something more than constitutional democracy. That was the historical function of *socialisation*. Especially in the nineteenth century, society developed as a system for generating value. The public realm came to be not merely a realm of power but a realm of value. Through the development of a professional bureaucracy, through the reform of the legal system, through the reform of parliaments, through the universalisation of elementary education, through the reform of secondary education and the reform of the universities, through the development of mass communications (in public libraries, mass production of books, mass circulation newspapers, and then radio and television) – through such means society became not merely a structure of political power but a system of shared social consciousness, a system for generating social values and social purposes. But communal values and social purposes would be generated not merely within the decision-making organs of government. They would be generated within the minds of the people. The social sharing of consciousness became the sharing of our most intimate consciousness.

14.30 The application of science and technology to agriculture and industry meant that the increase in social wealth was able to keep ahead of the increase in population, so that there was more wealth to be distributed, so that there was the possibility of social improvement not merely as an ideal but as an actuality. Society became a means for human self-creating, human self-perfecting through human interaction. And we have seen the wonderful results in the improvement of the living conditions and the opportunities of the mass of the people in a number of countries. The question is – what happened to the organising of the interaction between such societies, their international interaction, while all these developments were taking place internally?

14.31 What happened was that the sovereign was turned inside out and became the external manifestation of the society in question. What appeared on the international scene was not the totality of the evolved national societies. What appeared on the international scene was merely the internal public realms externalised. The internal public realms, the governments, were turned inside out like a glove.

14.32 Louis XIV is supposed to have said: *L'Etat, c'est moi* – 'I am the state'. He meant that he was the embodiment of the French nation, the embodiment of its public realm. He might have gone on to say: *Le monde, c'est nous, les états*, meaning that the international system should be regarded as consisting of the governments meeting each other externally.

14.33 The result was that we came to have an international system which was, and is, post-feudal society set in amber – undemocratised, unsocialised – capable only of generating so-called *international relations*, in which so-called *states* act in the name of so-called *national interests*, through the exercise of so-called *power*, carrying out so-called *foreign policy* conducted by means of so-called *diplomacy*, punctuated by medieval entertainments called *wars* or, in the miserable modern euphemism, *armed conflict*. That is the essence of the social process of the international non-society.

14.34 It is as if the external life of our societies were still a reflection of the internal life of centuries ago, a fitful struggle among Teutonic knights or European barons or Chinese feudal lords or Japanese shoguns. It is as if Thomas Hobbes were the world's only social philosopher. It is as if there had never been Locke and Rousseau and Kant and Hegel and Marx, let alone Plato and Aristotle and Lao Tzŭ and Confucius. It is as if the revolutions had never occurred – 1789 and 1917 and all the other dramatic and undramatic social revolutions.

14.35 Nowadays people believe that such an international system is natural and inevitable. Far from it. It is not necessarily natural and it was not simply inevitable. And this is where we get back to Emmerich de Vattel in his study. It is not difficult to unravel the story by which the misconceiving of international society was perpetrated. I will present it as a drama in five acts.

14.36 *Act One.* In the sixteenth century, a critical question for theologians and philosophers was the question of how there could be a law applying both to the nations of Europe and to the peoples of the lands which had been newly visited or revisited. It was necessary to reconsider the question, which had been familiar to ancient Greece and Rome and medieval Christendom, of whether there could be said to be a universal legal system. The idea was proposed, particularly in Spain and not for the first time in human history, that all humanity formed a sort of society and that the law governing the whole of humanity reflected that fact.

'[I]nternational law has not only the force of a pact and agreement among men, but also the force of a law; for the world as a whole, being in a way one single State, has the power to create laws that are just and fitting for all persons, as are the rules of international law'.[2]

14.37 Francisco de Vitoria (1492–1546) took the view that the basis of a universal law for all human beings was found in natural reason, the rational character of human nature, which generated what he called a law of natural society and fellowship which binds together all human beings and which survives the establishment of civil power (*potestas*) over particular peoples (*gentes*). The rules of the law of nations were to be derived from natural law and from a 'consensus of the greater part of the whole world, especially in behalf of the common good of all'.

[2] Francisco de Vitoria, *Concerning Civil Power* (1528), § 21; tr. G. L. Williams, in J. B. Scott, *The Spanish Origin of International Law* (Oxford, Clarendon Press, 1934) App. C, p. xc.

14.38 Francisco Suárez (1548–1617) conceived of a moral and political unity of the human race.

'The rational basis, moreover, of [the *ius gentium*, the law of nations] consists in the fact that the human race, into howsoever many different peoples and kingdoms it may be divided, always preserves a certain unity, not only as a species, but also a moral and political unity (as it were) enjoined by the natural precept of mutual love and mercy; a precept which applies to all, even to strangers of every nation.

'Therefore, although a given sovereign state [*civitas*] commonwealth [*respublica*], or Kingdom [*regnum*] may constitute a perfect community in itself, consisting of its own members, nevertheless, each one of these states (*communitas*) is also, in a certain sense, and viewed in relation to the human race, a member of that universal society.'[3]

14.39 *Act Two.* In the seventeenth century, Hugo Grotius (Hugo de Groot) (1583–1645) began the process of separating the law of nations from the law of nature, but he did so precisely in order to make clear to the new sovereigns that their will was not the sole test of what is right even if it was the practical basis of what is lawful under the law of nations. The nations are sovereign and independent of each other. They are all equally governed by the law of nations which is the product of the common will of nations acting in the common interest of all nations. And they are governed by natural law, which is the product of human nature and hence indirectly is the work of God who made human nature to be as it is, including its sociability and its rationality. And they are governed by a moral order which comes directly from God.

'But just as the laws of each state [*cuiusque civitatis*] have in view the advantage of that state, so by mutual consent it has become possible that certain laws should originate as between all states, or a great many states; and it is apparent that the laws thus originating had in view

[3] Francisco Suárez, *On Laws and God the Lawgiver* (1612) bk II, ch. 19.9 (tr. G. L. Williams; Oxford, Clarendon Press; 1944), pp. 348–9. The passage continues as follows:

'Consequently, such communities have need of some system of law whereby they may be directed and properly ordered with regard to this kind of intercourse and association; and although that guidance is in large measure provided by natural reason, it is not provided in sufficient measure and in a direct manner with respect to all matters: therefore, it was possible for certain special rules of law to be introduced through the practice of these same nations. For just as in one state or province law is introduced by custom, so among the human race as a whole it was possible for laws to be introduced by the habitual conduct of nations' (p. 349).

the advantage not of particular states, but of the great society of states [*magnae universitatis*]. And that is what is called the law of nations, whenever we distinguish that term from the law of nature.'[4]

14.40 *Act Three.* In the eighteenth century, an attempt was made by a German philosopher to construct a coherent and self-contained system of international law derived from natural law. That philosopher was Christian von Wolff (1679–1754). He proposed the view that the society of the whole human race continues to exist even after the creation of the nation-states.

'If we should consider that great society, which nature has established among men, to be done away with by the particular societies, which men enter into, when they unite into a state, states would be established contrary to the law of nature, in as much as the universal obligation of all toward all would be terminated; which assuredly is absurd. Just as in the human body individual organs do not cease to be organs of

[4] Hugo Grotius, *Of the Law of War and Peace* (1625), Prolegomena, 17, edn of 1646 (tr. F. W. Kelsey; Oxford, Clarendon Press; 1925) p. 15. The continuation of Grotius' argument should also be noticed.

'Many hold, in fact, that the standard of justice which they insist upon in the case of individuals within the state is inapplicable to a nation or to a ruler of a nation. The reason for this error lies in this, first of all, that in respect to law they have in view nothing except the advantage which accrues from it, such advantage being apparent in the case of citizens, who, taken singly, are powerless to protect themselves. But great states, since they seem to contain in themselves all things required for the adequate protection of life, seem not to have need of that virtue which looks toward the outside, and is called justice . . . '

'If no association of men can be maintained without law, as Aristotle showed by his remarkable example drawn from brigands, surely also that association which binds together the human race, or binds many nations together, has need of law; this was perceived by him who said that shameful deeds ought not to be committed even for the sake of one's country. Aristotle takes sharply to task those who, unwilling to allow anyone to exercise authority over themselves except in accordance with law, yet are quite indifferent as to whether foreigners are treated according to law or not . . . Bravery itself the Stoics defined as virtue fighting on behalf of equity. Themistius in his address to Valens argues with eloquence that kings who measure up to the rule of wisdom make account not only of the nation which has been committed to them, but of the whole human race, and that they are, as he himself says, not "friends of the Macedonians" alone, or "friends of the Romans", * but "friends of mankind". The name of Minos became odious to future ages for no other reason than this, that he limited his fair-dealing to the boundaries of his realm' (pp. 17–18).

(* Grotius' other notes cannot be reproduced here, but at this point he characteristically notes: 'Marcus Aurelius exceedingly well remarks: "As Antoninus, my city and my country are Rome; as a man, the world." Porphyry, *On Abstaining from Animal Food*, Book III: "He who is guided by reason keeps himself blameless in relation to his fellow-citizens, likewise also in relation to strangers and men in general; the more submissive to reason, the more godlike a man is."')

the whole human body, because certain ones taken together constitute one organ; so likewise individual men do not cease to be members of that great society which is made up of the whole human race, because several have formed together a certain particular society. And in so far as these act together as associates, just as if they were all of one mind and will; even so are the members of that society united, which nature has established among men. After the human race was divided into nations, that society which before was between individuals continues between nations.'[5]

14.41 *Act Four.* And then a critical event occurred. The trouble with Wolff was that his book on international law was the last volume of a nine-volume work on natural law. And it was written in Latin. Only the learned read it, among whom was Emmerich de Vattel (1714–67). He decided to communicate Wolff's volume nine to the world. But he decided not simply to publish a translation. He wrote his own book, using Wolff's ideas so far as he approved of them. On Wolff's essential theoretical point, Vattel explicitly parted company with Wolff.

14.42 Vattel agreed that there was a universal society of the human race governed by the law of nature, but the formation of the states made an important difference in the situation.

'[W]hen men have agreed to act in common, and have given up their rights and submitted their will to the whole body as far as concerns the common good, it devolves thenceforth upon that body, the State [*l'Etat*], and upon its rulers, to fulfil the duties of humanity towards

[5] Christian von Wolff, *The Law of Nations Treated According to a Scientific Method* (1749), Prolegomena, edn of 1764 (tr. J. H. Drake; Oxford, Clarendon Press; 1934), § 7, p. 11. Wolff also argues as follows:

'Nature herself has established society among all nations and binds them to preserve society. For nature herself has established society among men and binds them to preserve it. Therefore, since this obligation, as coming from the law of nature, is necessary and immutable, it cannot be changed for the reason that nations have united into a state. Therefore society, which nature has established among individuals, still exists among nations and consequently, after states have been established in accordance with the law of nature and nations have arisen thereby, nature herself also must be said to have established society among all nations and bound them to preserve society...

'Since nature herself has established society among all nations, in so far as she has established it among all men, as is evident from the demonstration of the preceding proposition, since, moreover, the purpose of natural society, and consequently of that society which nature herself has established among men, is to give mutual assistance in perfecting itself and its condition; the purpose of the society therefore, which nature has established among all nations, is to give mutual assistance in perfecting itself and its condition, consequently the promotion of the common good by its combined powers' (*Ibid.*, § 7, 8, p. 11).

outsiders in all matters in which individuals are no longer at liberty to act and it peculiarly rests with the State to fulfil these duties towards other States.'[6]

[6] Emmerich de Vattel, *The Law of Nations, or the Principles of Natural Law, applied to the Conduct and to the Affairs of Nations and Sovereigns* (1758) (tr. C. G. Fenwick; Washington, DC, Carnegie Institute; 1916), Introduction, pp. 5–7.

Other parts of Vattel's argument expose the tension between the universalism of the law of nature and the incipient individualism of the law of nations:

'Such is man's nature that he is not sufficient unto himself and necessarily stands in need of the assistance and intercourse of his fellows, whether to preserve his life or to perfect himself and live as befits a rational animal... From this source we deduce a natural society existing among all men. The general law of the society is that each member should assist the others in all their needs, as far as he can do so without neglecting his duties to himself – a law which all men must obey if they are to live conformably to their nature and to the designs of their common Creator; a law which our own welfare, our happiness, and our best interests should render sacred to each of us. Such is the general obligation we are under of performing our duties; let us fulfil them with care if we would work wisely for our greatest good.

'It is easy to see how happy the world would be if all men were willing to follow the rule we have just laid down. On the other hand, if each man thinks of himself first and foremost, if he does nothing for others, all will be alike miserable. Let us labour for the good of all men; they in turn will labour for ours, and we shall build our happiness upon the firmest foundations.

'Since the universal society of the human race is an institution of nature itself, that is, a necessary result of man's nature, all men of whatever condition are bound to advance its interests and to fulfil its duties. No convention or special agreement can release them from the obligation. When, therefore, men unite in civil society and form a separate State or Nation they may, indeed, make particular agreements with others of the same State, but their duties towards the rest of the human race remain unchanged; but with this difference, that when men have agreed to act in common, and have given up their rights and submitted their will to the whole body as far as concerns the common good, it devolves henceforth upon that body, the State, and upon its rulers, to fulfil the duties of humanity towards outsiders in all matters in which individuals are no longer at liberty to act, and it peculiarly rests with the State to fulfil these duties towards other States. We have already seen (s. 5) that men, when united in society, remain subject to the obligations of the Law of Nature. This society may be regarded as a moral person, since it has an understanding, a will, and a power peculiar to itself; and it is therefore obliged to live with other societies or States according to the laws of the natural society of the human race, just as individual men before the establishment of civil society lived according to them; with such exceptions, however, as are due to the difference of the subjects.

'The end of the natural society established among men in general is that they should mutually assist one another to advance their own perfection and that of their condition; and Nations, too, since they may be regarded as so many free persons living together in a state of nature, are bound mutually to advance this human society. Hence the end of the great society established by nature among all nations is likewise that of mutual assistance in order to perfect themselves and their condition.

'The first general law, which is to be found in the very end of the society of Nations, is that each Nation should contribute as far as it can to the happiness and advancement of other Nations.

14.43 Of Wolff's idea of a society of the nations, Vattel said: 'From the outset it will be seen that I differ entirely from M Wolff in the foundation I lay for that division of the Law of Nations which we term voluntary. Mr Wolff deduces it from the idea of a sort of great republic [*civitas maxima*] set up by nature herself, of which all the Nations of the world are members. To his mind, the *voluntary* Law of Nations acts as the civil law of this great republic. This does not satisfy me, and I find the fiction of such a republic neither reasonable nor well enough founded to deduce therefrom the rules of a Law of Nations at once universal in character, and necessarily accepted by sovereign States. I recognise no other natural society among Nations than that which nature has set up among men in general. It is essential to every civil society [*civitas*] that each member should yield certain of his rights to the general body, and that there should be some authority capable of giving commands prescribing laws, and compelling those who refuse to obey. Such an idea is not to be thought of between Nations [*On ne peut rien concevoir, ni rien supposer de semblable entre les Nations*].'[7]

14.44 Those words have determined the course of history. They have made the world we know. Vattel has used the sovereignty theory of the

'But as its duties towards itself clearly prevail over its duties towards others, a Nation owes to itself, as a prior consideration, whatever it can do for its own happiness and advancement...

'Since Nations are free and independent of one another as men are by nature, the second general law of their society is that each Nation should be left to the peaceable enjoyment of that liberty which belongs to it by nature...

'In consequence of that liberty and independence it follows that it is for each Nation to decide what its conscience demands of it, what it can or can not do; what it thinks well or does not think well to do; and therefore it is for each Nation to consider and determine what duties it can fulfil towards others without failing in its duty towards itself. Hence in all cases in which it belongs to a Nation to judge the extent of its duty, no other Nation may force it to act one way or another...

'Since men are by nature equal, and their individual rights and obligations the same, as coming equally from Nature, Nations, which are composed of men and may be regarded as so many free persons living together in a state of nature, are by nature equal and hold from nature the same obligations and the same rights...

'Since Nations are free, independent, and equal, and since each has the right to decide in its conscience what it must do to fulfil its duties, the effect of this is to produce, before the world at least, a perfect equality of rights among Nations in the conduct of their affairs and in the pursuit of their policies. The intrinsic justice of their conduct is another matter which is not for others to pass upon finally; so that what one may do another may do, and they must be regarded in the society of mankind as having equal rights.' (*Ibid.*, Introduction, pp. 5–7.)

[7] Preface, p. 9a.

state to disprove the possibility of a natural society among states. It is fascinating to see, through the course of his book, the word *state* coming to have its modern double meaning. It comes to refer both to the internal organisation of the public realm of a society and to the whole of a society when seen externally.

14.45 Vattel's book was written in French, which was in those days the international language of the ruling class from London to St Petersburg. The book was archetypally eighteenth-century – elegant, clear, rational, easy to understand, full of good sense and worldly wisdom. Vattel himself was the very model of an eighteenth-century gentleman – cultivated, leisured, occasionally leaving his study to take part in public affairs and diplomacy. And his book, unlike Wolff's, was read by everyone who mattered, was on the desk of every diplomat for a century or more. It was a book which formed the minds of those who formed international reality, the international reality which is still our reality today.

14.46 *Act Five.* In the nineteenth century, natural law ceased to have any hold on the mind of most philosophers, let alone diplomats and politicians. Natural law was swamped by utilitarianism, positivism and Marxism. Natural law was dead beyond resurrection.

14.47 Throughout the nineteenth century social and legal philosophers continued to emit streams of discordant ideas about the true nature of international law. They might have saved themselves the mental effort. Vattel-minus-natural-law filled comfortably the busy minds of those whose job it was to act internationally. And their seemingly rational reality became international society's actual reality. The natural-law framework of Vattel simply evaporated, leaving an international society consisting of so-called *states* interacting with each other in a social wasteland, subject only to a vestigial law created by their actual or presumed or tacit consent. International society would be, and would remain, an unsocial inter-statal system.

14.48 It must have been an agreeable discovery for post-revolutionary ruling classes when they found that, internationally, they could continue to deal with each other government-to-government, as in the good old days, free of the encumbrances of democracy and socialisation, and yet, oddly enough, sustained in the atavism of a permanent international old regime by such famously progressive words as *sovereignty* and *freedom* and *equality*.

14.49 In the course of the nineteenth century, the *law of nations* came to be known as international law, giving a veneer of spurious universalism to a law which knew itself now to be merely inter-statal.[8] The voice of invincible Anglo-American common sense became the representative voice of self-misconceiving international society and its law.

'International law consists in certain rules of conduct which modern civilised states regard as binding on them in their relations with one another with a force comparable in nature and degree to that binding the conscientious person to obey the laws of his country, and which they also regard as being enforceable by appropriate means in case of infringement.'[9]

14.50 Late in the nineteenth century there came to be newly unified and newly powerful states, bringing an immense increase of economic and political and military energy into an international system which was undeveloped, unsophisticated, unable to socialise the overwhelming volume of the new social energy. We have lived with the consequences in the twentieth century. We are living with the intolerable consequences today.

14.51 It is a speculation which is not only of intellectual interest. It is a might-have-been of history with a significance which is still practical.

[8] Jeremy Bentham (1748–1832) had proposed the change of name in his *Introduction to the Principles of Morals and Legislation* (1790; 1823 edn) II, p. 256. Cf. Bentham's footnote in the 1823 edition (W. Pickering & E. Wilson): 'The word *international*, it must be acknowledged, is a new one; though, it is hoped, sufficiently analogous and intelligible. It is calculated to express, in a more significant way, the branch of the law which goes commonly under the name of the *law of nations*: an appellation so uncharacteristic, that, were it not for the force of custom, it would seem rather to refer to internal jurisprudence. The chancellor d'Aguesseau has already made, I find, a similar remark: he says that what is commonly called *droit des gens*, ought rather to be termed *droit entre les gens* (*Oeuvres* (1773 edn) II, p. 337).' The substance of Bentham's proposal had also been anticipated by Zouche in his *Iuris et iudicii fecialis, sive iuris inter gentes* (1650), explicitly substituting the phrase *ius inter gentes* for the traditional *ius gentium*. See Wheaton, *Elements of International Law* (Lawrence's 2nd annotated ed, London, Sanson Low; 1864), pp. 19–20, where Lawrence's note traces the gradual acceptance of Bentham's proposal in English and other languages.

[9] William Edward Hall, *A Treatise on International Law* (Oxford, Clarendon Press; 1880), p. 1. Cf. L. Oppenheim, *International Law – a Treatise* (London, Longmans, Green & Co.; 1905):

'Since the Law of Nations is based on the common consent of States as sovereign communities, the member States of the Family of Nations are equal to each other as subjects of International Law. States are by their nature certainly not equal as regards power, extent, constitution, and the like. But as members of the community of nations they are equals, whatever differences between them may otherwise exist. This is a consequence of their sovereignty and of the fact that the Law of Nations is a law between, not above, the States.' (ch. 2, § 14, pp. 19–20).

If Christian von Wolff had written in simple lucid French like Vattel, or in excited and exciting French like that other Swiss citizen of great influence, Jean-Jacques Rousseau, the world's conception of itself might have been fundamentally different, the history of the world might have been different, the story of the twentieth century might have been different.

14.52 Instead, we have the world as it is, a human world which human beings in general think is natural and inevitable but which requires each of us to be two people – with one set of moral judgements and social aspirations and legal expectations within our own national society, and another set of moral judgements and social aspirations and legal expectations for everything that happens beyond the frontiers of our national society. And the post-Vattel ethos which supports this wretched spiritual and psychological dislocation has turned itself into an articulated system which is all too familiar. I will call it the *old regime* of the human world and of its law. I will epitomise it in eight principles. And then, finally and equally briefly, I will put before you a *new view* of the human world and its law.

14.53 The *old regime*, which subtends everybody's everyday view of the human world and its law, can be stated as follows:

- The human world consists of a collection of states, approximately 190 of them, together with a number of intergovernmental organisations (so-called international organisations).
- International law is made by and for the states and international organisations, which are the only legislators and the only subjects of international law.
- Individual human beings and non-governmental entities of all kinds, including industrial and commercial enterprises, are not subjects of international law.
- International law organises the interaction of the states, that is to say, the interaction of their public realms, the governmental aspect of their social activity.
- Other international transactions are a matter for international law only in so far as they involve action by governments, either international action, or consequential internal action.
- The internal realms of the state are independent of each other, protected by a formidable series of defensive concepts – sovereignty, the sovereign equality of states, sovereignty over territory, domestic

jurisdiction, political independence and territorial integrity, non-intervention. From behind these conceptual barricades, each state is free to formulate its own policies and pursue its own interests.

- States are thus, as Vattel proposed, inherently free and equal and independent sovereigns. International law is accordingly conceived as an act of sovereignty by which states choose to accept limits on the exercise of their natural freedom.
- The only international responsibility for governmental activity is thus a form of legal responsibility, called state responsibility, for a breach by one state of another state's rights. And that breach takes one of three forms – a breach of territorial rights (property wrong), a breach of a general duty owed to another state (delictual wrong), a breach of a treaty (contractual wrong).
- Beyond this, there is no systematic conception of an international society at all – no international social purposes, no international morality, no international moral responsibility, no international social accountability, no systematic international economy, no systematic international culture. And the people of the world do not govern themselves internationally. If anything, they have only a marginal effect on the international activity of their own government.
- International social progress comes, if at all, as an incidental external consequence of internal activities, and as a more or less random outcome of so-called development assistance, and, especially, as a by-product of the wealth-creating and wealth-distributing effects of international capitalism, including rudimentary co-operation among some of the governmental managers of international capitalism (in GATT, the IMF, OECD, the European Community, the Group of Seven).

14.54 What can we do about it? What should we do about it? You will not be surprised to hear that the solution I propose is conceptual. I do not propose institutional change, whether root-and-branch or Fabian. I do not propose that we take up arms to expropriate the expropriators. I do not propose that we use the power of the people to disempower the powerful. What we will take up is not the power of arms but the power of ideas. We will let our best ideas of society and law flow into our imagining and our understanding of the human world. By *best ideas* I mean ideas that are philosophically fruitful, psychologically empowering, morally inspiring, practically effective. Within ourselves we can find unrealised *best ideas of society and law* which are an inheritance secreted from more than 5,000 years of intense social experience. We will, at last, take up our best ideas of society and law. We will make them into humanity's ideal. We will choose them as the programme of a revolution.

14.55 The *new view of the human world and its law* may also be expressed in the form of eight principles.

- International society is the society of the whole human race and the society of all societies. In other words, everything human that happens in the world is part of the social process of international society.
- We, the people, are members of international society – as are all the countless subordinate societies that we form, including, among many others, the family, the industrial and commercial corporation, the state-societies, and non-governmental and intergovernmental international organisations.
- International society has a constitution like every other society, which carries the systematic structure of society from its past to its future, determining the way in which all social power is created and distributed throughout the world.
- The state-societies and intergovernmental organisations are constitutional organs of international society, with special functions and powers in relation to the world public-realm, functions and powers delegated by international society under the international constitution and under international law.
- International law is the law of international society, the true law of a true society. It is made, like all other law, through the total social process of international society, in which we all participate, the people of the world and all our subordinate societies, including the state-societies.
- The constitution of international society, like any other constitution, is not finally fixed. It is a dynamic thing, liable to unceasing change under the pressures of international society, constantly reformed by the ideas and aspirations of humanity. The era of unsocial inter-statal society is ending – the era of international relations, state-power, foreign policy, diplomacy and war, the era of the old international law. The era of social international society has begun.
- The responsibility of the state-societies, as organs of international society, is not merely a matter of property, delict and contract. Nor is

their responsibility merely legal responsibility. Their primary responsibility is for abuse of power. All governments everywhere are socially and legally responsible for the way in which they exercise the powers delegated to them by international society. And the same is true of all those individuals and societies, including industrial and commercial corporations, which exercise social power affecting human survival and prospering.

- International law, like all law, is inherently dynamic – developing structurally and systematically, developing substantively, flowing into new areas, embodying and responding to the social development of the world – human rights law, environment law, natural resources law, sea law, space law, telecommunications law, intellectual property law, economic law of all kinds, and international public law to control the use and abuse of public power.
- International society and international law embody the social purposes which humanity chooses for itself and which are realised in the social power, legal and non-legal social power, which human beings exercise with a view to human survival and prospering.

14.56 Our consciousness extends throughout the world, passing freely across political frontiers. Our sympathy extends to the whole of humanity. Our moral and social responsibility extends to the whole of humanity and to the whole of the physical world which we transform by our actions. But our social ideals and our social possibilities are trapped and stifled within the mental structures which divide and disable the human world, structures which human consciousness has made and which human consciousness can remake.

14.57 The necessary revolution will free human consciousness from its self-subjection, from its self-disabling, from its self-destroying, allowing our ideas and our ideals, as well as our willing and our acting, to include the whole world, the physical world and the human world. The necessary revolution will leave us free to make and remake a human society which does not abolish our national societies but embraces and completes them.

14.58 The necessary revolution is a world revolution. The world revolution is a revolution not in the streets but in our minds.

The scales of the understanding are not quite impartial, and one arm of them, which bears the inscription: Hope of the future, has a mechanical advantage.. This is the sole error which I cannot set aside, and which in fact I never want to.

Immanuel Kant (1724–1804), *Dreams of a Spirit-Seer*, pt. 1, ch. 4 (tr. E. Goerwitz, ed. F. Sewall; London, Swan Sonnenschein; 1900), p. 365.

Self-love but serves the virtuous mind to wake,
As the small pebble stirs the peaceful lake;
The centre mov'd, a circle strait succeeds,
Another still, and still another spreads,
Friend, parent, neighbour, first it will embrace,
His country next, and next all human race . . .

Alexander Pope (1688–1744), *Essay on Man*, Ep. 4, lines 361–72.

That thy way may be known upon earth, thy saving health among all nations.

Book of Psalms (tenth–fourth century BCE), Psalm 65, v. 2 (King James version, 1611).

INDEX OF NAMES

References are to paragraph numbers.

INDEX OF SUBJECTS

References are to paragraph numbers.